MAYA 4.5
FUNDAMENTALS

Contents at a Glance

MAYA 4.5 FUNDAMENTALS

Jim Lammers with Lee Gooding

201 West 103rd Street, Indianapolis, Indiana 46290

An Imprint of Pearson Education

Boston • Indianapolis • London • Munich • New York • San Francisco

New Riders

Maya 4.5 Fundamentals

Copyright © 2003 by New Riders Publishing

International Standard Book Number: 0-7357-1327-8

Library of Congress Catalog Card Number: 2002114510

Printed in the United States of America

First edition: January 2003

07 06 05 04 03   7 6 5 4 3 2 1

Interpretation of the printing code: The rightmost double-digit number is the year of the book's printing; the rightmost single-digit number is the number of the book's printing. For example, the printing code 03-1 shows that the first printing of the book occurred in 2003.

Trademarks

Warning and Disclaimer

Publisher
David Dwyer

Associate Publisher
Stephanie Wall

Production Manager
Gina Kanouse

Senior Product Marketing Manager
Tammy Detrich

Publicity Manager
Susan Nixon

Senior Acquisitions Editor
Linda Anne Bump

Senior Editor
Sarah Kearns

Project Editor
Kelley Thornton

Senior Indexer
Cheryl Lenser

Composition
Gloria Schurick

Manufacturing Coordinator
Dan Uhrig

Cover Designer
Aren Howell

Cover Art
Michael Sormann

Media Developer
Jay Payne

To my mother and father, for their love and support.
—Jim Lammers

———————— ❖ ————————

To Damon Feuerborn, for introducing me to 3D, and my parents, for their support.
—Lee Gooding

Table of Contents

About the Authors

Jim Lammers is an animator, instructor, and reseller of Maya based in Kansas City, Missouri. A graduate of the University of Missouri's Electrical Engineering program, he switched to freelance animation within a few years of graduation and formed his company Trinity Animation in 1992. Since then, Jim has combined animation production with training and 3D software sales. Trinity Animation's web site is a popular source worldwide for 3D software and related tools. Jim coordinates an active animation user's group in Kansas City, and continues to produce animation. He created 3D effects for the Sony/TriStar film *Starship Troopers* in 1997 under renowned Hollywood effects veteran, Peter Kuran, and his company, VCE. Jim's other past animation work includes visualization projects for clients such as Nestle, McDonald's, and Butler Manufacturing. Jim can be reached at jim@trinity3d.com.

Lee Gooding is currently studying Computer Graphics Technology at Purdue University in Lafayette, Indiana, where he works with a variety of graphics-related technology. Lee is a self-taught Maya user, who first explored 3D animation at Blue Valley High School—one of the first high schools to teach this new visualization technology. Gooding worked with Lammers at Trinity Animation in 2000, developing training materials for Maya. He is currently focusing on completing his education and developing his own 3D projects. Lee has hopes of mastering MEL to become a true Maya guru. Lee can be reached at slgooding@jphreak.com.

About the Technical Reviewers

These reviewers contributed their considerable hands-on expertise to the entire development process for *Maya 4.5 Fundamentals*. As the book was being written, these dedicated professionals reviewed all the material for technical content, organization, and flow. Their feedback was critical to ensuring that *Maya 4.5 Fundamentals* fits our reader's need for the highest-quality technical information.

Shawn Dunn has been involved in the CG industry for over ten years. Presently he is a Professor at Seneca College in Toronto Canada and is teaching and developing the curriculum for the Character Animation course. Shawn also has a company called Get 3D that builds educational material and consults for the 3D market (www.get3D.ca). Prior to Seneca, Shawn worked for five years at Alias|Wavefront consulting, building, and delivering educational content for Maya such as *MEL Fundamentals*; *Rendering*; *Character Rigging and Animation*; and *The Art of Maya* to name a few. Prior to Alias|Wavefront, Shawn worked in production for four years in different roles focusing on 3D. Shawn has also taught at Sheridan College in Toronto.

Tom Harper's interest in 3D graphics began in the 1980s while working for a product design company in New York City. His reputation for expertise in 3D development grew, and he was eventually invited to become a member of an advanced technology group at Spectrum HoloByte, a games company in Alameda, California. After a year or so, Tom received a phone call from LucasArts Entertainment, inviting him to join the core development team for the blockbuster N64 title, *Star Wars: Shadows of the Empire*. When *Shadows* shipped in late 1996, Tom left LucasArts and joined Alias|Wavefront, where he was one of a team of product specialists working on Maya, which was still in the early alpha stages. Tom is currently the North American Developer Relations Manager for Criterion Software, the makers of the Renderware family of products for game development.

Chaz Laughlin is the owner/CEO of RPM, a 3D Communications Company. Chaz holds two B.F.A.s in computer graphics, his first from the design and illustration department at Kansas State University, headed up by Bob Hower, and the second from the film and animation department at the Kansas City Art Institute, headed up by Patrick Clancy. He was initially brought into the field of 3D animation through working at a company that designed wargames and battle simulations for the U.S. Army. Chaz's love for what computer graphics are capable of has fueled his success in 3D.

Eric Pavey has been professionally involved in CG since 1993. He received his degree in graphic design from Al Collin's Graphic Design School and completed two CG animation courses from The School of Communication Arts. Previous employment includes Square and Neversoft; Eric is currently working for Ronin Entertainment. He gives thanks to his wife and son for putting up with the long hours, and to New Riders for putting up with his bad comedy. Eric can be reached at e_pavey@yahoo.com.

Acknowledgments

I'm proud to have been associated with the creative and excellent *Maya Fundamentals* team assembled by New Riders. I wish to thank them as a group and also individually: The first edition's Development Editor Lisa Lord improved the book immeasurably with her quick perception of Maya (without ever using it!) and amazing attention to detail. This 4.5 edition was edited by Sarah Kearns, who helped coordinate a large number of changes and additions. Senior Acquisitions Editor Linda Bump piloted our project, keeping us on the right track and offering kind encouragement when we needed it. And this book would not be possible without the confidence from New Riders executive management, Publisher David Dwyer. First edition technical editors Chaz Laughlin and Eric Pavey were immeasurably helpful in guiding our approach, as well as checking every technical detail. Thanks also to the technical editors for this edition, Shawn Dunn and Tom Harper.

The developers of this book's tutorials made a major contribution—Lee Gooding and Garry Lewis. Lee developed a continuing "Spooky World"-themed tutorial that teaches many concepts and yields some attractive results with a minimum of complex steps. Garry Lewis of Mind's Eye 3D (www.me3d.tv) helped create the character animation chapter that is new to this edition. Garry's organized approach to character rigging and animation make a potentially painful subject fun and straightforward.

I am indebted to the artists who have contributed imagery to this book, in particular cover artist Michael Sormann (see www.sormann3d.com for more of his images and movies) for giving us a book cover to promote *Maya 4.5 Fundamentals* before there were any words for the pages inside. The artists' inspirational images prove that lone artists can create stunning 3D art and animation using Maya, in an age where large teams of animators often work on single scenes for 3D animated movies.

Thanks to Alias|Wavefront for their help; particularly David Lau and Leilei Sun for keeping my software humming between new beta releases.

Here at home, Pam Willis managed sales for my company Trinity Animation while I was preoccupied with creating a new edition. Michael Rucereto compiled the FAQ for the book's web site that helped drive some of the changes we made to this new edition. Amber West also helped in compiling the CD-ROM movies for this book and in development of the book's web site. I'm blessed to have such outstanding help with my business and book projects. My deepest thanks to Pam, Michael, and Amber.

My gratitude and affection also goes out to those who have inspired me creatively and otherwise: my high school art teacher Sherryl Knox, who gave me the eyes to understand visual expression; my guitar teacher and lifelong friend Scott Roby, who taught me to teach; my elementary school music teacher Mrs. Young, who showed me how technology and creation can go together; Bill Allen of 3D Artist magazine, who encouraged me to write about 3D computer graphics; my father, who introduced me to computing when I was still in junior high school (with a Sinclair ZX-81, which would be somewhat sluggish if it could run Maya today!); my mother, who taught me to read before kindergarten, and also taught me the principles of art and music from before I can remember; my sisters Diane, Tracy, and Tonya, who have always treated me like a star even when it was quite clear I *was not*; and my wife, who showers guidance, support, and encouragement upon me at every turn.

Tell Us What You Think

As the reader of this book, you are the most important critic and commentator. We value your opinion and want to know what we're doing right, what we could do better, what areas you'd like to see us publish in, and any other words of wisdom you're willing to pass our way.

As the Associate Publisher for New Riders Publishing, I welcome your comments. You can fax, email, or write me directly to let me know what you did or didn't like about this book—as well as what we can do to make our books stronger. When you write, please be sure to include this book's title, ISBN, and author, as well as your name and phone or fax number. I will carefully review your comments and share them with the author and editors who worked on the book.

Please note that I cannot help you with technical problems related to the topic of this book, and that due to the high volume of email I receive, I might not be able to reply to every message.

Fax: 317-581-4663

Email: stephanie.wall@newriders.com

Mail: Stephanie Wall
        Associate Publisher
        New Riders Publishing
        201 West 103rd Street
        Indianapolis, IN 46290 USA

Introduction

Maya 4.5 Fundamentals is designed to help new animators quickly grasp the main tools and techniques that production Maya animators use. This book is not a collection of dabblings in Maya, and none of the tutorials start with loading a prebaked scene. As gently as possible, we shove you into the water and teach you to swim like a pro.

Maya has historically been targeted to larger effects studios and animation houses. To some extent, that targeting continues in the current version, in that no complex sample scenes are included, and material libraries, marking menus, and hotkeys are minimal. In this book, we supply you with all these aids to help you absorb the working methods of a Maya animator.

A Brief History of How Maya Came to Be

While we're on the subject of history, take a look at what has led to the current state of computer graphics in general and Maya in particular. It will give you some perspective for the choices made in Maya's design.

The "Olden Days"

Electronic computers have been with us since the 1940s, but have been applied to imaging for aesthetics only recently. By the 1950s the idea of combining technology with visuals could be seen in television, oscilloscopes, and radar screens. The first major step was probably Ivan Sutherland's Sketchpad electronic drawing system, created in 1961. This vector-based system worked with a lightpen, allowing users to create art directly on a display screen. *Vector graphics* are primitive line art, common in early video games and movie effects.

In 1967 Sutherland joined David Evans at the University of Utah to create a computer graphics curriculum that merged art and science. The university developed a reputation for computer graphics research and attracted some of the future principle players in the CG business: Jim Clark, founder of Silicon Graphics, Inc. (SGI, today the parent company of Alias|Wavefront); Ed Catmull, an early developer of computer-animated movies; and John Warnock, founder of Adobe Systems, developers of such industry-defining products as Photoshop and Postscript.

Algorithms, Invented and Improved

CG pioneers developed the 3D concept: using a computer to form a perspective drawing from whatever theoretical set of geometry was entered—usually triangles, but sometimes spheres or paraboloids. The geometry was depicted as solid, with foreground geometry obscuring background geometry. Next came the creation of virtual "lights," producing flat-shaded 3D elements that gave the earliest computer graphics a hard-edged, technical look (see Figure I.1).

FIGURE I.1   *Rendered polygons.*

Averaging the shading from corner to corner produced a smoother look, an innovation called *Gouraud shading* (for its inventor, Henri Gouraud). This form of smoothing polygons is computationally minimal and is used for real-time smoothing in most 3D video cards today (see Figure I.2). When Gouraud proposed it in 1971, computers could render only the simplest scenes at a glacial pace.

FIGURE I.2   *Gouraud shading achieves a smoother look.*

In 1974, Ed Catmull introduced the concept of the Z-buffer—the idea that if an image has horizontal (X) and vertical (Y) picture elements, each element could also have depth embedded. This concept speeds the removing of hidden surfaces and is now standard in real-time 3D video cards. Catmull's other innovation was wrapping a 2D image onto 3D geometry. *Texture mapping*, as shown in Figure I.3, is fundamental to attempting realism in 3D. Before texture mapping, objects had only one solid color, so creating a brick wall might require each brick and bit of grout to be modeled individually. Now, by applying a bitmap image of brick to a simple rectangular object, you can build a wall with minimal computation and computer memory, not to mention less frustration for the animator.

Bui-Toung Phong improved on Gouraud shading in 1974 by interpolating shading across the entire polygon instead of simply using the corners (see Figure I.4). Although this render method can be up to 100 times slower than Gouraud shading, it yields the hyper-real "plastic" look that characterized early computer animation. Two variants of Phong shader types are built into Maya.

FIGURE I.3   *Texture mapping—applying a 2D texture to a 3D surface.*

FIGURE I.4   *Phong shading yields a plastic look.*

James Blinn combined elements of Phong shading and texture mapping to create *bump mapping* in 1976 (see Figure I.5). If the surface normals are already being falsely smoothed via Phong shading, and you can wallpaper 2D imagery over your 3D surfaces, why not use a grayscale image to perturb the normals and give the illusion of bumpiness rather than smoothness? A gray level higher than medium gray is treated as bumped up, and darker is bumped down. As with Gouraud and Phong shading, the geometry is unaffected, and the trick is revealed in the object's silhouette. However, Blinn's innovation added a new realism to 3D rendering. When effective, coordinated texture and bump maps are combined with a moderately detailed 3D model, and realistic 3D rendering comes within reach.

Figure I.5   *Bump mapping gives the illusion of surface detail.*

Blinn also developed the first method of *environmental reflection mapping.* He proposed creating a cubic environment by rendering six views outward from the center of a object. These six images are then reverse-mapped back to the object, but with fixed coordinates so that the imagery does not move with the object. The result is that the object appears to be reflecting its environment, an effect that holds up well unless parts of the environment are moving or changing rapidly during animation.

In 1980, Turner Whitted proposed a new rendering technique called *raytracing*; it works from the camera's render plane, tracing each pixel of the final image into the virtual scene. The rays ricochet through the scene, striking surfaces or lights and modifying the pixel's color accordingly (see Figure I.6). Reflective and refractive surfaces create more rays that modify the pixel's color. Although computationally expensive, the results are quite realistic and accurate for reflections and refractions. Raytracing is used particularly for chrome and glass effects.

FIGURE 1.6   *A raytraced all-CG image that really uses the effect!*

The 1980s: Pretty Pictures at Last

In the early 1980s, as PCs became more common in business, some early attempts at including computer graphics in entertainment included the movies *Tron* and *The Last Starfighter*. These attempts used specialized hardware and supercomputers to create a few minutes of film-resolution computer graphics, but the way had been shown.

By the mid-1980s, SGI had begun to build high-powered personal workstations for research, science, and computer graphics. In 1984, Alias was founded in Toronto, combining two meanings for *alias*: as a "pseudonym" (the founders were moonlighting then) and to describe the jagged appearance of CG images that aren't sampled enough. Initially, Alias focused on CAD-oriented use of its software, mostly for modeling and designing complex surfaces. Later Alias created Power Animator, a powerful and expensive software product that many production houses regarded as the best 3D-modeling package available.

Also in 1984, Wavefront was founded in Santa Barbara, named for the front edge of a light wave. This company immediately began developing software for creating 3D-rendered visual effects and produced opening graphics for Showtime, Bravo, and National Geographic Explorer. Wavefront's first software program was called Preview. Another 3D software package called SoftImage, released in 1988, was also popular and renowned for its power with animation. The software and hardware used for professional animation throughout most of the 1980s was specialized and expensive. By the late 1980s, only a few thousand people worldwide were creating visuals, almost all using SGI computers with 3D software from Wavefront, SoftImage, and many other competing products.

The '90s: Innovation Leads to Popularization

Soon this small animation clique began to expand quickly, thanks to the desktop computer invasion: IBM PC, Amiga, Macintosh, and even Atari computers produced their first 3D software applications. In 1986 AT&T introduced the first desktop animation package, called TOPAS. This $10,000 package was a full-blown professional animation system that would run on DOS-based computers with an Intel 286 CPU. TOPAS made freelance animation possible on a large scale despite primitive graphics and relatively slow computation. Electric Image, another desktop-based animation system, was developed the following year for the Apple Macintosh. In 1990 AutoDesk began to sell 3D Studio, created by the Yost Group, a small independent team that had created graphics products for the Atari. At $3,000, 3D Studio competed with TOPAS for the PC user. NewTek's Video Toaster came out the following year, bundled with an easy-to-use 3D software product called LightWave; both worked only on Amiga computers. NewTek sold thousands of these packages to aspiring video producers, wedding videographers, and music video enthusiasts.

By the early 1990s, computer animation was no longer an elite enthusiasm. Hobbyists everywhere began experimenting with raytracing and animation. Even users with no money could download such raytracing software as Stephen Coy's Vivid or the Persistence of Vision Raytracer, better known as POVRay (POVRay continues to be an excellent free way for kids and beginners to explore 3D computer graphics). Movies with groundbreaking and stunning effects, such as *The Abyss* and *Terminator 2*, illustrated that a new kind of imagery and visualization process—based on computers—had become possible. Unfortunately, most people gave all the credit to the transistors and none to the toiling animators, a misconception that continues to this day.

Alias Meets Wavefront

As the market for 3D applications matured and competition intensified, many of the older companies merged to pool technologies. In 1993, Wavefront acquired Thompson Digital Images, which offered interactive rendering and NURBS-based modeling, features that evolved into Maya's Interactive Photorealistic Renderer (IPR) and NURBS modeling. Microsoft purchased SoftImage in 1994 and ported the software to the Pentium-based Windows NT platform, marking the arrival of top-tier 3D software on inexpensive and generic PCs. SGI reacted by purchasing and merging Alias and Wavefront in 1995, presumably to prevent further erosion of 3D applications that worked exclusively on SGI's specialized graphics computers. Almost immediately the new company (renamed Alias|Wavefront) began to consolidate its collective technologies into a completely new program.

Finally, in 1998, Maya was released, priced at $15,000 to $30,000 and available only for SGI workstation's IRIX (a variation of UNIX). A complete ground-up rebuild, Maya pointed the way to the future of animation with an open application programming interface (API), dependency-graph architecture, and enormous extensibility. Despite SGI's original intent of protecting its platform exclusivity, in February 1999 it changed direction and the software was released for Windows NT. The old price structure was discarded, and Maya's base package was set at a radically lower $7,500. In April 1999, Maya 2 was released with many major enhancements and refinements. In November 1999, Maya 2.5 was released, adding a still unrivaled feature called Paint Effects. In the summer of 2000, Maya 3 was released, adding the nonlinear animation feature TRAX to many other enhancements. Ports of Maya to Macintosh and Linux were announced early in 2001, and by June 2001, Alias|Wavefront had shipped Maya 4 for IRIX and Windows NT/2000. In April of 2002, Alias|Wavefront again instituted a major price reduction, setting Maya Complete's price to just $1,995. A watermarked but otherwise full version of Maya Complete was also made freely available at this same time to any visitor of the Maya home page. Clearly, Alias|Wavefront sees a large market beckoning for Maya.

What Is Maya?

Maya is a software program for producing images and animations based on what the user has created in the virtual 3D workspace, lit with its virtual lights, and photographed from its virtual cameras. Maya is offered in two versions for animators: the basic Maya Complete version, and the enhanced Maya Unlimited version that adds several major features outlined later in this introduction. Maya runs on normal PC-type computers (using the NT/2000 compile) as well as Linux, SGI's IRIX, and Macintosh. With Maya, you can create images that border on photo-real by creating bitmap images like those that a digital camera produces. Maya's world is virtual, however; you create each light, camera, object, and material yourself, starting with an empty black void. Any parameter can be set to change over time, creating animation when you render many images in sequence: The camera can move and rotate, textures can change from chrome to wood, objects can fly apart or assemble, and much, much more. The possibilities truly challenge the imagination. Here are some popular uses for Maya:

- **Cartoons and movies** The most well-known use for Maya is 3D cartoon-style animation, such as in *A Bug's Life*, *Toy Story*, and *Shrek*. Another movie-related application is creating photo-realistic elements that are combined with film or video to create a special effect that would otherwise be impossible, expensive, or dangerous, such as explosions, background sets, spacecraft fly-bys, and so forth. With the film *Final Fantasy* (created by SquareSoft, primarily using Maya), a new use has emerged—the completely synthetic but utterly realistic feature film.

- **Computer games** As home computers have become more powerful, with 3D accelerated video cards commonly included, game developers have relied more on 3D applications such as Maya to create game entities. Earlier games used 3D software only for static backdrops and movies shown between game levels. Most modern computer games are of the real-time immersive 3D variety, and the objects and textures experienced in the game engine are prepared in a 3D application such as Maya. In fact, a reduced Maya version known as Maya Builder is offered to game developers for this function.

- **Advertising** TV commercials and network ID spots are punctuated by frequent use of 3D animation. The earliest uses were for show titles and announcements such as "The ABC Monday Night Movie," with big beveled chrome letters flying through the air. The series of commercials featuring the flying Listerine bottle also broke ground for 3D animation on television. Computer graphics are ideal for advertisers because they can capture viewers' attention with compelling imagery unlike any earthly scene.

- **Promos** Maya can be used in this area for flashy effects, such as graphics to play on stadium scoreboards, to start a large meeting in an upbeat manner, or to produce a dazzling logo treatment for a company's presentations.

- **Architectural animation** Typically, this use is for sales or zoning purposes to a small audience, where a virtual version of a proposed design is created as a large poster or a fly-through animation on videotape.

- **Forensic animation** Animations are sometimes used in lawsuits when a sequence of events needs to be played out for the jury; usually these applications are used for accident re-creations or technical explanations.

- **Industrial design** This is similar to architectural animation, in that a design is being considered for a product to be mass-produced; Maya's virtual method is a much faster, cheaper way to review a design than building prototypes. Industrial design encompasses anything sculpted and mass-produced—cars, boats, perfume bottles, blenders. A|W's Studio Tools software focuses more on this use of computer-based 3D design, but some people prefer using Maya for this task.

- **Industrial animation**   A catch-all phrase for the work requested by people giving business presentations—animated graphs, metaphorical explanations, "eye-candy" visuals, and so on.

Maya is the pre-eminent off-the-shelf 3D animation software. It finds use in nearly every major effects film, has a large market share in the preceding categories, and many consider it to be the best overall 3D animation program, despite a comparatively difficult learning curve. Maya's primary competitors are currently LightWave, SoftImage XSI, and 3ds max, which all fall in the $2,000 to $7,000 range. The under-$1,000 3D programs include trueSpace, Inspire 3D, Cinema 4D, Bryce, and Animation Master. Most of these programs work on the PC platform, and many have versions for other operating systems, such as Macintosh. Comparisons are difficult, but in general the best 3D programs enable more complex animation and offer more ease of use and automation when creating complex objects or animation.

Who Should Read This Book?

Maya 4.5 Fundamentals is designed for the beginner, but many segments are worthwhile for an intermediate Maya user. Maya is a complex package, and even seasoned animators who use Maya might find that some areas of the software are unexplored. Maya is well designed and uses similar conventions throughout, so you'll find that the more you know about Maya, the easier it is to learn more Maya. It's consistent and logical, so you don't need to memorize endless exceptions to the rule.

The 3D beginner should not be a beginner at both computers and art, however. Ideally, you'll bring to this book some skills with traditional art and a basic knowledge of a computer operating system. The animator is at heart an artist, though, and must embrace principles of color, design, contrast, motion, direction, and other creative aspects. The animator's primary tool is the computer, so you must be able to at least navigate its storage areas and perform the tasks that don't happen in Maya.

Most 3D animators come to Maya by way of 2D bitmap image-editing programs, such as Photoshop, Fractal Painter, and Corel Photo-Paint. Many also use 2D vector art ("line art") programs, such as CorelDraw, FreeHand, or Illustrator. Some have experience with animation in compositors, programs that combine a timeline with a bitmap editor, such as After Effects or Combustion. Some Internet-oriented animators have experience with products that combine a timeline with vector art, such as Flash animation. Experience with these software programs helps you understand parts of Maya. At a minimum, you should investigate bitmap image editors; for example, Paint Shop Pro is available at http://www.jasc.com in an evaluation version. Bitmaps are used frequently in creating 3D animation.

Bring tenacity: 3D animation is challenging because it requires using both technical and artistic mindsets, often simultaneously. Don't be discouraged if you struggle at times; all computer animators hit challenges that take some time to solve. As you progress through this book, and through Maya, remember to allow time to reinforce the concepts you learn and to consolidate your learning frequently with small projects and experiments. Each chapter includes "Going Further" sidebars to give you some ideas for this sort of excursion. Complete the experiment and move on: If some rendered results look promising, you can return to them after you have more mastery over other parts of Maya, and beautify the project to make it worthy of your portfolio. You need to get the big picture of animation production before working in earnest on a single project, and you should have that overview by the time you complete the tutorials in this book.

How This Book Is Organized

Maya 4.5 Fundamentals is composed of four parts. Part I, "A Quick-Start Guide to Maya," gives you the basics of using Maya and creating 3D animation with it. Chapter 1, "Pre-Maya: A Primer," gives some guidance to users who are weak in one of these areas. It's for people who are skittish about computers or people who didn't like art in school and have avoided it ever since. Chapters 2, "A Tour of Maya," and 3, "Maya Interaction," give you the basics of navigating through and interacting with Maya so that you can begin your 3D creating. Chapter 4, "Diving In: Your First Animation," consolidates all the steps of modeling, texturing, animating, and rendering with Maya into one tutorial that gives you an overview of the entire process.

Part II, "Maya Basics," is where you become proficient at using Maya. You'll revisit the major stages of creating animation with Maya by working through tutorials in each chapter, and move into a more sophisticated mode of using Maya. As Chapter 5, "NURBS Modeling Basics," begins, the tutorial workflow moves from the simple pull-down menus to a more professional marking-menu approach, designed to immerse users in real-world workflow. Because Maya offers both NURBS and polygonal modeling, both forms are covered in separate chapters. Chapter 6, "More NURBS Modeling," delves into NURBS modeling in more detail, with a tutorial that involves building a house. In Chapter 7, "Modeling with Polygons," you'll model a creature to see the techniques of organic modeling with polygons. Chapter 8, "Materials," explains how to create all kinds of standard surfaces with Maya's Hypershade. In Chapter 9, "Lighting," you see how to get dramatic and realistic lighting results with Maya's virtual lights. Chapter 10, "Animation Basics," demonstrates Maya's strength with animation and automating animated responses. Chapter 11, "Character Animation," teaches the techniques for getting your models to animate in a lifelike way. In Chapter 12, "Cameras and Rendering," you learn to finalize a project by fixing a viewpoint and producing your final rendered results from it.

Part III, "Going Further with Maya," begins with Chapter 13, "Paint Effects," which demonstrates this powerful module, capable of creating all manner of plants and trees, natural media, and even clouds, stars, and nebulae. Chapter 14, "Particle Systems and Dynamics," shows you methods for creating complex animation in an automated way. At the end of Chapter 14, you will have completed the book's projects and produced a sophisticated animated sequence from beginning to end in Maya, starting from an empty screen. Chapter 15, "Your Next Steps: Efficiency and Artistry," offers guidelines on speeding and simplifying the animation process and steers you away from common traps.

Part IV, "Appendices," includes several useful reference appendixes. Appendices A, "Maya Headstart for Max Users," and B, "Maya Headstart for LightWave Users," give 3ds max and LightWave users brief compare-and-contrast guidelines to help adapt more quickly to using Maya. Don't forget to browse through this book's color insert to see a collection of inspiring images created by professional Maya artists. We've also included some figures and sample renderings from the book's tutorials to give you a chance to see them in full color.

Conventions Used in This Book

Translating software interaction to text (when we write) and back (when you read) can be difficult. To make it easier for you to understand, we've adopted certain typographic conventions in this book:

- A monospace font is used for text you type in, such as values changed in a dialog box or filenames used to save projects.
- A **bold** font is used for hotkeys.
- *Italics* are used to introduce new terms or for emphasis.
- The pipestem character (|) indicates Hotbox or menu choices.

We've also iconized certain tidbits of information: Tips, Traps, Notes, Going Further sidebars, CD files, and CD movie files.

tip
As you're working through tutorials, this is where you'll find helpful guidelines or reminders of how to perform certain techniques.

trap

Pointers on potential trouble spots are highlighted as traps.

note

General comments in a tutorial or interesting background comments are often highlighted as notes.

Going Further

We've added tips on personalizing your Maya experience and ideas for further exploration at the conclusion of some tutorials and chapters.

This symbol indicates when to load a scene file from the book's CD-ROM. In most cases, you can continue with your previous work, but if you're having trouble, you can dissect your problems by examining the scene file or just forge ahead by loading the next scene. Tutorials are saved at several points so that you can easily move around the book if you want.

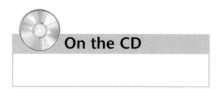

Full-resolution movies with audio are included on the CD, too. These movies should prove invaluable in speeding your progress. Instead of translating a complex series of moves and mouse clicks from the book's text, you can actually look over our shoulders while we perform each step in the tutorial and explain what we're doing. See the next section if you have any difficulties playing these .wmv files.

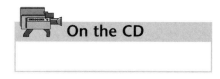

Movies on the CD-ROM: How to Play Them and Use Them

The movies on the CD-ROM were created with Camtasia from Techsmith. With this utility, users can capture movies from a computer desktop with perfect fidelity, while simultaneously recording audio. To help you understand offscreen actions, left mouse clicks are designated with a blue circle that emanates from the pointer, and right mouse clicks show up as red circles. Unfortunately for Maya, the middle mouse click is not circled, but we've verbally cued you when the middle mouse button is being used. Camtasia also overdubs noises of key clicks and mouse clicks to clue you in to what's going on. You can easily shuttle these movies forward or backward if you want to replay difficult parts or skip sections you've already learned. Nearly every chapter in the book has supporting movies that are worth exploring, totaling over a dozen hours of direct instruction.

To make these movies multi-platform, they have been recompressed into WMV for-mat, a streaming media format that plays with Windows Media Player. The Windows Media Player is available for PC and Macintosh, as well as Sun Solaris. The WMV screen codec is very clean and compresses tightly for the maximum amount of recording time in a fixed storage space. The full 800×600 capture is crisp and clear and the audio is distinct. If the movies are noisy or inaudible, check your system for speaker power, connection, speaker volume, and desktop volume. Right-click the speaker icon in Windows so that you can adjust both overall volume and "Wave out-put" volume. Distortion could occur in the audio if the computer volume is set too high, but the amplified speakers' volume knob is set too low. Adjust both to a mod-erate level for the best results.

Because the video will be playing back at 800×600 resolution, you need to set your desktop resolution to 1024×768 or larger so that you have access to the Media Player controls that appear below the movie. If you must view them at 800×600 or smaller (as with laptops), set your player to resize the movie player to 50%. You'll get some image degradation, but you'll still be able to view the movie. After playback starts in Media Player, toggle the full-screen mode.

If you get errors such as "invalid file type" when attempting to play the movies, you simply need to download the latest Media Player version from Microsoft. Point your web browser to `http://www.microsoft.com/windows/windowsmedia/` and download the latest player for your operating system.

You might also want to check this book's web site (see more about it in the section "This Book's Web Site") for other tips for movie playback, as well as new free movies for you to download: `http://www.mayafundamentals.com`

Maya and Hardware

Because of the relatively high cost of the Maya software, you might have the impres-sion that some sort of super-computing PC is required to run Maya. On the contrary, virtually any modern PC from any discount supermart will suffice, with the excep-tion of the video card, as you'll learn in the next section.

3D Video Cards

Your Maya experience will be much better if you start with one of the better 3D video cards, and eventually you'll probably need to buy a professional 3D video card to use Maya. See the compatibility guide that Alias|Wavefront keeps updated at its web site, or navigate from `Aliaswavefront.com` to Maya Support and search for "Qualified Hardware."

In general, 3D Labs, nVidia, and ATI cards targeted to professional users are going to be most compatible. Check with the maker to find out its specific driver modes. If it offers a driver mode specifically designed for Maya, it will almost certainly work well for you. Many offer taskbar mode switching, as shown in Figure I.7. A key feature to look for is "overlay planes"; without it, all the interactive paint functions will be painfully slow. You'll probably need to budget a few hundred dollars at minimum for your video card. See http://www.pricewatch.com to price these pro-level 3D video cards from hundreds of retailers.

FIGURE I.7   *Resetting the video driver mode to work with Maya.*

A few tips on video cards: Be sure to visit the web page of your card's manufacturer often to find the latest drivers. After installing the drivers, in Windows, you can right-click on the desktop and choose Properties. In the Display Properties dialog box that opens, select the Settings tab, where you set resolution and color depth. Click the Advanced button to display the customization settings for your video card, so you can test that its OpenGL 3D acceleration is functioning correctly. This is also where you find program-specific settings, with a preset for Maya. Test your card at 1024×768 or less at first; some cards have trouble when set to high resolutions. Acceleration is usually designed for a specific color depth: 15/16-bit (32,000 color) or 24/32-bit (16 million color). Most newer cards are 24-bit (also known as Truecolor), but some less expensive cards accelerate only in 15-bit mode.

A Three-Button Mouse

A minor expense is a three-button mouse. Most computers have at most a two-button mouse with a scroll wheel between the buttons. The scroll wheel button can substitute for the middle mouse button, but it may become awkward after the frequent use that Maya makes of this button. Using Maya is much more natural with a three-button mouse, like that shown in in Figure I.8.

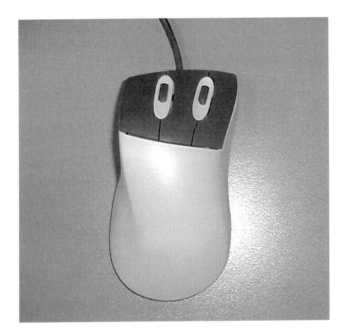

FIGURE I.8 *An inexpensive three-button mouse with two scroll wheels.*

Some mouse drivers have caused problems, such as not recognizing the middle mouse button in a mode compatible with Maya, or not recognizing a button release when two mouse buttons are used at the same time. These functions are too fundamental to Maya to work around, so download newer or different drivers for your mouse if this problem happens. If it persists, buy a new mouse.

Tablets

Another recommended hardware purchase is a tablet. All the paint tools in Maya—Artisan, 3D Paint, Paint Weights, Paint Effects, and so on—are pressure enabled. A tablet gives you much greater control over the results because you can make your paint strokes change along their length based on stylus pressure. Typically, brush size or opacity is made to vary based on stroke pressure, but any variable you see in Maya that appears twice with a (U) and (L) after the parameter name can vary between these upper and lower limits based on stylus pressure. If you're using a mouse, it simply uses the upper value for all parts of all strokes—a fairly ham-fisted way to do business! A tablet can cost from $100 to $4,000, but Wacom's Graphire 4x5 and Intuos 6x8 lines are $100 and $300, respectively, and yield excellent results. It's worth the investment if you plan to make use of Maya's paint tools.

Minimum Requirements

Maya 4.5 for Windows officially requires the following:

Pentium II, III, 4, and AMD Althon processors, 600 MHz or faster.

128MB of RAM (256 strongly recommended).

CD-ROM drive.

Hardware-accelerated OpenGL graphics card: mid- to high-performance overlay plane capability recommended.

About 400MB of disk space for a full installation.

Windows 2000 Professional with Service Pack 2 or later, or Windows XP Professional.

Netscape 4 or higher or Internet Explorer 4 or higher to view online documentation.

Optionally, a sound card.

Maya 4.5 for Macintosh requires:

G4 chipset (450, 500, 533, 633, 733, 800, 867, and so forth).

Specified ATI or NVida graphics card.

Three-button USB mouse (such as Contour Design UniMouse).

Mac OS X 10.1.5 or 10.2. Mac OS X must be installed on its own disk partition. Do not install Mac OS X on the same partition as Mac OS 9.

Local Mac OS extended-formatted drives.

Minimum 512MB of memory.

At this writing, requirements for Maya 4.5 for Linux and IRIX have not been announced.

Regardless of the OS you are using, most animators consider it essential to have a scanner, a ZIP drive, a CD burner, Internet access, and possibly a video capture and output device. If your budget at the beginning is tight, you can add these items as needed in your work.

System Recommendations

We've outlined our unofficial recommendations for PC hardware in this section. It's not "blank check" advice; these tips are based on experience and current prices in relation to Maya software.

- **Processor** Get a dual-processor system if you can afford it. On the PC, Athlons have only recently offered dual-processor motherboards, but Pentium systems have been multiprocessor for years. Dual CPUs make your system much more robust at multitasking, if you want to let Maya render while you browse the web, work in Photoshop, or even start a new session of Maya on the same machine! Maya's batch rendering mode can use the number of processors that you tell it to, so you can let Maya work with one when it's in the background, and set it to use both when you won't be sitting at the computer (nearly doubling rendering power).

- **RAM** 512MB is typical for most users because the price of RAM remains relatively low. For Macintosh, 512MB is the minimum. If you'll be working with huge models, you might opt to get 1GB or more, if your motherboard supports it. RAM acts as a bottleneck if your needs exceed what you have installed, but doesn't help if you have more than necessary. Simply watch your physical RAM use and if it often runs low, buy more RAM. In Windows, check the Performance tab in Task Manager to view the available physical RAM. Usually it won't go to zero even when you have far too little RAM. Instead, you'll see it drop to 10MB or lower and then vary up and down. Also, you'll notice the hard drive light flashing constantly and a fidgety response from your computer when it is RAM-malnourished. This is because RAM needs will be met by paging memory to the hard drive, a progressively sluggish function.

- **Video card** Don't use a video game–oriented card; buy a professional CAD and 3D video card. Also, consider the geometry and texture RAM available on the 3D video card. If you use big scenes or make lots of large textures visible in your Maya shaded viewports, you could overrun the video card's available RAM. If you do that, your shaded views will become extremely slow to interact with. If you're certain you will be using large scene files, choose a video card with an abundance of RAM. Typical pro 3D video cards have 64MB or more of fast onboard RAM.

note
The "3D acceleration" afforded by a fast 3D video card applies to one function only: interacting with shaded views. All computational functions of Maya including rendering are dependent on the CPU only. If you don't use interactive painting in Maya and prefer to work in wireframe modes, you may need only the most basic video card.

- **Network card**   Although Alias|Wavefront will still offer the hardware lock, it's advisable to get a network card for your Maya authorization. Because network cards have unique internal ID numbers, they can be used in lieu of a hardware lock, also known as a *dongle*. The reasons for using the network card include the hardware lock's possible exposure to damage and theft, the $150 charge from A|W to get a hardware lock, and the potential for parallel port trouble when the dongle is put between the device (usually a printer) and the parallel port. Most PCs are now equipped with a network card, but you can buy one for $20 or less; any PCI Ethernet 100BaseT card will do. The one benefit of having a hardware lock is that it's easier to use Maya on multiple machines; you can simply take the hardware lock with you wherever you go. Note that A|W also offers a "floating" license option for an additional charge when you want to allow the license to work on any one machine in a large LAN.

Where to Weight Your Computer Budget

If your budget is on the low end, prioritize as follows:

1. First, choose the best video card possible. Check this book's web site for more up-to-date advice on card choice; 3D video technology changes rapidly. Consult the officially approved video card list at Alias|Wavefront's web site. Then check prices and hardware evaluations to narrow your selection.

2. For this book's tutorials, in Windows, 256MB should be enough RAM to create and render all the projects. If you have 128MB of RAM, upgrade to 256. For Macintosh, the 512MB minimum is sufficient.

3. Next, get a tablet. They are relatively inexpensive and enable you to really take off with 3D Paint and Paint Effects.

4. Last, consider replacing your CPU; making a major leap on CPUs usually requires a complete new system. Simply raising a Pentium 3 500MHz to a Pentium 3 700MHz is not going to make a big difference. Older motherboards might not support the fastest clock rates; for example, your old P3-500 motherboard may not allow you to switch it to 1000MHz. Check before you buy a new CPU! In general, it's better to buy a complete new integrated computer than to try to upgrade because of the inevitable hardware incompatibilities when you push new hardware to work with older hardware and firmware.

A luxury item for animators to consider is a second monitor. This usually means replacing the entire 3D video card with a new video card that supports dual monitors, preferably with full 3D acceleration on at least one of the two monitors. Adding a second monitor gives you the ability to move any of Maya's floating palettes and windows to the second screen where they don't obscure your 3D views of the scene and can stay open all the time. Almost every Maya panel or menu can be "torn off" to float. Note that on the Macintosh, Maya's Paint FX feature can cause problems on dual-display systems.

What's New in Maya 4.5?

A large amount of the work you do in Maya is moving, rotating, and scaling things in 3D space. New features in this area include special new tools for aligning and snapping objects that will make it much easier to accomplish relative positioning of scene objects:

- **Align tool**   You can quickly and interactively align any number of objects of any type with the Align tool. It offers min/max/center alignments, as well as an opposite edge alignment for any axis. The tool is totally graphical; you don't need to think about left and right in XYZ space.

note   The Align tool will not work in Component mode, but will work on any scene element—lights, curves, and so on.

- **Snap Together tool**   Like the Align tool, the Snap Together tool is completely visual. After activating the tool, an arrow will appear to indicate the point that will touch the second object. Next, click on the surface of the second object, and a dotted line will indicate the pending movement while you adjust this second target point.

- **Discrete Move, Rotate, and Scale**   When the move, rotate, and scale icons in the toolbox are double-clicked, the tool settings appear; here you will find a new option for discrete snapping. This allows the object to snap in increments as you adjust it. The increments may start at zero, or you can enable the relative option to cause the transform to start the increments based on the object's current transform.

- **Polygonal Snap**   Below the discrete move settings, the new polygonal snap options appear. You can select a polygonal object and make it "live" with the Make Live button, and then other objects will snap to either the vertices or face centers when moved.

- **New marking menus for component selections**   Maya has a built-in set of marking menus for editing the components of polygons, NURBS, or Sub-Ds. In all cases, using Ctrl-right click brings up the new marking menus, which offer options for expansion or contraction of the current selection, or conversion of one type of component to another. This allows you to select a set of vertices, for example, and then convert this selection to the group of faces encompassed by the vertices.

- **Node notes in Attribute Editor**   Now appearing at the bottom of the Attribute Editor is a notes area. Each node of a scene can have unique notes. This can be invaluable for group work, sharing files with friends, or just keeping track of scene development as you go.

- **Presets in Attribute Editor**   You can build a set of presets for any node and later load them or even blend them with the current settings. You can use this button to save the current settings as a preset, edit presets for this node type, or select a preset and either load or blend it at 10%, 25%, 50%, 75%, or 90%.

- **New display features**   Maya's 3D viewports can exhibit some new features as well. If you need to call attention to a specific object by name, you can use annotated labels. This lets you have a floating text label pointing at something in all 3D views. Use Create | Annotation for this feature. Wireframes may now display in a pseudo-antialiased mode. This is in the panel's Shading pull-down and is called smooth wireframe. Another new panel menu feature is Use No Lights—something that might be helpful with the new Ramp shader materials.

- **New polygon-editing tools**   New polygon-editing tools such as poly cut, poly poke, poly wedge, and poly edit by painting allow you to make fast edits in a single step to your polygonal models. Cut allows you to make a linear slice across any selection of polygons, with the option to discard polygons from one side. Wedge allows for easy rounded extrusions from a face, where one edge of the face acts like a hinge. Poke will add a vertex to the center of a polygon, connecting all the polygon's edges to the vertex as triangles. All of these polygon-editing features will prove helpful for modeling with the smooth proxy approach, described later and employed in Chapter 7, "Modeling with Polygons."

- **New NURBS modeling tools**   Maya 4.5 sports an integrated "bevel plus" feature for beveled NURBS objects, which is particularly helpful for logo creation.

- **Smooth Proxy**   This feature allows for fast setup of polygon mesh creation via a smoothed object that is controlled by a lower-resolution but easier-to-edit mesh. This technique is explored in Chapter 7 of this book. The smoothed mesh can now use either Linear or Exponential smoothing to allow more modeling flexibility. The Exponential and Linear smoothing algorithms both smooth equally, but they offer different controls for the resulting topology. For example, Exponential has an option to maintain soft and hard edges, while Linear has options to better control the number of resulting faces.

- **New animation features**   Maya 4.5 adds new marking menus for adjusting tangents or editing keys. For dynamics, a new rigid body hinge constraint has been added that will rotate on its axis when torque is applied. This allows for superior dynamics simulation when your hinge is moving or bouncing at some point in the simulation. The old hinge constraint is now called "Directional Hinge." Maya 4.5 also adds a function called Mirror Joint for easier character construction because most jointed characters are vertically symmetrical. In addition, Maya 4.5 adds new minor features to Trax and the Graph Editor.

- **Lighting**   New volume lights. This means you can visually fill an area with a light with built-in falloff. These are scalable and offer volumetric shapes such as sphere, cone, cube, and cylinder. For most lighting work, users will prefer the ease and control of this new light type where point lights might have been used in the past.

- **Particles**   Now, particles may cast shadows in hardware shading.

- **New Ramp shader**   A type of shader where all the attributes have ramps assigned. This new shader allows for easy creation of new material types including glass, stone, x-ray, and toon-shading. The toon or "cel" shading look is the most common use for this shader, achieving a look that mimics the ink and paint appearance of traditional 2D cartoons.

About Maya Personal Learning Edition (PLE)

To help students and interested artists explore and learn to use Maya, Alias|Wavefront took the unprecedented step of releasing a full, free version of its software. Anyone can download the installer (at 140MB, this download is not for the broadband-impaired) or purchase a CD with the installer from Alias|Wavefront for a nominal price. After installation, a one-year license of the software is free from Alias|Wavefront. The software is not licensed for any commercial purposes; it is for learning Maya only. This student version, known as *Maya Personal Learning Edition* (or PLE for short), is identical to Maya Complete, with a few exceptions:

- PLE cannot load or save standard Maya *.ma or *.mb files. It can only load and save files in its own *.mp format.

- PLE is watermarked—every screen and dialog within Maya has a large repeating diagonal Alias|Wavefront brand that fills the frame.

- PLE will not allow plug-ins to run.

At this writing, only Maya 4.0 is available in the Personal Learning Edition, and only for Windows or Macintosh (as yet, there is no IRIX or Linux version of PLE). The *.mp-formatted files on this book's CD-ROM were created in Maya PLE 4.0, but should also load for PLE 4.5. Consult the book's web site where modified PLE scene files are posted if you encounter problems loading the scene files into Maya PLE 4.5.

Maya Complete Versus Maya Unlimited: What More Would You Get?

Maya Complete contains a majority of Maya's features, and most animators are fully served by it. This book covers only the features of Maya Complete. Four unique modules are added for those who purchase the upgrade to Maya Unlimited:

- **Cloth** This module allows the user to define a clothing pattern and stitch it to a character, and have the cloth move realistically in reaction to the character's motions. You can simulate cloth-like effects with good results using Maya Complete's soft-body dynamics, but for characters wearing clothes, Maya Unlimited offers an elegant and complete solution.

- **Fur** Like cloth, the fur applied with this module moves realistically in reaction to motions of the character it's applied to. It also calculates and renders quickly. It's not designed to create the effect of long hair. You can simulate fur with good results using Maya Complete's Paint Effects, but it doesn't bounce in reaction to character movement and takes longer to render.

- **Live** This module can analyze live-action footage, deduce the camera position, and then create a virtual camera in Maya that's animated exactly the same as the real-world camera. This feature enables perfect compositions of CGI elements into filmed real-world backgrounds, as well as putting filmed foreground objects (usually filmed against a blue screen) into CGI environments.

- **Fluids** New for version 4.5, fluids allow quick and realistic simulations of smoke, fire, clouds, liquids, lava, and other viscous materials. Also included is a water and terrain simulator for making such environments as turbulent oceans or craggy mountainscapes. A full palette of settings appears in Visor for installations of Maya Unlimited 4.5.

These modules, when enabled, appear seamlessly in Maya as additional pull-downs or modes. A few other features are included only with Maya Unlimited: NURBS booleans, the Round tool, and Global Stitching. These features are timesavers, but their essential function is available in Maya Complete by taking several steps to accomplish the same end result.

Help Within Maya

Since Maya 4.0, the voluminous manuals are available online only. The set of documents supplied with Maya are just get-started material, such as "Instant Maya," how to install, what's new, and release notes. The online documentation, however, is thorough and detailed. Press F1 in Maya to bring up Maya Documentation. You should get in the habit of having the documentation open all the time in the background. When you start work in an area where you're not confident about the exact meaning of each variable label or pull-down option, do a little reading. The search utility built into the documentation is fast and reliable. There's no need for confusion or uncertainty about the many (often strangely named) variables. Just look them up as you go to get a complete grasp of every part of Maya.

This Book's Web Site

To interact with our readers and improve their understanding of Maya, we have created a supporting web site for this book. Visit it at `http://www.mayafundamentals.com`. Here you can pick up additional tips and ideas, new movies and other new supporting content, and links to helpful sites and focal points for the Maya online community. Any important corrections to the book will be listed here, too.

Please note that we'll try to help you when possible, and we're curious to know where we can improve on future editions of this book, but we can't act as unlimited advisors and e-teachers for your personal projects.

Reaching the Authors

Contact the authors at:

Jim Lammers
`jim@trinity3d.com`

Lee Gooding
`goodings@purdue.edu`

If things change, our most current contact information is kept at the book's web site at `http:\\www.mayafundamentals.com`.

A Last Note

This book is not about making spreadsheets or designing newsletters. 3D animation programs in general, and Maya in particular, can lay claim to something no other software can—the ability to create and visualize entire worlds, full of detail and realistically imaged, all from your own mind. Between the price/power ratio of modern computers and Maya's lower price point, we're entering an era in which one person can create fully realized environments, characters, and stories, all from four simple resources: a desktop computer, Maya software, time, and talent. There may be moments of difficulty mixed with other moments of triumph as you progress from neophyte to master. For the most part, however, we have found that the primary emotion is the joy of creation as we get better. We hope you find your journey to be every bit as rewarding and pleasurable as we have.

PART I

A Quick-Start Guide to Maya

Pre-Maya: A Primer

In This Chapter

Not everyone with a passion for 3D animation has spent hundreds of hours directing films, painting or drawing portraits, coordinating interior decoration colors and patterns, and lighting and shooting photographs. Nor have they necessarily built a computer, set up a network, installed an operating system, or written a software program—but it would help! Seriously, computer graphics combines so many disciplines that practically everyone has at least a little relevant experience. So many combined skills are needed to master 3D animation, however, that it's helpful to review a list of them.

The end result of 3D animation is nearly always a 2D image—a still image or a movie (although the 3D models themselves are in some cases distributed, for example, to examine a modeled stereo system on an e-commerce Web site for audio equipment). In most respects, Maya-created art isn't different from any other traditional media. The same principles of design apply: those learned from thousands of years of painting and at least 100 years of still and moving photography. Many aspiring animators have had only brief exposure to these design concepts, so this chapter provides a concise overview. At the end, you'll find a bibliography that points the way to more information.

A final section covers the basics of computer graphics. The ABCs of computer graphics include terms like pixels, resolution, color depth, and bitmap. If these words are foreign to you, read this section carefully as a starting point for the rest of this book.

Color Basics

If you took anything away from your childhood art class, it was probably learning the *primary* colors: red, yellow, and blue. A color wheel, shown in Figure 1.1, puts these three colors in the corners of a triangle, and the results of mixing these colors appear between those three points: the *secondary* colors orange, green, and violet. Colors from green to violet are called *cool,* and those from red to yellow are *warm.* Colors that are opposite each other on the wheel, such as blue and orange, are considered *complementary* colors. They tend to clash when combined; for example, an orange ball in a blue room might look harsh. The general palette of color used in a composition is called a *color scheme,* and a composition's overall color scheme can be said to be warm or cool, depending on the predominant color. In general, a color scheme appears more harmonious if you avoid large overlapping areas of complementary colors. However, used judiciously, complementary colors can be useful if you want to make objects seem to "pop" from the background.

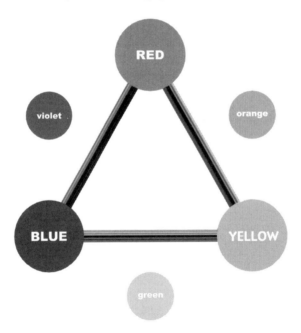

Figure 1.1   *The color wheel.*

Color Mixing: Subtractive and Additive

The familiar primary colors are known as *subtractive color,* a form that's not used in computer graphics. It is called subtractive because with paints and crayons, the pigments are applied to a reflective surface, usually white paper. Light travels through the pigment, tinting it, and then reflects from the white surface and back through the pigments, tinting the light again before it reaches your eye. The pigments absorb and subtract certain colors, leaving the observed colors to pass through. Add enough pigments of different colors, and you get black.

With computer graphics, color is *additive*. The monitor is black by default, and you create color by adding three colors of light. The primary additive colors are red, green, and blue, which changes the way you think about color when you work with computer graphics. The mixed colors of red, green, and blue are yellow, cyan, and magenta (see Figure 1.2). Add enough light of different colors, and you get white.

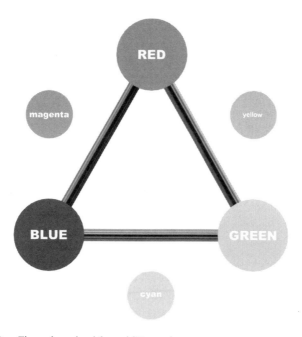

FIGURE 1.2   *The color wheel for additive color.*

note

Printing a hard copy of a digital image does not require the artist to go back to a subtractive-color mindset. The computer software automatically adjusts the colors to a "CMYK" mode that is appropriate for putting the image on paper before sending the image to the printer. CMYK (which stands for Cyan, Magenta, Yellow, and Black) is similar to the red-yellow-blue color wheel, using cyan for blue and magenta for red. An overall black value is used to darken and create rich blacks.

HSV and RGB

When setting a color in Maya, you can edit colors in RGB or HSV mode (see Figure 1.3). In RGB mode, you set the power of the red, green, and blue values independently, from 0 to fully on (fully on can be normalized to 1.0 or to 255). The HSV mode, however, is much more intuitive for tuning color. *HSV* stands for "hue, saturation, and value." *Hue* is the root color tint; for example, a pastel pink has a red hue. *Saturation* defines the color's purity compared with grayscale; the less saturated it is, the more it looks like a monotone grayscale image. *Value* defines the color's brightness compared with black, and can be thought of as a black mix value. As you mix colors for your scenes, you'll notice that colors in reality are rarely fully saturated or desaturated. There's a tendency to think of a red flower or stop sign as a pure red, but a pure, fully saturated red looks too intense in computer graphics. If you want a natural look, avoid extreme settings in any of the HSV sliders, particularly saturation.

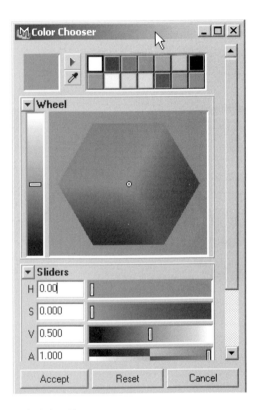

FIGURE 1.3   *Maya's Color Chooser.*

Image Composition

A key part of framing your shots is *image composition*—the placement of the subject and its surroundings within the image's rectangular frame. Another element of composition is how you use color and contrast to direct the viewer's eye. Areas of similar colors, or similar brightness, with low contrast are de-emphasized in relation to other areas of the composition.

Brightness and Contrast

In general, you want your images to run the gamut from very white to very black, but you might choose a washed-out (the darkest dark is medium gray) or underexposed (the brightest bright is medium gray) look. However, usually you want to have some areas of your image remain quite dark and others more fully illuminated so that the image doesn't look dull or washed out. Contrast can be used to focus the viewer's attention. Low-contrast areas of a composition (for example, a large unadorned beige wall that dominates one part of the frame) are often more bland and uninteresting than high-contrast areas (such as a shiny red car with black tires). However, in general you should avoid making your entire composition high contrast and busy; it can detract from the composition's focus and look harsh.

With 3D, the usual danger is a washed-out appearance (see Figure 1.4). To avoid this, take care not to overlight your scenes, and be sparing about *ambient* light (a type of light in Maya that shines on all surfaces at all times). Work up from darkness, adding many local lights of low strength to bring out the areas of interest. You should almost always apply some amount of *falloff* (decreasing the light's intensity) to any point lights, the type that shine in all directions. Otherwise, each light is like a sun, in which the intensity seems not to diminish at any distance.

FIGURE 1.4   *Brightness and contrast: The leftmost image has areas of nearly maximum and minimum brightness, the middle image is overlit, and the right image is underlit.*

Lighting in 3D is completely different from lighting in the physical world. The tiniest lightbulb creates trillions of photons that scatter throughout the environment, reflecting color and light in all directions. Any simulation of natural light would be too intensive for current computers. Instead, simple mathematical simulations of light sources that do not scatter are used. In the real world, the sunlight shining through a window lights a darkened room and reflects from the floor. In 3D, the light would affect only the floor, and the room would remain dark!

note   Some third-party renderers, such as Mental Ray for Maya, do support simulations of reflected light, but this usually comes with greatly increased computational burden during rendering.

Negative Space

Negative space is the term for less complicated and eye-catching areas of the image. In other words, it's the space that fills the image where the subject does not appear. Usually it means a neutral look—flat walls, empty sky, and so forth. However, negative space is as important as the subject. An image swirling with complex images everywhere creates a visual effect akin to 100 radios on different stations all playing at once. Use negative space to accentuate and focus on the important parts of your composition, as shown in Figure 1.5.

FIGURE 1.5   *Negative space adds emphasis to the busier, high-contrast areas.*

Sometimes a scene is detailed and complicated, so how do you create negative space then? Combining techniques of photography and *post-processing* (the digital equivalent of the darkroom), you can find new ways to create the emphasis you want. You can use *depth of field* to blur foreground and background areas so that the subject is in focus against a blurry field. You can desaturate areas that should be negative space by using post-processing techniques. With this approach, the surrounding environment's color is muted and appears somewhat pastel (halfway to a grayscale look) while the subject is fully saturated. Instead of black-and-white grayscale, you could use a monochrome theme, such as shades of blue, blended in the background to make it less interesting. With Maya, you can fully control your 3D world and the resulting 2D images for maximum artistic impact.

Dividing the Canvas

Putting the subject right in the center of your frame like an amateur photographer is not always the best approach. If you take a tour of an art museum and look at the way painters position an image's focal point, you'll find some interesting patterns. Observing paintings and film will give you helpful ideas on how to say something about your subject by the way you frame the image or action. A common principle of composition is dividing the canvas into thirds and putting key parts of the image into these vertical or horizontal areas (see Figure 1.6). This division helps avoid a boring symmetrical look and forces the artist to think about putting the subject in the appropriate portion of the image. Is the character alone in a big world? Then he might be in the bottom third of the frame. Is the image a closeup of a strong character? Then it might take up the vertical two-thirds of the frame. You can find many examples and explanations in a good art history or cinema history book to give you a palette of ideas for how you'll divide your own canvas.

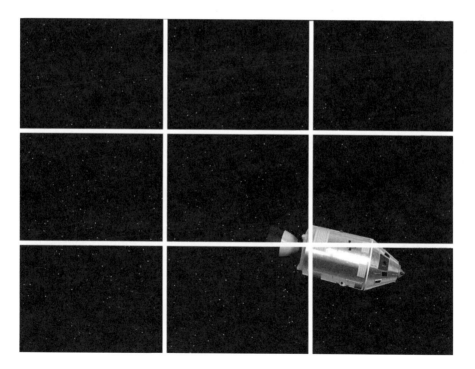

FIGURE 1.6   *The canvas divided into vertical and horizontal thirds.*

Lighting 101

Most photographers, cinematographers, and stage-lighting designers will tell you that lighting is an art in itself. The photographic process is more sensitive than the virtual cameras you use in 3D animation, however, so you have more options than a photographer does. For example, you can create lights that don't cast shadows, objects that are not affected by a specific light, or lights that never fade in intensity. However, you can still learn some useful tips from the basics of photographic lighting.

Standard Lighting Model

Every scene you create has its own unique lighting requirements, but for standard lighting of a typical subject, photographers generally use a *three-point lighting approach*. This method is good for computer animators, too. These are the three points (see Figure 1.7):

- **Key light** A primary front light source, it's the dominant light source in a scene. It's usually set some distance to the left or right of the camera so that its shadows are apparent. In Maya, the key light is normally set to cast shadows.

- **Fill light** A secondary front light source used to counter the shadows cast by the key light. It's usually less bright and is often placed at the opposite side of the key light. You can determine whether the fill light casts shadows in Maya. Generally, only one or two lights should cast shadows on the same area in a scene. Too many shadows weaken the effect and slow down image calculation.

- **Back light** A background wash of light used to bring out the subject's back side and the backdrop. You can set Maya's back light to not create specular highlights, meaning it won't create highlights on shiny surfaces.

Another light often used for 3D animation is the *rim light*. Like a crescent moon, the rim light is positioned to accentuate the subject's visible perimeter. A common approach is to tint the rim light, often light blue. In Maya this light can be set to illuminate only the subject so that the backdrop doesn't exhibit illumination from a tinted light. The color contrast of a tinted rim light on the subject can make it pop out from the background, particularly if the rim light is a complementary color of the background.

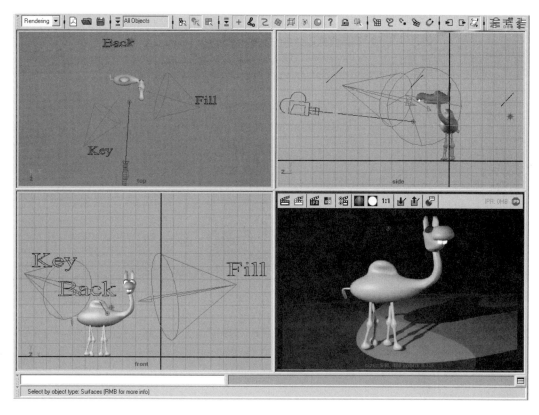

FIGURE 1.7   *A three-point lighting approach.*

Cameras and Perspective

The camera's positioning can imply certain characteristics or traits about the subject. The camera can be close to or far from the subject. It could be under the subject looking up or above the subject looking down. In addition, cameras—both real and virtual—have a field of view or, as it's called in Maya, *angle of view*. That means the camera can be wide-angle or telephoto. The viewer's perception is the intensity of the perspective effect; that is, as the camera views a wider field, the perspective becomes more exaggerated. Normal human vision applied to a typical viewing plane (TV, movie screen) uses a roughly 50-degree viewing angle. Larger angle values view a wider area and produce a stronger, more exaggerated perspective effect, and vice versa, as shown in Figure 1.8.

FIGURE 1.8   *Angle of view and apparent perspective: On the left is a 20-degree angle of view, and on the right, an 85-degree angle of view.*

Angle of View and Perspective

Relative height can imply importance. For example, if you want your subjects to look mighty, you photograph them from underneath, as though looking up at a giant statue. To create a lonely or isolated effect, you can photograph the subject from above at some distance.

Perspective implies drama and action. You may have noticed that sleek cars and planes are sometimes photographed from the front at an extremely wide angle quite close to the vehicle body. This gives a wildly exaggerated perspective, as though the vehicle is coming right at you. Telephoto views at a very low angle value diminish perspective until the objects in view are so flattened that it's hard to tell which objects are closer. The lack of perspective tends to give a sterile, "schematic view" look to your scene.

Perspective can also impart a sense of scale. Because 3D worlds have no reference point for size, sometimes it's difficult to communicate whether you're looking at a toy car, a normal full-sized car, or a giant car. There are many cues to size, such as the intensity and size of details in a surface (for a car, scratches, metallic flake, and dirt). Using a wider angle lens is an easy way to impart scale quickly, however. Be careful not to overdo it; generally, angles should range from 25 to 80 degrees. For closeups, you are usually better off with a narrower angle on a camera that's farther away because putting a standard or wide-angle camera very close to an object always results in exaggerated perspective, as shown in Figure 1.9.

FIGURE 1.9   *Same subject, but different camera position and angle of view.*

Vanishing Points and Perspective

Renaissance-era artists began to realize the key to realistic landscape painting when they discovered the *vanishing point*. An image can have one, two, or three vanishing points, depending on the camera's orientation. If the camera is perfectly level, only a single vanishing point is apparent. If the camera is rotated left or right (the camera in Figure 1.10 was rotated left), you get a second vanishing point. If the camera is then rotated up or down, a third vanishing point is introduced.

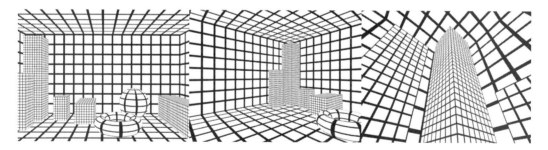

FIGURE 1.10   *Using 1-, 2-, and 3-point perspective.*

In some cases, you might need to position the camera in a place that forces 2-point perspective, but you want only one vanishing point. This often happens in architectural images, when you don't want the buildings to appear to converge at the top, but do want to render the building from a low point of view. Maya can solve this problem with a camera attribute called *film offset*.

Directing 101

Having learned about camera placement from a still photographer's point of view, now add the dimension of time. Objects can move and change shape or color over time, and the camera can move around the scene. You can also edit together several sequences with cuts or dissolves between different camera passes. At this point, you are in the realm of the movie director. Film direction has some rules that are good to know for shooting 3D action.

Cutting and the "Line of Action"

Generally, when starting a scene, the viewer needs a frame of reference. Directors usually provide it with what's called a *master shot*, a brief shot of the majority of the setting to give an idea of the layout.

If characters will interact, the master shot usually begins with the *two shot*, a view of both characters that establishes their relative positions. If a single character is moving around, the full-body shot is referred to as a *wide shot*. A *medium shot* shows a character from waist to head, and a *medium closeup*, from chest to head. The *closeup* includes the neck to the top of the head, but the *extreme closeup* crops from above the eyes to below the lips. These descriptions apply to humans, of course; your alien character's body and facial parts might be in quite different places! At least you have a starting point to describe the shot sequence for telling your story, though.

note

The *line of action* refers to maintaining the camera on one side of the scene action to avoid disorienting the viewer. As in a stage play where the audience is fixed on one side of the action, it is easy to confuse the viewer if the camera crosses the line of action between characters, as shown in an establishing shot. For example, if two characters are conversing, the camera will stay on one side of an imaginary line between the characters, as in Figure 1.11.

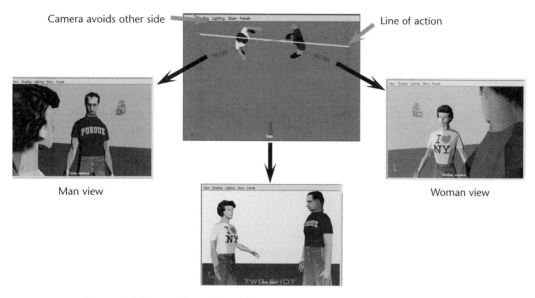

FIGURE 1.11   *An illustration of line of action.*

Scene Motion

A problem that animators of all kinds have is imparting mass and momentum to characters. In life, objects and people rarely start or stop moving instantly, but when they do stop abruptly, things attached to them often wobble or fall off. None of this happens automatically in animation, however, so you must remember the dynamics of real-life motion and simulate it with the motions you create. In cartoons, this motion is often exaggerated: A character's height and width vary radically as she walks, or she spreads out and loses height when hitting the ground.

Center of gravity is also important. For example, if a character rears back, it puts a leg out as a counterbalance; otherwise, it would fall over. Animators often act out their characters' motions and film them for reference to remember these subtle but important facets of real-world movement.

Camera Motion

The camera can move as well, and in a 3D program there are no limitations—it can fly through keyholes, move as fast as a jet and stop instantly, or rotate in place at 100 spins per second. Unless you want your human audience to become upset or ill, however, you should adhere to the same principles as real-life camera operators. If you rotate in place, you must move very slowly, for example. Don't roll (tilt) the camera in relation to the horizon unless you are doing a special effect, like a fighter jet or roller coaster point of view.

As an animator, you should give the camera mass so that it doesn't start or stop "on a dime." The camera should go from fixed to moving or rotating with gradual acceleration, and go from moving or rotating back to a fixed position with gradual deceleration. You can put the camera on a *path*, a curvy line that passes through your scene like a roller-coaster rail. Be careful not to force the camera to look forward, though, or the results will be a whiplash experience for your viewers. Instead, leave the camera rotation as floating so that the virtual viewpoint is moving, but its rotation is smooth and fluid.

Computer Graphics Primer

If you've used a product such as Photoshop, you probably already know the terms and general methods of computer graphics and can skim forward, but these terms are so fundamental to progressing with computer graphics that we've supplied a recap of them in the following sections.

Vectors and Pixels

You approach computer graphics in two primary ways: vectors and pixels. *Vectors* are a connect-the-dots approach; a fixed point on a picture has a connecting line to the next point. After several lines are made, you can close the line and then fill in the resulting shape with color. This approach is sometimes called *line art*. Because the endpoints and lines are at absolute points in space, you can create line art at any scale without loss of quality. This approach is excellent for hard-edged graphics, such as signs and logos, and programs such as CorelDraw and Illustrator use this method. All TrueType fonts are vector-based.

The pixel (for *picture element*) approach uses an array of rectangular dots called *pixels* to make up a *bitmap* image. The dots can be any of a multitude of colors, and viewed together from a distance, the array of pixels can produce any sort of image or photograph. The more pixels, the more detailed the resulting image, if the image's absolute printed or projected size stays the same. The image's absolute pixel array size is called its *resolution*, and densely pixeled images are described as high-resolution or sometimes "high-res" (for example, 35mm motion picture film is usually at 2048 pixels across by 1536 pixels high). Bitmaps are not *scalable* like vector art. If you enlarge a bitmap enough, or zoom in far enough, it *pixelates*; in other words, you can see the squares of solid color that make up the image. Bitmaps are ideal for photographic imagery, and programs such as Adobe Photoshop and Corel Photo-Paint are popular software for creating and editing bitmaps. For the most part, vector art is not used in 3D applications, but most vector art programs allow you to *rasterize* the image—turn it into a bitmap at some chosen resolution.

The files for bitmaps are usually much larger than line art files. For example, a typical small 640×480 pixel color image contains 307,200 pixels, and each pixel has a data byte for each of its red, green, and blue colors. The raw file size is, therefore, 921,600 bytes! This size issue was a real problem in the early computer graphics, but data compression techniques (described in "Image File Formats," later in this chapter) and the ever-larger-capacity computer have solved that problem.

Both types of graphics files come into play in Maya. You might need to create a logo from line art, create text from a font, or import a 2D floor plan from a drafting program like AutoCAD. All have vector files as sources, which is a good thing; you can easily take these 2D shapes and use them as modeling curves. You might need tools such as Okino Polytrans to make these translations because Maya's capability to import vector files is minimal. You'll use bitmaps far more often in your 3D work, mostly to apply to surfaces in a manner similar to decals or wallpaper. Also, Maya's actual output (its *renderings*) is bitmaps, the 2D pictures taken in its 3D world.

2D and 3D

It's possible to confuse 2D and 3D computer graphics because artists often strive for a 3D "look" but use 2D tools exclusively. When we speak of 3D, we're referring to a fully three-dimensional virtual space where objects, lights, and cameras can be placed anywhere. You'll see the three dimensions referred to as x, y, and z, taken from the mathematical subject of geometry. Helpers appear in Maya to indicate these axes, as shown in Figure 1.12. Which direction is represented by which letter? It usually depends on the user's discipline. For animators, the 2D screen had an x-axis going from left to right and a y-axis for up and down. The screen faces the animator, so y was always the up and down vector. When 3D arrived, the z-axis added the factor of depth—into or out of the screen. CAD users saw it differently, however. They were always looking down on their floor plans from above—the plan view—so x and y were indicators of north/south and east/west. The z axis for these users indicated height. Maya allows the user to switch the up axis between y and z, and you'll find this feature necessary to change to the z-axis when you work on CAD-related scenes. Other 3D programs mix these axes up, too (again, usually based on the program's pedigree—drafting versus art), so you might need to change the y/z up setting when importing from other packages.

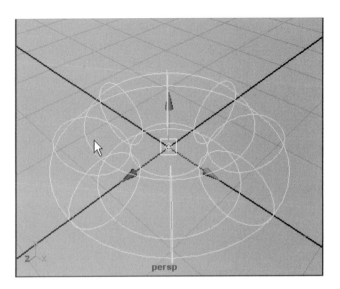

FIGURE 1.12   *Maya's axes are displayed in the corner of any 3D view, and selected objects can display their own axes.*

Input and Output

Much of the time, you work in Maya from a completely blank scene and build up your world from this black empty void. When the scene is finished, a still image or a series of stills is *rendered*—that is, the computer calculates a 2D bitmap of the scene from the camera view, taking into account all lights, objects, and material properties assigned to objects. A series of stills is used to create animation by playing them back quickly in sequence. Movies can be viewed from sequences by using the computer to play them back or by output to videotape or movie film.

Don't confuse the fast shaded views of Maya's interactive 3D panels with rendering. Although a reasonably high-quality image can be produced in real time from a modern 3D accelerated video card (like those Maya requires), the image quality is no match for what the slower software rendering looks like (see Figure 1.13). Each new generation of video cards increases the capacity and quality of the shaded view (also known as hardware or real-time rendering), but the quality of software rendering cannot be achieved in anything close to real time for a typical scene file. Animators are always wanting more, and soft shadows, volumetric lights, depth of field, and other effects are render killers. The software renderer can handle them, but it can take several minutes more per frame to compute.

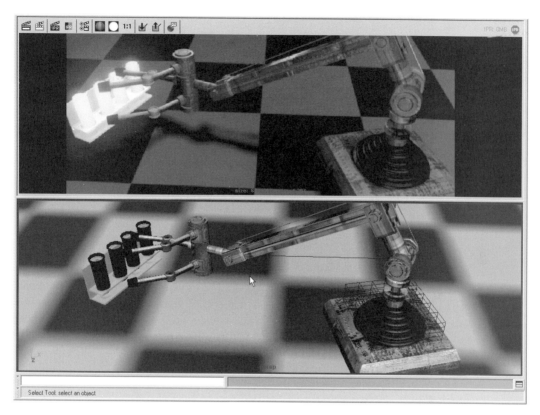

FIGURE 1.13   *The interactive shaded view at the bottom looks nice, but it's no match for the quality of actual final renderings.*

Often you need to bring data, particularly images, into or out of Maya. Every time you apply an image to a surface as part of a material, you need to load the image, and every time you render an image that you plan to keep, you need to save it as a file. Also, you can create scenes from real-world objects (known as scanning) or create real physical objects from 3D modeled objects in Maya.

3D Scanners

Wouldn't it be nice if you could scan in a plastic model of a car rather than painstakingly hand-draft each part? Actually, there are several technologies for doing this, but there are also drawbacks.

The laser scanner is the fastest and most expensive method, ranging from a few thousand to a few hundred thousand dollars. An array of data called a *point cloud* is collected from the laser's scan of a region. Multiple scans must be stitched together to create an object's outer surface. The point clouds are necessarily dense, so the usual result is a huge mesh data file that requires a lot of editing to make it usable in a 3D program. Often the point cloud functions as a reference, and the model is created over it.

A stylus device uses a pointer to take data from an object. These devices are usually cheaper than laser scanners, but thousands of points must be carefully captured before an object of any real detail emerges. The stylus can be connected by an armature that calculates position, or it might use a kind of radio field so that you can use a portable wand to capture points. Less editing is required than with laser scanning, but it's a slow process to touch a probe to 10,000 points on a plastic model! Inaccuracy can also be a problem, making the 3D-sampled version of a perfectly smooth car body appear warped and dented.

3D Printers

An even more amazing technology can generate a solid physical object from any object made in a 3D program. The leader of these technologies is called *laser sintering* and involves the use of a laser to harden specified areas of a photosensitive viscous amber fluid. A small platform in the fluid slowly submerges after each laser pass, pulling the partially completed object down so that the laser can create a new layer on the top. The result is a kind of amber plastic solid model of your object!

These devices remain expensive and are mostly owned by service bureaus that charge by the object's size and complexity. Sintering is also time consuming; it might take days to create large objects. Manufacturers, in particular, appreciate the ability to create a physical version of an object modeled in a 3D program, such as Maya, for the purposes of prototyping or design evaluation.

Image File Formats

The usual output of your efforts in Maya is in the form of 2D bitmaps. Many different file formats are offered in Maya, and you need to know the basics of how they store data. Some formats discard parts of the image, so you might be disappointed when you see the saved version of the image that seemed so perfect in its raw state from the Maya renderer. These are the file formats available in Maya:

- **One bit**   Pixels are either on or off, either black or white. These images look like a fax.
- **Grayscale**   No color information; only the value component (as in HSV color) of the color is used. Grayscale depth is important, too; typically 256 shades of gray are possible.

- **Paletted** A limited number of colors are used to create the image. Think "paint by number." Sometimes the colors are *dithered* (randomly scattered in a controlled way) to achieve a better approximation of the image.

- **Truecolor** An 8-bit byte that allows 256 shades is allocated for each of a pixel's RGB components. This format allows 16 million colors and is a good-quality mode to reproduce nearly any image. The three 8-bit bytes for red, green, and blue are 24 bits combined, so this format is sometimes called 24-bit color.

- **48-bit color** Instead of 24 bits, 48 bits are allocated to a color image; 16 bits per channel. This allows for 65,000 shades for each of red, green, and blue, making for a much higher-quality image that will be twice the file size as with 24 bit. This higher depth can be helpful when you are seeing a banding effect caused by brightening a dark area. Programs like Photoshop will allow you to load a TIFF 16 format file created by Maya, although many filters and options are disabled. However, you can adjust the image levels and brightness before changing the image back to an 8-bit/channel standard image to continue editing.

Images can be compressed in several ways, but you need to be aware of whether the compression is *lossy*, which means some image degradation is allowed to achieve a smaller file size. *Non-lossy* compression schemes can reduce file size by minimizing redundant data, but files are always retained at the original quality. Samples of the image formats listed previously and of lossy image compression artifacts are available on this book's CD-ROM (in the folder below the CD file icon).

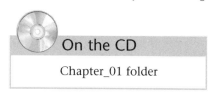

On the CD

Chapter_01 folder

Maya images that are added to other images later might have an *alpha channel*, an optional attribute for each pixel that defines the transparency. For example, if you want to render a character in Maya and then have him cavort around in the real-world video footage, it would be a pain to cut the character out from each frame by hand. The alpha channel lets you instantly cut the mask for the character. Make sure you save the image sequence using an image file format that supports the inclusion of an alpha channel, or it will be lost when you render the character.

Let's review the image file formats offered by Maya:

- **Alias PIX** A truecolor format that's backward-compatible with older Alias products.

- **AVI** A movie format that's usually truecolor but usually has a lossy compression scheme. Don't use movie file formats when you are rendering and saving only one frame. Other popular movie formats are MPG and QuickTime MOV. They are not supported by Maya, so you need other software to import or export these formats.

- **Cineon**   A truecolor still image format used frequently for output to celluloid movie film.

- **EPS**   Usually for vector files, such as logos, but also allows bitmap images to be embedded. If Maya outputs an EPS file, it's a bitmap with an EPS "wrapper" around it. Just because a bitmap image is in EPS format doesn't mean the image can be scaled larger without pixelating—it can't.

- **GIF**   A paletted image used for the Web. GIFs can be made to animate crudely, but Maya doesn't support this kind of GIF. It supports only still image output to GIF.

- **JPEG**   A truecolor format with a lossy compression scheme. Does not support alpha channel.

- **Maya IFF**   A truecolor format specific to Maya. Optionally includes an alpha channel.

- **Maya 16 IFF**   A 48-bit format with 16 bits per red, green, and blue channel. Optionally includes an alpha channel, also in 16-bit format.

- **Quantel YUV**   A truecolor format that converts the image from RGB to another colorspace called YUV, used for specialized video encoders.

- **RLA**   A truecolor format supported by many compositors, it can embed extra information such as depth and is sometimes used when the image from Maya needs special editing, such as blurring objects in the background. Optionally includes an alpha channel.

- **SGI**   A truecolor format popular on Silicon Graphics workstations. Optionally includes an alpha channel.

- **SGI16**   A 48-bit color format. Optionally includes an alpha channel, also in 16-bit format.

- **SoftImage pic**   A truecolor format used by the 3D animation application SoftImage. Optionally includes an alpha channel.

- **Targa**   A truecolor format, usually the rendered output format of choice. This format has few variations and is almost guaranteed to work with anything that reads targa (TGA) files. Optionally includes an alpha channel.

- **TIFF**   A truecolor noncompressed format. Maya saves TIFF only in truecolor and high-color format, but the TIFF image file can be almost any type of file format—paletted, one-bit, and so on. Usually the compression schemes are non-lossy, but newer TIFF formats sometimes use a JPG-like lossy compression mode. If you get a TIFF file from a source other than Maya, it might be in a mode Maya can't read. Typically, you convert it to a compatible format with Photoshop or another bitmap editor. Optionally includes an alpha channel.

- **TIFF16**   A 48-bit color format of TIFF. Optionally includes an alpha channel, also in 16-bit format.

- **Windows BMP**   A truecolor noncompressed format. BMP is like TIFF, with many variants allowed. Does not offer support for an alpha channel.

Using a movie file format for later output to video is usually a bad idea because most movie formats often have lossy compression schemes. For output of animations to video or film, the usual route is sequential TIFF or TGA. Dozens or even thousands of individual numbered files are rendered and saved on the hard disk. Later, these images are loaded by specialized hardware that can then play back video at full speed or burn the images to movie film.

Going Further

Take an art class. Many community colleges offer reasonably priced classes that meet in the evenings. Look for classes in figure drawing, art history, or art appreciation. These classes can hone your sense of color and design and possibly spark ideas about how to approach new problems as you encounter them.

Request the books listed in the "Bibliography" section (on the following page) from your library. For hard-to-find books, most libraries offer interlibrary loans.

Bibliography

Art Books

The Artist's Complete Guide to Facial Expression, by Gary Faigin. Watson-Guptill, 1990. ISBN: 0823016285.

Atlas of Facial Expression: An Account of Facial Expression for Artists, Actors, and Writers, by Stephen Rogers Peck. Oxford University Press (Trade), 1990. ISBN: 0195063228.

Dynamic Figure Drawing, by Burne Hogarth. Watson-Guptill, 1996. ISBN: 0823015777.

Dynamic Light and Shade, by Burne Hogarth. Watson-Guptill, 1991. ISBN: 0823015815.

Dynamic Wrinkles and Drapery, by Burne Hogarth. Watson-Guptill, 1995. ISBN: 0823015874.

The Human Figure in Motion, by Eadweard Muybridge. Dover, 1989 (originally published in 1887). ISBN: 0486202046.

Art History and Appreciation

Arts and Ideas, by William Fleming. HBJ College & School Division, 1997. ISBN: 0155011049.

History of Art, by H. W. Janson and Anthony F. Janson. Harry N. Abrams, 2001. ISBN: 0810934469.

Learning to Look at Paintings, by Mary Acton. Routledge, 1997. ISBN: 0415148901.

Creativity and Visual Psychology

Color, Environment, & Human Response, by Frank H. Mahnke and Rudolf H. Mahnke. John Wiley & Sons, 1996. ISBN: 0471286672.

Conceptual Blockbusting: A Guide to Better Ideas, by James L. Adams. Perseus Press, 1990. ISBN: 0201550865.

The New Drawing on the Right Side of the Brain, by Betty Edwards. J. P. Tarcher, 1999. ISBN: 0874774241.

Ways of Seeing, by John Berger. Viking Press, 1995. ISBN: 0140135154.

Film Direction

Directing: Film Techniques and Aesthetics, by Michael P. Rabiger. Focal Press, 1996. ISBN: 0240802233.

Film Directing Shot by Shot: Visualizing from Concept to Screen, by Steven D. Katz. Focal Press, 1991. ISBN: 0941188108.

Lighting

Digital Lighting & Rendering, by Jeremy Birn. New Riders Publishing, 2000. ISBN: 1562059548.

Light Fantastic: The Art and Design of Stage Lighting, by Max Keller and Johannes Weiss. Prestel Publishing, 2000. ISBN: 3791321625.

A Practical Guide to Stage Lighting, by Steven Louis Shelley. Focal Press, 1999. ISBN: 0240803531.

Set Design and Interior Design

Colour Art and Science (The Darwin College Lectures), by Trevor Lamb and Janine Bourriau (eds.). Cambridge University Press, 1995. ISBN: 0521499631.

Living Colors: The Definitive Guide to Color Palettes Through the Ages, by Margaret Walch and Augustine Hope. Chronicle Books, 1995. ISBN: 0811805581.

3D and Computer Graphics

The Art of Maya, by T. Hawken et al. Alias|Wavefront Education, 2000. ISBN: 0968572510.

The Art and Science of Digital Compositing, by Ron Brinkmann. Morgan Kaufmann Publishers, 1999. ISBN: 0121339602.

The Art of Visual Effects: Interviews on the Tools of the Trade, by Pauline B. Rogers. Focal Press, 1999. ISBN: 0240803752.

Summary

A combination of art and technology goes into 3D animation. At this point, you have learned the basics of computer graphics terminology and are ready to start working with Maya. You can explore these topics in more depth with other books if you want to.

- **2D and 3D computer graphics terms**   A common language to start with.
- **Still image composition**   What appears where in your frame.
- **Lighting and directing**   Thinking like a movie-maker!
- **File formats for bitmap images**   The pros and cons of each format.

Don't feel like you need to be an expert in every subject of technology and art. Learn the basics and, just as important, learn what else there is to learn. If you know the range of possibilities in a discipline, you can explore more deeply in specific areas to solve problems as they come up.

CHAPTER 2

A Tour of Maya

In This Chapter

It's time to start Maya and learn how to move around in it. Before we begin discussing how to make anything, though, this chapter introduces you to Maya's structure and design. You'll learn all the interface elements and start to get a feel for getting around in the panels. You'll also look at playing back animation and the Shaded and Wireframe modes of viewing objects. These are the primary parts of any 3D program, and after you gain some comfort with these *true* fundamentals of Maya, you'll be poised to move on to specifics:

- **The Maya interface** Take a tour of each feature as we describe it and name the parts.

- **Manipulating views** Learn how to tumble, track, and dolly your 3D view.

- **Detail and shading** See how any 3D panel can be displayed in several different modes.

- **Changing your interface** Learn how to quickly change the Maya interface to suit the task at hand by resizing and reassigning the panels and by minimizing or maximizing any single panel.

Key Terms

Attribute Editor The primary interface for changing objects and such in Maya, available as a floating window or docked at the interface's right side.

Channel Box Used to view and edit the variables of your currently selected item, usually accessed at the interface's right side.

Key Terms

Hotbox   A workflow speedup that many Maya animators love—an overlaid menu triggered by holding down the spacebar.

tumble   The official term for spinning or rotating around in a view.

track   The official term for panning or moving linearly across a view.

dolly   The official term for zooming into and out of a view (technically, the term for moving the camera into or out of a scene).

zoom   Used for actions in which you draw a window to magnify or reduce.

LMB   The left mouse button, the primary action-taking button.

MMB   The middle mouse button, often a secondary or alternative action-taking button. On a mouse with a scroll wheel, the scroll button acts as the MMB.

RMB   The right mouse button; usually provides options to select with the LMB (as with most Windows applications).

Wireframe mode   Viewing a 3D scene as lines that make it look as though the objects are made from a wire screen mesh. Until the fairly recent advent of higher powered 3D graphics cards, the only interactive way to work with 3D scenes.

Shaded mode   Lets you view geometry in a crudely rendered interactive way (not to be confused with the high-quality renderer). Any 3D view panel in Maya can be in Wireframe or Shaded mode.

Gouraud shading   A crude form of smooth shading that adds highlights to polygonal objects by averaging the polygon corners. It renders quickly and is the method used for interactive shaded mode in Maya panels.

Hotkeys to Memorize

Alt+LMB   orbit

Alt+MMB   pan

Alt+LMB+MMB   zoom

Ctrl+Alt+drag window with LMB zoom window

Ctrl+A   activate the Attribute Editor

f   use the Frame Selected Object option (zoom in or out to the boundaries of the current object)

a   use the Frame All Objects option (zoom in or out to the boundaries of the scene)

spacebar tap   toggle full-screen mode of selected panel

spacebar hold   open Hotbox

1   NURBS at low detail

2   NURBS at medium detail

3   NURBS at high detail

4   Wireframe mode for selected 3D view panel

5   Shaded mode for selected 3D view panel

6   Shaded and Hardware Textured mode for selected view panel

7   use scene lights

q   Select mode - pointer

w   Move mode

Hotkeys to Memorize

e	Rotate mode	**F3**	Modeling mode
r	Scale mode	**F4**	Dynamics mode
t	Manipulator mode	**F5**	Rendering mode
F1	Help	**Ctrl+z**	undo
F2	Animation mode		

Maya Overview

Maya's core design takes an approach called the *dependency graph*. The idea is that everything in the scene—every curve, object, link, image, texture, keyframe, and so forth—and every tweak made to those items would be considered one "thing." Actually, not "thing"; the name they use is *node*, but it means about the same. It's one building block of the scene. These building blocks link to create ever more complex things. For example, when a line is drawn in Maya, it becomes a node. When the line is 3D-revolved to create, for example, a vase, the underlying line is still there. Further, the revolve operation creates a "revolve" node, placed in history, thus letting you modify the original line and the revolve parameters independently.

Modifications made to the line immediately affect the vase's shape, and the modifications themselves create a node so that you can undo or modify anything you've done before. This flexibility underlies the entire Maya product, and includes the option to disable or delete history, which animators often use for efficiency.

The dependency graph architecture is simple to understand and allows tremendous flexibility. Maya allows the animator to view a scene file with every dependency revealed by using a view called the *Hypergraph*. There, links can be broken and reconnected so that any variable can control virtually any other variable. This feature illustrates one reason for Maya's popularity with Hollywood: A technician can set up dependencies so that the animator's work is minimized. When a character tilts her head back, the skin stretches, the muscles appear to move and bulge—and this all happens automatically because it has been set up to work that way in Maya. Naturally, setting up complex dependencies takes time, but the investment is easily justifiable for a character that will be used often. Programming skills are rarely required, however. It's simply a matter of learning what's possible and becoming proficient in setting up these dependencies. As Maya becomes more popular with animators of all types, this type of "TD work" (named for the technical directors of projects that typically perform this work) is becoming something everyone does, so long as it saves time and effort overall.

Hand Positioning

Most of the time when you animate with Maya, your right hand controls the three-button mouse, and your left hand is at the left side of the keyboard. This puts your left hand in position to operate the primary hotkeys, the spacebar, the Alt and Ctrl keys, and other keyboard shortcuts that get heavy use. Left-handed users who keep the mouse at the left of their keyboard probably will want to reprogram the default hotkeys that put all the primary keys at the keyboard's left side.

Using the Three Mouse Buttons

Maya uses all three buttons of the mouse constantly. The left mouse button (LMB) is used to select and pick things, and often it's used to take actions such as moving or rotating an object. The right mouse button (RMB) usually brings up a selection list (which you might be familiar with in other programs as a pop-up menu or a context-sensitive menu) for you to pick from with the LMB. The middle mouse button (MMB) is used for adjusting interim things—for example, dragging and dropping materials to the scene or moving part of an object with snapping temporarily engaged.

Using the Spacebar

The spacebar has two functions. The first is the full-screen window toggle, where a brief tap of the spacebar causes a window to toggle to full screen. The window that switches to full screen is always the one that the mouse cursor is currently hovering over. When a fresh install of Maya starts, it's in the typical Four View mode, with Top, Side, Front, and Perspective views; however, the Perspective view is maximized. If you briefly tap the spacebar, the four screens appear. You can then maximize any of the other views.

The other function of the spacebar is to open the Hotbox by holding down the spacebar. The Hotbox is described in detail near the end of this chapter.

Manipulating a View

As you build and manipulate objects, you need to be able to quickly adjust your viewpoint interactively. A primary part of knowing Maya is its window manipulation method. You can position yourself anywhere in a scene by using tumble, track, and dolly controls.

Tumble

With the tumble control, also known as *orbit* or *spin*, you move your orbital position in relation to the scene. Hold down the Alt key with your left hand while you click and drag with the LMB in a perspective viewport.

Track

With the track control, also known as *pan* or *move*, you laterally move your view of the screen. That is, without changing angle or zoom level, the viewpoint moves up, down, left, or right. Hold down the Alt key with your left hand while you click and drag with the MMB in any viewport.

Dolly

With the dolly control, also known as *zoom*, you can interactively zoom in and out of a scene. Hold down the Alt key with your left hand while you click and drag with both the LMB and MMB pressed. You can also zoom into or out of a drawn rectangle by using these methods:

- **Zoom window**   You can click-drag a window that outlines an area you want to zoom into, a technique that CAD users are particularly fond of. To zoom into a window, hold down the Ctrl and Alt keys with your left hand while you drag a window with the mouse holding down the LMB. Drag the rectangle from the upper-left corner to the lower-right corner.

- **Zoom out window**   If you perform the same steps for a zoom window but drag the rectangle from the lower-right corner to the upper-left corner, the window is zoomed back. The smaller the window, the greater the zoom outward.

Saving a View

Every panel has its own Bookmark Editor so that you can save your views. This can be a big timesaver when you have perfectly aligned some objects in a panel and then need to adjust the panel to edit something else. To add a bookmark for a panel, open the Bookmark Editor with View | Bookmarks | Edit Bookmarks. You can type in the bookmark name and even include a description. Now the bookmark will appear above the Edit Bookmarks item under View | Bookmarks in that panel.

trap

You cannot tumble an orthogonal view because Side, Top, and Front views by default do not rotate (orthogonal camera settings are discussed in Chapter 12, "Cameras and Rendering"). These views are locked in place. The term *orthogonal* means the views have no perspective or vanishing point.

tip

All these tools except the tumble work throughout Maya. That is, every graphical Maya dialog box that appears, from Render windows to Hypershade and even the Paint Effects palette, can be tracked and dollied and zoom-windowed. You will use these tools constantly to focus your work area and also to avoid eye strain. Don't forget this when a dialog box appears with text so tiny that it's unreadable!

trap

Each panel has its own bookmarks, exclusive of the others. If you can't find a bookmark you made, you are probably looking in the wrong panel or originally made the bookmark in the wrong panel.

The Maya Interface

When you start Maya for the first time, it looks like the window shown in Figure 2.1. We'll take you on a tour of the interface now and explain what it all means. Some elements of the interface are explained in more detail in the sections that follow. If the need or use for some features seems hard to fathom, just file it away for future reference. As you get the bigger picture, the logic of this layout will make more sense.

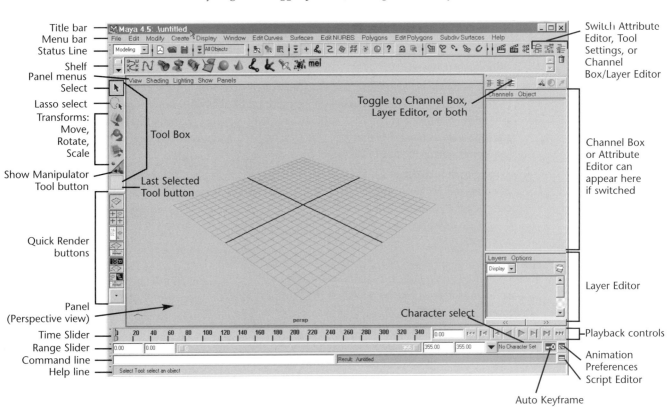

FIGURE 2.1   *The Maya interface.*

Coming down the left side of Figure 2.1, at the top is the title bar, followed by the menu bar—features common to all computer applications. The Status Line contains most of the toggles and buttons used for object manipulation and frequently used functions, such as the Quick Render button (the director's clapboard icon). Below the Status Line is the Shelf, a Maya innovation that lets you easily add customizable quick buttons. Depending on the project you are working on, you might have several custom "macros" you keep visible in the Shelf to speed up your work.

Moving down the left side, next is the vertical dialog box called the Tool Box. The top half of the Tool Box consists of the select and transform tools, which are used constantly to move, rotate, and scale things (collectively, the position, rotation, and scale of an object is known as its *transform*). The Show Manipulator Tool and the Last Selected Tool buttons round out this section. The Show Manipulator Tool button lets you adjust the "history" of an operation, such as when you previously applied a texture to an object and now need a manipulator to change where that texture is applied. The Last Selected Tool button is just that—a quick way to get back to the last tool you used. It's helpful for speeding up your workflow. The icon in this box changes to match the last tool used.

The bottom half of the Tool Box consists of a set of Quick Layout buttons, which adjust the panel layout to several popular configurations. Below those buttons is the Time Slider, which serves several functions: first, to show the current time point of the animation, and second, to allow the animation to be *scrubbed* (that is, click in the Time Slider and drag the mouse left and right to see the animation move forward and backward).

Next down is the Range Slider, which allows the animator to focus on a specific part of the animation. Numerical entries at either end of the Range Slider set (from left to right) the overall animation start frame, the focus range start frame, the focus range end frame, and the overall animation end frame. If you were working on a cartoon scene for TV that lasted one minute, you would probably set the overall start and end to 0 and 1800 because there are 30 frames per second and 60 seconds in a minute. If a problem occurred at the 12-second point, you would want to look at frame 360 and would probably set the range to frames 300 and 420; this makes it much easier to see what's going on. Below the Range Slider is the Command Line and the Help Line. The Command Line is helpful because it's where Maya talks back to you, confirming whether things are working or letting you know when it's detecting errors with what you're asking Maya to do. The Help Line also gives you feedback, letting you know what Maya expects you to do next.

On the right side of the interface, at the far right of the Status Line, are three toggle buttons for picking what will appear at the far right of the interface. You can also choose to have nothing at the right side of the panel, for maximum 3D panel space.

The toggle choices are Attribute Editor, Tool Settings, or Channel Box/Layers, from left to right. In earlier versions of Maya, it was always the Channel Box, and many users will probably favor that mode. Here's what these features are used for:

- **Attribute Editor**   This is another, more detailed way to adjust the settings for an object. Most of the time you use the Attribute Editor as a floating window.

- **Tool Settings**   This window is where you adjust such things as angle snaps for the Rotate mode.

- **Channel Box**   The Channel Box has a toggle at the top for adding the Layer Editor to the bottom or switching entirely to the Layer Editor. There are two types of layers in Maya: display and render (accessed with the Layers pull-down at the top of the Layer Editor). *Display layers* are used for organizing your work; for example, you might put your guidelines for a model in one layer so that they can be hidden or locked (Template mode, in Maya's terminology) while you build based on the lines. *Render layers* let you easily set some objects to be renderable or non-renderable, often useful in complex scenes when you want to render only certain objects.

At the lower right are the playback controls for animation. The outermost buttons rewind to start or fast forward to the end. The next buttons in move the time one frame backward or forward. The next buttons in go to the last or next *keyframe*, the adjacent point in time where the animator has set a "pose" for the object in question. In computer animation, the computer handles all the interim motion, and the animator sets only the most extreme or "key" positions. The two innermost buttons (the simple triangles) are the play forward and play backward buttons. The speed of playback is adjustable, set by clicking the Animation Preferences button. Two other buttons in this area enable Auto Key mode and the Script Editor, which are discussed later (Auto Keyframe mode is covered in Chapter 10, "Animation Basics," and scripting is described briefly in Chapter 15, "Your Next Steps: Efficiency and Artistry").

The Menu Bar

A few things are useful to note about the menu bar. First, the six leftmost entries in the menu bar—File, Edit, Modify, Create, Display, and Window—always stay the same, but the others change based on the mode you are in. The mode is set in the list box at the far left in the Status Line. The four modes in Maya Complete are Animation, Modeling, Dynamics, and Rendering (see Figure 2.2). The hotkeys for these four modes are F2, F3, F4, and F5. Also, you can *tear off* any menu item that has double lines above it to create a customized mini-Tool Box, so that frequently used tools can float on your desktop, as shown in Figure 2.3.

FIGURE 2.2   *Changing modes. Compare this to Figure 2.1 and notice that the first six menu items are the same, but the others have changed.*

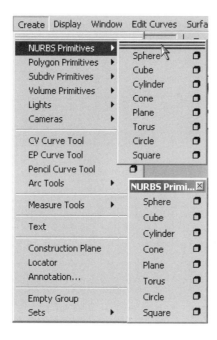

FIGURE 2.3   *Click on the double lines to tear off a dialog box. Note the floating dialog box at the bottom right.*

The Option Box

Many menu items have a small box to the right of the command name (see Figure 2.4). This is the *option box*, which you click to open a dialog box containing all the creation settings for the command. Whenever the option box is used, the settings become the new defaults for that tool.

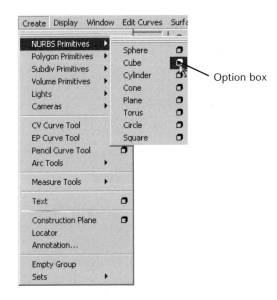

FIGURE 2.4   *Choosing the option box.*

tip

When in doubt, you should always choose the option box and then reset it when you're following tutorials in this book because Maya remembers option box settings even after restarting. That means you won't get the result you expect if the tool has been adjusted before by anyone using your copy of Maya! Simply choose Edit I Reset Settings from the menu bar in the option box to put it back to factory-installed values (see Figure 2.5). In the long run, you'll customize the tools you use frequently so that you don't need to always reset the option box. As a beginner, however, it's easy to forget that you previously changed the settings, and the tutorial you're following in this book might assume they remain in their default settings.

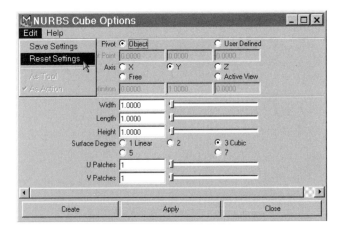

FIGURE 2.5   *Resetting the option box.*

The Status Line

Let's take a closer look at the Status Line shown in Figure 2.6 and explain a few of its alien-looking controls. At far left is the mode selector, described previously in "The Menu Bar" when we explained changing modes.

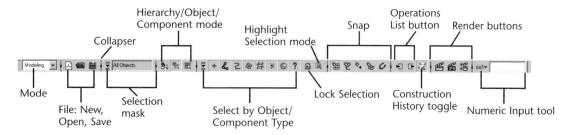

FIGURE 2.6   *Maya's Status Line, a collapsible bar of buttons.*

Next is an arrow bar—a collapser that is a clickable switch used to hide a section of the Status Line. These collapsers let you display what you need and hide items that clutter the Status Line for your current work. When the vertical line has a right-pointing arrow in it, something is hidden within it. Next are the typical File icons for New, Open, and Save.

After the File icons is another list box that controls masking "presets" for object selection, which enables you to ignore certain types of objects when trying to select them. The icons to the right of the list box show the masking selections that have been made. Because animating with Maya relies on selecting the right things in the right order, switching off the ability to select only certain types of items makes the process much easier. The selection mask list box acts as a preset for the buttons in the Select by Type area farther to the right. For example, in Animation mode, only joints and handles can be selected (the character's "pull points" for animation) in the Select by Type area; you wouldn't want to select anything else when posing and keyframing. The three buttons to the right of the selection mask enable you to switch between three modes: Hierarchy, Object, and Component mode.

At the beginning, you usually remain in Object Selection mode. Here, you can select whole objects and mask your selection to pick only certain kinds of objects—lines, surfaces, lights, and so forth.

Component Selection mode allows you to adjust subcomponents of an object, such as pulling a sphere into a capsule shape by picking just the top half of the sphere and stretching it out.

Hierarchy is the animation term for linking one object to another. For example, you link the car's tires to the car body so that you need to animate only the motion of the car body—the tires follow automatically. In this case, you say that the tires are children of the body, and the car body is the parent to the tire objects. Maya also uses a tree metaphor with the words *root* and *leaf*. In Hierarchy Selection mode, selection masks let you pick only the parent ("root") or only the children ("leaf")—most helpful when you're setting up object hierarchies, which are discussed in more detail in Chapter 10, "Animation Basics."

The range of buttons to the right of the Hierarchy/Object/Component switches changes depending on which of these three modes you have chosen. When a button describing a type of entity such as curves, surfaces, lights, or cameras (when in Object Selection mode) is pushed in, it can be selected. When it's not pushed in, it cannot be selected. For example, you might want to pick a vase object that was created from a profile spline, but you could accidentally pick the spline instead of the vase object because both coexist, even after the spline has produced the vase. One solution is to hide objects not being edited. However, it's usually more expedient to set the selection mask so that you can pick only surfaces, not curves. If there are many different kinds of objects cluttering the scene, selection masks can become invaluable.

tip

Some selection mask buttons cover several things; for example, the Select by Object Type-Rendering mask covers lights, textures, and cameras. If you right-click over the button, you get the option to enable or disable each of these subtypes. When some subtypes are on and some are off, the button turns brown. For example, if you keep lights selectable but not cameras or textures, the little sphere icon on the button has a brown background to indicate a partially enabled selection.

Next is the Lock Selection button, handy for avoiding accidentally clicking off an object and deselecting it. When you know you want to work on something for a while, you lock it. Next is the Highlight Selection Mode button, a toggle to highlight the selected object in the display, which is on by default. Next are the snap tools, which ease modeling and modifying objects by making it seem as though an object or part of an object is drawn toward another; when the mouse approaches within a certain distance, the entity being moved by the mouse jumps to the nearest snap-to element. The snap-to element could be curves, points, view planes, the grid, or any combination of them. The rightmost snap icon (the big U magnet by itself) makes an object "live," thus turning the object itself into a building template. With this mode, you might use a human face mesh to create a Lone Ranger mask; curves would automatically snap to the face surface.

You use the Operations List buttons to view upstream and downstream connections and enable or disable them. The Construction History toggle is next, and Maya uses it to record construction. All the parameters used to make an object are stored with the object, allowing you to change them later. Having it on can make files large and slow to load, however, so you might opt to turn it off sometimes. More often, the animator deletes an object's history when the object has been built successfully, instead of turning off all history with this button.

tip

History is not related to the Undo operation. You can have history off and still use Edit I Undo to undo anything. History only embeds the construction history in an object, such as how many divisions are used to create an extruded object. With history on, the animator can return to the project at any time and set more or fewer segments.

The hotkey for undo is Ctrl+z, as in nearly all Windows programs. By default, the Undo option records your last 10 edits, but it can be set to any value, including indefinite, by using Window I Settings/Preferences I Preferences I Undo.

Next are the Quick Render and IPR (Interactive Photorealistic Renderer) rendering buttons. Clicking them pops up a window, and the computer then takes a few seconds to a few minutes (or even hours) to compute a full-quality render. IPR rendering is slower, but when finished, it can update the rendering in near real time as you adjust lights and materials in a scene. The size of the rendering and many other parameters are controlled by the Render Globals window; a button to open this window appears to the right of the IPR button.

Finally, at the rightmost side of the Status Line is the Numeric Input tool. It can operate in four modes:

- **Selection by name**   Used to type in a prefix or common letters and select all the objects you want quickly. For example, typing in *Torus* would select any object with the letters *Torus* anywhere in the name.
- **Quick rename**   Used to rename the currently selected object.
- **Absolute entry**   Used to enter an exact value for the current highlighted transform. For example, you can select the Y move arrow when in Move mode, and it turns yellow. Entering a value then forces it to move immediately to that value for the Y-coordinate.
- **Relative entry**   Similar to absolute entry, but in this case, the amount entered is added to the current value.

Panel Menus

Every view panel you work in has a common set of pull-down menus listed above it, as shown in Figure 2.7.

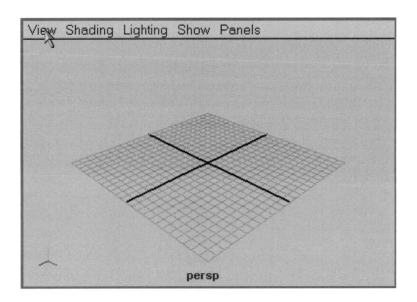

FIGURE 2.7   *The panel menu that appears in any view of the 3D scene.*

If the panel pull-downs are not appearing, you can enable them in Window | Settings/Preferences | Preferences, and then click the Interface entry under the Categories list on the left side of the dialog box. Make sure there's a check mark in the Show Menubar – In Panels check box.

A few of the more important panel menu items are described in the following list:

- Under the View pull-down, you'll see options for Look At Selected, Frame Selected, and Frame All. These options are helpful for finding an item and focusing on it. The Look At Selected option centers the selected object in the view. Frame Selected (hotkey: **f**) centers the object and zooms to the object's extents. Frame All (hotkey: **a**) centers and zooms the extents of all displayed objects in the currently active panel. These same hotkeys apply in other types of Maya panels, such as Hypershade.

All hotkeys are case sensitive. If you accidentally have your Caps Lock toggled on, it will seem as though the hotkeys aren't working or aren't doing what you expect them to.

- Under the Shading pull-down, the first two entries are Wireframe (hotkey: **4**) and Smooth Shade All (hotkey: **5**). These options toggle a viewport between viewing objects as lines only or as Gouraud-rendered real-time shaded images.

An important option to note is the NURBS detail mode. When you're working with NURBS, you can display them in three detail levels: low (hotkey: **1**), medium (hotkey: **2**), or high (hotkey: **3**). These hotkeys work only with NURBS.

- The Lighting pull-down has an option for using the lights in the scene (hotkey: **7**) with this panel's Shaded mode. Normally, Shaded mode uses default lights, which are minimal and serve to get some light in the scene when you just need some fast calculating light.

- The Show pull-down lets you selectively hide all entities of a certain type. For example, you often use it to hide cameras and lights, just to clean up the view so that you can focus on the objects. At the bottom of this pull-down is an option to hide the grid, which is useful when you want simplicity in the view.

- Under the Panels pull-down (see Figure 2.8), the top three options allow you to select what the panel is seeing in a 3D view. The first option is for Perspective, with the option to use any predefined Perspective view or add a new one. If you do add a new one, you'll see it listed the next time you look at the Perspective view options. The second option is similar; for orthographic views, you have the option of existing Top, Side, or Front views, but you can create new ones. The third option, Look Through Selected, works with Directional and Spot lights so that you can see exactly where they are pointed. It also works with nearly any object type, merely placing you at the pivot point of the entity, looking in the negative-Z direction.

The next three options let you change the entire layout of the panels. The Panel item displays options that let you switch the selected panel to some other window, such as a rendered view or the Graph Editor. Note that all these other panel types can also be activated as floaters under Window on Maya's main menu bar. However, any panel that's already open as a floater is unavailable in a fixed panel position and will be grayed out in this dialog box. Next is Layouts, used to determine how the view area is split into windows. Below it is Saved Layouts, which is similar to the Quick Layout buttons below the Tool Box. Ten popular layouts are listed, as opposed to the six that appear as hot buttons below the Tool Box. You can create your own custom layouts, too.

FIGURE 2.8   *The Panels pull-down on the panel menu.*

 tip   You can LMB-click and drag at the dividing line between any two or more panels and move it to favor one panel over the other. You can also do this at the center point of four panels.

Tutorial: Interacting with Maya

This tutorial gives you a chance to try out some of these hotkeys and key combinations. Because these actions are the most fundamental ones in Maya, run through this tutorial a few times so that it becomes more of an internalized skill, like typing or playing a musical instrument. As any typist or musician knows, repetition is the key!

1. Load the scene file called ch02tut01.mb from the CD-ROM. It has some NURBS and polygon primitives already created for you to interact with.

On the CD

Chapter_02\ch02tut01.mb

2. Hold the cursor over the Perspective view and tap the spacebar. The view should toggle to full screen.

3. Hold down the Alt key and use the LMB, MMB, and both mouse buttons together to navigate around the objects. Try to get a good view of the NURBS torus.

On the CD

Chapter_02\movies\ch02tut01.wmv

4. Select the NURBS torus. It should become outlined in green. Press **2** and notice the improvement in detail. Then press **3** to see it improve again (see Figure 2.9). To put it back into its original state, press **1** again. Leave it in "3" mode—the highest detail.

FIGURE 2.9   *A NURBS torus in high-detail mode.*

5. Use the Alt key with the MMB to pan to other NURBS objects and adjust their display detail. Note that the plane and the cube do not gain detail despite the added divisions because they have no curved edges. Also note that the NURBS cube is created as six separate NURBS planes.

6. Press **4** to switch the panel to Wireframe mode. Press **a** to use the Frame All (also known as Zoom Extents for All Objects) option. Hold down Ctrl+Alt and drag a window to zoom in on the six leftmost objects.

7. Click on the polygonal cylinder to select it, and press **f** to use the Frame Selected (Zoom Extents of Selected Object) option (see Figure 2.10).

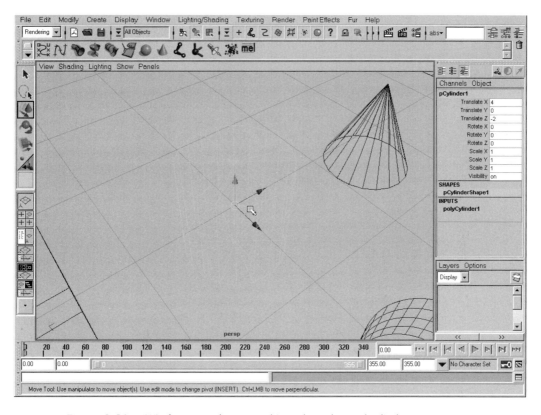

FIGURE 2.10   *Wireframe mode, zoomed into the polygonal cylinder.*

8. Tap the spacebar with the mouse cursor placed over the perspective panel to reveal the four views. Go to any of the four panels, and in the panel menu, choose Panels | Layouts | Three Panes Split Top.

9. Place the cursor on the horizontal split point of the panels, and LMB-click and drag downward to make the bottom panel smaller. Set the bottom panel to view the front orthogonal view by choosing Panels | Orthographic | Front in the panel menu.

10. Right-click in the Top view to activate it. Notice that right-clicking enables you to activate a view without deselecting a currently selected object. LMB-click and drag a rectangle around the letters at the right of the geometric primitives (see Figure 2.11).

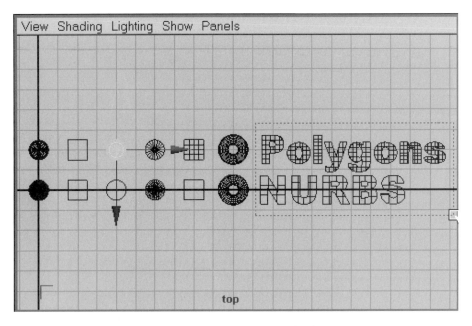

FIGURE 2.11   *Dragging a rectangle to select multiple objects.*

11. In the Top view's panel menu, choose View | Look At Selection. The text items will be centered. Tap the spacebar with the mouse cursor placed over this panel, and the view will switch to full screen. Press **5** to switch this view to Shaded mode. Press **1**, **2**, and **3** to watch the NURBS text display different detail levels. Notice that the polygonal text is unaffected.

12. Click on the number 0 in the Time Slider, and while holding down the LMB, drag the mouse slowly to the right. You should see the polygonal torus move. This object had animation applied to it when you loaded the scene. Drag the Time Slider back to the far left, and the torus should return to its original position. Now select the torus by clicking on it. In the Time Slider, vertical red lines should appear to indicate the frames at which keys have been created (see Figure 2.12).

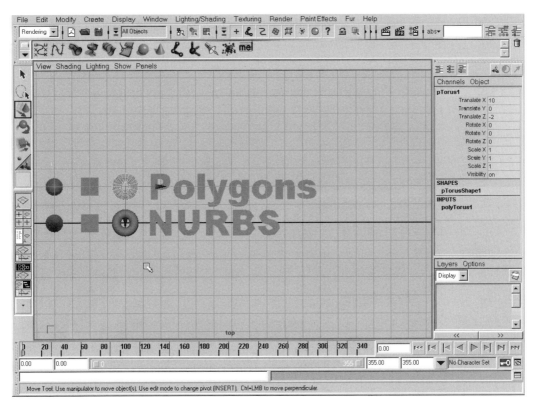

FIGURE 2.12   *The Time Slider displays keyframes for the selected object with a vertical line.*

13. Click the next key button at the lower right: the play button pointing right, with the vertical red line at the point. This hops you forward in time to the next key point. Repeat to see the jumps. Then click the play button, the right-pointing arrow. View the animation playing back. The play button becomes a red square during playback—the stop button. You must click it to stop playback.

14. Change this view to the Perspective view by choosing Panels | Perspective | Persp from the panel menu. Play the animation again. Tumble, track, and dolly the view as the animation plays to center the action and get a good idea of what's going on. Stop the animation playback.

tip   You can stop playback with the Esc key or by clicking the stop button (the same button clicked to begin play).

15. Press **f** to zoom to the polygonal torus. Now bring in the time ranges to 250 to 320; to do that, type those numbers in the two inner number fields below the Time Slider, or LMB-click and drag the little boxes in the Range Slider. Scrub the

On the CD

Chapter_02\ch02tut01end.mb

Time Slider to see what happens by LMB-clicking and dragging left and right. Begin playback again, and adjust the view during playback. Figure 2.13 shows what the scene should look like when you're done. If you like, load the file noted below the CD icon to compare it to your work.

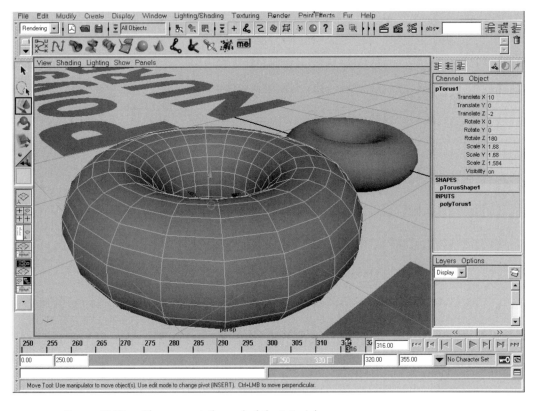

FIGURE 2.13   *The scene at the end of the tutorial.*

Going Further

Repeat the tutorial several times, and each time try to manipulate things differently. Explore the zoom-window option for zooming in and out of a rectangular selection window you've drawn. Try some of the different panel layouts (in any panel, choose Panels | Saved Layouts), including Hypershade and Hypergraph, and note how you can zoom and pan these panels the same as with 3D view panels.

The Hotbox

Maya's Hotbox is another way of getting to the same pull-downs as in the menu bar. To activate it, hold down the spacebar. The Hotbox is centered over the mouse cursor's position at the time the spacebar is pressed, so you'll want to be somewhat in the center.

To see the entire Hotbox, click in the Hotbox Controls section on the right-hand side of the window, and drag the cursor over the Show All option (see Figure 2.14).

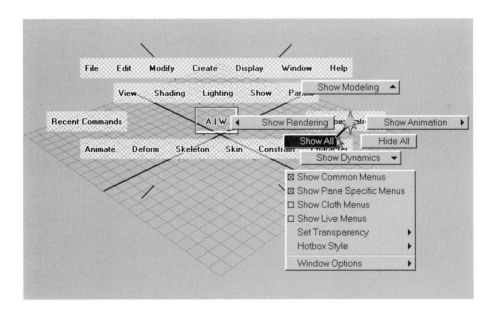

FIGURE 2.14   *Turning on all Hotbox options.*

Now the Hotbox displays every option. Here, in one panel, is every single Maya command. In addition, there are five zones with special options. To see them, click on the top, bottom, right, left, and center (the A|W logo box) of the Hotbox. New menus will appear, as shown in Figure 2.15.

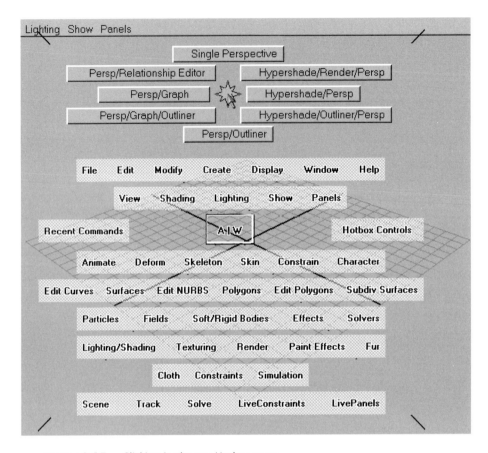

FIGURE 2.15   *Clicking in the top Hotbox zone.*

Going Further

We have only touched on the Hotbox in this chapter, but use this opportunity to explore it more. Try each of the five Hotbox zones, and activate the modes that appear there. You can change panel layout, panel view, and enable and disable parts of the user interface, among other things.

Summary

Having toured the interface, you have learned to interact with Maya's virtual world so that you can see the things you want to see, from the angle you want to see them, and shaded the way you want. You have also begun to develop a common language for the parts of Maya so that you can tell the Tool Box from the Channel Box. Here's a short list of what you've been exposed to and, we hope, have begun to internalize:

- **3D manipulation with Alt+mouse button**   A core skill you will need every time you want to change the view in a Maya panel.

- **The Hotbox**   Even if you aren't using it yet, you can begin to explore what it does and see how it can make working with Maya more efficient.

- **Playback, scrubbing, and time range**   Essential skills for creating, editing, and viewing your animation.

- **The names**   A common language for the Maya interface components so that you can understand the rest of this book.

- **Zoom windows, zoom extents**   When you get lost in a 3D view panel, these actions bring you back to your work quickly and easily.

- **Panel layouts**   You'll use them to quickly reset the interface to one that's optimal for the task at hand.

These are truly the fundamental tasks and concepts of Maya. The key point to take from this chapter is 3D view manipulations. After practicing the Alt+mouse movements for a few hours, they should start to become second nature, and you'll benefit from a more instinctive use of the Alt+ manipulations as you move on to learn new things. From this point, you're ready to learn how to create and modify scene elements, such as objects, lights, and cameras, and to round out your knowledge of Maya's pull-down menus.

CHAPTER 3

Maya Interaction

In This Chapter

Now that you've learned the layout of Maya, it's time to start creating and interacting with objects in Maya. This chapter will prepare you for the next chapter, in which you'll create a complete animation from beginning to end. To get there, you'll need a few more tools under your belt:

- **Creating scene elements** Learn Maya's approach to creating the different types of scene elements you'll need—objects, lights, cameras, and so forth.

- **Selecting scene elements** Maya has several methods for selecting objects, lights, and other parts of your scene file. You'll need to know them all when your scenes get complex.

- **Transforming scene elements** Maya offers a number of useful enhancements to moving, rotating, and scaling your scene elements.

- **Duplicating scene elements** An easy way to speed up creation is to build elements by copying existing ones.

- **Modifying pivot points** Rotating and scaling occur around a pivot point (a sort of "anchor"), so by adjusting this pivot point, you can control how an object or other scene element is transformed.

- **Hierarchy** Scene elements can be set to have relationships to each other so that they inherit transforms made to objects above them in the hierarchy.

- **Extra display modes** Panels can display a 3D view in a number of ways to help with visualization or speed the screen display of complex scenes.

Key Terms

hierarchy   Connections between scene elements in which one object dictates the transforms of all objects below it in the hierarchy.

transform   The combined position, rotation, and scale of an object; the information about where an object is, how it is oriented, and how it has been sized.

scene element   A term we use in this book to refer to all the things you can make in Maya: objects, lights, cameras, and other entities that exist in 3D space.

parent   The higher member of a hierarchy relationship between two scene elements.

child   The subordinate member of a hierarchy relationship between two scene elements. The child can move freely, but any transforms made to the parent are made to the child.

pivot point   The point around which an object rotates or scales; also where the transform manipulator appears, and the reference point for the values that appear in the Channel Box. The pivot point is where the object "lives" in 3D space.

group   An organizational option to create a new scene *node* or handle that represents a collection of scene elements and is the parent of those scene elements.

instance   When duplicating a scene element, a special kind of duplicate that can have its own unique transform but echoes all edits (except for transforms) made to the original object.

snap   An option that forces your mouse cursor to "jump" to specific points. For example, grid snapping, when enabled, tugs your mouse cursor toward grid points when you are moving an object. Maya also offers rotation snaps that force rotation changes to switch in fixed angle increments.

Hotkeys to Memorize

Insert key   toggle Pivot Editing mode

Ctrl+q   select with lasso

Shift-select   toggle object selection

p   parent

Shift+P   unparent

x   temporary snap to grid

c   temporary snap to curve

v   temporary snap to point

Ctrl+d   duplicate

Creating Objects

Instead of creating objects in the viewports, Maya creates them at the center of the Maya world space—the 0,0,0 (or *origin*) point by default. From there, it's up to you to move the object and place it in the position you want.

All the basic scene elements that can be rendered are listed under the Create menu: NURBS, polygons, subdivision surfaces, lights, cameras, curves, and text. Most have option boxes where you can change the default type of object that's created. There are many other scene elements, such as joints, deformers, and lattices, that do not render but assist animation or modeling. Other renderable scene elements that don't appear in the Create menu include particles and paint effects.

Creating Primitives

The types of objects you'll see under NURBS, polygon, and subdivision surface creation are called *primitives*: sphere, cube, cylinder, cone, plane, and torus. These shapes might not seem like a useful starting point for your project, but they are very malleable with Maya's object editing tools; with some experience, you can sculpt a sphere into a rock or a head or a bowl. However, usually you model by creating curves (construction lines that are infinitely thin and do not render) and then using the Surfaces functions to extrude, loft, or perform another function that builds an object from a curve.

When you create a new primitive in Maya, it becomes the selected object. In the Channel Box, you can access the object's creation parameters, the ones used most often to modify a new shape. After you create an object, you open the Inputs node in the Channel Box and edit the object's creation parameters. For example, you might change a sphere's Sweep value to quickly convert it to a hemisphere.

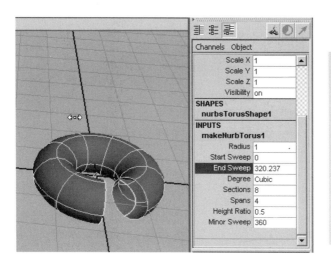

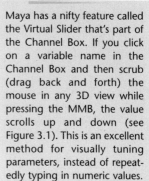

tip

Maya has a nifty feature called the Virtual Slider that's part of the Channel Box. If you click on a variable name in the Channel Box and then scrub (drag back and forth) the mouse in any 3D view while pressing the MMB, the value scrolls up and down (see Figure 3.1). This is an excellent method for visually tuning parameters, instead of repeatedly typing in numeric values.

FIGURE 3.1   *Maya's Virtual Slider in action: The MMB is being dragged left and right to adjust the End Sweep parameter.*

Creating Lights

When you're creating lights, Maya doesn't create any real geometry. The Light icon that appears shows where the virtual light source will radiate from, but it's merely a placeholder that doesn't render.

There are six types of light you can create. For three of these types—Directional, Spot, and Area—you can scale their icons. For the Directional and Spot types, you can use the Scale tool to make the Light icon larger so that it's easier to see and select. For the Area light, you would scale it to make more light, emanating from a larger surface area. For the Volume light, you would scale it to adjust the outer range of the light's falloff area. You can't scale the Point and Ambient lights larger with the Scale tool, and the icons that represent these light types stay at a fixed size regardless of how close or far the lights are from any panel's viewpoint. Lights are described in detail in Chapter 9, "Lighting."

Creating Cameras

You can create three types of cameras:

- Camera
- Camera and Aim
- Camera, Aim, and Up

When you create each camera type, an icon that looks like a movie camera appears at the origin. This icon, like the Light icons, can't be rendered. It can be scaled to a convenient size to ease selecting the camera. Cameras are described in detail in Chapter 12, "Cameras and Rendering."

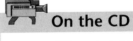

On the CD

Chapter_03\movies\ch3select.wmv

Selecting Objects

Before you can change or delete a scene element, you need to be able to select it. As scenes become populated with many objects, it can get surprisingly difficult to select the items you want to focus on. Fortunately, Maya offers a variety of selection options.

Single Selections

A click of the mouse on an object selects it. If the object is displayed as a wireframe, you must click on a line. The wireframe changes color to indicate it's selected; by default, this color is green. If the object is displayed in Shaded mode, you can click anywhere on its surface to select it. The shaded object's wireframe is displayed to indicate when it's selected. Clicking anywhere that's not on a line (in Wireframe mode) or not on a surface or other scene element (in Shaded mode) deselects everything.

trap
If you find yourself unable to select other objects in Maya, you're probably in Component Editing mode, as shown in Figure 3.2. Note that the selection mask icons in the Status Line have changed, and the word *Components* appears in the space that normally says "All Objects," for example. Maya has locked the object as the selection and is expecting you to select parts of the object; for example, you might be selecting and moving an object's control points to reshape it. To get out of this mode, press the F8 key, a toggle for Object mode and Component mode. You'll use it frequently in the modeling chapters of this book.

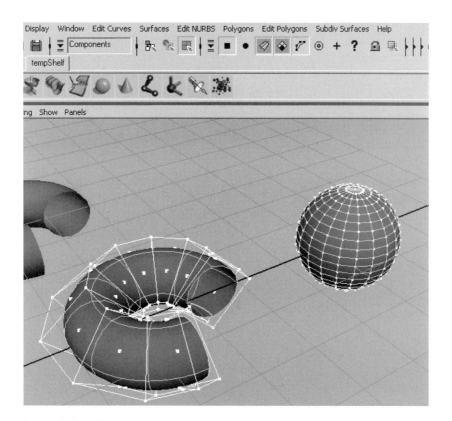

Figure 3.2   *When you see purple dots or lines, and you can't select other objects, you're probably in Component Editing mode.*

Adding and Subtracting Selections

You have the following options for adding and subtracting selections:

- **Toggling the selection**   Use the Shift key to select and deselect objects. Each click on the same object toggles its selection. The last object selected is a unique color (green by default), and the other selected objects indicate their selection by a color change in the wireframe (white by default).

- **Subtracting from a selection** Ctrl+clicking on an object (or Ctrl+ marquee selecting over multiple objects) in the viewport always deselects.
- **Adding to a selection**   Shift+Ctrl+click (or Shift+Ctrl+marquee selecting over multiple objects) always selects objects.
- **Inverting the selection**   Shift+clicking on an object (or Shift+marquee selecting over multiple objects) reverses its selection state.

Edit Menu Selection Options

There are some helpful selection options under the Edit menu. Select All selects all scene elements, including lights, cameras, and objects. Select All by Type allows you to select all elements of a given type, such as lights or geometry (all objects).

Select Invert is useful to reverse a selection, but all scene elements are included in the reversal, even if all your viewports are set to not display certain items, such as cameras. However, there are two ways to hide objects from view *and* from editing: You can use the Display | Hide menu choice to hide an object or objects or to globally hide all lights or cameras. Another method is to toggle the visibility of entire layers in the Layer Editor to hide groups of scene elements. We'll demonstrate this technique in Chapter 5, "NURBS Modeling Basics."

Marquee Selecting Objects

An easy way to select several objects at once is to LMB-click, hold, and drag. A drawn rectangle—the *marquee*—appears to indicate a rectangular selection. Any object that even slightly overlaps the marquee will be selected when you release the mouse button.

Lasso Selecting Objects

Sometimes a rectangle is not the best shape for selection. Your scene objects might require a more complicated selection shape for elements that overlap or are arranged more haphazardly. In these cases, you can select objects with a Lasso tool—a free- form drawn boundary. The Lasso Select icon appears in the Tool Box just below the Select (Arrow) icon. As with marquee selections, any object that slightly overlaps the shape you draw will be selected. The hotkey for this tool is **Ctrl+q**, worth memoriz- ing for when the Tool Box is hidden.

Quick Selection

As you create objects, you should name them to make it easier to navigate through your scene. Another benefit of naming objects is that Maya includes a tool to pick objects with wildcards: the Numeric Input tool, at the far right of the Status Line. You might need to collapse some of the Status Line options (click on the vertical line dividers) to see this area. To use this tool with wildcards to select objects, click the down-arrow icon next to the entry area to choose the Selection by Name mode.

There are two kinds of wildcards: * and ?. The * stands for any number of characters, and the ? stands for a single character. So if you have objects named

1. front_tire
2. front_tire01
3. rear_tire
4. rear_tire_right
5. side_tire
6. front_right_head_light

You would use wildcards as shown here:

You can select items 3 and 4 with rear*.

You can select items 1, 3, and 5 with *tire.

You can select items 4 and 6 with *right*.

You can select items 1, 2, 3, 4, and 5 with *tire*.

You can select items 3 and 5 with ?????tire.

Keep this in mind as you name your scene elements; making careful choices about a name's prefix or suffix can make it easier to select the groups you need to work on.

Quick Select Sets

Another helpful tool is the Quick Select Set. These are named selections of objects or other scene elements that work like a bookmark. To create one, choose Create | Sets | Quick Select Set. In the dialog box that opens (see Figure 3.3), you can enter the name of the set. Be sure to use Maya "legal" naming, meaning you should avoid spaces and characters other than letters, numbers, and the underscore, and don't start the name with a number. To use this named selection later, choose Edit | Quick Select Sets on the menu bar, and all the named sets will appear for you to select from. To delete or rename your selection sets, use the Outliner, which is described in the section "Selection from a List: The Outliner."

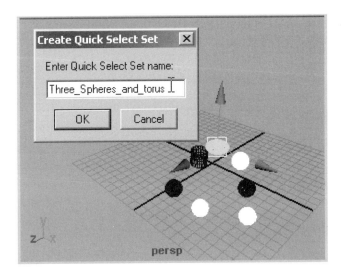

FIGURE 3.3   *The Create Quick Select Set dialog box.*

Selection Masks

When you are in Object Selection mode, a set of buttons appears on the Status Line for limiting what can be selected in the viewports with clicks, marquees, and lassos. Each button contains several subtypes that can be individually enabled or disabled by RMB-clicking on the icon. For example, if you'd like to be able to pick everything but lights, RMB-click on the Select by Object Type-Rendering button, and then uncheck Lights in the list that appears, as shown in Figure 3.4.

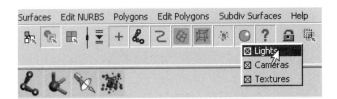

FIGURE 3.4   *RMB-clicking on any of these Selection Mask buttons displays the subtypes that are included.*

Selection from a List: The Outliner

You can also select and deselect objects from a list that shows every scene element by name. This dialog box, called the Outliner, is activated by choosing Window | Outliner on the menu bar. In the Outliner, selected items have a gray bar over them. You can select and deselect in groups just as you do in Windows lists: Click a node, and then Shift+click somewhere else in the list to select an entire range, or Ctrl+click to select items that aren't adjacent. If you simply click on an item, all the others are deselected. Another option is to click and drag up or down to select everything in the drag range (and deselect your previous selection). Selecting in the Outliner works even when selection masks (described in the previous section) prevent you from clicking on an item. You'll use the Outliner extensively in Chapter 5.

Transforming Objects

An object's "transform" sounds like it should mean its position, but it actually describes three functions: position, rotation, and scale. Each function has three components—for X, Y, and Z—so the transform is made up of nine variables. When you create a scene entity, its transform appears in the Channel Box.

You change an object's transform with the Move, Rotate, and Scale buttons in the Tool Box. More often, you'll use the hotkeys for these modes: **w**, **e**, and **r**. When you're changing any of these three transform types, a manipulator appears that enables you to modify the object's position, rotation, or scale constrained to one axis at a time. The axis you are adjusting on turns yellow to indicate the constraint. If you click at the center of the manipulator, you can adjust on all three axes at once. The manipulator's handles appear in three colors: red, green, and blue. These colors correspond with X, Y, and Z. It's easy to remember: X-Y-Z, R-G-B. Say it three times.

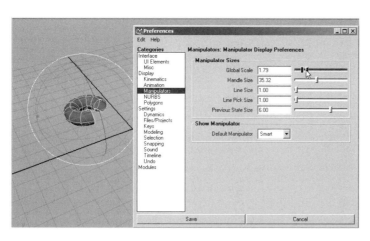

FIGURE 3.5   *Adjusting the size of the manipulators in the Preferences dialog box.*

tip

Sometimes you'll find that the manipulator handles are too small or large for your liking. You can adjust their size easily with the + and – keys. If you want more control over the exact size and appearance, you can edit this setting by choosing Window | Settings/Preferences | Preferences on the menu. In the Categories list under Display, click Manipulators to open their settings (see Figure 3.5). Here you can adjust the manipulators' global scale, handle size, and other helpful attributes.

Using Transforms

When you are in the Move (hotkey: **w**), Rotate (hotkey: **e**), or Scale (hotkey: **r**) mode, you have several options for transforming the object, described in the following sections. Generally, if you click and drag on the surface of a selected object, or on the center point for the manipulator handles, you can freely move or rotate the object. In Scale mode, the object scales uniformly. You can also click and drag on any of the handles to have the action constrained to that axis.

The Move Tool

Click-dragging on the center point in the middle of the manipulator moves the object in relation to the screen, and click-dragging on one of the axis arrows moves the object along that axis. Clicking on one of the axis arrows selects it, and an MMB-drag anywhere in the viewport causes the object to move along that axis.

Ctrl+clicking on an axis arrow changes the center point to be constrained to a plane perpendicular to the selected axis. For example, if you Ctrl+click on the Y axis, and then click+drag in the center point, your translation is constrained to the X-Z (ground) plane. A little yellow plane appears at the center of the manipulator to indicate the plane that movement is constrained to. Normally, this yellow indicator faces the viewer and looks like a square, indicating screen-relative movement mode. If you are in planar movement mode, Ctrl+clicking on the center point resets it to screen-relative movement.

MMB-dragging in the viewport moves the object in relation to the current settings for the center point. You don't have to select the object or center point of the manipulator to move the object; any part of the viewport will work. For example, if you have just moved the object in one direction, that arrow remains yellow, and MMB-dragging anywhere in the viewport moves the object constrained to that axis.

Shift+MMB+drag moves the object along the axis that most closely aligns to the drag direction. You don't have to click on the object or the manipulator to do this; again, anywhere in the viewport will work. By aligning the drag direction to one of the three XYZ axes, you can move the object on that axis. This is the most efficient way to quickly move objects constrained to one axis.

The Rotate Tool

Click-dragging on the outer blue ring rotates the object in relation to the screen, and click-dragging inside the manipulator produces free rotation.

Click-dragging on a particular rotation axis constrains the rotation to that particular axis. When an axis or the outer ring is selected, MMB-dragging in the viewport constrains the rotation to that axis.

The Scale Tool

Click-dragging on a particular scale axis constrains scaling to that axis, and click-dragging on the center of the manipulator constrains rotation to all three axes for uniform scaling.

After a manipulator axis has been selected, MMB-dragging in the viewport constrains the scale to that axis.

Rotation Snapping

If you double-click on the Tool Box icons for move, rotate, and scale, you'll get options for the tools (none appear for scale, but at least an empty dialog box appears). For rotate, you'll find the option to set snaps, which is helpful when you want to rotate objects in discrete increments. A good setting might be 15 degrees, to make it easy to rotate objects to precise 30-, 45-, 60-, and 90-degree positions. Note that this snapping happens only when you use a manipulator's axis handle.

Transforming Multiple Objects

When you have selected multiple objects, you can apply transforms to them together. For Move and Rotate mode, you'll want to revisit the tool options so that you can choose whether your changes happen to the objects locally or globally. For example, after you've rotated an object, if you add another object to the selection and move them in *local* mode along the Z axis, each object moves along its local Z axis—completely different directions, as shown in Figure 3.6. *Global* mode movement forces them all to move together as though they were one object. Double-click the Move button in the Tool Box to switch between modes.

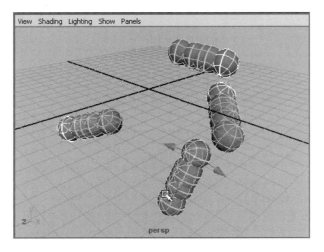

FIGURE 3.6 *Movement along the Z axis means something different to each sphere when moving in local mode.*

Duplicating Objects

You'll often create new objects by starting with existing objects. Sometimes you need to copy an object many times to create a complex object. Maya's object duplicator is under Edit | Duplicate on the menu. The default is to duplicate an object in place, and you can do this with the hotkey **Ctrl+d**. The new duplicate appears by default exactly over the original object, so you normally follow a duplication with a transform.

Advanced Duplication: Array Duplication

In some cases, you want to create more than one duplicate. Use the Edit | Duplicate option box to modify how duplicates are made. You can make each copy with an incremented transform from the previous one, as shown in Figure 3.7. Maya makes only linear *arrays*—duplicates that appear in a line. To fill an area or a volume with objects, you simply choose Edit | Duplicate | option box again with the line or area of objects duplicating along a perpendicular axis.

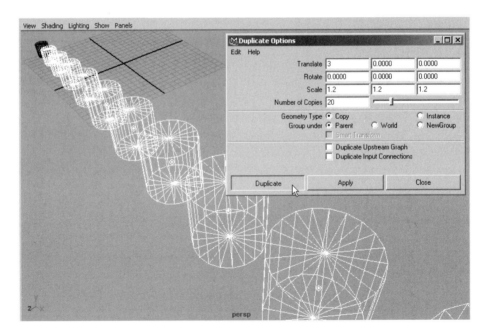

FIGURE 3.7 *The Duplicate Options dialog box, with each new copy increasing its scale by 1.2 and moving three units in X.*

Duplicating Instances, Upstream Graph, or Input Connections

In Figure 3.7, you'll notice that there are options for creating instances rather than copies. You'll also notice two check boxes at the bottom of the dialog box, one for duplicating the Upstream Graph and one for duplicating the Input Connections; these options are explained in the following sections.

Instance Copies

Instances are different from copies. Instances appear as unique objects, but Maya is actually referencing the original object's geometry (in Maya terminology, its *shape node*) exactly for each instance. The instances can have unique transforms and have different materials applied, but any change to the source's (or any of the instances') geometry is reflected in all instances. This can be a big timesaver when you need to change an object's design after you have positioned many copies of it in your scene. If they are instanced, you can update all of them at once!

Upstream Graph

If you look back at Figure 3.1, you can see how an object normally maintains its creation history so that you can edit its creation parameters later. When creating duplicates, however, the new copies have none of these options in the Channel Box. In other words, their *upstream graph* does not exist. If you duplicate with this option checked, each duplicate gets its own duplicated creation options.

Input Connections

In this duplication mode, you get a result similar to instancing, in which the source's creation parameters are copied to all the objects. In this mode of duplication, however, all the copies are unique objects, and you can modify each copy in different ways without affecting the other copies or the original.

Deleting Objects

For deleting objects, you simply select them and press the Delete or Backspace key. You can also choose Edit | Delete on the menu. All selected objects, lights, or other scene elements are removed permanently from the scene.

Deleting by Type

Just below the Edit | Delete menu item is Delete All By Type, which allows you to quickly get rid of all lights, objects, or other scene element types. If you look down this list, you'll see many other types of scene elements: Joints, Lattices, Clusters, Wires, and many others.

Pivot Points

When you transform an object, you'll notice that it usually seems to place the manipulator right in the center of the object, but sometimes that's not the ideal place. For example, if you had modeled a rectangular slab to be used as a door, you might want its rotational pivot to be at one edge of the door. You can edit the pivot point of objects in Maya by using the Insert key, which toggles you in and out of Pivot Editing mode. Whether you are moving, rotating, or scaling, when you are in Pivot Editing mode, you see only the pivot point icon (as shown in Figure 3.8) and can only move it. Although the pivot point handles work similarly to the move icon, with X, Y, and Z constraints, you might find that you need to align the pivot perfectly to some corner or edge of your object. The next section explains the technique for solving this problem.

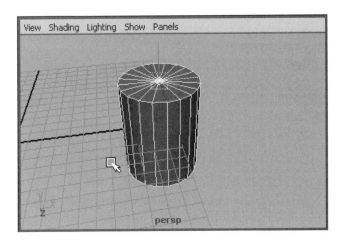

FIGURE 3.8   *Pivot Editing mode has a unique icon.*

Temporary Snapping

As described in Chapter 2, "A Tour of Maya," often you need Maya to help you place things precisely, especially when you're creating or editing mechanical or man-made objects. For example, if you're editing the pivot point of a door, you want the pivot to be exactly on the door's corner edge. Maya's snaps pull you toward a grid point, object edge, or object point when needed. Instead of enabling snapping permanently, you can temporarily engage the type of snap you want as you move scene elements around. The hotkeys for snapping are **x** (grid), **c** (curves), and **v** (points).

To use temporary snapping, you need to already be in Move mode and have something selected. If you hold down the x key, you'll see the square at the center of the transform icon become a circle. If you try to move the selected item, you'll find that it snaps to the grid. Curve and point snapping are similar, but you need to specify the curve or point of a deselected object. To do this, you hold down the snap-to key (c or v) and then MMB-click on the edge or point of the target object. Further movement of the object is now constrained to the curve or point.

Hierarchy

Sometimes you have groups of objects in your scene that are related to each other without being connected as a single entity. For example, you might have a bouquet of roses that more or less translate together, or you might have a car object with four wheel objects, and the wheels are stuck to the car's position but rotate independently of the car object. In cases like these, Maya's hierarchies come into play as you apply groups and parenting.

Grouping Explained

Any collection of objects can be selected and made into a group by choosing Edit | Group on the menu. This makes a new, single node (in Maya terms, a *transform node*) that connects to all the members of the group, and transforms the group's members as the group node is modified. Note that the objects are not tied up into this bundle; you can still select them independently. There's simply a new object that stands for the collection.

At first, this doesn't seem to be an improvement in scene organization, but navigation to the group is not difficult. The group node is "over" the members of the group, and the up and down arrow keys enable you to navigate up or down through your selection. So you merely select a member of the group and press the up arrow, and the entire group is selected. In fact, the grouping is created by making a new group node (which can't be rendered) and then parenting each member of the group to this node. The members of the group are the children, and the group node is the parent.

Parents and children in hierarchies work as follows: Where the parent goes, the child must follow, but the child is otherwise free to roam. Therefore, any animation or transform applied to the parent node ripples to any child object. The child objects can still be animated independently, however, without affecting the parent or other siblings. With groups, the group node can be animated and all the members of the group follow the group node, but the group's members can still animate independently of the group.

Normally, when Maya creates objects, it links a shape node to a transform node to define a single object. The shape node defines the object's geometry, and the transform node defines its transform. When you create a group, you create a node that is an empty transform; it has no linked shape node, so there's nothing to render of the group node itself. However, it can be made a parent or child of any other object in the scene, which is often helpful in organizing or animating a scene.

Parenting and Unparenting Objects

You can directly assign hierarchical relationships to objects by selecting the child object(s), Shift-selecting the parent, and then choosing Edit | Parent (hotkey: **p**). Any transform applied to the parent will then be reflected in the child. Note that the child transforms around the parent from the parent's pivot point. This makes sense because you would want the child object to seem connected to the parent when the child object is not animated to transform independently of the parent. In the previous example, a car's four wheels would be parented to the car body, so the car wheels were children to the body. Now the wheels can be animated (rotating to spin and steer), but will follow the body wherever it moves.

You can also break this bond by using Edit | Unparent (hotkey: **Shift+P**). This works only when the child object or objects are selected.

Parenting and Grouping: What's the Difference?

Parenting creates individual parent-child relationships between the objects in your scene. Creating a group is a special kind of hierarchy that's automatically created. When you group several objects, Maya creates the group transform node, which can't be rendered. Its pivot point is usually placed at the geometric center of all the objects, but you can move it to another position in the usual Pivot Editing mode. Grouping creates a parent-child relationship, with each of the group members parented to the group node. To sum up, parenting is the general concept of creating a hierarchy between scene elements, and grouping makes all the grouped objects siblings that are parented to a new unrenderable scene element.

FIGURE 3.9
The Outliner shows parent-child relationships by indenting. Notice the transform icon that appears beside the group node.

If you open the Outliner (Window | Outliner), you'll see the group object with a + beside it. Clicking this + in the Outliner opens the group list so that you can see the members. If you have hierarchies that are several layers deep (children of children of children of children), the Outliner makes it easy to see the relationships (see Figure 3.9). If you select a child object, its parent is also selected but in a different color (by default, a light green).

Displaying Objects

In Chapter 2, we showed you how to switch from Wireframe to Shaded mode (hotkeys: **4** and **5**) and how to change the detail level of NURBS objects (hotkeys: **1**, **2**, or **3**). There are some other display options that can help you see your object more clearly or speed up interaction.

If you choose Shading | Shade Options in the panel's menu, you'll find options to display Wireframe on Shaded Objects and X-Ray mode. These options can be helpful when you need special, slower rendering display modes in Shaded mode to help solve a problem. Wireframe on Shaded Objects can help you visualize curvatures better and see the effects of editing an object's shape more clearly. X-Ray mode makes the shaded objects in the 3D view semi-transparent. You can see through all objects without giving up the three-dimensional look of Shaded mode.

Other options speed the interactivity of shaded views. Under Shading | Interactive Shading on the panel menu, you'll find four options for degrading the display update when you are moving scene elements. As soon as you stop transforming objects or changing the view, the full shaded view returns. Often, complex scenes bog down the 3D shaded views so badly that you cannot easily move objects; the shaded view stops the movements constantly to refresh the display. That mode is called Normal in the Interactive Shading options. The other options—Wireframe, Bounding Box, and Points—switch the display to view the scene in those visual styles during viewport or object changes.

Another interactivity speedup is under Display | Fast Interaction. When it's enabled, the shaded views simplify objects and textures under certain conditions to speed up the display. This option is very popular and saves time without being too intrusive in its degradation of the displayed image during changes.

Tutorial: Create, Select, Transform, Duplicate!

Now you can apply some of what you've learned to a brief, simple tutorial. You'll use a little bit from each of this chapter's sections to build a door object.

1. Start with a blank, empty workspace in Maya. Confirm that your history is on by making sure the Construction History button in the Status Line is activated. Choose Create | Nurbs Primitives | Cube to create a cube object at the origin point that will be your door.

On the CD

Chapter_03\movies\ch03tut01.wmv

On the CD

Chapter_03\ch03tut01start.mb

2. The object is named nurbsCube1, which you can see at the top of the Channel Box. Click on the name so that you can rename it as door.

3. Right-click in the Perspective view to activate it without deselecting the cube object. Press **5** to switch to Shaded mode.

4. Switch to Scale mode (hotkey: **r**), and scale the box vertically (in the Y direction) by dragging on the green box that's the manipulator handle. Scale it repeatedly if necessary to achieve a height of roughly 16 units.

trap

NURBS cube objects are already "groups" of six sides. If you accidentally deselect the cube by clicking elsewhere in the view, it takes two steps to reselect the entire cube: First select one side of the cube, and then press the up arrow to navigate to the top of the group hierarchy, selecting all six sides automatically. You can also select it in the Outliner.

5. Click on Scale X in the Channel Box, and then MMB-drag left and right in the Shaded view to see how Maya's Virtual Slider works. You can adjust any parameter this way. Set Scale X to roughly 8.

6. Having roughed in the size of the door, type in the values 8 and 16 in the Scale X and Scale Y entries in the Channel Box. This is how you set a numerical value precisely. Remember, you must press the Enter key after typing in the value!

7. Set Translate X for the door to 4 units, and Translate Y to 8 units, so that it's placed on the origin point, as shown in Figure 3.10.

8. Create a cylinder with Create | Polygon Primitives | Cylinder. In the Channel Box, change the name from pCylinder1 to knocker_stub. Then open the Inputs section by clicking on the polyCylinder1 text just below the Inputs label, where you'll see five creation parameters: Radius, Height, and three subdivision settings. Set Radius to .25 and Height to 0.5.

9. Next you'll put the knocker stub into position. Switch to Move mode and position the cylinder horizontally at the center of the door and vertically three-fourths of the way up the door. You'll also need to move the knocker stub outward a little so that it protrudes from the door. Position it by changing the values in the Channel Box to 4 for Translate X, 12 for Translate Y, 0.75 for Translate Z, and 90 for Rotate X.

10. Create a torus with Create | NURBS Primitives | Torus, and rename it knocker in the Channel Box. Click the makeNurbTorus1 label under Inputs to open the Inputs section, and set the Height Ratio to 0.1. Position the torus by changing the transform settings in the top section of the Channel Box: Translate X to 4, Translate Y to 11, Translate Z to .75, and Rotate X to 90. To check what the knocker looks like in other views, tap the spacebar to switch to Four View mode, and then check the other views to see the relative positioning of the objects, as shown in Figure 3.11.

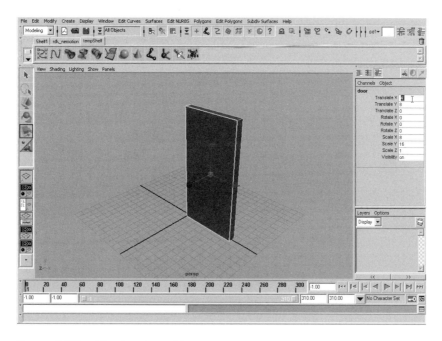

FIGURE 3.10   *The door in position.*

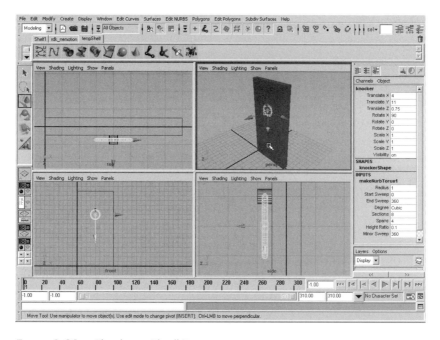

FIGURE 3.11   *The door with all its parts.*

11. Next you'll adjust the pivot points for the knocker and the door. Start with the knocker, which should still be selected. Then switch to Move mode (hotkey: **w**) and press the Insert key to switch to Pivot Editing mode (you must always be in Move mode before attempting to change the pivot). The transform icon on the knocker switches to look like the move transform, but without arrows on the ends of the three axes. Use the Front view, and zoom close to the knocker. Now, while in Move mode, click directly on the vertical green line of the pivot point. This constrains your movements to the vertical (Y-axis) direction. Now you can raise the pivot point until it's centered on the cylinder that is the knocker stub. Press Insert to exit Pivot Editing mode.

12. With the knocker still selected, switch to Rotate mode (hotkey: **e**) and click on the red circle to rotate constrained to the X-axis. You can now knock on the door with the knocker. Rotate the knocker so that it's slightly off axis, for a natural look.

13. Select the door next. Click on any one of the six sides of the cube object that makes up the door, and then press the up arrow to select the entire door object. You should still be in Rotate mode, and you'll notice that the rotational handles are on the center of the door. You don't want the door to rotate on its center point; the hinges should be at the left edge of the door's front. Engage Pivot Editing mode by pressing Insert. Note that you are automatically in Move mode with the pivot, despite being in Rotate mode overall. Pivots can only be moved, not rotated!

14. Next you'll place the pivot point precisely at the bottom corner of the door by using curve snapping. Each corner edge of the door is considered a snappable curve when in Curve Snap mode. Go to Perspective view, and orbit the view to a position in front of and to the left of the door. Hold down the **c** key, MMB-click directly on the door's upper front edge, and then MMB-drag to the left. The pivot will be constrained to the front edge of the door and slide easily to the far left, where the pivot should be located. Press Insert to exit Pivot Editing mode.

15. Test the door rotation by clicking on the green circle (to constrain the rotation to the Y axis) and dragging. The knocker stub and knocker do not turn with the door (see Figure 3.12), however. They need to be parented to the door so that they rotate when the door rotates. Press **z** to undo your rotation.

16. Go to Select mode (hotkey: **q**), select the knocker, and then Shift-select the knocker stub. The stub will be green and the knocker will be white. Now choose Edit | Parent, or simply press the hotkey **p**. Now when you select the knocker stub, the knocker is also selected. Also, any time you transform the knocker stub, the knocker follows as though it's part of the knocker stub.

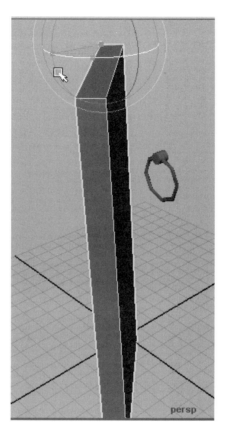

FIGURE 3.12   *Rotating the door on the corrected pivot point; the knocker is not following the door's rotation.*

17. Select the knocker stub (the knocker seems to be selected, too, but if you check the Channel Box, you'll see that only the knocker stub is selected). Shift-select the front panel of the door, and press the up arrow key to select the entire door. Then parent the knocker stub to the door (hotkey: **p**). Now you can select any side of the door object, press the up arrow to select the entire door, and then switch to Rotate mode. Rotate with a Y constraint (click and drag on the green circle of the rotation manipulator), and you'll see that the entire assembly rotates as one (see Figure 3.13). Success! If you test it, you'll find that you can still correctly rotate the knocker regardless of the door's angle.

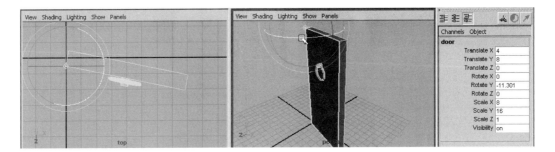

FIGURE 3.13   *All the parts now rotate together—a linked hierarchy!*

18. Open the Outliner (Window | Outliner). Click the + to the left of the door object to expand it. You'll see the six sides of the door cube; one side has a + next to it, indicating that it's the side the knocker stub is parented to. Open this object and the knocker stub to see that the knocker is embedded four levels deep in the hierarchy: door, leftnurbsCube1, knocker_stub, knocker. This display gives you a visual cue to the hierarchy, as shown in Figure 3.14.

On the CD

Chapter_03\ch03tut01end.mb

You can explore the scene further and observe the parenting effects for object transforms of the door's parts. If you'd like to load a completed file, find the scene file on the CD-ROM (noted below the CD icon) and load it.

FIGURE 3.14
The Outliner displays the full hierarchy you created.

Going Further

Explore all of Maya's display modes to see the advantages of each one. Test the interactive speedup options to learn what they do to the Shaded view and to recognize the look. You might also want to test the duplication options to learn some of the possibilities they offer.

Summary

Now that you've gotten an overview of Maya's creating and editing functions, you're ready to delve into using Maya. This chapter has demonstrated the following concepts and techniques:

- **Creating primitives and other objects**   Use these objects as the building blocks of your scene.

- **Selecting objects**   You now know a variety of ways to get to the object or objects that you want to act on.

- **Transforming objects**   Use the Channel Box or the transform manipulator to move objects as you build your scenes.

- **Duplication of scene elements**   Copying parts of your scene to build new parts is a helpful feature.

- **Adjusting pivots**   You can set an object to rotate or scale about any point in space by repositioning its pivot point.

- **Hierarchy**   Linking objects into parent-child relationships is an essential technique of scene setup and preparation for animation.

Now that you've had a chance to learn Maya's design and basic methods, it's time to get your feet wet. In the next chapter, you'll progress through every step of creating a full-blown animation in Maya. This upcoming tutorial will seem easier if you've become familiar with each of the tools described in this chapter as well as Chapter 2.

If upcoming chapters seem challenging, come back to this chapter and try to step through it again. You'll get more comfortable with navigating through your scene and having control over what mode you are in and what Maya is doing. Gain some confidence with these core skills, and you'll then be ready for a new challenge.

CHAPTER 4

Diving In: Your First Animation

In This Chapter

The time has come to step into the realm of Maya and create your own world, top to bottom. Being told what Maya can do is one thing, but you can learn much more by diving in, exploring its features, and discovering what it's capable of. To the uninitiated, it might seem as though not that much goes into the production of a project. As you will find out in this chapter, however, there's a lot to it. Besides engaging the creative side of your brain, you also have to apply your organizational and problem-solving skills. You can create amazing scenes, but if they aren't organized efficiently, they can cause problems for coworkers or others who must work with your scenes. Or it could be troublesome for you when you return to edit your scene three months later!

We're going to familiarize you with the steps that CG artists typically go through in Maya when building a project from scratch. Even if you already have some Maya experience, you might learn something. One of the best ways to learn new techniques is by watching what other people do—sometimes you'll discover alternative, better ways of accomplishing things.

This chapter is going to be an exciting opportunity for you to discover what Maya has to offer as you complete a small project from beginning to end. You'll get a feel for the workflow the software package has right out of the box and will be introduced to the following concepts:

- **Getting more comfortable with the Maya interface**   In the previous chapters, you've learned the basics of the Maya interface. In this chapter, you'll apply that knowledge and increase your comfort level when working with Maya.

- **Learning the steps of the animation process** In completing this mini-project, you'll model, light, texture, animate, and render—all the major steps every animation project requires.

- **A little bit of everything** Work through a tutorial that touches on most of the basic and intermediate features Maya has to offer. You will have the opportunity to use soft body dynamics, path animation, NURBS, texturing, and more!

- **Basic scene organization** You'll learn how to work with layers for organizing your scene efficiently.

- **Simple modeling and editing with NURBS** Using one of Maya's two main modeling tools, you will go through a tutorial to create objects for your scene.

- **Render your first scene in Maya** After finishing the tutorial in this chapter, you will have an impressive animation to render and show off!

Key Terms

isoparm A curve on a NURBS patch that helps give a visual indication of surface topology.

vertex An X, Y, Z description of a point's location in 3D space. Vertices can be connected with line segments known as edges. Three or more edges connected in a polygon shape represent a polygon face (which produces the surface).

control vertices (CVs) Very similar to the vertex for a polygon, except CVs are used with NURBS.

material A surface definition, including such factors as color and shininess. Phong, Blinn, and Lambert are examples of different material types you work with in Maya.

raytracing A rendering method used to create realistic reflections and refractions on surfaces such as mirror and glass. Raytracing also renders more realistic shadows. As a high-quality alternative to reflection mapping, raytracing needs more computation, thus causing longer render times.

dynamics A physics simulation. Rather than manually animate, you apply mass to objects, add gravity and other factors, and let Maya figure it out.

soft body dynamics Dynamics applied to "squishy" objects. When the object collides with something, it not only rebounds, but also flexes and jiggles.

project A way to organize your scene information. Made up of several folders, a project contains a collection of scene files and other files, such as textures, generated for your scene.

Hotkeys to Memorize

spacebar hold   Hotbox

q   Select mode

w   Translate mode

e   Scale mode

r   Rotate mode

t   show manipulators

4   change current view to Wireframe mode

5   change current view to Shaded mode

F2   Switch to Animation user interface

F3   Switch to Modeling user interface

F4   Switch to Dynamics user interface

F8   Component Selection mode

spacebar tap with mouse cursor over a view   maximize or minimize viewport

Alt+v   play or stop Time Slider playback

Ctrl+a   open Attribute Editor

f   focus on object

right-click on object   display a shortcut menu of available functions

Ctrl+d   duplicate

g   repeat last command

p   create a parent object

z   undo

Shift+Z   redo

b+LMB-drag   resize brush when sculpting an object

Starting a New Project

Maya works best with a project structure. This is a folder you put somewhere on your hard drive and specify as the project root. Maya can then create subfolders to organize the different files that will be created for the scene.

A little planning never hurts before starting, either. 3D images can be a little harder to visualize than 2D images. It's often a bad idea to just sit down and start creating something—you end up having to start over because you forgot a beginning step. Most CG artists take pencil to paper for at least a few sketches and timing notes before hitting the power switch on the workstation.

The first project you're going to create is an animation of a boat floating on an ocean. You'll model the ocean and boat and then make the boat travel around the ocean. You'll apply wood materials to the boat and water materials to the ocean. Then you'll animate the boat traveling around the ocean and render a movie of the result.

Tutorial: Initial Setup

The first step in creating this scene, as with any other scene in Maya, is to create a new project. Don't forget that if any of the steps in this tutorial confuse you, you can see them performed and explained by playing the movie noted below the CD movie icon. The introduction to this book includes tips on getting the movie to play on your computer.

On the CD

Chapter_04\movies\ch04tut01.wmv

1. With Maya open, choose File | Project | New on the menu, or press and hold the spacebar to open the Hotbox and then click File. After you have opened the New Project dialog box, click the Use Defaults button (see Figure 4.1), which automatically creates organizational folders for the project components.

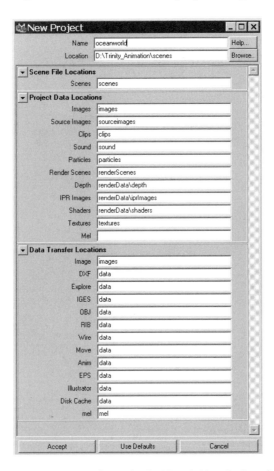

FIGURE 4.1   *Setting up project directories in Maya's New Project dialog box.*

2. Next, name your project by typing oceanworld in the Name text box. In the Location text box, you should enter the default directory you'll use for all Maya projects. The default for Windows 2000 and Windows XP is C:\Documents and Settings\user\My Documents\maya\projects. You should create your projects in this folder with a meaningful project name to make it easier to identify folders containing your projects.

note
You cannot have any spaces in filenames because Maya doesn't recognize the space character. You can use an underscore (new_scene, for example) or a mixture of uppercase and lowercase letters, such as NewScene, to name your files.

3. After naming your project, click the Accept button to have it automatically created.

Organizing Your Project Folders

When you created your new project, you told Maya to specify a default file structure. Your project directory is an organized method for storing and retrieving information about a project and its scene files so that Maya knows where to look for information about a particular component in a scene. Look over the folders that have been created in your project directory; most of the names are self-explanatory. The most important one is the Scenes folder, where you save your scene files and information for your project.

In addition to having your project folders organized, it's important to continually save your scene as you develop your project. Saving in increments allows you to go back to a previous stage in your project by opening a scene you saved earlier in your project development, and saves you remodeling time if something didn't work out as expected. The incremental save was a new feature in Maya 4. To use it, choose File | Save Scene | option box to open the Save Scene Options dialog box, and select the Incremental Save check box. This creates a backup folder in your project's scenes folder (\scenes\incrementalsave\). Each time you save your scene, a backup file is placed in this folder, numbered with an incremental extension (for example, filename.000.mb, filename.001.mb). By default, you have an unlimited number of incremental saves, but you can specify a limit to conserve hard drive space. You'll activate incremental save as the first step in the next tutorial.

Creating Scene Elements for Your Project

With your project created, start off by saving the scene (File | Save Scene) and naming the file ch04oceanScene. As you go through the following tutorials, you can save as often as you like. Usually, it's a good idea to save after performing several operations on an object or the scene.

The next time you open this saved file, choose File | Project | Set on the menu. This specifies the project you're working with and points Maya to the correct location of files in the project. You can also choose File | Recent Projects to choose from a list of the most recent projects you have worked on.

With the project set, and your initial scene file saved, you're ready to begin modeling the scene! You'll start by creating the water and then adding some motion to the water to bring some life to the scene. This is the outline of steps for creating the water:

1. Choose your geometry (in this case, a NURBS plane).

2. Specify the density (number of patches) of the geometry. To make the water's little peaks appear smooth and detailed, you'll need more density than the default.

3. Change the plane into a soft body so that you can have a "ripple" effect for the water.

4. Add dynamics to "shake" the plane to create motion for the water.

Tutorial: Creating the Water's Plane

The first step in creating the water is deciding which type of geometry to use. For water, a plane is good because water doesn't need volume; by simply creating the water's surface with a plane, you can get the right visual effect. For this tutorial, you'll use a NURBS plane instead of a polygon-based plane because a NURBS surface can automatically subdivide to provide more detail at render time. Because the water will have all those little wavelets, this is a good thing.

On the CD

Chapter_04\movies\ch04tut02.wmv

note
The Hotbox is often a faster way to create objects in your scene. To see all the features in Maya in the Hotbox, click Hotbox Controls | Show All. All the menus are displayed so that you don't have to press keys to switch between animation, rendering, modeling, and so forth. For now, however, leave the Hotbox at its default settings.

1. Go ahead and turn on the Incremental Save feature so that you'll have files to fall back on if you run into a problem. Choose File | Save Scene | option box to open the Save Scene Options dialog box, and select the Incremental Save check box.

tip
Professional users usually save with incremented filenames as they build a scene. The filenames have an inserted number, such as "bob_smile.004.mb." Saves are advisable after major edits, deletions, or history clearing. This allows you to import an earlier version of an object if necessary, or revert to an earlier scene file if a disk becomes corrupted. If you limit the number of saves, Maya will overwrite the oldest file once the limit is reached.

2. To create a NURBS plane, first make sure you're in Modeling mode (hotkey: **F3**). Using the menu bar or the Hotbox, click Create | NURBS Primitives | Plane | option box to open the NURBS Plane Options dialog box. Later you'll be changing the plane into a soft body and then adding a dynamic force to it to produce a wavelike water effect. To have enough dynamic particles to add motion to the water, you'll need to increase the number of patches to have more CVs, which define the location and number of particles for the soft body you will create; enter 30 in both the U Patches and V Patches text boxes (see Figure 4.2).

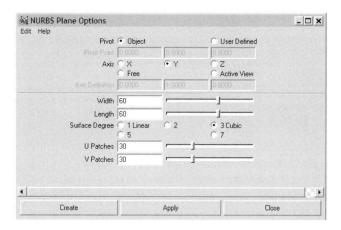

FIGURE 4.2   *Using the NURBS Plane Options dialog box to change values used in creating a surface.*

3. Next, you need to define the plane's size. In the Length and Width text boxes, enter 60 and then click the Create button. By default, the newly created object will be selected. In the Channel Box, name the NURBS plane WaterPlane.

At this point, you should hide the default grid so that you can see the plane more clearly (choose Display | Grid on the main menu, or on the panel's menu bar, choose Show | Grid).

Converting the Plane into a Soft Body

4. By converting your NURBS plane into a soft body, you get a particle-based replica with particles placed at each of the CVs of the NURBS plane. This enables you to add dynamic effects to the plane to achieve a more realistic water effect. To work with soft bodies, you need to switch to Dynamics mode (hotkey: **F4**). With the plane selected, open the Hotbox and click Soft/Rigid Bodies | Create Soft Body | option box.

5. In the Soft Options dialog box (see Figure 4.3), change the following settings: In the Creation Options drop-down list, select Duplicate, Make Original Soft; select the Hide Non-Soft Object and Make Non-Soft a Goal check boxes; and enter .25 in the Weight text box. Click the Create button. This creates a hidden duplicate of WaterPlane and converts the original plane to a soft body.

FIGURE 4.3   *Use the Soft Options dialog box to specify how you want the soft body to be created.*

The particles from the soft body will be attracted to the hidden plane, which keeps the water's surface from deforming too much. The goal weight controls the particles' attraction to the goal. Without setting a goal, the plane would distort uncontrollably after you applied a dynamic field to it. Setting a value of 1 causes the particles to immediately jump to the goal, and a value of 0 has no effect on the particle position. Values from 0 to 1 create a bounce-like effect that's good for rolling waves.

6. Open the Outliner (Window | Outliner on the menu) and look for the new group called WaterPlane. Expand this group by clicking the + next to its name, and you'll see the particle soft body—WaterPlaneParticle—that was created. Below the original WaterPlane is the goal surface, copyOfWaterPlane (see Figure 4.4). To see the particles for the soft body, select WaterPlaneParticle in the Outliner. The plane in the viewport will clearly show all the particles.

7. Before adding motion to WaterPlane, you should figure out how long you want your animation to be. By default, animation is set to play at 24 frames per second (fps). You'll be playing the animation for 15 seconds, which means a total of 360 frames will be created. Go to the Range Slider at the bottom of the Maya window, under the Play buttons (Time Slider), and enter 360 for the end time of playback and animation.

FIGURE 4.4
The Outliner clearly shows the structure and components of the scene. WaterPlane is now a soft body.

If you click Play on the Time Slider, however, nothing happens because no dynamics are affecting the soft body particles yet. In the next tutorial, you'll see how to add dynamics so that you can see the water moving the next time you play the animation. If you have had trouble with this tutorial, you can copy the scene file (noted below the CD icon) from the Maya Fundamentals CD-ROM and use it to continue to the next tutorial.

On the CD

Chapter_04\ch04tut02end.mb

Tutorial: Adding Motion to the Water

The ocean plane is now set to "jiggle" because you made it a soft body, but to set it moving, you have to do something to it. One option is to animate it shaking back and forth, to get water motion like rocking a tub of water. It would probably look just like a tub of water being shaken, though! Luckily for this project, Maya provides "influences," such as wind and gravity, that you can apply to soft bodies to make them do something even when they're standing still. To create dynamic water motion, you'll use the one called turbulence. Turbulence creates a "noise field" that causes random motion. There are two settings you'll change to modify the turbulence field: its *magnitude*, which represents the strength of the turbulence field, and its *attenuation*, which affects how the turbulence is distributed across the surface of the plane. For instance, an attenuation value of 0 causes the turbulence to be spread evenly across the surface. If the value is increased, you get strong waves in the middle that die out around the edges of the water plane.

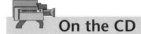

On the CD

Chapter_04\movies\ch04tut03.wmv

1. In the Outliner, under the expanded WaterPlane item, select the WaterPlaneParticle soft body.

note

When you select WaterPlaneParticle, notice that the information in the Channel Box changes. That's because the Channel Box is displaying all the particle attributes that can be modified by default. You can also display these properties by opening the Attribute Editor (hotkey: **Ctrl+a**) and clicking the WaterPlaneParticleShape tab.

2. Make sure you're in Dynamics mode (hotkey: **F4**). With WaterPlaneParticle select-
ed, open the Hotbox and click Fields | Turbulence to attach a Turbulence field to
the soft body particles. You should see a small circular icon appear at the scene
origin, indicating that the field has been created. With the turbulence field selected, go to the Channel Box, and name the field `WaterWavesField`.

tip   You can also attach the turbulence field to the soft body particles with the Dynamic
Relationships Editor (Window | Relationship Editors | Dynamic Relationships). For
more information on this, see Chapter 14, "Particle Systems and Dynamics."

3. Now try playing the animation again to see the plane move ("deform"). If you
don't see it moving, try zooming in closer to the plane. It doesn't move the way
you expect an ocean to move, so to fix that, you need to modify the settings for
the turbulence field. In the Outliner, select WaterWavesField. In the Channel Box,
set Magnitude to 6 to create a stronger force on the soft body. Set Attenuation to
0, as shown in Figure 4.5, to distribute the turbulence evenly across the surface.

4. Play the animation again and look at the difference. The soft body deformation is much more
evident now that the turbulence is evenly
distributed. If you haven't done so already,
save your scene.

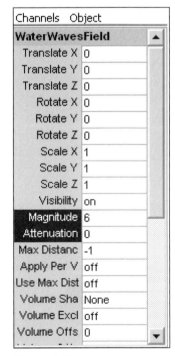

warning   In some cases, instead of rippling water, you'll
see a progressively chaotic tsunami! If this happens, the water is becoming unstable because
the turbulence that was added to the water
calculates the motion based on the previous
frame of animation. This means that the play-
back speed in Windows | Settings/Preferences |
Preferences | Timeline needs to be set at "Play
Every Frame" in order to get the correct calculation for animation.

Going Further
You might want to try adding other fields such as Air
(for a wind effect) or Vortex (a whirlpool!) to the
scene and play the animation to see the results. Also,
you can achieve some interesting results by tweaking
just a few settings in your turbulence field. Try modifying values for the Frequency, Attenuation, and
Magnitude settings.

FIGURE 4.5
*Changing settings for turbu-
lence in the Channel Box.*

If your animation plays back slowly or choppily, you might need to change the animation playback speed or your computer might not be powerful enough to play the animation smoothly. Click the Animation Preferences button to the right of the Range Slider or choose Window | Settings/Preferences | Preferences to open the Preferences dialog box. In the Categories list, scroll down to Settings, and click the Timeline entry (see Figure 4.6). Under the Playback section, select Play Every Frame in the Playback Speed drop-down list, and then click the Save button to save these preferences. These changes should have the animation playing more smoothly.

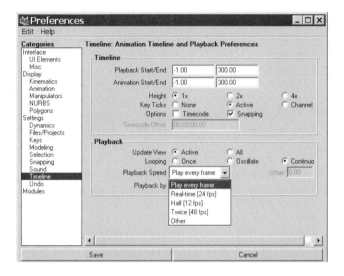

FIGURE 4.6   *Changing the playback setting in the Preferences dialog box.*

tip

If your animation still plays back very slowly, you can playblast your scene (Window | Playblast | option box). Playblasting takes a copy of each frame from your viewport and plays it back in your default media player or the FCheck utility. It's an accurate method for testing the playback speed of your animation.

Tutorial: Creating the Ground

In this tutorial, you'll learn how to create a layer, which allows you to organize scene elements so that they're easier to manage. You'll also see how grouping objects makes it easier to select items in the Outliner or Hypergraph because you wind up with fewer objects cluttering the windows. You can continue from the previous tutorial, or load the scene file noted.

On the CD

Chapter_04\movies\ch04tut04.wmv

1. To create the ground, you need another NURBS plane. On the menu bar, choose Create | NURBS Primitives | Plane, with the same settings you used for the water.

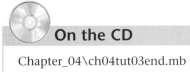

On the CD

Chapter_04\ch04tut03end.mb

2. In the Channel Box, name the plane GroundPlane. Because it's created at the scene origin (the 0,0,0 point), it's in the same position as WaterPlane. The ground needs to be under the water, however, so you need to move it in the -Y direction. To do that, enter -2 for Translate Y in the Channel Box.

3. Because the ground is created from a plane, it's completely flat. To get a more realistic bumpy surface and add a small island, you'll sculpt the NURBS plane. It's difficult to do that with the water in the way, so you need to hide it or create a layer. You'll use the Layer Editor at the bottom of the Channel Box (see Figure 4.7) to create a layer for the water. Make sure the water plane is selected, and on the Layer Editor's menu bar, choose Layers | Create Layer.

note Remember to set the Time Slider back to zero for your scene if you have been playing an animation. The leftmost playback button (double left arrows) is the quick button for this. Don't forget to stop playback first! Some geometrical deformations will remain unless you "rewind." The water is a good example of this.

4. Double-click on the new layer to open the Edit Layer dialog box where you can change settings for the layer (see Figure 4.7). Name the layer WaterL, and change the color of the layer to blue; any objects associated with this layer will now be blue in Wireframe mode. Click the Save button to keep changes to the layer. Then toggle visibility of the layer.

note Sometimes hiding a layer causes all newly created objects to disappear. This is caused by a toggle in the layer options. Look at the Layers panel, in Options, as shown in Figure 4.8, and note that if you have either option checked, it will cause newly created objects to fall into the current layer. Turn off both options to keep new objects from being inadvertently assigned to a hidden layer.

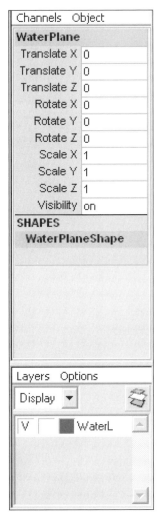

FIGURE 4.7

Use the Layer Editor to organize your scene elements.

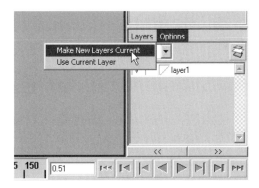

FIGURE 4.8   *Enabled layer options can be a source of confusion when layer visibility is toggled off, so make sure both options are unchecked.*

5. Before adding the water to the layer, you'll group all the parts of the water together so that they appear as one object (which reduces clutter in the Outliner). In the Outliner, Ctrl+click to select WaterPlane, copyOfWaterPlane, and WaterWavesField.

6. In the Hotbox, click Edit | Group, and name the group WaterGroup. Check the Outliner, where you'll see the water components under WaterGroup.

> If you now select WaterPlane in one of the viewports, the other components of the water group wouldn't be selected. However, you can click any one component of the group and then press the up arrow to easily select the entire group. Grouping the objects creates a hierarchically higher "group node," instead of bundling all the objects into a single object. You can also use the arrow keys to navigate to other hierarchically arranged objects in the Outliner. For example, expand WaterGroup, select WaterPlane, and press the left and right arrow keys. You'll see the highlighted selection move to other parts of WaterPlane. The left and right arrow keys let you move to siblings of the selected object, the up arrow takes you to the parent, and the down arrow takes you to a child.

7. Next, you need to assign WaterGroup to the layer. Make sure WaterGroup is selected in the Outliner, right-click on WaterL in the Layer Editor, and click Add Selected Objects on the shortcut menu. WaterGroup is added to the water layer, so it's no longer visible. Because the layer is hidden, you can view and modify the ground plane easily.

8. Now you can sculpt GroundPlane to give it some shape: Select GroundPlane, and in the Hotbox, click Edit NURBS | Sculpt Surfaces Tool | option box to open the Tool Settings window for the Sculpt Surfaces Tool (shown in Figure 4.9). Click the Sculpt tab if it's not displayed.

 **tip**   If you have a pressure-sensitive graphics tablet (such as Wacom Intuos or Graphire), this would be a good time to use it because you'll have more control with the Sculpt Surfaces Tool. In the Tool Settings window for the Sculpt Surfaces Tool, click the Stroke tab. Under the Stylus Pressure section, set the pen to be sensitive to Opacity, Radius, or Both.

9. Under the Operation section, click the Pull radio button, and leave everything else at the default settings (see Figure 4.9). Minimize this window, and move the mouse cursor across the ground plane. You should see a red circle that represents the area to be sculpted.

10. If you don't see the red cursor moving across the plane, you probably don't have the ground plane selected. Press q to get the selection cursor, click on the plane, and then press y to get the last-used tool. As you click and drag across the ground plane to make it look like an ocean floor, you should see the surface being pulled upward (in the Y direction). Switch to Shaded mode (hotkey: **5**) to make it easier to see changes to the surface. The radius of the Sculpt Surfaces Tool is a little too small, however, so adjust it by pressing b and LMB-dragging left and right.

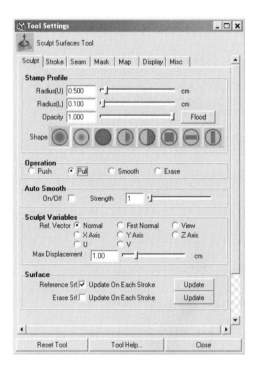

FIGURE 4.9   *The Tool Settings window for the Sculpt Surfaces Tool.*

11. Continue sculpting the surface, occasionally switching the operation to Push in the Tool Settings window or with the **u** hotkey for the marking menu. Pull up some to edges of the ground plane, but don't pull them up so much that the ground penetrates the water plane. Eventually, you should have a surface similar to Figure 4.10. You can display the water layer to get an idea of which portions of the ground will be above the water line. In the Layer Editor, double-click WaterL and select the Visible check box in the Edit Layer dialog box. You can also toggle the visibility by clicking on the square to the far left of the layer's name in the Layer Editor. When you click on the square, it should display a V for "visible."

tip

You can interactively change the current function of the Sculpt Surfaces Tool by pressing u and clicking on the surface you're sculpting. This displays a marking menu with options for the tool.

12. To exit the Sculpt Surfaces Tool, press q. Just as you did for the water, you need to create a layer for the ground plane. Create a new layer, name it GroundL, set the color to brown, and assign GroundPlane to it.

13. If you haven't done so already, save your scene.

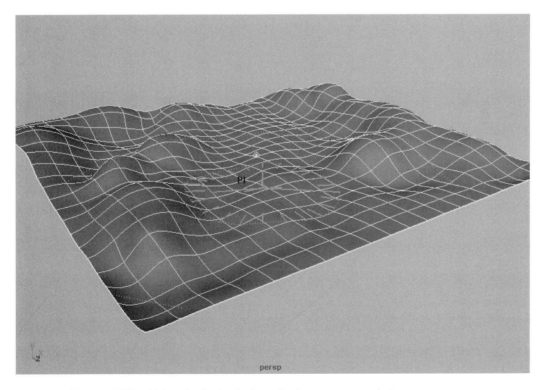

FIGURE 4.10   *Using the Sculpt Surfaces Tool on your ground plane.*

Tutorial: Creating the Boat

Finally, you get to create the boat that will float through your scene. You'll construct the boat from NURBS. Hide all the layers in your scene, and then switch into Four View mode. You can continue from the previous tutorial, or load the scene file noted here.

On the CD

Chapter_04\movies\ch04tut05.wmv

1. The boat you'll create resembles a split cone, so first create a NURBS cone by choosing Create | NURBS Primitives | Cone | option box. In the NURBS Cone Options dialog box, click the Z radio button to change the axis, and enter 180 in the End Sweep Angle text box (this tells Maya to

On the CD

Chapter_04\ch04tut04end.mb

   create a surface that's only half-spun—180 degrees). Next, select the Bottom radio button for Caps, select the Extra Transform on Caps check box, and enter 4 in the Number of Spans text box.

2. Click the Create button to create half a cone with a cap on one end. If the cone seems too far away, select it (by clicking on the cone, not the end cap) and press f. Name the cone BoatOutside.

3. Next, you need to shape the cone to resemble a small boat. Maximize the Side view by placing your cursor over it and tapping the spacebar. Make sure the cone is still selected, and in the Channel Box, set Scale X to 0.5, Scale Y to 0.75, and Scale Z to 1.5 to begin shaping the cone.

tip

Because viewports are sensitive to mouse cursor location, place the mouse cursor over the view you want to focus on. You can then press f to affect that particular viewport.

4. In the Perspective view, the cone doesn't look like the curved bottom hull of a small boat. To correct this, you need to move and scale CVs. With the cone selected in the Side view, switch to Component Selection mode (hotkey: **F8**). Right-click on the cone, and select Control Vertex. You will see columns of CVs sloping down toward the back of the cone.

5. The CVs control the shape of the cone. In the Side view, marquee-select each bottom set of CVs (two CVs are visible, but you're selecting three), and switch to the Move tool (hotkey: **w**). Start with the CV pair at the far right, and work forward until the cone has a flat bottom that suddenly curves up to shape the front of the boat, as shown in Figure 4.11. Note that in the figure all the modified CVs are selected, but the CVs were moved only as groups of three for each "rung" of the boat.

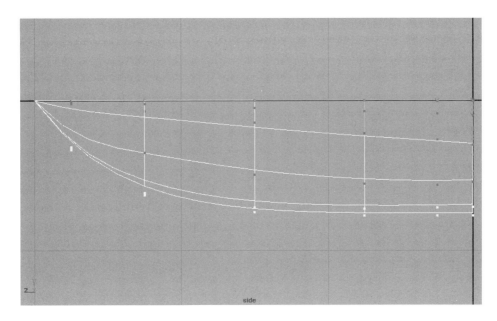

FIGURE 4.11   *The CVs at the bottom of each column of CVs have been moved down to shape the profile of the boat.*

6. Switch to the Top view and maximize that viewport. You can see that the cone is still too narrow at the front. Make sure you're still in Component Selection mode with the CVs selected so that you can scale rows of CVs to further shape the cone. Starting with the row at the cone's wider end, marquee-select all the CVs in that row. Then scale them along the X axis (the red arrow) by switching to the Scale tool (hotkey: r) and sliding the red X axis handle sideways. Referring to Figure 4.12 as a guide, scale the CVs to achieve a smoothly rounded boat shape.

7. Now you can work on the inside of the boat. Exit Component Selection mode (hotkey: **F8**), and restore the Top view so that you have all four viewports visible. Select BoatOutside and duplicate it by clicking Edit | Duplicate (hotkey: **Ctrl+d**). The duplicate will be automatically selected. In the Channel Box, name it BoatInside, and set Scale X to 0.44, Scale Y to 0.45, and Scale Z to 1.321 so that it fits inside BoatOutside. The back side of BoatInside is still on the same plane as Boat Outside, however, so move BoatInside forward by setting Translate Z to 0.12. You should now have the outside and inside of the boat created from the original cone (see Figure 4.13).

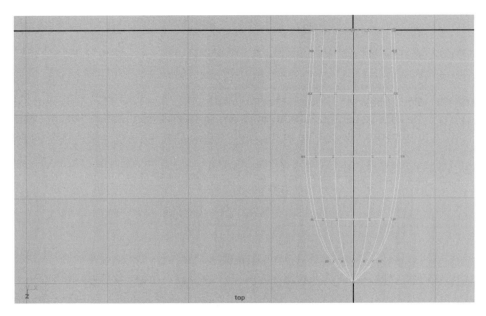

FIGURE 4.12   *In the Top view, you can see how the CVs have been scaled in the X axis to shape the cone.*

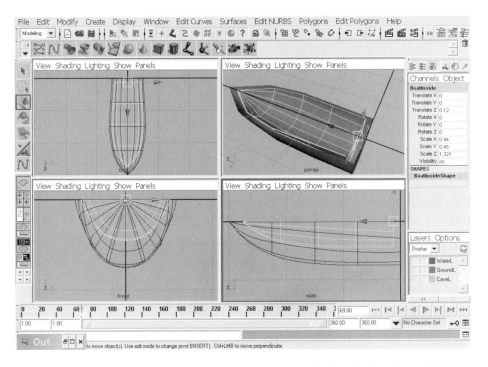

FIGURE 4.13   *The inside of the boat is now positioned within the boat's outside "shell."*

8. To close the gaps between BoatInside and BoatOutside, you'll use a loft. Return to Component Selection mode (hotkey: **F8**), RMB-click on BoatOutside, and choose Isoparm on the shortcut menu. BoatOutside's wireframe will turn blue. Select the isoparms at the edge of one side of BoatOutside (a yellow line appears to represent the isoparm you have selected). Next, you need to select an isoparm on the parallel edge of BoatInside. Right-click on BoatInside, choose Isoparm, and Shift+click on the edge isoparm parallel to the isoparm you selected on BoatOutside. With both isoparms selected, go to the Hotbox and click Surfaces | Loft to fill the gap, as shown in Figure 4.14.

9. Repeat on the other side of the boat, selecting the isoparms at the edges and then lofting them together.

10. Just as you did with the two sides of the boat, you need to loft the end caps at the back of the boat together. Select the edge isoparm on the inner and outer end caps, and then loft them together. You will have to do this twice on each side of the boat. When you're finished with the lofts, switch out of Component Selection mode (hotkey: **F8**).

tip

Remember that you can change the display's level of detail by selecting the boat and pressing **1**, **2**, or **3**.

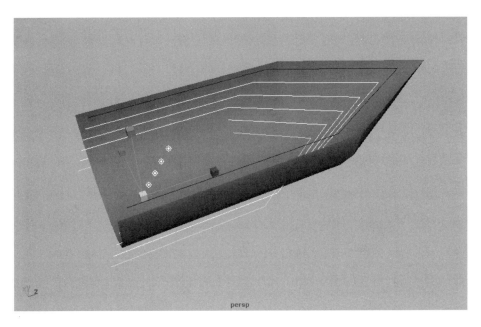

FIGURE 4.14   *Lofting isoparms together to close gaps between BoatOutside and BoatInside.*

11. If you click to select the boat, only portions of the surface instead of the entire boat are selected because you constructed the model from two separate objects: the cone you started with and the duplicate you made for the inside. You need to group them together to appear as one surface. Before doing that, though, you need to delete the construction history. If any history remains, scene elements can still be influenced by the objects that created them, meaning you could get random changes you don't expect. Select all surfaces of the boat, and choose Edit | Delete by Type | History. Next, group the surfaces by clicking Edit | Group. The boat turns into one selected object called Group1. Change the name of Group1 to BoatG in the Channel Box. If you deselect the boat and click it again to select it, you're still selecting only part of the surface because the surfaces have been placed in a hierarchy under the group's parent. Press the up arrow to move up the hierarchy until BoatG is the name at the top of the Channel Box; now the BoatG group is selected.

 tip   With the Outliner, you can easily clean up a lot of clutter in your scene. Look at all the objects listed in the Outliner, which include unused remains of objects and other elements created earlier in this chapter. With all the layers visible in your viewports, click on a surface in the Outliner that you don't recognize. By having all the layers visible, you can see if something is selected when you click the surface. You might want to press f to focus in a viewport in case the object isn't in the viewable area. If no actual surface is selected, feel free to delete that surface from the Outliner—just be careful that you don't delete a vital part of your scene!

12. Hide all the layers again and create one for your boat. Name the layer BoatL, and add BoatG to the new layer. Be sure to save your scene again.

Adding More Animation to Your Scene

Making a plane "live" turns it into a modeling aid, and is an easy way to draw a curve directly on a surface. By adding a curve to the water plane, you can attach BoatG to it so that the boat follows along the curve (the animation path). Because the curve is drawn on the water, it will also deform with the water's motion.

Tutorial: Animating the Boat Along a Path

To animate the boat, you'll create a motion path along the water and attach the boat to it. You can continue from the previous tutorial, or load the scene file noted here.

On the CD

Chapter_04\movies\ch04tut06.wmv

1. Hide the BoatL layer and display WaterL. Make sure the Time Slider is set to the first frame, 0, which sets the plane to its original shape before deformation. Open the Outliner, expand WaterGroup, and select WaterPlane. In the Hotbox, click Modify | Make Live. The plane turns a dark green color by default to indicate that it's live.

On the CD

Chapter_04\ch04tut05end.mb

2. Display the GroundL layer, and switch to the Top view. You can work in Shaded mode (hotkey: **5**) and enable wireframes, too, with Shading | Shade Options | Wireframe on Shaded. Create a CV curve (Hotbox | Create | CV Curve Tool), and click along the top of the water, making a path with CVs that will go across the water (see Figure 4.15). Note that the curve won't appear until you've created the first four points, and then it updates with each new click. If you want to go back one step on the curve drawing, press the Backspace key. Press Enter when you're done drawing the curve. Try to create the path so that you don't click on the "islands" so the boat doesn't run ashore. Don't worry about your curve being perfect; you can always tweak it later. Name the curve BoatPath.

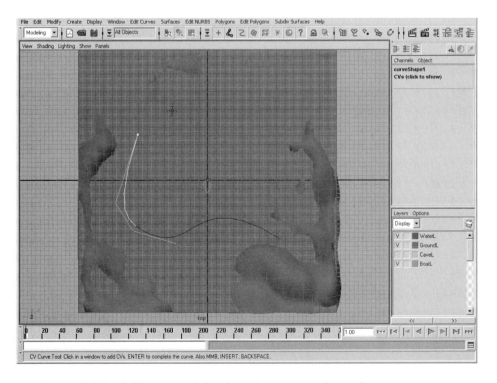

FIGURE 4.15   *A CV curve path has been drawn onto a live surface.*

3. The curve is still not part of WaterPlane and will not be until you make the plane *not* live. Deselect the curve you created by clicking on a blank area of the viewport, and in the Hotbox, click Modify | Make Not Live. You now have a curve drawn directly on the surface. Although the curve is part of the plane, you can select it separately by clicking on it.

4. Display the BoatL layer, and select the BoatG group in the Outliner. Zoom in on BoatPath and Shift+click to select the curve. The boat and the curve should both be selected. Switch to Animation mode (hotkey: **F2**). Attach the boat to BoatPath by choosing Animate | Motion Paths | Attach to Motion Path on the menu. Restore the view to Four View mode, and play the animation in the Perspective view (hotkey: **Alt+v**). BoatG will now follow along the path as the animation plays.

5. After watching the animation, you probably noticed a few problems. The boat is under the water because of the pivot location for BoatG. When an object is attached to a path, the point of attachment is at the object's pivot point. To fix this, set the animation frame to 0 in the Time Slider, and zoom in on BoatG in the Perspective view. With BoatG selected, switch to the Translate tool (hotkey: **w**), and press the Insert key to enter Pivot Editing mode. Translate the pivot along the –Y axis until the boat is sitting on top of the water. Leave the boat submerged a little, just as a real boat would be. When you have the boat positioned (see Figure 4.16), press Insert again to exit Pivot Editing mode.

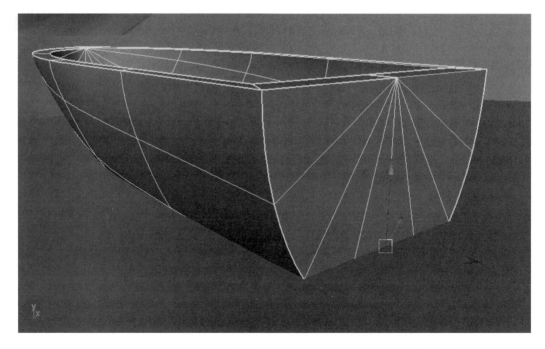

FIGURE 4.16   *By moving the boat's pivot point, you can position it above the water.*

6. The next problem is that the boat floats sideways along the path. To correct the direction in which the boat is facing, with BoatG selected, open the Attribute Editor (hotkey: **Ctrl+a**), and click the motionPath1 tab to display the list of options for the motion path. Select Z in the Front Axis drop-down list and change World Up Type to Normal (which orients the object's Y axis to the curve direction). Click the Close button at the bottom of the Attribute Editor. The boat should now be facing in the correct direction, as shown in Figure 4.17.

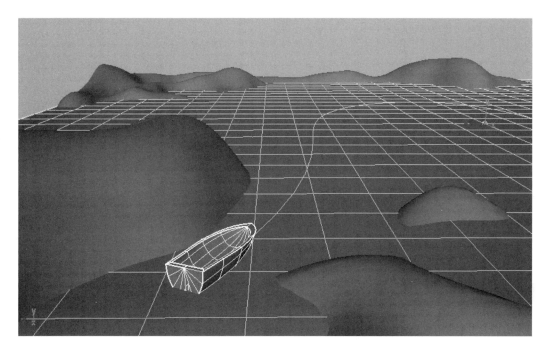

FIGURE 4.17   *The boat is now facing in the right direction.*

tip

If you play the animation and the boat jerks back and forth, check the CVs on your motion path. Clustering them too closely together could be the cause of this problem. Also, avoid scrubbing the Time Slider because it can have negative effects on an object's dynamics.

Tutorial: Placing the Camera

In this tutorial, you're going to render a scene from the perspective of someone riding in the boat. The camera you add will be a major step in creating that illusion. You can continue from the previous tutorial, or load the scene file noted here.

On the CD

Chapter_04\movies\ch04tut07.wmv

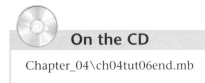

On the CD

Chapter_04\ch04tut06end.mb

1. Switch back to the Four View layout by tapping the spacebar. First, create a locator to lock the camera onto by clicking Create | Locator, and name it `CameraHinge` in the Channel Box. With the locator selected, you need to position it directly above the boat. Using the Move tool (hotkey: **w**), position the locator so that it's directly above the boat, near the back end, as shown in Figure 4.18. The camera will be placed inside the boat attached to the locator.

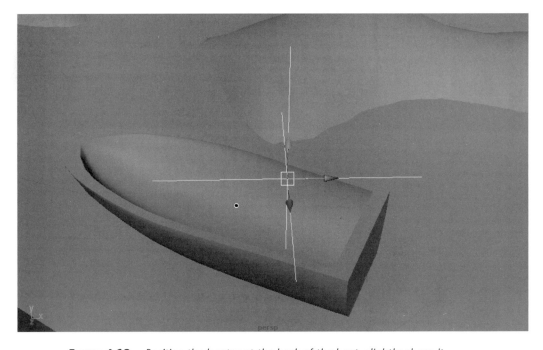

FIGURE 4.18   *Position the locator at the back of the boat, slightly above it.*

2. Next, you'll attach the locator to the boat so that it moves with BoatG along BoatPath. Open the Outliner, select CameraHinge, and MMB-drag it on top of BoatG.

3. Next, you'll import a camera that's already set up for the scene. With the Maya Fundamentals CD-ROM in the drive, go to File | Import. Browse to the file noted below the CD icon, select the file, and click the Import button. This camera is now located at the scene origin and has an environmental sky attached to it. In the Outliner, expand BoatG, select CameraHinge, and then Ctrl+click on BoatCamera so that both items are selected.

On the CD

Chapter_04\BoatCamera.ma

4. To attach the camera to CameraHinge, you need to set a constraint, which enables you to lock an attribute to a specific value, position, orientation, or scale. Make sure you're in Animation mode (hotkey: **F2**), and click Hotbox | Constrain | Point to place the camera directly on the locator. Now the camera will follow the locator and, therefore, the boat.

5. In the Perspective view, select the camera and choose Panels | Look Through Selected to change the current view to that of the camera. You can change to the camera at any time by choosing Panels | Perspective | BoatCamera. If you don't have all your layers visible, display them all in the Layer Editor. Play the animation, and watch the viewport from the BoatCamera perspective.

tip

The reason you didn't parent the boat to the camera is that the child of a parent inherits the parent's attributes. So if you scaled your boat, for example, it would affect the camera in a way you don't want.

6. You might have noticed that the camera follows the boat, but doesn't change its orientation during the animation the way it should. To fix the camera problem, you'll set an orient constraint on the locator. In the Outliner, select CameraHinge and then BoatCamera, and click Hotbox | Constrain | Orient. Now the camera will change its orientation according to the locator.

7. If the camera is pointing the wrong direction, you can easily fix that by selecting CameraHinge and using the Rotate tool (hotkey: **e**) to rotate around the Y axis until BoatCamera is pointing toward the front of the boat. As you rotate and adjust the camera, watch the view from BoatCamera.

8. Select the BoatCamera in the Outliner and right-click in the Channel Box over the Translate Y label. This brings up an option menu; choose Break Connections, as shown in Figure 4.19. This lets the camera's height float free, making for a less jerky ride on the boat when viewed from this camera.

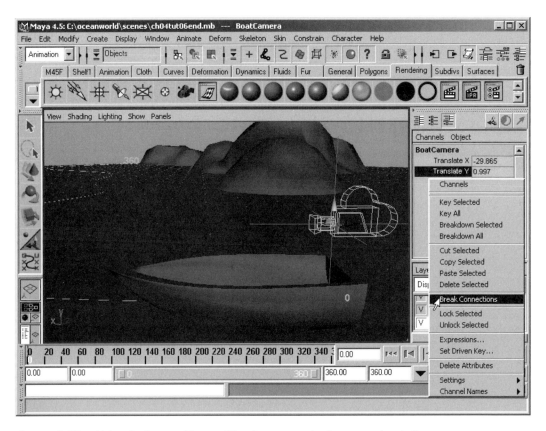

FIGURE 4.19   *Using the locator (CameraHinge) to constrain the camera's rotation.*

tip   Play back the animation and watch it carefully. If the front of the boat goes under water, try moving BoatG's pivot point toward the front of the boat. If the boat is moving too fast, you can modify BoatPath by deleting CVs on it to shorten the length of the path. Traveling a shorter path in the same amount of time (360 frames) means the boat will move slower.

Adding Materials and Lighting Your Scene

Next, you'll make the scene objects a little prettier than light gray. Materials not only give color, but also add surface attributes, such as shininess or transparency. By adding materials to your scene, you can create contrast among the scene elements and make them look more realistic. In this section, you'll explore Hypershade to create and apply materials. In Hypershade you can also work with "rendering nodes," which are used to modify textures, materials, lights, special effects, and other scene elements. You'll also work with adding materials and lighting the scene. You'll apply materials to objects and then do some quick renders so that you can see where you might need to make adjustments. Materials and lights go hand in hand because lighting affects the appearance of any materials you apply.

Tutorial: Adding Lights and Materials

Before you render anything, you need to create at least a simple lighting system, so for this tutorial, you'll add a Directional light to simulate sunlight. You'll then import some shaders to add texture to objects in your scene. You can continue from the previous tutorial, or load the scene file noted here.

On the CD

Chapter_04\movies\ch04tut08.wmv

1. First, add a simple Directional light to the scene (Create | Lights | Directional). In the Channel Box, change the light's name to SunRays. You can see the effect of this light by pressing 7 on your keyboard to turn off the default lighting and using only the Directional light you added.

On the CD

Chapter_04\ch04tut07end.mb

2. Next, you'll need to change some settings for the Directional light. Its location doesn't matter because you can aim a Directional light anywhere you like, no matter where it's placed. To adjust the light's focus, in the Channel Box, set Rotate X to 0, Rotate Y to -132, and Rotate Z to -38.

3. Next, set Scale X, Y, Z to 10 to make the Light icon bigger and therefore easier to select. With the light still selected, under Shapes in the Channel Box, change Use Ray Trace Shadows to On. You now have enough light to render the scene and view your textures, so you can move on to texturing.

4. Maya has a predefined layout for texturing that includes Hypershade, the Render View window, and the Perspective view. To open this layout, on any viewport menu bar or in the Hotbox, click Panels | Saved Layouts | Hypershade/Render/Persp. The interface will change to the predefined layout (see Figure 4.20).

5. Texturing is a complex process, so for this tutorial, you'll work with *shaders* we've already created. A shader defines the materials, volume, and other attributes for a material. To import these shaders, choose File | Import | option box on the menu bar. In the Import Options dialog box,

On the CD

Chapter_04\Shaders\OceanWater.ma

select the Group check box; under the Name Clash options, it should read "Resolve clashing nodes with this string." Change both list boxes in the dialog box to match this statement. In the This String text box, enter Water, and then click the Import button. Insert the Maya Fundamentals CD, browse to the file noted previously, select it, and click the Import button. In the Materials tab in Hypershade, you should now see a shader material called OceanWater (see Figure 4.21).

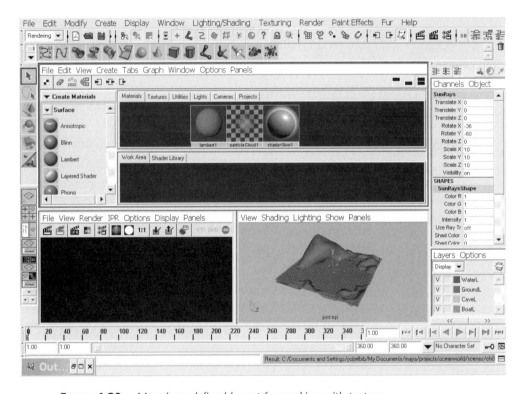

FIGURE 4.20   *Maya's predefined layout for working with textures.*

6. In Hypershade, right-click on OceanWater, and choose Graph Network. The Work Area in Hypershade displays all the nodes used to create that shader. You can use this information to figure out how the shader works and eventually create one of your own.

7. OceanWater is ready to be applied to the water in your scene. In the Perspective view, select WaterPlane. Then right-click on OceanWater in Hypershade, and choose Assign Material to Selection. The water is now textured!

8. With Maya's IPR rendering, you can see how textures and lights affect the scene by automatically updating the render with each change you make. First, position your scene in the Perspective view so that you're zoomed in close on an area where you can see part of the ground and the water.

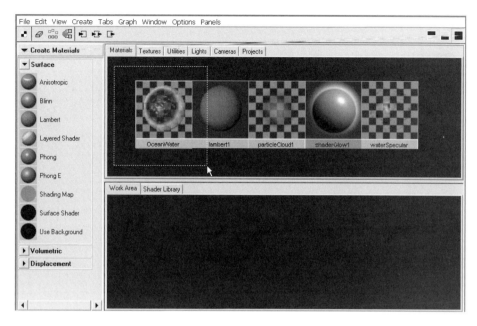

FIGURE 4.21   *Importing OceanWater.ma into Hypershade.*

9. Click the Play button on the Time Slider and stop about halfway through the animation. In the Render View window, click the IPR button to start the IPR render. This render takes longer than a normal test render because the IPR render has to store more information about the scene so that it can update when you make changes. When the IPR render is finished, marquee-select the entire rendered image (dragging from the upper-right to the lower-left corner) in the Render View window to be updated with IPR. You should see a green border surrounding it (see Figure 4.22).

10. Open the Outliner, select the place3dTexture17 node, and MMB-drag it into the WaterGroup group.

11. Next, you'll import the shaders for the ground. As you did in Step 5, choose File | Import | option box, change the text box from Water to Ground, and click the Import button. On the Maya Fundamentals CD, browse to the file noted here, select it, and click the Import

On the CD

Chapter_04\Shaders\OceanGround.ma

button. A new shader named OceanGround is added to Hypershade. Select the ground plane in your scene, RMB-click on OceanGround in Hypershade, and choose Assign Material to Selection on the shortcut menu. You'll see the IPR render update and show the ground textured. Save your scene.

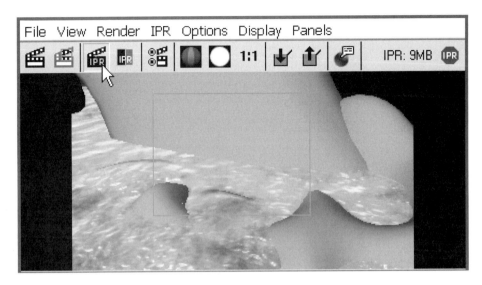

FIGURE 4.22   *Selecting a region to be automatically updated with IPR rendering.*

12. Hide all the layers except BoatL. Import OceanBoat.ma (use the same procedure as in Step 5), and be sure to change the text box in the Import Options dialog box to Boat. After importing OceanBoat.ma, you'll see it available in Hypershade. In the Outliner, select BoatG, and then focus on BoatG in the Perspective view (hotkey: **f**). With BoatG selected, RMB-click on the OceanBoat shader in Hypershade, and choose Assign Material to Selection.

> **trap**
>
> To have the textures loaded correctly, you must have the CD-ROM in the drive.

13. Make sure the animation playback is rewound to frame 1, and IPR render the boat. The texture doesn't look right because the texture placement nodes, which show you how a texture is placed on an object, are not aligned correctly with the boat. To position the texture, in

On the CD

Chapter_04\Shaders\OceanBoat.ma

Hypershade, right-click on the OceanBoat shader, and choose Graph Network. In the network for OceanBoat is a node called place3dTexture_boat. You need to adjust the values for the position of this node (see Figure 4.23).

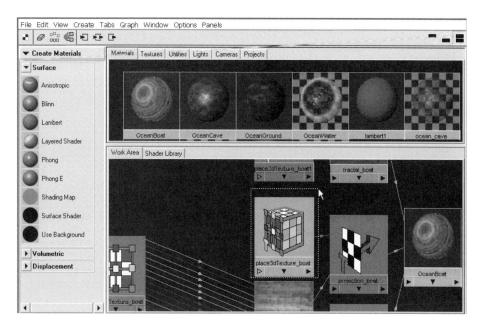

FIGURE 4.23   *The place3dTexture_boat node shows the placement of the texture on the boat.*

14. With place3dTexture_boat selected, open the Attribute Editor (hotkey: **Ctrl+a**). Under the 3D Texture Placement Attributes section, click the Fit to Group Bbox button. In the Perspective view, you'll see a green frame (the projection frame) at the side of the boat that represents how the 3D texture is placed on your object.

15. The green projection frame is not parallel to the side of the boat because the boat is attached to a path and has been rotated to fit. You'll need to temporarily align BoatG back to zero rotation, and then apply the placement node. Select BoatG again in the Outliner, and change all the rotation values in the Channel Box to 0. Those values have an orange background, so you know they are keyframed, meaning that when you play the animation again, the boat will return to its proper position.

16. Select the place3dTexture_boat node in Hypershade again, open the Attribute Editor if it's not open, and click Fit to Group Bbox again. Now the texture fits correctly on the boat (see Figure 4.24).

17. If you were to play the animation now, the boat would move but the textures would stay in the same place, giving the effect of textures sliding across the water's surface. To prevent that, you need to set BoatG as a parent of the place3dTexture_boat node. In the Outliner, expand the Group2 group to display

the place3dTexture_boat item. MMB-drag Group2 on top of BoatG to parent the boat to the texture node. When you play the animation, the textures will now animate with the boat along the motion path.

18. Now would be a good time to save your scene.

Figure 4.24 *Adjusting the position of the place3dTexture_boat node.*

Finishing the Scene

You're almost finished with your scene. All you have to do now is finish the lighting and render your scene. Because lighting can be a complex task, we've made it easier in this chapter by supplying a file with the lights already set up. You'll learn more about lighting in Chapter 9, "Lighting."

Tutorial: Importing the Lights and Rendering the Scene

You can continue from the previous tutorial, or load the scene file noted here.

1. Display all your layers. Switch back to the standard Four View layout (Panels I Saved Layouts I Four View).

2. To import the lights into the scene, choose File I Import I option box on the menu bar. Leave the options the same as they were in the previous tutorial, but change the text box with the word *Boat* in it to Lights. Click the Import button, browse to the Maya Fundamentals CD-ROM, select the file noted here, and click the Import button.

3. All the lights for your scene have been imported and are already positioned. Check out their settings in the Attribute Editor, and save your scene.

On the CD

Chapter_04\movies\ch04tut09.wmv

On the CD

Chapter_04\ch04tut08end.mb

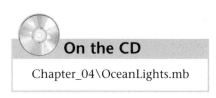

On the CD

Chapter_04\OceanLights.mb

All your hard work will finally come together when you render your scene. During rendering, Maya calculates each frame in your scene and saves it as a file. You then sequence those files together to play the animation in FCheck (Maya's image viewing program). Before you render the scene, however, you need to change some of the rendering settings, explained in the following steps.

4. Open the Render View window (Hotbox I Window I Rendering Editors I Render View), and then open the Render Globals window (Options I Render Globals on the menu), which contains the settings for your render. To specify a name for the images that will be rendered, under Image File Output, enter OceanWorld in the File Name Prefix text box, and select name.#.ext in the Frame/Animation Ext list box as the naming convention for files created during a batch render. For instance, frame 67 would be named OceanWorld.067.tif.

5. To specify the number of frames to be rendered, enter 360 in the End Frames text box. Next, change Frame Padding to 3 (for 3 digits) to have preceding zeros added for numbers below 100. This will ensure that the numbering system works for all image compilation programs.

6. Next, you need to choose an image format. If you don't have much disk space, you might want to select JPEG, but TIFF/TIF is usually a good choice (refer back to Chapter 1, "Pre-Maya: A Primer," for information on different file formats). Most important, be sure to select the correct camera for rendering: In the Camera list box, select BoatCamera. Uncheck the Alpha Channel (Mask) check box because you won't need it in this render. For Anti-aliasing Quality, select Production Quality in the Presets list box. Next, under the Raytracing Quality section, select the Raytracing check box. Finally, select the Motion Blur check box and select the 2D radio button (see Figure 4.25). After you've made these changes, close the Render Globals window.

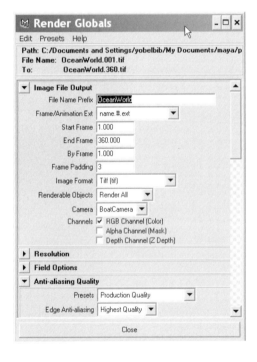
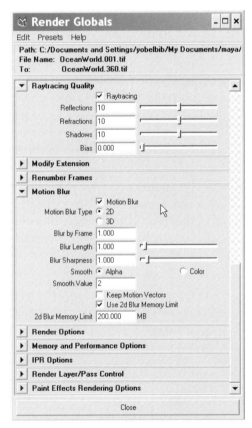

FIGURE 4.25   *Using the Render Globals window to specify settings for a batch render.*

7. Save your scene.

8. In the Render View window, click the Render button. If the wrong view is rendered, right-click with your mouse cursor placed over the image, and choose Render | Render | View (for the view you want to render).

9. To render the animation, click Hotbox | Render | Batch Render. Maya will begin the render, and the images will be stored in your Project directory in the Images folder. You can watch the progress of your render by opening the Script Editor (Window | General Editors | Script Editor).

On the CD

Chapter_04\ch04tut09end.mb

Viewing Your Render

In this example, you've rendered a frame sequence rather than a movie file. Now that you've waited for all the frames to render, you'll want to see it played back. This is where FCheck comes into play. This little utility is Maya's animation viewer. It allows you to load a sequence of images you have rendered and play them in order.

When you install Maya, shortcuts to the FCheck utility are placed in your Start menu. Go to the Start menu and then the menu item where Maya is placed. Click the shortcut named FCheck to open the utility. Open your animation by choosing File | Open Animation on FCheck's menu bar, browse to the Images folder in your project directory, and select the first image file, OceanWorld.001.tif. Click the Open button, and then watch as the animation is loaded into memory. FCheck loads the entire sequence and then plays it back at full speed.

Alternatively, you can set the file type to a movie type, such as AVI, and play it back from a movie player. For maximum compatibility between platforms, we've converted our AVI to WMV format (with Microsoft's free WMV conversion utility) and put it on the CD-ROM (see file noted here).

On the CD

Chapter_04\ch04oceanworld.wmv

Summary

In this chapter, you have taken your first steps into the full Maya experience. You were introduced to the vast number of techniques and tools Maya has to offer and have learned about the basic workflow. By using just one of the many animation methods—path animation—you were able to create an interesting scene. Along the way, you learned about the following concepts and methods:

- **Introduction to modeling**   The foundation of your scene comes from the objects you model.

- **Working with layers and groups**   You learned how to separate scene components into layers or group them together to make it easier to work with scene elements and keep things organized.

- **Soft body dynamics**   You learned how easily you can deform a simple object to get a more complex effect and create the illustration of motion.

- **Using constraints**   You have seen alternative ways of setting up object relationships, which give you more control over your scene.

- **Basic animation**   You learned to use path animation as a simple way to animate objects.

- **Adding shaders with Hypershade**   You learned how to import shaders and apply them to objects in your scene to add texture.

- **Using IPR rendering**   Your ability to texture and light a scene in Maya is augmented by real-time previewing, which gives you instant updates of changes you make in your scene.

- **Rendering**   You have seen how to set up a scene for final rendering and use Maya's FCheck utility to view the render.

It's always a good idea to stay organized as you work—name the things you create; group objects, lights, and other scene elements when it makes sense; and so forth. It'll make all the other steps easier, as you've seen in this project when you hid layers or moved groups around. As you continue with *Maya 4.5 Fundamentals*, you're going to find that working in Maya becomes easier with time. It's even fun because Maya simplifies the process of translating complex visions into reality. Moving forward from here, you'll investigate each of the steps touched on in this chapter's project: modeling, adding materials, lighting, animating, and rendering.

PART II

Maya Basics

CHAPTER 5

NURBS Modeling Basics

In This Chapter

Having glimpsed all the Maya animation steps in the preceding chapter, we'll explore each major task in detail in the upcoming chapters: modeling, materials, lighting, animation, and rendering. We'll start at the beginning, with modeling. Modeling fundamentals are the basis for everything you create in Maya. Whether you're creating an entire world, a character, or a simple project, the first step is to sculpt in virtual space each of the objects that appear in your project. In 3D computer graphics, modeling is defined as the process of creating object surfaces.

Also, you begin working with Maya in a more professional manner in this chapter, with the Hotbox, hotkeys, and custom-built marking menus. Unlike many hobbyist-oriented 3D programs, Maya does not come fully preconfigured. Professional Maya users rely on the Hotbox and usually configure their own hotkeys in addition to those supplied with Maya. Marking menus are a special Maya innovation that greatly speed your work. To guide the way, this book includes a set of marking menus like the ones professionals create. In Chapter 15, "Your Next Steps: Efficiency and Artistry," we'll show you how to build your own marking menus.

Here are some of the concepts and techniques covered in this chapter:

- **Installing presets** See how to load a set of customizations for Maya's marking menus, hotkeys, and other preferences.

- **The Hotbox and hotkeys** Learn to use Maya's Hotbox, along with the hotkeys and marking menus we supply, to increase your efficiency.

- **NURBS modeling basics** Learn to construct 3D models from primitive objects, such as spheres and cubes, and learn to manipulate the parts of those objects.

- **Choosing a modeling technique**   Compare the strengths and weaknesses of different modeling techniques to decide which method will give you the effect you want.

- **Putting it together**   Walk step by step through this chapter's tutorial—creating the basics of an old house—to see how all these skills come together.

This chapter helps you understand the basics of NURBS modeling techniques in Maya and gives you some guidelines for the approach you should take with different types of objects. By understanding the principles of NURBS modeling, you can create lighter and more efficient models that are easier to manipulate and faster to render. Maya offers so many features and capabilities with NURBS modeling that you will never get bored!

Key Terms

node   The basic building block of Maya, it's a place to store information and related actions. A simple object might be made up of its creation, or "shape," node, and its transform is a different but connected node. The variables set in a node are called *attributes*, and a node's attributes can be connected to other nodes to create a network, or web, of nodes. When you work with Maya, behind the scenes it is creating, connecting, evaluating, and eliminating nodes.

NURBS   Non-Uniform Rational Basis Splines, the term for modeling 2D or 3D shapes with curves.

spline   A curved line with its curvature dictated by control points.

surface direction   A NURBS surface always has a top side and a bottom side that give you the surface direction, defined in U and V coordinates. Similarly, curves have a direction. Trouble can occur when the direction is flipped from what you expect.

normal, surface normal   Because objects are made up of surfaces that are always infinitely thin sheets, one side is defined as "out" and the flip side is defined as "in." The "out" side is where the surface normal points out. Think of a surface normal as a ray that emanates perpendicularly from its surface.

Hotkeys to Memorize

spacebar hold   Hotbox

up arrow   selects the entire group when a group member has been selected (the group node is the parent of all the member nodes, and the up arrow is used to pick the parent)

z   undo

F8   toggle Component mode or Object mode

F9   NURBS component editing: CVs

Hotkeys to Memorize			
x	snap to grid	**r**	scale
w	move	**Ctrl+z**	open the NURBS Primitives marking menu (a custom one created for this chapter)
e	rotate		

What Are NURBS?

Modeling comes in three flavors in Maya: NURBS, subdivision surfaces, and polygons. Most 3D animation products work entirely with polygons, objects made from fixed 3D triangles. Subdivision surfaces are a kind of variation on polygons where a smooth surface is controlled by a coarse surface. Maya offers a more complex and powerful modeling system known as NURBS—Non-Uniform Rational B-Splines. Think of them as 3D curvy sheets in space. They have their own rules and limitations about how you can build, attach, and cut them, but in general, they are very flexible. A major advantage of NURBS is that they remain as pure curves—mathematical constructs—in Maya. You can choose to have more or less detail in your 3D views or renderings at any time. The faceted, low-resolution look that often occurs when creating curved surfaces with polygons is easily handled in NURBS models, which can display curved surfaces as virtually any number of polygons.

NURBS modeling is not simply putting objects together. Unlike fixed polygons (covered in more detail in Chapter 7, "Modeling with Polygons"), NURBS create 3D objects from curves and surfaces. Therefore, NURBS can be modeled in a variety of ways. Those who enjoy architectural designs and problem solving will definitely like NURBS modeling.

Although the term *NURBS* sounds a little silly (try delicious new nacho cheese NURBS!), it's actually a rather complex concept. To make it a little simpler, however, NURBS are simply a variation of splines, which are used to define a curve. Curves are the basis for the underlying mathematical structure of what makes up a NURBS surface, and in this chapter, you get to see how they actually work (instead of wading through pages of theory). In computer graphics, the best way to learn is through trial and error, so this chapter gives you the opportunity to work through a detailed tutorial. We'll supply constant reminders along the way on where to find certain settings or commands to help you remember them. To ease your absorption of so much detail, we try to mention every action, location, hotkey, and value you'll need. As you progress through this book, you won't need these reminders as often, but we've included them anyway to ease the learning process.

Choosing NURBS as a Modeling Technique

Each modeling technique has its own strengths and weaknesses, and deciding on the best method is a matter of experience. When choosing a method to use for a specific object, you need to consider several factors. Generally, NURBS are best for organic objects, such as animals, fruits, and vegetation—objects with smooth-flowing surfaces that run together. Ideal candidates for NURBS are industrial surfaces (defined as curvy and mass-produced) that require both precision and flowing curved surfaces: vehicles, molded parts, appliances, and other man-made curvy objects.

If you're in doubt about which modeling technique to use, it's okay to start with NURBS and convert to subdivision surfaces or polygons later. A major advantage of modeling with NURBS in Maya is that you can convert any NURBS object to subdivision surfaces (also called "SubDs") or polygon surfaces at any time. For instance, if you're modeling a character and find that you can't get rid of a seam between multiple NURBS surfaces in the limbs, you might want to convert that character to polygons so that you can weld it into a single object, instead of multiple surfaces. By using Maya's construction history, you can later deform and animate the original source NURBS surfaces, and the converted surface follows automatically!

Using NURBS can have its drawbacks, too. When modeling a character that needs to be animated, you might notice the seams between NURBS surfaces or even visible gaps between NURBS surfaces (see Figure 5.1). As a result of the way NURBS are constructed, you rarely come up with an object composed of a single surface, and the surfaces must mate together exactly to avoid these problems.

Using NURBS also adds to your model's complexity. It can be hard to modify an object if you have a large number of curves that define the shape. A complex NURBS surface can also make your model so hefty that it becomes difficult to interact with it in real time (depending on the power of your 3D accelerated video card). Another major drawback, especially in a production environment, is rendering time, which is when NURBS must tessellate. The ideal mathematical curves that define the surface shape are fleshed out with polygons, and this process can be time-intensive when a lot of polygons are required.

In this chapter, you start creating an old house from NURBS, the foundation of a scene that you'll build on throughout this entire book.

Figure 5.1   *A surface with visible seams.*

Marking Menus and the User Interface

Maya has the potential for a quick and efficient workflow. Watching an experienced user interact with Maya looks like magic because good work takes shape quickly, with a minimum of keystrokes and mouse presses. The key to this efficiency is creating custom marking menus that increase productivity and speed. When you press and hold a key on the keyboard, and then left-click and hold on the mouse, a kind of compass appears onscreen. You can then drag with the mouse toward a command to execute it. If you perform the action a little faster, you'll see only a short drawn line onscreen and a brief flash of the command name (such as "Create Cube") as the command is executed.

After a few weeks, you'll have memorized your marking menus and will be able to zip through creating and editing. Because the marking menu is a two-choice combination (first the hotkey, then the mouse selection), you can group related commands on a single hotkey. The mental relationship is very natural and fast if you assign your marking menu actions and hotkeys logically. For example, you might choose Alt+c as a hotkey for the Curve Editing marking menu, and assign the most frequently used menu items directly to the left and right (at the 9 o'clock and 3 o'clock positions), as shown in Figure 5.2. Therefore, a simple Alt+c and LMB-drag to the left puts you in the correct edit mode—ergonomically efficient and, in time, blindingly fast. If you've ever learned to play a musical instrument, you know the power of internalizing motions through repetition.

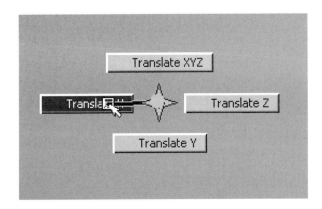

FIGURE 5.2   *One of the built-in marking menus: Translate X is at the 9 o'clock position.*

For this chapter, and the rest of the book, we have constructed a set of marking menus specific to the tasks you're learning how to perform. They are available on the book's CD-ROM; by loading them before you start the tutorials, you'll get a good idea of the many ways marking menus can be used. These marking menus also give you a good starting point for building your own set. Learning Maya's hotkeys and adding new hotkeys will also add to your creation speed. We've included a few hotkeys in addition to the ones used for the custom marking menus. Let's load them now.

Customizing the Interface and Loading the Marking Menus

First, you need to import the marking menus and hotkeys for this chapter. Chapter 15 explains how to create your own marking menus and assign them to hotkeys, but to save time, we've put them on the CD-ROM for you to load in a few steps. Remember that when you see the little CD movie icon like the one listed here, that means you can load a movie from the book's CD-ROM that corresponds to the skill being presented.

Note that the directions are for Maya users

On the CD

Chapter_05\movies\ch05tut01.wmv

on Windows-based operating systems. If you are using Maya on Linux, Mac OS X, or IRIX, you'll find analogous folders and files on your hard drive. Consult your reference manual if in doubt.

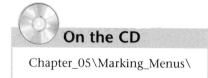

On the CD

Chapter_05\Marking_Menus\

1. Make sure you have closed Maya 4.5, and then when you start Maya again, it will load the files you're about to change.

2. With this book's CD-ROM in the drive, open the folder called Marking_Menus, which contains all the marking menus. Click the first file in the folder, hold down the Shift key, and then click on the last one. All the files should now be selected. Right-click on the selected files, and choose Copy.

3. Next you need to locate your preferences folder for Maya. In Windows NT, it should be in My Documents\Maya\4.5\prefs\Marking Menus, or winnt\ Profiles\Administrator\maya\4.5\prefs\markingMenus. In Windows 2000, it might appear under Documents and Settings\Administrator\MyDocuments\ maya\4.5\prefs\markingMenus. If you're on a networked multiuser system, the preferences appear under your login name rather than the administrator's (a nice feature that lets each logged-in Maya user have unique settings). In any case, the folder is usually on the C drive. An easy way to find the folder is to have your operating system search the hard drive for `windowprefs.mel`. Browse to that directory, and paste the files there.

On the CD

Chapter_05\Hotkeys\

4. Files pasted from a CD will be set to "Read Only," which must be toggled off. For Windows, you must right-click the selected files, choose Properties, and uncheck the Read-only attribute. If you accidentally unselect the pasted files, you can reselect them with the Ctrl key.

5. Access the CD-ROM again, open the Hotkeys folder, select all the files in that folder, and copy them.

6. Browse to the Maya preferences folder on your hard drive, and paste the files in that directory to load your custom hotkeys. As in Step 4, right-click the posted files, choose Properties, and uncheck the Read-only option.

7. Now open Maya. Before you load the marking menus, you need to hide some unnecessary user interface (UI) components so that you have more area to work with. First, hide the entire user interface by opening the Hotbox (hotkey: **spacebar hold**) and clicking Display | UI Elements | Hide UI Elements. Notice how much larger the work area is now.

8. You should have a couple of UI elements visible, however. In the Hotbox, click Display | UI Elements again, and in the list, check the boxes for Help Line and Command Line. When you're constructing something in Maya, these two elements display help information and error messages. You still need to hide the File and Panels menus. To do that, use the hotkeys **Ctrl+m** and **Shift+M**, respectively.

 tip

> You can also access detailed UI controls in the Preferences dialog box. On Maya's main menu, click Window | Settings/Preferences | Preferences. In the Categories list, click Interface. Modify the general interface preferences by unchecking the options for Show Menubar in Main Window and In Panels. You could go even further and hide Maya's title bar if you like, but if you need multiple applications tiled onscreen, hiding the title bar makes it a little more difficult to work with Maya.

9. Click the Save button. You have now simplified the Maya interface for the tutorials in this chapter.

 tip

> Replacing all your Maya settings can point some parts of Maya to the wrong folder—for example, your Visor brushes for Paint Effects. If this happens, you can fix it easily by choosing Tabs | Revert to Default Tabs in the Visor menu.

Customizing the Hotbox

At first, the Maya interface might seem intimidating, because hiding all those UI elements makes it seem as though you have less control over the software. However, you actually have access to every menu with the Hotbox. Follow these steps to customize the Hotbox so that all your options are showing:

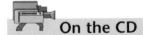 On the CD

Chapter_05\movies\ch05tut02.wmv

1. To make sure all the menus are enabled, hold down the spacebar to display the Hotbox, click the Hotbox Controls section, and then click Show All. You can see that all the elements are available. When you need to access a feature that doesn't have a hotkey or marking menu, you can simply use the Hotbox. When you find yourself using the Hotbox repeatedly for a certain group of commands, you can create marking menus and/or hotkeys to handle them.

If you own the Maya Unlimited package, you should hide a few of the Hotbox items for now so that the Hotbox displays only the functions you are using. To do this, open the Hotbox, click Hotbox Controls, and uncheck the boxes Show Cloth Menus and Show Live Menus.

2. Before you go any further, save your preferences by clicking File | Save Preferences.

You can't access the Hotbox with the spacebar unless one of the panels is active. When you have a dialog box open on top of the panels, none of the panels is considered active, so right-click on any panel to make it active. This activates the panel without selecting or deselecting any objects (left-clicking a panel activates it, too, but is a bad habit because it could cause accidental selects or deselects). Notice that the panel's border turns blue to indicate that it's active. You can then hold down the spacebar to open the Hotbox.

Here are the marking menu hotkeys you've loaded:

Marking Menu	Hotkey
mfNURBSPrimitives_Press:	**Ctrl+z**
mfNURBSediting_Press:	**Alt+z**
mfNURBSsurface_Press:	**Ctrl+Alt+z**
mfPolygonPrimitives_Press:	**Ctrl+x**
mfPolygonEditing_Press:	**Alt+x**
mfCurvesCreation_Press:	**Ctrl+c**
mfCurvesEditing_Press:	**Alt+c**

You can test out your new hotkeys by pressing the key combination and then LMB-clicking on your viewport (see Figure 5.3). Keep the mouse button pressed, and suddenly a menu will pop up! Drag the mouse toward any of the menu options to take that action. Try each of the hotkeys for your marking menus.

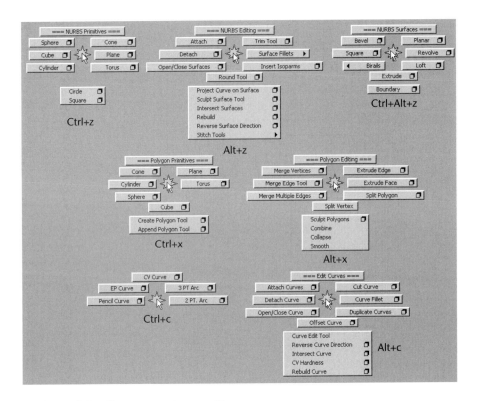

FIGURE 5.3   *Your new custom marking menus.*

Here are the other hotkeys we've added or reassigned:

Function	Hotkey
Script Editor	**Shift+S**
Hypergraph	**Shift+H**
Attribute Editor	**Ctrl+a**
Show/Hide Channel Box	**Shift+C**
Hypershade	**Shift+T**
Outliner	**Shift+O**
Toggle the Time Slider on/off	**Alt+t**
Undo	**z**
Visor	**Shift+V**

The hotkeys have been positioned so that they are more easily accessible to the left hand for right-handed mouse users. You can always reassign them to other keys if you choose. You would also want to move the translation hotkeys (**q**, **w**, **e**, **r**) because they too are on the left side of the keyboard. By keeping your hand in one area, you can work even more quickly. The objective is to be able to press the primary hotkeys without having to look at the keyboard. We'll add more hotkeys as you get further into the book, after you have memorized the ones just assigned.

The first of the hotkeys you'll use and memorize in this chapter's tutorials are as follows:

- **Ctrl+z**   Gives you access to a menu containing NURBS surface creation tools.

- **Alt+z**   Brings up the marking menu for editing NURBS surfaces.

- **Right-click in a panel with a NURBS object selected**   Brings up the marking menu for selecting elements of a NURBS mesh, such as an isoparm or a control vertex.

trap

If you accidentally press **Alt+v**, Maya begins playing the animation. This can be frustrating because you don't have the Time Slider visible, so you won't be aware that Maya has started playback—you haven't created any keyframed animation yet. You lose the ability to create and edit most objects when the animation is playing. You can bring back the Time Slider in the Hotbox, using Display | UI elements | Time Slider to confirm that Maya is playing back. We have also mapped a hotkey that toggles display of the Time Slider: **Alt+t**. Pressing **Alt+v** or the Esc key stops the playback if Maya has started it.

You can reprogram this default hotkey to some other key by using the Hotkey Editor. In the Assign New Hotkey section of the dialog box, enter v as the key, select the Alt check box, and click the Find button. Now you can easily reassign or unassign this hotkey.

Creating the Old House

You're ready to start building the "Spooky World" project by creating the creature's house. At first, the house is made of simple NURBS objects, but it gets more complicated as you add detail. We're not going to exhaustively list and explain every possible Maya tool—you can get that in the Maya reference manual. However, we'll explain the primary tools and a few of the more arcane ones, in the process imparting a feel for Maya's working mode.

Normally, a rigid and flat object like a house might be best modeled with polygons. However, this *spooky* house will later warp and bend. And when it does, the fact that it is made of NURBS will ensure that it warps and bends smoothly.

To get started working with NURBS, you'll create the beginnings of an old house, using the Hotbox, hotkeys, and marking menus to navigate. You'll continue adding to the house in subsequent chapters, and by the time you finish this book, you'll have an elaborate scene file that renders to an impressive animation.

Starting a New Project

Unlike typical Windows programs that let you load and save files anywhere on your drive, Maya always points to the folders designated under the project folder. You can still load or save files anywhere, but it always points back to the project folders. Why *folders* rather than *folder*? Because Maya creates a number of subfolders to manage all the files that can be created when generating a complex animation. Some of the folders include those for scene files, material texture images, rendered images, and so forth. Generally, when you are starting a new project, you create the project folder somewhere on your hard drive, and Maya then assists in creating all the subfolders.

On the CD

Chapter_05\movies\ch05tut03.wmv

1. First, choose a spot on your hard drive to designate as your Maya 4.5 Fundamentals tutorial folder. Create and name a folder there using the standard file browser for your operating system. We named our folder book_project, and put it on the C drive of our Windows computer.

trap   Avoid the use of the space character in folder and filenames; instead, substitute underscore characters. Parts of Maya do not function well with file paths that include spaces!

2. To create a new project for your scene, activate the Hotbox and click File | Project | New.

3. Enter the name of the project as OldHouse, and click the Use Defaults button.

4. Check the location of your project to make sure it's the folder where you want to store the files. Click the Browse button to find the folder you created, and double-click it so that the icon appears as an open folder. Then click the Accept button. If you revisit the project folder in a file browser, you'll see all the subfolders that have been created.

5. Next, set the measurement units for your project to work in nonmetric units (it's an old house, after all). To change the units that Maya works with, in the Hotbox, click Window | Settings/Preferences | Preferences.

6. In the Categories list, select Settings. In the Working Units section, change the Linear setting from centimeter to inch.

7. In case the grid has been adjusted, reset it to make sure we're at the same starting point. Click Hotbox | Display | Grid | option box, and then reset the settings. Choose Edit | Reset Settings in the dialog box, and then click the Apply and Close button at the bottom.

8. Click the Save button at the bottom of the Preference dialog box to save the preferences and close the dialog box. If you want to start the tutorial from this point, load ch05tut03end.mb from the CD.

On the CD

Chapter_05\ch05tut03end.mb

trap

You might notice some problems when you try zooming in and out now that you have changed the units. Your viewport might look as though it's cut in half as you zoom farther away (see Figure 5.4). This is because the value for the perspective camera's Far Clip Plane is set too low. Make sure the Perspective panel is active. Then open the Attribute Editor for the perspective camera by choosing View | Camera Attribute Editor in the Hotbox. Under the Camera Attributes section, change the Far Clip Plane value to a higher number, such as 10000. That should give you plenty of far-field viewing distance before the camera cuts out. If near objects seem to disappear as you get closer to them, correct this the same way by adjusting the Near Clip Plane value to a smaller value.

Making the Roof

When making the roof, you'll use two NURBS primitives: a cube and a plane. When you create a cube from NURBS, it's composed of several NURBS planes placed together in a group, therefore creating a cube. If you were to click on the cube, only one side would be selected. You need to select the top of the hierarchy—the parent object of all the cube's six sides. Bump your selection to the top of the group with the up arrow to select all the sides at once.

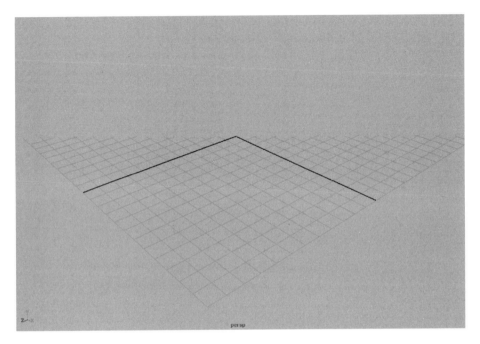

FIGURE 5.4   *The grid plane appears to cut off because the Far Clip Plane value for the perspective camera is not set high enough.*

Tutorial: Creating the Shingles

Remember, before you start a tutorial, you can load the movie noted below the CD movie icon to watch us go through the steps before you try it.

On the CD

Chapter_05\movies\ch05tut04.wmv

1. To make the roof, you start by using a NURBS cube. Rather than using the Create menu item in the Hotbox, begin by applying and getting used to your new marking menus. Access the NURBS Primitive Creation marking menu by pressing Ctrl+z and LMB-clicking and holding. Drag left to the Cube option box. In the NURBS Cube Options dialog box, change the Surface Degree to 1 Linear, and then click the Create button.

2. Open the Channel Box (hotkey: **Shift+C**) so that you can modify the cube's settings. In the Name text box, enter RoofTile, set Scale X to 150, set Scale Z to 12, and set Rotate X to –6. You now have a long flat board, slightly angled, to use as a roof shingle slat.

3. Next you're going to duplicate the cube so that you have multiple copies of the RoofTile object; this will make laying the shingles for the roof faster and easier. In the Hotbox, choose Edit | Duplicate | option box to duplicate the shingle slat. In the Duplicate Options dialog box, reset the settings (Edit | Reset Settings). If you have used Maya before to create duplicates, resetting the settings gets you back to the default mode so that you don't create duplicates with previously used settings.

4. Change Translate Z to 8 (the rightmost column is Z), and then set Number of Copies to 15. Leave all the other settings at their defaults, and click the Duplicate button. You should end up with 15 angled shingles, as shown in Figure 5.5.

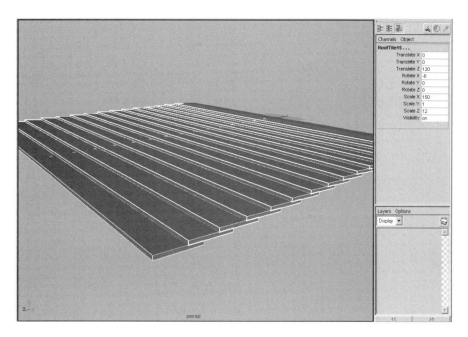

FIGURE 5.5   *Duplicated cube objects to create a roof side made of shingle slats.*

5. You now have rows of cubes overlapping each other. Zoom out to see everything (hotkey: **a**). Now select all the cubes by LMB-dragging a rectangle around them. Press the up arrow to select the entire box hierarchy of each member of the group, and then group them together by clicking Edit | Group | option box. In the Group Options dialog box, change the Group Pivot radio button to Center, leaving the rest at their default settings, and click the Group button to create a group. (See Figure 5.6.) This gives you a single entity for all the roof slats, making it easy to rotate and move them. Having just created the group, it will remain selected.

Next, change the group name from Group1 to Shingles in the Channel Box. It's good form to name everything you make in Maya; it's even better form to name things immediately, instead of putting it off!

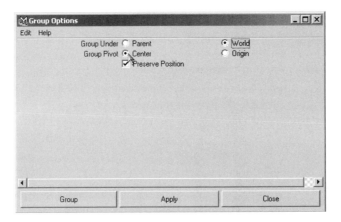

Figure 5.6   *Set the Group Pivot to Center or it will be created at the 0,0,0 point—a bit confusing because new objects are also created at the origin.*

Tutorial: Finishing the Roof

If you'd like, you can load the scene file ch05tut04end.mb to start the tutorial at this point.

On the CD

Chapter_05\movies\ch05tut05.wmv

On the CD

Chapter_05\ch5tut04end.mb

1. To finish the roof, you need to give the shingles a surface to lay on—the roof slab. This helps prevent being able to see inside the house between the shingles. Create a new NURBS cube with the marking menu (Ctrl+z | LMB-drag | Cube). Rename the cube as RoofSlab.

2. You want the RoofSlab cube to fit under the Shingles group, but be a bit smaller so that the shingles stick out. This is most easily done by using all four views and interactively scaling and translating the cube along the X and Z axes. Tap the spacebar to go to Four View mode, and zoom all views to Frame All (hotkey: **Shift+A**). Then, using the Move tool (hotkey: **q**) and then the Scale tool (hotkey: **r**), position the cube as shown in Figure 5.7. You can also use the Channel Box to enter these exact values: Translate Y to -2, Translate Z to 58.5, Scale X to 143, and Scale Z to 129. Ultimately, you want to position the RoofSlab cube right under the shingles, aligned with the first cube you created.

tip

The transform marking menus are helpful when you're zoomed in close and want to constrain a transformation tool to one axis. By pressing and *holding* the corresponding hotkey for a transform tool (**w** for Translate, **e** for Rotate, **r** for Scale), and then LMB-clicking and holding, you open a marking menu that allows you to constrain the translation along any axis (see Figure 5.8). Select one, and then use the MMB to transform the object on that axis.

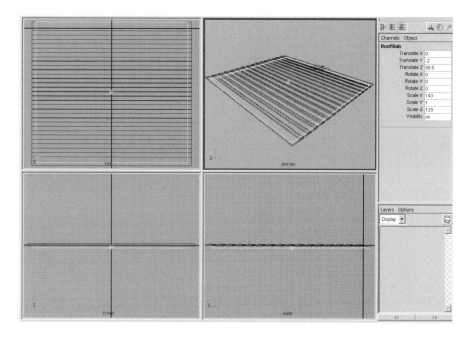

FIGURE 5.7   *Scaled and repositioned roof slab. The Perspective view is set to Wireframe mode (hotkey: 4) to see under the shingles.*

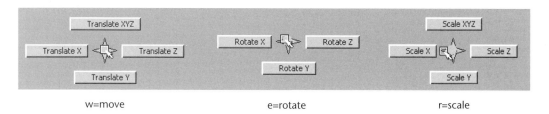

FIGURE 5.8   *The three marking menus for transformations.*

3. Zoom out so that you can select the RoofSlab and the Shingles, and then LMB-drag a rectangle around everything. Now group them together for easy manipulation: Press the up arrow to select the entire cube object for each of the selected surfaces. In the Hotbox, choose Edit | Group | option box; in the Group Options dialog box, select the World radio button for the Group Under option. If you kept Group Under as Parent, you would lose the grouping for the shingles and slab. Name the group RoofSide in the Channel Box.

4. Rotate the group by adjusting the Rotate X value in the Channel Box to 35.

5. You need to create the other side of the roof, which is done simply by duplicating RoofSide and scaling it with an opposite value. With RoofSide selected, open the Duplicate Options dialog box (Hotbox | Edit | Duplicate | option box). Reset the settings with Edit | Reset Settings. Set Translate Z to -109.3, Scale Z to -1, and Rotate X to -70. Click the Duplicate button, and you now have the other side of the roof. Group both sides together by using Frame All (hotkey: **Shift+a**), LMB-dragging a rectangle around all the parts, pressing the up arrow two times to select every cube in the scene, and then choosing Hotbox | Edit | Group. Name the new group Roof.

note

Remember: Try to get in the habit of resetting your option box settings, as in Step 5. In that step, the Duplicate Options settings had already been set when making the shingle slats earlier, so the number of copies, for example, was still set to 15. Resetting your settings put you back to a single-copy duplication mode.

6. Next you'll move the center of the Roof group to the Maya origin point to ease the modeling work to come. Be sure the Move tool is active (hotkey: **w**). In the Side view, press and hold **x** for Grid Snapping—you'll know snapping is enabled because the center of the Move tool changes from a square to a circle. Click on the center of the Move tool where the axes meet and drag to the origin, where the bold black lines of the grid intersect (see Figure 5.9). Snapping helps you put it right on the spot.

7. Now you'll tidy up the roof peak. In the Side view, zoom in to the top point of the roof by drawing a zoom box (hotkey: **Ctrl+Alt+LMB-drag**), and then select the area you want to zoom to. After zooming in, you can see that the shingles on each side don't meet, and some of the cubes are going through each other, as shown in Figure 5.10. To fix that, you need to grab the vertices of the Shingles cubes and snap them to the grid until they intersect.

trap

If the viewport camera's Far Clipping Plane is set too low, in addition to the viewing troubles described previously, you can select only to a certain depth. If you are in the Side view and picking overlapping elements near and far, you won't be aware that your selections aren't getting the rear elements!

It's a good practice to check your selections in other viewports before acting on them. Pop back to Four View mode and check out the Side and Perspective views to make sure your selections are what you think they are. Adjust the clipping plane for the side camera (Hotbox with mouse over Side view | View | Camera Attribute Editor, and increase the Far Clip Plane value).

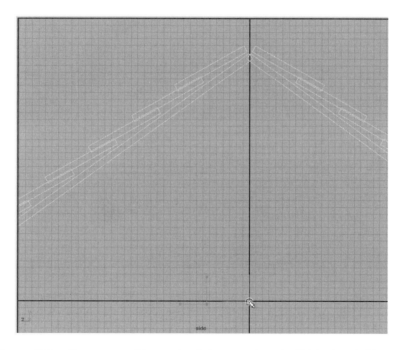

FIGURE 5.9   *Temporary grid snapping helps you place the finished roof object at the origin for easy additional modeling.*

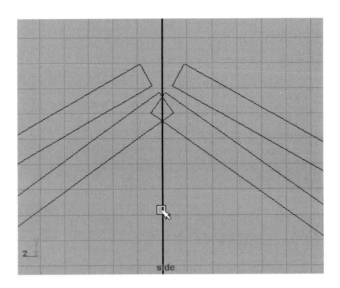

FIGURE 5.10   *A zoomed-in Side view reveals a sloppy roof peak.*

8. Select the top cube shingle object on each side of the roof (hotkey: **Shift** to pick additional selections), and then press the up arrow to get both RoofTile objects. Next, press **F9** to switch to editing components of these NURBS objects. F9 activates CV Editing mode—the endpoints of the NURBS objects. The CVs appear in purple. Drag a little box around the CV at the highest corner of one of the sides. This selects all the vertices that control that edge of the cube object, turning them blue. Check the Perspective view to make sure all four vertices are selected: two in front and two in back.

9. With the Move tool activated (hotkey: **w**), press and hold **x** for the temporary snap to grid. Now MMB-click on the blue CVs in the Side view, and snap to the first grid intersection up and to the right, as shown in Figure 5.11.

10. Repeat Step 9 for the top tile on the other side of the roof: Drag a selection around the other CVs, press and hold **x**, and MMB-drag the selected CVs to the same center point.

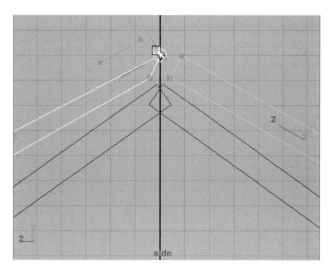

FIGURE 5.11   *Temporary snap helps move the upper edge of the RoofTiles to a center point.*

11. Now you want to snap the CVs under the top ones, just to make things tidy. Snap them exactly one grid unit below, as shown in Figure 5.12. Press **F8** to get out of CV Editing mode so that you can select other objects.

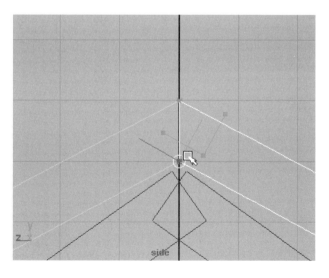

FIGURE 5.12   *Snapping the bottom edge of the RoofTiles.*

12. Repeat the entire process (Steps 8–11) for the RoofSlab objects. See Figure 5.13 for the final result. Press F8 to get out of Component mode.

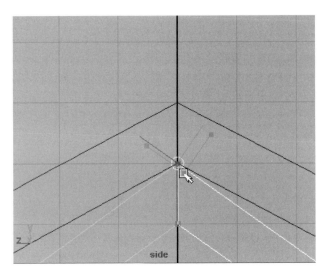

FIGURE 5.13   *All the CVs are now vertically aligned.*

13. Make sure the Channel Box is open (hotkey: **Shift+C**), and in the Layer Editor, create a layer (Layers | Create Layer). If the Channel Box isn't currently displaying the layers, click the rightmost button just above the Channels pull-down in the Channel Box to make both the Channel Box and Layer Editor visible. Double-click on the created layer named "layer1" to open its properties. Name the layer RoofL and assign the wireframe color. With the roof selected, right-click on the newly named layer RoofL in the Layer Editor, and choose Add Selected Objects to assign the Roof group to the layer. Click the V (for visibility) box to display and hide the roof to check that it was assigned properly.

14. Save your scene now (Hotbox | File | Save Scene As), and name it ch05oldHouse.mb. Note that the Oldhouse\scenes folder is automatically chosen because you are saving a scene and Maya has been set to work on the project Oldhouse. Remember that you can turn on the Incremental Save feature (Hotbox | File | Save Scene | option box, and select the Incremental Save check box) to help ensure that you have plenty of backups in case something corrupts your scene.

Adding to the House

If you want to start fresh at this point, you can load the saved file from the end of the last tutorial, ch05tut05end.mb.

On the CD

Chapter_05\ch05tut05end.mb

Tutorial: Creating the Walls and Foundation

You'll start by creating the walls for the house:

1. If it's not already hidden, hide the RoofL layer. Create a NURBS square by using the NURBS Primitives marking menu (Ctrl+z | LMB-drag south | Square). Name this nurbsSquare1 as `OuterWallcurve1` in the Channel Box. The square is made up of four curves that are grouped together to shape a square.

2. You'll adjust this square to form the bottom edge of the house foundation. Set the Scale X to `140` and the Scale Z to `200`. Set the Translate Y to `–159`. This will make a rectangle that is slightly inside the edges of each side of the roof as seen from the Top view.

tip

> When you are in Wireframe mode, it might be hard to see your selection if you have the display set to its lowest level of detail. Remember that you can always press keys **1**, **2**, or **3** to change the display detail. If you set the detail level higher, you can see more divisions on that surface, making it easier to see what you have selected in Wireframe mode.

3. You'll duplicate the existing square to form the outlines of the wall's structure. Later, the curves can be lofted together to form the walls' surfaces. Select OuterWallcurve1, if necessary, by clicking one edge and using the up arrow to select the entire square. Then duplicate it to an object with the same transform with Hotbox | Edit | Duplicate (reset option box). Set the Translate Y to `–111`.

4. With the OuterWallCurve2 rectangle still selected, perform a Duplicate again. Adjust the Translate Y to `–107` and the Scale X and Scale Z values to `138` and `198`. With this rectangle, OuterWallCurve3, still selected, Duplicate again. Set the Scale X and Scale Z values to `136` and `196`. Duplicate one more time and set the Translate Y to `–33`. This will give a total of five OuterWallCurve objects (see Figure 5.14).

5. With the wireframe you have created, you can now loft the curves from these squares together to form the surfaces. Start with OuterWallCurve5 (the top rectangle) and click on the long side of the square on the –X side, selecting one of the rectangle's four curves. Check the name of the curve—it should be leftnurbsSquare1. Shift+click on the edge of OuterWallcurve4 that's directly under the current curve selection. You'll need to zoom closer before picking, to avoid accidentally selecting OuterWallCurve3. Loft across the two curves by using the

NURBS Surfaces marking menu (Ctrl+Alt+z I LMB-click I Loft I option box). Reset the settings for the loft (Edit I Reset Settings), and change Surface Degree to Linear. Click the Loft button. The first wall has been created, as shown in Figure 5.15. This is your first wall, so name it Wallside_1. You can turn on the Shaded mode to see the surface (hotkey: 5).

6. Moving clockwise and using the same method as for Wallside_1, loft the next side from its two top curves. Just to be sure, verify that the top curve (first curve for lofting) is named bottomnurbsSquare1. If not, select the curve on the opposite side of the square. Then select the curve below it and loft them together. Instead of using the Loft Options box, simply repeat the last action performed (hotkey: **g**). Name the resulting loft Wallside_2. Repeat the procedure two more times to finish the other sides of the wall, and name them in order as Wallside_3 and then Wallside_4. By lofting in this manner, it ensures that all the surfaces created have identical parameters that can be textured easily.

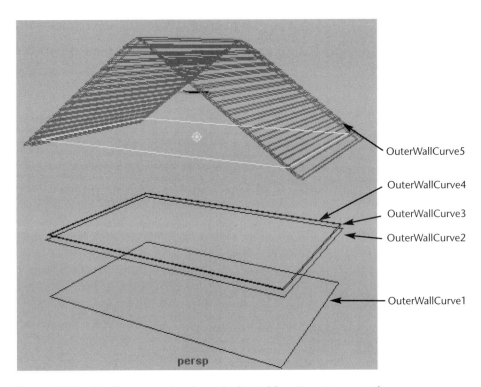

OuterWallCurve5

OuterWallCurve4

OuterWallCurve3

OuterWallCurve2

OuterWallCurve1

persp

FIGURE 5.14   *The first square has been duplicated four times to create the wall's wireframe outline.*

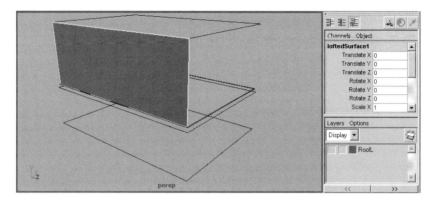

FIGURE 5.15   *The first side of the wall has been created by using a loft.*

Remember: You can always press **g** to quickly reuse the last action performed. Also, the Hotbox has a list of recent commands (Hotbox | Recent Commands). You can choose one in the list to repeat it.

7. The outside wall of the house will be complete after you group the wall's four sides together (Edit | Group). Make sure you don't accidentally select the curves. Name the group `OuterWall` to finish. Having a cube with the bottom and top cut out gives you the walls you need for the house.

8. Create another layer in the Layer Editor, as in Step 13 of the previous tutorial. Name the new layer `OuterWallsL`. Select and assign the OuterWall group to this new layer; make sure you have the parent node for the walls selected (press the up arrow with a side selected). Hide the layer so that curve selection is easier.

    The next component to add to the outside is the foundation, which you'll create with the same method you used in the previous tutorial. However, the foundation is made up of the bottom four curves.

9. Start by selecting the side curve, leftnurbsSquare1, from OuterWallcurve4. It's the same curve that was used to create Wallside_1 (the bottom, or second, curve used in the loft). Shift+click on the curve below it, leftnurbsSquare1, from OuterWallcurve3, and then Shift+click the curve below, leftnurbsSquare1, fromOuterWallcurve2, and finally Shift+click the curve below, leftnurbsSquare1, from OuterWallcurve1. See a pattern here? Each side curve has the same name as the previous one. The names define each of the four sides for a NURBS square. Because they are all the same name, you know you have selected a curve on the same side as a separate square. Loft the four curves together as before, and name the resulting surface `FoundationSide_1`.

10. Work your way around clockwise, lofting and then naming each side, until all the sides of the foundation are created. Group the foundation, name the group Foundation, and assign it to the OuterWallsL layer along with the five OuterWall curves. Save your scene.

11. Display both layers in your scene. Notice that you need to fill the triangular gap between the roof and walls (see Figure 5.16).

On the CD

Chapter_05\ch05tut06end.mb

note

With the construction history in Maya, you can modify the new surface by changing the source curves used to create that surface. They are still in the scene, and they are still linked to the surface that was created. Try this with different objects you create; it's easy to undo by pressing **z**. You could get some impressive results and open your mind to the variety of modeling and animation techniques with NURBS.

persp

FIGURE 5.16   *The walls and foundation are now set up properly, except for the huge holes between the roof and the walls.*

Tutorial: Filling the Gaps and Adding the Inner Wall

Don't forget you can load the scene file from the end of the previous tutorial (ch05tut06end.mb) to start fresh, and check out the movie file noted here to watch the tutorial in action.

On the CD

Chapter_05\movies\ch05tut07.wmv

1. Select the first curve, leftnurbsSquare1, that was used to create Wallside_1. Temporarily hiding the OuterWallsL layer can make it easier to select the curve. Use the Channel Box to change Translate Y to 80. Even though Wallside_1 was not selected, the curve caused a modification to it because of its construction history (the curve helped create Wallside_1).

2. With the wall penetrating the roof, you can intersect the surfaces and trim off the extra part of the wall that's sticking through the roof. Intersecting creates curves on a surface based on the surfaces that penetrate or cross through other surfaces. By intersecting Wallside_1 with the roof, you'll add curves that define exact points (on a curve) of surface penetration on the wall (see Figure 5.17). To do this, select Wallside_1, and Shift-click the bottom plane of RoofSlab on one side of the roof. Intersect the surfaces by using the NURBS Editing marking menu (Alt+z+LMB-click | Intersect Surfaces | option box). Reset the settings, and set the Create Curves option to First Surface. Click the Intersect button. Next, intersect the wall with RoofSlab on the other side of the roof.

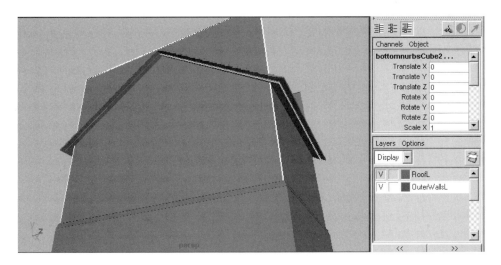

FIGURE 5.17   *Notice that the top of the wall penetrates the roof.*

3. Select Wallside_1, and use the Trim tool from the NURBS Editing marking menu (Alt+z+LMB-click | Trim Tool). This tool allows you to "slice" off portions of a surface with curves drawn on it. When the Trim tool is focused on a surface, you'll see a white grid. Using this grid, click on the surface area you want to keep (see Figure 5.18). In this case, you want to click somewhere under the roof, and press Enter. The edges are gone and the wall now fits perfectly! Now that you know how to fix the problem, repeat on the opposite side of the house. Select and delete the two raised curves.

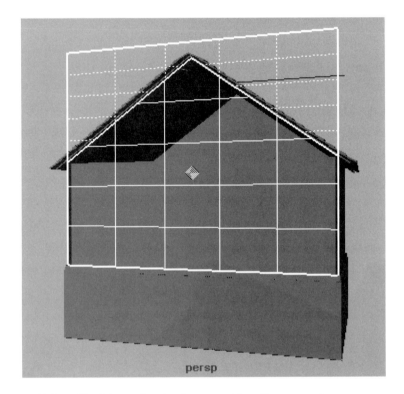

FIGURE 5.18   *The Trim tool makes it easy to trim off excess surfaces.*

4. Now you can add the inner walls, which is straightforward. Create a NURBS cube (Ctrl+z | LMB-click left | Cube), and name it InnerWalls. In the Channel Box, set Translate Y to –89, Scale X to 132, Scale Y to 112, and Scale Z to 192.5. The top of InnerWalls should line up with the corner where the outside walls meet the roof.

5. Assign the InnerWalls cube to a new layer named InnerWallL. To do that, after creating the layer, select the group in the Outliner (hotkey: **Shift+O**), and assign it by right-clicking on InnerWallL in the Layer Editor, and choosing Add Selected Objects (see Figure 5.19).

6. Save your scene (Hotbox | File | Save Scene), and load the scene file (ch05tut07end.mb) from the CD if you want to compare your end result.

On the CD

Chapter_05\ch05tut07end.mb

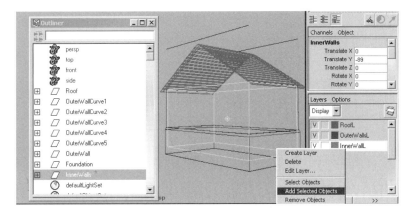

FIGURE 5.19 *Adding an object to a layer after selecting it in the Outliner.*

Tutorial: Creating the Porch

Now you'll put a porch on the front of the house.

On the CD

Chapter_05\movies\ch05tut08.wmv

1. Hide RoofL Layer because you don't need it right now, and it's taking up memory. Tap the spacebar to go to Four View mode, and then press the spacebar again with the mouse held over the Front view.

2. Check to make sure the grid is turned on (Hotbox | Display | Grid).

3. Zoom to the house's lower-right corner, which is in the positive X direction. Zoom enough so that the squares on the grid are clear and easy to see.

4. You're going to use the EP (edit point) Curve tool to create the boards on the porch. Activate the EP Curve tool from the CV Curve marking menu (Ctrl+c hold | LMB-drag to EP Curve | option box. In the Tool Settings window, change the Curve Degree to 1 Linear. Click the Close button to close the Tool Settings window.

5. Each square on the grid represents an inch, and you want to create a porch about 6 feet wide. Using grid snapping (hotkey: **x**), you'll click and place points to create a curve that represents the side view of boards laid across the ground. To do that, press the x key, and click at a point 2 inches above and 2 inches to the right of the inner walls' lower-right corner (16 inches above the foundation). Create the next point 4 inches (grid divisions) to the right. Now click down 2 units, to the right 1 unit, and then back up 2 units to create a groove 2 inches deep and 1 inch wide. Repeat to get 14 downward-pointing bumps, to create a shape like the one in Figure 5.20.

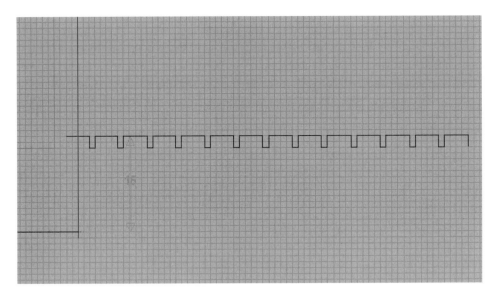

FIGURE 5.20   *A side view of the 14 boards, each 4 inches wide with a 1 inch gap between the boards.*

tip

If you happen to place a point incorrectly, you can press **Backspace** to delete the last placed point. Another option is to press the **Insert** key for repositioning, and move the point where you want it, without having to finish the curve first. Just press **Insert** again when you have positioned the point correctly. You can press **x** for grid snapping, as long as you press it before using the LMB to start moving the point.

note

Remember: When you are placing points and start to run off the screen, just move the screen as you normally would to view another area: Alt+MMB-drag.

6. When you have finished placing the points, press Enter to finish the curve. The curve turns bright green. Name this curve porchProfile.

7. When you create a curve that isn't at the origin, the pivot is still placed at the origin. To center the pivot in the object so that moving, scaling, and rotating are easier, click Hotbox | Modify | Center Pivot. If you switch to Move mode (hotkey: **w**), the transform icon appears at the pivot point and you can observe its repositioning to the center of the green curve.

8. Tap the spacebar to go to Four View mode, and then press the spacebar again with the mouse over the Top view to bring it to full screen.

9. You need to move the curve almost to the edge of the house, but first zoom in so that you can see the grid.

10. Switch to the Move tool (hotkey: **w**), and translate downward along the Z axis, using the blue arrow to constrain movement. Move it to 6 inches from the edge of the outer wall. To set it manually, enter 94 for Translate Z in the Channel Box (see Figure 5.21).

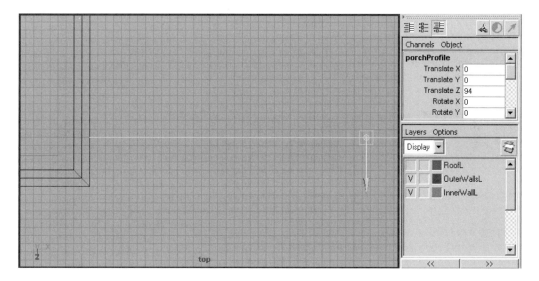

FIGURE 5.21   *Positioning the porch profile curve to the right spot in the Top view.*

11. Restore the view to Four View mode by tapping the spacebar.

12. The curve you just created is the profile of the porch surface you'll be creating. To create the porch surface, you have several options, but for this tutorial, you'll perform an extrude. Open the Extrude Options dialog box by using the marking menu (Ctrl+Alt+z | Extrude | option box). Change the following options: Style to

Distance, Direction to Specify, and the Direction Vector (the direction you want to extrude, along the side of the house) to Free. Set the extrusion vector in the three spaces below the radio buttons (use 0, 0, and –1), and set Surface Degree to Linear. Setting the –1 tells the surface to extrude in the –Z direction. Do not extrude yet, however.

13. You need to change one more option: the Extrude Length. The extrusion should end 6 inches from the other side of the OuterWall. There are a couple of methods you could use, but for this tutorial, you'll use the Distance tool (Create | Measure Tools | Distance Tool). From the Top view curve, snap (hotkey: **c** and LMB-drag along a curve) the first locator at the edge of porchProfile. Move the view so that you're zoomed into the opposite side of the house you need to measure to. Shift+LMB-drag at an estimated point. Move the cursor until it's 6 inches from the wall's edge (you have to do this visually, and you can snap to the grid with the x key as before). Now zoom out from the view, and the distance is shown to you—188 (see Figure 5.22). After you have the distance, you no longer need the measurement. Click the number to select the distanceDimension, and press Backspace to delete it. Open the Outliner and check for any extra locators. Delete any you find.

14. Select porchProfile again and go back to the Extrude Options box. Using the Distance value, go back to the Extrude Options window and enter it as the Extrude Length. Click the Extrude button to create the surface. Name the extruded surface PorchFloor, and center its pivot (Hotbox | Modify | Center Pivot).

15. In the Layer Editor, create a layer and name it PorchL. Assign porchProfile and PorchFloor to this layer.

16. Save your scene file again (Hotbox | File | Save Scene). If you want to compare your scene to the book's tutorial, load ch05tut08end.mb from the CD.

If you want to see the construction so far, make all the layers visible and check it out. A few test renderings might be worthwhile to check how the geometry renders.

On the CD

Chapter_05\ch05tut08end.mb

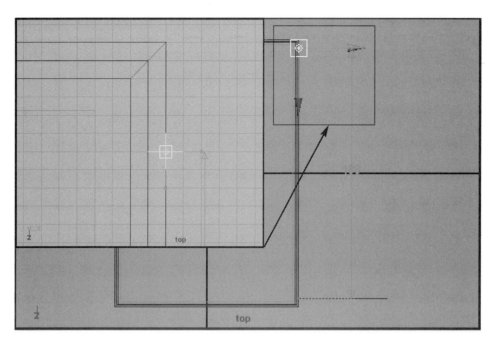

Figure 5.22   *By using the Distance tool and placing the second locator visually, you can come up with a fairly accurate distance between the opposite walls.*

Going Further

Start a new scene file and try to create some similar types of objects on your own. Explore the options of the Loft and Extrude tools, and see how they work on other types of curves you can draw.

In most of the tutorial's steps, we set the curvature to 1 (or linear) from 3 (cubic), thereby forcing flatness. See what happens when you draw lines in cubic mode. Try extracting and projecting curves onto other NURBS primitives, such as spheres.

Summary

In this chapter, you have explored the standard approaches to modeling with NURBS, focusing on architectural modeling. You have also practiced the following techniques:

- **Creating and editing NURBS primitives**   You learned to use cubes as a starting point for modeling, and then how to delete parts of primitives or take their endpoints and move them around.

■ **Engaging snapping when needed**   You can temporarily turn on grid snapping to make more precise model edits.

■ **Using the Channel Box for numeric entry**   You can use this tool to enter precise size and position settings.

■ **Creating curves**   You can draw lines that are later used for extrusion, lofting, or many other modeling creation methods.

■ **Merging surfaces**   You merge surfaces to get a temporary surface on which to project a line.

■ **Extruding curves**   You learned this skill for simple extrusions from any curve.

■ **Lofting to connect lines**   Any two lines can be lofted together to create a surface.

■ **Using Construction History to manipulate surfaces**   The history allows you to work with previous steps that have led to an object's current state (for example, moving a CV on a curve that created a loft will change the lofted surface).

■ **Basic trims**   Trimming allows you to "slice" off portions of surfaces.

■ **Using layers**   You can easily hide scene elements and organize your scene.

Now that you have built some basic and flat objects, you'll continue to explore NURBS modeling in Chapter 6, "More NURBS Modeling," with more complex methods and some curved surfaces. Looking at the house at this point, you can see that you'll need some new techniques to be able to cut precise holes in the walls to accommodate windows, doors, and other objects. You'll also finish the porch with rails and posts, and add other details to complete the house.

CHAPTER 6

More NURBS Modeling

In This Chapter

Having worked through the basics of modeling with NURBS in the previous chapter, you're ready to explore more complex surfaces and advanced modeling techniques. You'll continue modeling the house, adding a detailed front porch, stairs for the porch, a chimney, and doors and windows. Along the way, you will see the rest of the main methods for modeling with NURBS. Here are some of the concepts and techniques covered in this chapter:

- **Using curves to create complex surfaces** You can connect, spin, or extrude curves in many ways to model complex surfaces.

- **Snapping** You can snap elements (such as CVs) or objects to any NURBS-based CV, edge, or curve for precise placement.

- **Rebuilding** You can re-create NURBS surfaces with more or fewer divisions to retain the current shape and to add or remove detail in specific areas.

- **Modeling from existing objects** You can start a surface with the edge of any existing NURBS object to quickly model new details in a specific place.

Key Terms

edit point A point that lies on a curve or surface, displayed as a small × in Maya. You create a shape by creating sequential edit points. Moving these points changes the shape of the curve or surface.

control vertex (CV) A NURBS control point that defines the shape of a curve or surface. CVs often float somewhere in space, seemingly tugging on the fabric of the NURBS surface.

Key Terms

isoparms   The curves that define the surface topology of a NURBS object. These NURBS "dividers" create the surface as a sheet, with U and V directions that make up the sheet.

span   The part of a curve between two edit points. Spans are not directly edited; they "react" to changes you make to the edit points.

hull   A visualization enhancement in which the CVs are connected with lines to yield a kind of imaginary cage that shows the CV influence across a surface.

multiplicity   A factor specific to each point on a curve that determines its strength or hardness—how "pointy" it can be.

pivot point   The designated center point of an object or a curve, which rotates or scales around that center point.

Hotkeys to Memorize

Insert   adjust pivot point toggle

Ctrl+g   group selected objects

g   repeat last action

x (with Move)   snap to grid

c (with Move)   snap to edges or curves

F9   edit NURBS object CVs

F8   exit Component Editing mode of NURBS objects

t (on revolved objects) adjust the revolve axis

Custom Marking Menu Hotkeys

Custom hotkeyed marking menus used in this chapter:

Ctrl+c   Create NURBS Curve

Alt+c   Edit NURBS Curve

Ctrl+z   Create NURBS Primitive

Alt+z   Edit NURBS Surface

Ctrl+Alt+z   Create NURBS Surface

This chapter uses custom marking menus that were loaded at the beginning of Chapter 5, "NURBS Modeling Basics." These commands can be found readily in the Hotbox (mainly in the fifth row, under Edit Curves, Surfaces, or Edit NURBS) if you do not have the marking menus loaded.

More NURBS

You've seen some of the basic methods of modeling with NURBS in the previous chapter, starting with primitives: editing components of those primitives, projecting curves onto surfaces, and building surfaces based on curves. Now you'll follow up those techniques with other kinds of complex surface creation: revolves, lofts from existing surfaces, and sculpting surfaces by rebuilding and editing CVs. These techniques will be your basic toolkit for NURBS modeling.

Refining the House

Now that you have the primary parts of the house built, it's time to add some details to make it more realistic, starting with the porch. If you worked through Chapter 5, you can continue with your current scene file. If you skipped Chapter 5, or want to start fresh, you can load the scene file from the CD-ROM.

On the CD

Chapter_05\ch05tut08end.mb

Tutorial: Adding to the Porch

The next stage in creating the porch is constructing the rails, steps, and porch roof.

On the CD

Chapter_06\movies\ch06tut01.wmv

1. Hide all the layers in your scene by clicking the V toggle next to each layer in the Layer Editor under the Channel Box. The viewports should have nothing in them. Frame all objects in all viewports (hotkey: **Shift+A**) to see if anything remains unassigned to the four layers created in Chapter 5. If so, you can easily assign them to the correct layer. Switch to the Front view. Zoom into the scene origin (where the bold lines intersect) until you can easily work with the grid. If the grid is not displayed, turn it on (Hotbox | Display | Grid).

    To create the poles for the porch's side rails, you'll use a Victorian-style design that adds to the ambience of this spooky shack. To do this, you'll draw a profile curve and then revolve it to get a lathe effect.

2. Switch to the CV Curve tool (Ctrl+c+LMB-click | CV Curve | option box). Under the CV Curve Settings section, click the Reset Tool button, and then close the dialog box.

3. Grid snap (hotkey: **x**) the first CV at the scene origin. Snap another CV a couple of inches to the left of the origin point. Begin to create the profile curve for the rail by placing CVs as you move up the Y axis, as shown in Figure 6.1. Don't worry about the size of the curve in relation to the house; you can always scale the surface you end up with later. Be sure not to cross the Y axis—keep all points on the left side of the bold line. At the end of the profile curve, make sure you snap the last CV onto the Y axis, above the first CV you placed, so that when revolved, the top of the pole will be closed because the Y axis *is* the axis of revolution. Press Enter to complete the profile curve.

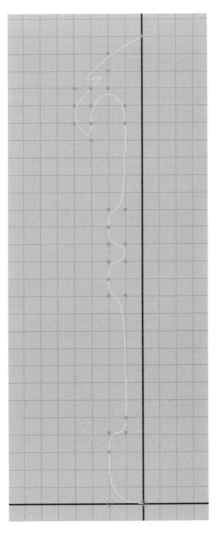

FIGURE 6.1   *The initial profile curve that will be revolved to create railing posts.*

4. Usually, after you create this type of curve, you edit it before creating a surface with it. The first edit you'll make is to the bottom of the pole, where you want a hard corner at the lower-left point. Right-click on the curve, and choose Control Vertex. This puts you in Component mode, where you are editing CVs. Click on the bottom CV you placed at the scene origin point, and press the Delete key.

5. Right now, the curve is rounded all the way through, but for this pole, you want some sharp edges on it. This is where the CV Hardness tool comes in handy. When you begin creating a CV curve with its degree set to 3 Cubic (the default choice in the CV Curve Tool dialog box when you create a curve), Maya sets a Multiplicity value (the pull strength) of 3 to the starting and ending CVs. The arcs between these CVs have a Multiplicity value of 1. When you change a CV's hardness, the Multiplicity value is changed.

6. Select the second downward-pointing tip's CV point (shown in Figure 6.2), or other points you want to be sharp edges, and use the Edit NURBS Curve marking menu (Alt+c+LMB-click | CV Hardness) to sharpen the point.

7. To create a surface from this profile curve, you need to perform a revolve. Get out of Component Selection mode (hotkey: **F8**), and select the curve—it should be displayed with a solid green line. Open your NURBS Surface marking menu (Ctrl+Alt+z+LMB-click | Revolve | option box), reset the settings (Edit | Reset Settings), and then click the Revolve button. To get a look at the surface, make sure the surface is selected, set the detail to high (hotkey: **3**), and then go back to Four View mode (hotkey: **spacebar tap**). Frame the selected object in all four views (hotkey: **Shift+F**), and it should look like Figure 6.3. You can orbit the surface in the Perspective view set to Shaded mode (hotkey: **5**) to inspect the results.

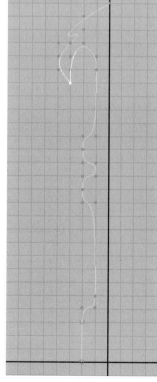

FIGURE 6.2

The rounded tip is hardened to a point.

 tip

The CV Hardness tool works only if there are two CVs on each side with a multiplicity of 1 (that is, CVs other than the start and end points).

When you're creating a curve, you can always press Backspace to delete the last point you placed or press Insert to move the point.

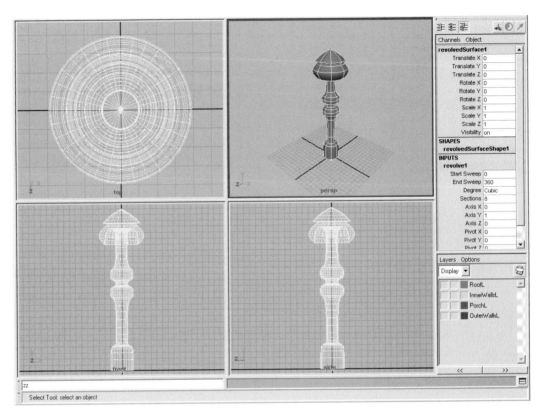

FIGURE 6.3   *The newly revolved surface.*

tip

Now that you can see the surface created from your profile curve, you might think it looks different than you expected. If you have history enabled (the button with the scroll icon at the far right of the Status Line), you can select the original curve and alter the revolved surface in real time—a good way to work with a surface because you get instant results when the surface is simple and your CPU is fast. You can also interactively modify the revolution axis. To do this, under Inputs in the Channel Box, select revolve1, which is the revolve input node. Then activate the Front view, and press **t**. You will see three handles appear—two for moving the endpoints and one to translate the entire axis. If you move them around, you can see how the axis orientation affects the revolve.

8. In the Front view, select the profile curve, right-click, and choose Control Vertex. All the purple CVs appear, and you can move them to adjust the shape until it looks similar to Figure 6.4. To make it easier, you can configure Maya so that you can select only CVs: Bring back the Status Line if you currently have it hidden (Hotbox | Display | UI Elements | Status Line), then click the Select by Component Type button (hotkey: **F8**), and make sure all the filters are deselected except for

the far-left button points (check the Status Line in Figure 6.4). After you finish tweaking the pole CVs to look like the pole in Figure 6.4, press F8 to get out of Component Editing mode. Now delete the revolved surface history to make its design permanent: With the surface and curve selected, click Hotbox | Edit | Delete by Type | History. Open the Outliner and delete the profile curve because it's no longer linked to the revolve.

> **tip**
>
> The extra views shown in Figure 6.4 are Shaded (persp panel) and X-Ray Wireframe on Shaded (persp1 panel). The X-Ray and Wireframe on Shaded view options are in Hotbox | Shading | Shade Options. The view must be in Shaded mode to see these options (hotkey: **5**). These view options can help you see objects you're adjusting more clearly.

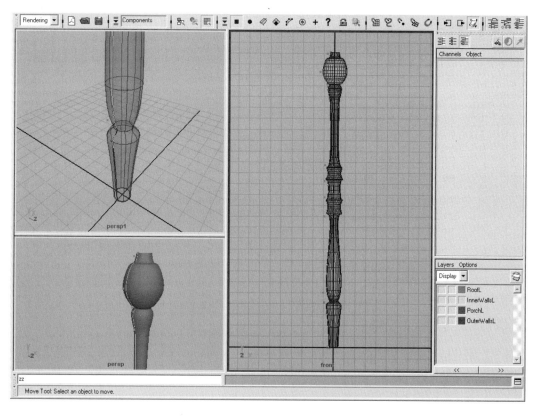

FIGURE 6.4   *The modified revolve, a Victorian railing post.*

9. Name the pole PorchPole, and save your scene as ch06tut01a.

10. Next you need to position the pole on your porch. Display the OuterWallsL and PorchL layers in the Layer Editor below the Channel Box. Maximize the Front view. Move the pole so that it's 1 inch (one grid square) above the top of PorchFloor. To do this, press **w** to enter Move mode, and then press and hold **x** (for the grid snap) before clicking on the object to move it into position. Your movements will snap to the grid.

11. Depending on the pole's size, you might need to scale it to fit. We used a height of 4 feet. Your grid is set to 1-inch divisions, so you could count them to scale to 4 feet, but there's an easier way to do it. The Distance tool creates a measuring tape with locators as movable endpoints that display the calculated distance. To use it, click Hotbox | Create | Measure Tools | Distance Tool, and click and drag the tool in the Front view (roughly placed; you'll fix it in the next step). The measurement should then be displayed (if it's not, make sure Show | Dimensions for the current panel is active). Confirm that you are in Move mode (hotkey: **w**), and then press and hold x while you click the first locator to the grid, 1 inch above PorchFloor. Move the other locator, with snap, to a point 48 units directly above the first locator. This gives you a guide as to how tall the pole *should* be.

12. Now that you have a visible goal with the Distance tool, you can scale your PorchPole to the correct height. This scaling will be an approximate adjustment made in the viewport; in this case, close is close enough! Switch to Scale mode (hotkey: **r**), and click and drag from the center (yellow box) of the Scale transform axis; the pole should scale uniformly upward because its pivot point is 0,0,0 (see Figure 6.5). If it doesn't scale uniformly, use the Channel Box (hotkey: **Shift+C** if it isn't already displayed), and change Scale X and Scale Z to match the adjusted Scale Y. When you've finished scaling the pole, delete all parts of the Distance tool. You'll find the distance dimension nodes in the Outliner (hotkey: **Shift+O**) as locator1, locator2, and distanceDimension1.

13. The PorchFloor currently looks like a corrugated panel hovering in the air, so you need to add a frame and some supports. To do that, you add some cubes around the porch floor and scale them to fit. Create a NURBS cube (Ctrl+z+LMB-click | Cube), and name it PorchPanel.

14. The PorchPanel cube is too small and not scaled the way you want. In the Channel Box, set Scale X to 68, Scale Y to 4, and Scale Z to 2.

15. Position the cube on the positive-Z axis side of the porch. Look at the Top view and the blue axis of the icon in the panel's lower-left corner. Press and hold **x** while moving the cube to snap its position to the grid. Use Figure 6.6 as a guide for placement.

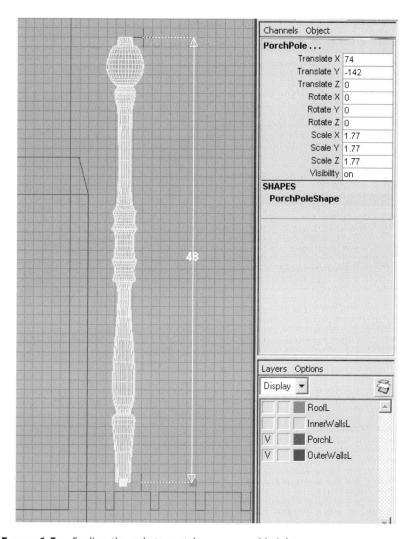

FIGURE 6.5   *Scaling the pole to match a measured height.*

<table>
<tr><td></td><td>Channels Object</td></tr>
</table>

tip

Sometimes it's helpful to view your scene in other panel layouts, such as in the scaling operation in the next step. With Maya's predefined layouts, you can easily switch to a two-view setup and have the Front and Top views stacked (Hotbox | Panels | Layout | Two Panes Stacked). After you display the new layout, you can switch what's in a viewport (Front, Side, and so on) by making the view active (hotkey: right-click over the panel), and then clicking and holding on the center AIW in the Hotbox. A marking menu with the Orthographic and Perspective view options opens, where you select the view you want.

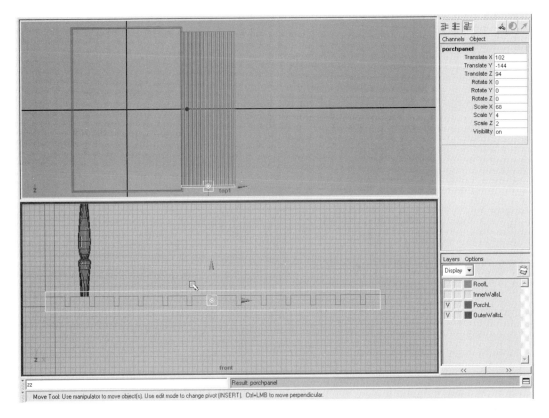

FIGURE 6.6   *The positioned side frame for the porch.*

note

Remember: If you deselect a cube and want to select it again, you must first pick one of the sides and then select the top node in the group (press the up arrow). If the Outliner is open, you can avoid this step by selecting the cube by name.

16. Switch the Top pane to Perspective view in Shaded mode so that you can easily select the two small planes at the ends of the stretched cube and delete them (you might need to temporarily hide the porch and wall layers to get at the face that touches the house foundation). The open-faced ends of the frame will be covered with vertical posts, so it's not a problem to delete both ends.

17. Select the PorchPanel cube. Open the Duplicate Options dialog box (Edit | Duplicate | option box), reset its settings, and then click the Duplicate button. The copy will be directly on top of the original, so switch to the Move tool and translate it along the Z axis a few units. If you lose track of the duplicate, you can find it in the Outliner with the name PorchPanel1.

18. Position the duplicated PorchPanel on the opposite end of the porch in the same manner as your original, using **x** to grid snap as you move it. The house is aligned to the X axis, so Translate Z is set to -94 for the duplicate because the original cube's Translate Z was set to 94.

tip
When moving objects, the default is to move the object in world coordinates. This is a Move tool setting, adjusted by double-clicking the Move icon. You can use the Reset Tool button in the Tool Settings window if you need to reset the Move tool to its default settings.

19. Duplicate PorchPanel one more time, and in the Channel Box, set Rotate Y to 90. Move the new panel, PorchPanel2, to the front of the porch. Grid snap the pivot point to the bold X axis line in the Top view and then translate along the X axis until PorchPanel2 is directly in front of PorchFloor. It should not be overlapping, but there shouldn't be a gap. Scale the length of PorchPanel2 so that it meets the other two panels: Set Scale X to 190, as shown in Figure 6.7. You can save your scene again as ch06tut01b.mb, as good practice for keeping a backup. If you want to compare your work to the book file, load the file noted below the CD icon from the CD-ROM.

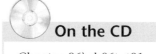

On the CD

Chapter_06\ch06tut01end.mb

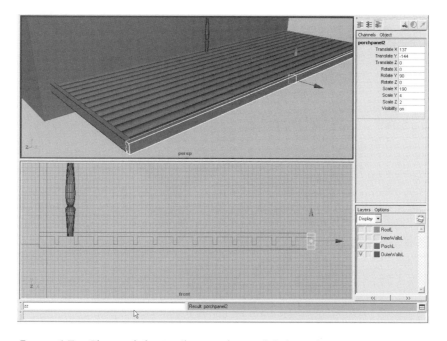

FIGURE 6.7   *The porch front rail—now the porch is framed.*

Tutorial: More Porch Details

All the PorchPanels are created. The next thing you need to do is create the legs that hold the porch up.

On the CD

Chapter_06\movies\ch06tut02.wmv

1. Switch back to the standard Four View mode (Hotbox | Panels | Saved Layouts | Four View). Create another NURBS cube and name it PorchLeg. Set Scale X and Z to 6 and Scale Y to 20.

2. In the Top view, move PorchLeg to the porch's lower-right corner. Snap it in position so that it's sitting on the corner, as shown in the Top view of Figure 6.8. In the Front view, move PorchLeg along the Y axis until its top is 3 inches above the porch (refer to the Front view of Figure 6.8). Make sure the bottom of the porch leg is even with the bottom of the house foundation. You can temporarily drag the leg right toward the house to check it, and then use Undo (hotkey: **z**) to undo the movement.

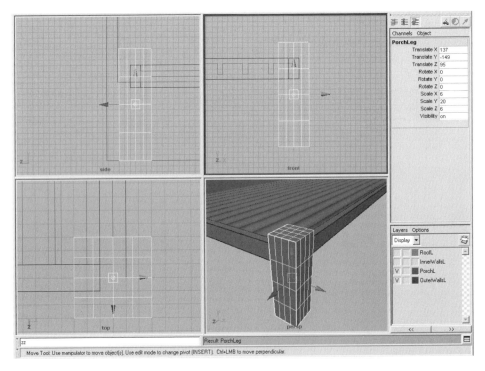

FIGURE 6.8   *The porch leg after using the Rebuild Surface function.*

3. The porch leg is rather simple, so you'll modify some of its CVs to give it more complexity. If you switch to the CV Component Selection mode (hotkey: **F9**), you'll see that there are no CVs in the middle of the cube's surfaces to allow sculpting. However, the Rebuild Surface function enables you to change the options for a surface that's already created. First, make sure you're not in Component mode (hotkey: **F8** to exit). Open the Rebuild Surface Options dialog box (Alt+z+LMB-click | Rebuild | option box) and reset the settings (Edit | Reset Settings). To add more detail to the cube, you need to change its number of spans. The options Number of Spans U and Number of Spans V set the number of divisions on your surface. The default is 4, which works fine for your purposes. Select the 1 Linear radio button for both the Degree U and Degree V settings. Click the Rebuild button, and the cube changes to display more curves (and therefore more CVs) on its six planes, as shown in Figure 6.8.

4. Switch back to the CV Component Selection mode (hotkey: **F9**), and scale or position the top three rows of CVs, as shown in Figure 6.9, to make the porch leg look like a carved pole. Use the Front and Top views and turn on the Status Line so that you can limit component selections to points only—the far-left selection mask button (see Figure 6.9).

trap
It is easiest to deform the post by selecting horizontal rows of CVs in the Front view, and then scaling them to a new size. If you select more than one row of CVs to scale, you can accidentally adjust their height in Y because the Scale function bases its pivot on the center of the selection. If the position of the bottom row of CVs is adjusted in Y, it will no longer match the base of the foundation, so it's best to select and edit single rows of CVs only.

5. Next you need to duplicate the porch leg and make four copies: Open the Duplicate Options dialog box (Hotbox | Duplicate | option box), change the Translate Z setting to -47, and enter 4 in the Number of Copies text box. Click the Apply button, and four copies of the leg will be created, lining up evenly along the edge of PorchFloor (see Figure 6.10). Notice that the dialog box stays open; that's because in Maya, the Apply button performs the function without closing the dialog box. Reset the Duplicate Options dialog box (Edit | Reset Settings) so that future duplications create a single copy, and close the dialog box.

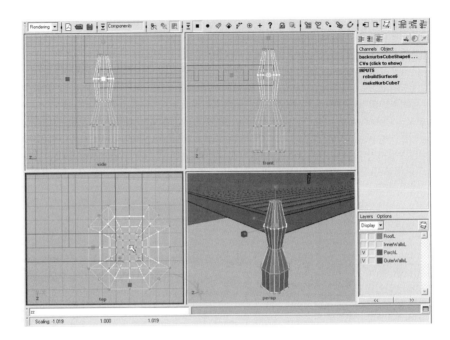

FIGURE 6.9   *The modified porch leg.*

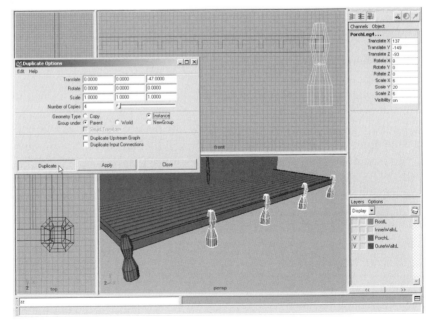

FIGURE 6.10   *The duplicated porch legs in place.*

6. You need to duplicate and position two more porch legs. Select and duplicate the original PorchLeg (hotkey: **Ctrl+d**). Measuring the distance from Foundation to the edge of the porch leg yields 64 inches, and you want to position a porch leg in the center of the Foundation and PorchLeg. Make sure the PorchLeg you just created is still selected, and in the Channel Box, click in the box for the Translate X value. The entire value should turn blue, and when you begin typing, the current value disappears. Type in -=32, and then press Enter. The current value will be decremented by 32 to equal 105. These relative-value entry functions work in any variable. You can use -=, +=, /=, and *= for the different math functions.

7. Repeat Step 6 on the other corner post.

8. In the Top and Front views, move and snap the PorchPole directly on top of one of the legs. Duplicate (hotkey: **Ctrl+d**) the PorchPole and snap-move (press and hold **x** before moving the pole) to place a pole on top of each leg, as shown in Figure 6.11.

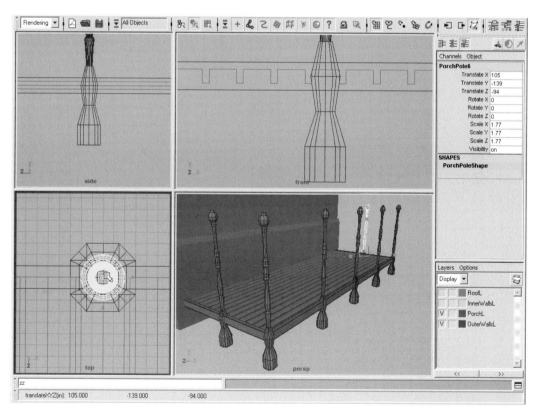

FIGURE 6.11   *All poles positioned.*

9. To complete the railing, you need to create the handrails. Create a NURBS cube (Ctrl+z+LMB-click | Cube), and size it as follows: Scale X to 36, Scale Y to 1, and Scale Z to 4. Move it over to the porch area by setting Translate X to 86, Translate Y to -97.5, and Translate Z to 94. Name the cube HandRail.

   You'll now put HandRail objects between the two leftmost poles of the porch and the front of the house.

10. Adjust the railing width (Scale X) so that it fits with the PorchPoles. Scale and move the cube so that it's between the house and the left rear pole, as shown in Figure 6.12. When placing the HandRail between the house and the pole, avoid letting the edge of the HandRail penetrate the walls.

11. To add some detail to the HandRail, again start by rebuilding the surface for more CVs. Select the HandRail object, and in the Rebuild Surface Options dialog box (Alt+z | Rebuild | option box), select the 3 Cubic radio button for both the Degree U and Degree V settings, and reduce the number of spans to 3. These settings create more CVs to give you more control over the shape and also change the degree so that the cube adds roundness between CVs. Move the CVs to create boards that flare out in the middle, as shown in Figure 6.12. Also, pull the handrail's end CVs slightly so that the end of the HandRail fully intersects the pole, almost to the center (see the Top view in Figure 6.12).

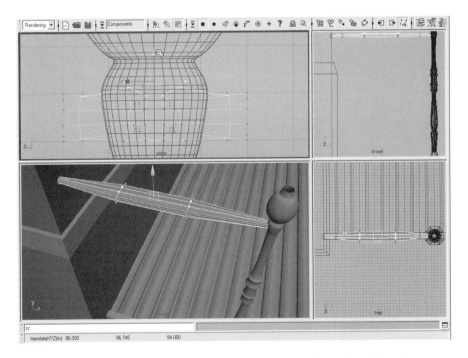

FIGURE 6.12   *The HandRail after modifying CVs; now it's a sculpted board.*

12. Duplicate the HandRail and move it along the Y axis until it's about 8 inches from the PorchFloor. An easy method is to put the HandRail on the porch floor, and then enter +-8 for Translate Y in the Channel Box.

13. Shift-select the two handrails and duplicate them. Then move them along the X axis until they are between the next two poles. Scale the new rails as necessary to fit them between the poles (we set Scale X to 31). You might need to select the CVs on one side and pull them along the X axis.

14. Duplicate one of the handrails to serve as a vertical slat. Change the duplicate's Rotate Z to 90, and rename it as RailBar. Adjust Scale X and move the RailBar in Z so that it neatly intersects both top and bottom HandRails, as shown in Figure 6.13. Place the RailBar at the side of the house. We set Translate X to 68, Translate Y to -116.5, and Translate Z to 94. Now move the RailBar out exactly 7 inches by typing +=7 for the Translate X value in the Channel Box (see Figure 6.13). Press Enter to finish the calculation and move the rail into place.

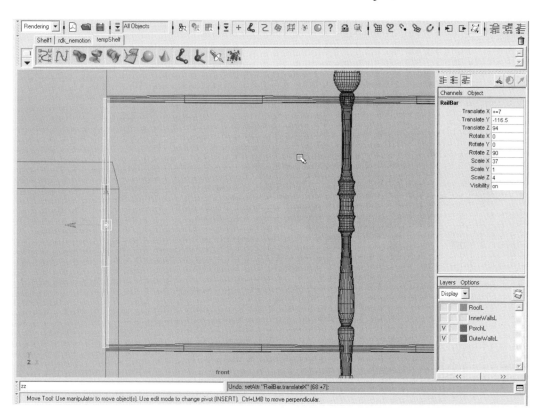

FIGURE 6.13   *The RailBar just before repositioning in X.*

15. Duplicate the RailBar (hotkey: **Ctrl+d**) and move it by typing +=8 for the Translate X value in the Channel Box. Duplicate the new RailBar and move it eight more units, and then repeat once more. Your settings might not be exactly the same, but the objective is. Try to evenly space the four RailBars between the pole and the side of the house (see Figure 6.14). Between the two side poles, position a duplicated RailBar and copy it twice with similar spacing as before. This gives you three bars between poles and four bars between the house and the pole, as shown in Figure 6.14.

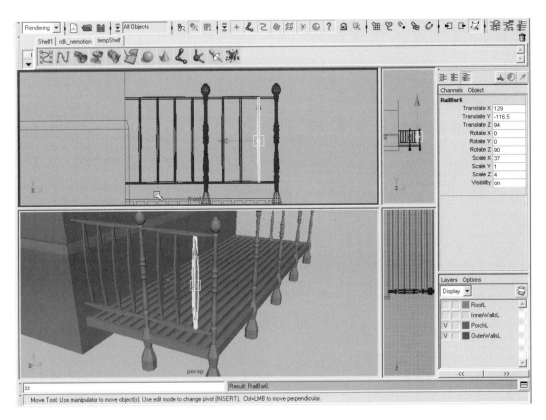

FIGURE 6.14   *Seven vertical RailBars more or less evenly spaced.*

16. Now with all the RailBars positioned on the left side of the porch, you can select all the HandRails and RailBars and duplicate them to the opposite side of the porch. An easy way to select them is to open the Outliner and Ctrl-click to select the 11 objects that start with HandRail or RailBar. You can also select them by Shift-clicking on a single side of each cube object, and then pressing the up arrow so that each selected side becomes the complete selected object. Shift-select anything you missed, press the up arrow again if necessary to include all parts of all cube objects, and then duplicate the objects with Ctrl+d. In the Channel Box, change Translate Z from a positive to a negative value (for example, from 94 to –94), and the instance-duplicated rails will move to the opposite side of the porch, as shown in Figure 6.15.

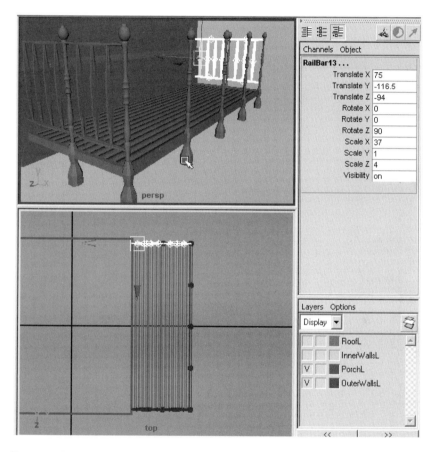

FIGURE 6.15   *The handrails and railbars from one side of the porch have been duplicated and placed on the opposite side.*

17. Next, you need to place rails along the front of the porch. Shift-select a pair of HandRails—a bottom and a top. Press the up arrow to make sure you have the complete objects. Duplicate them and rotate them on the Y axis by 90—you can do that in the Channel Box while both objects are still selected.

18. Position the duplicated HandRails between two of the poles at the front of the porch, and scale them to fit. We set Translate X to 137, Translate Y to -97.5, and Translate Z to 71. Scale X was set to 46 so that the rails would reach from pole to pole.

19. Duplicate a vertical RailBar, and change its Rotate X setting to 90. Position the duplicated RailBar at the center of the corner post, and enter -=8 for Translate Z. Your first RailBar on the front was positioned at Translate X 137, Translate Y -116.5, and Translate Z 86. Next, duplicate the RailBar four times by using the Duplicate Options dialog box, setting Translate Z to –8 and Number of Copies to 4 (see Figure 6.16).

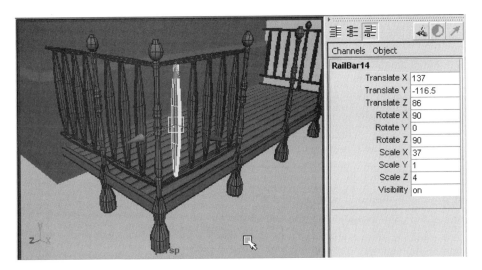

FIGURE 6.16   *First railbar selected, showing the Channel Box settings. The duplication to fill in the rest of the gap has already been performed.*

note   We've used the Wireframe on Shaded mode for clarity in some of the figures. To enable this mode, choose Shading | Shade Options | Wireframe on Shaded on the menu.

20. Having completed one section of the front rails, you'll fill the next two gaps similarly. The last gap will be left open for the porch entrance. Shift-select a portion of each RailBar and HandRail of the just-completed section—a top, a bottom, and five vertical rails. Press the up arrow to select the entire cube object for each piece. Duplicate the selection, and move it to the next set of poles. Position them accordingly, and repeat once more (see Figure 6.17).

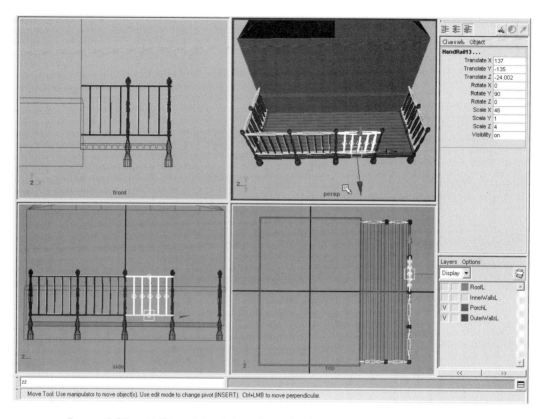

FIGURE 6.17   *At this point, all the rails are in place.*

21. Hide all the layers in your scene by clicking the V next to each layer in the Layer Editor. Drag and select all the poles, handrails, and bars. Group them together (hotkey: **Ctrl+g**), and name the group `PorchRailings`. With the group still selected, Shift-select the remaining PorchPanels and PorchLegs, and assign them to the PorchL layer.

On the CD

Chapter_06\ch06tut02end.mb

22. Save your scene again (hotkey: **Ctrl+s**).

Tutorial: Creating the Stairs

Now that you have finished the porch, you can make some stairs to lead up to it. You'll do it like a carpenter—two side supports and two stairs.

1. Display the PorchL layer. Switch to the Front view and activate the EP Curve tool (Ctrl+c+LMB-click I EP Curve I option box). Set the Curve Degree to 1 Linear.

2. Snap the first edit point so that it's 3 inches lower than and 3 inches to the right of the PorchPanels—the position of the × in Figure 6.18. Place another point 2 inches above the first. Start grid snapping the next edit point 8 inches across and the next edit point 6 inches down. Create another step 8 inches over and 6 inches down, and you should be at the horizontal level of the PorchLeg. Then place a point 4 inches to the left. Snap the last point to the starting point, as shown in Figure 6.18. Press Enter after placing the last point to close and complete the shape. Center the pivot point on the curve (Hotbox I Modify I Center Pivot).

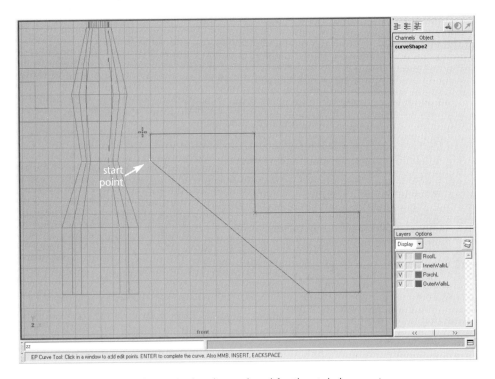

FIGURE 6.18   *The last point has been placed for the stairs' support curve.*

3. Switch to the Side view, and move the curve in front of the gap in the porch at the front, as shown in the Side view in Figure 6.19. Be sure not to move the curve in the Y direction because you already have it aligned correctly on that axis. Next, you'll zero the transforms by using the Freeze Transformations command, which leaves the object in place but resets all the transform values. Freeze the transformations for the curve with Hotbox | Modify | Freeze Transformations.

4. Open the Duplicate Options dialog box, and reset the settings. Duplicate (hotkey: **Ctrl+d**) the curve, and then set Translate Z to -2 in the Channel Box.

5. Select both curves and loft them together (Ctrl+Alt+z+LMB-click | Loft) to create a surface between the two curves.

6. Select one of the curves and apply a planar trim (Ctrl+Alt+z | Planar | option box). In the Planar Options dialog box, reset the settings, and change the Degree to Linear. Click the Planar Trim button. This creates a trimmed flat surface with the boundary as the curve, as shown in Figure 6.19.

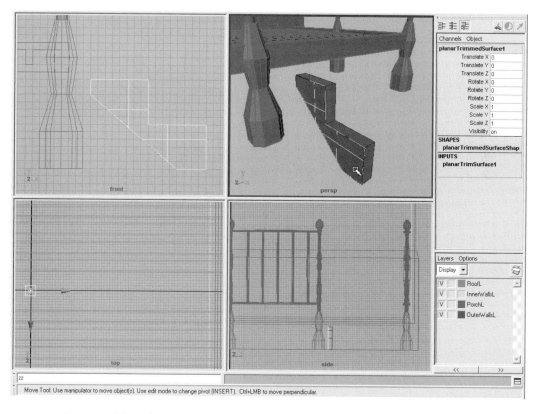

FIGURE 6.19   *The CV curve has been lofted and a front face has been put on the loft.*

7. Select the curve on the other side and create another planar surface. Now the stair support object is complete.

8. To delete the history for the curves, trims, and loft, marquee-select them all and then click Hotbox | Edit | Delete by Type | History. With all parts still selected, group them together (hotkey: **Ctrl+g**), and name the group StepFrame. Now delete the original curves you used to create the loft and trims by Shift-selecting them and pressing Delete. (You can also use the Outliner: Expand the group listing in the Outliner to see the curves that are part of the group, and then select and delete them.)

9. For StepFrame, change Translate X to –3 so that it's touching the front of the porch panel.

10. Duplicate StepFrame and translate it along the Z axis until it's next to the PorchLeg on the other side of the opening at the front of the porch, as shown in the side view of Figure 6.20. We set Translate Z for the StepFrame1 duplicate to –37, but your value could vary because you're placing the step supports by "eyeballing" them.

11. Create a cube and name it Step.

12. Next, you'll scale and place the step on top of StepFrame. Set Scale X to 10, Scale Y to 1.5, and Scale Z to 41. Maximize the Front view (hold the mouse cursor over it and tap the spacebar), and set Translate X to 143 so that the step lines up with the edge of StepFrame and PorchPanel. Then set Translate Y to –146.25 so that the step is positioned on top of StepFrame.

13. In the Side view, center the step on StepFrame by setting Translate Z to –70.5 (see Figure 6.20).

14. Duplicate Step and place it on the next edge down. We used the following settings: Translate X to 151 and Translate Y to –152.25.

15. Add the Steps and StepFrame to your PorchL layer. Then open the Outliner and select all the surfaces in PorchL and group them together (hotkey: **Ctrl+g**). This will make your scene a lot easier to work with in the Outliner. Name the group PorchGroup.

16. Save your scene again (hotkey: **Ctrl+s**).

On the CD

Chapter_06\ch06tut03end.mb

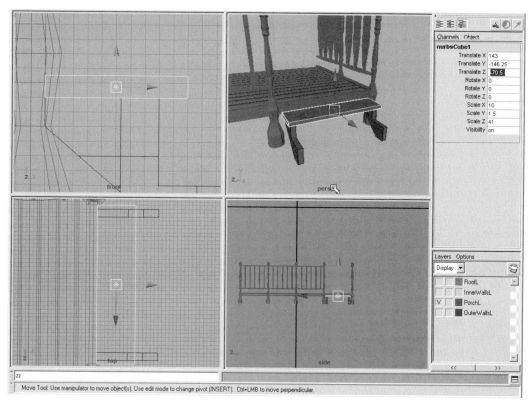

FIGURE 6.20   *Positioning the step.*

Building a Chimney for the House

Next you'll add a chimney to the shack. You'll create it by editing a NURBS cube in some new ways.

Tutorial: Creating the Chimney

The porch is complete, but the house needs more detailing, so next you'll add a chimney to the back of the house.

1. Hide the layer PorchL. Make all other layers visible except for RoofL.

On the CD

Chapter_06\movies\ch06tut04.wmv

2. Create a NURBS cube (Ctrl+z+LMB-click | Cube), and name it Chimney.

3. To move the cube behind the house, set Translate Y to -89 and Translate X to -100.

4. Make the cube the rough proportions of the chimney: Set Scale X to 40, Scale Y to 140, and Scale Z to 40.

5. Now you're going to move the pivot point to the chimney base. With the cube selected, switch to the Move tool (hotkey: **w**), and press Insert on your keyboard. The manipulator handles will no longer have arrows on their ends, which indicates you're in Pivot Editing mode. In the Front view, click and drag the pivot to the bottom of the chimney, grid snapping (hotkey: **x**) it near the center of the base. Press Insert again, after you have positioned the pivot, to get out of Pivot Editing mode.

6. The chimney doesn't reach the roof, so you need to scale it more along the Y axis. Instead of changing the values in the Channel Box, switch to the Scale tool (hotkey: **r**), and drag the green Y axis handle up. Notice that the chimney now scales in Y from the base upward. This is caused by moving the pivot point—the object scales from the pivot point. Set Scale Y to 225 so that the chimney is about a foot or two above the roof.

tip

Depending on where you want an object to rotate or scale from, you might find it helpful to repeatedly reposition the object's pivot point.

7. The Chimney cube is fairly rough, so you need to modify its shape to look more like a real chimney. There are not enough CVs on the cube, so open the Rebuild Surface Options dialog box (Alt+z+LMB-click | Rebuild | option box). Change the Number of Spans U to 6 and the Number of Spans V to 6. Check to make sure the 3 cubic radio button is selected for both Degree U and Degree V, as shown in Figure 6.21, and click the Rebuild button. There should now be enough curves to modify the chimney. The chimney is made cubic so that we can bend it in a later tutorial.

8. Delete the cube's top and bottom planes. You don't need the bottom plane because it's not going to be visible, and you will change the top of the chimney later. It's easier to select these parts if you use the Perspective view in Shaded mode. In Shaded mode, you can click anywhere on a surface to select it; in Wireframe mode, you must select the edge of an object.

9. Make sure the entire chimney is selected by selecting a side and pressing the up arrow. The Channel Box displays "Chimney" when the entire object is selected. Switch to CV Component Selection mode (hotkey: **F9**). In the Side view, marquee-select the bottom three rows of CVs. Increase Scale Z for the CVs by moving the blue modifier handle. You can see the Scale factor in Maya's Help Line; a Scale Z of about 2 should work.

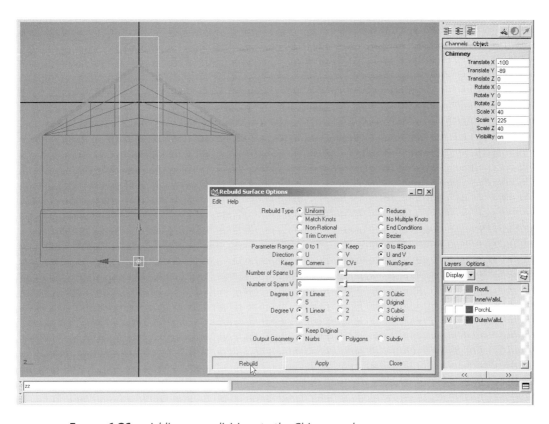

FIGURE 6.21   *Adding more divisions to the Chimney cube.*

10. Next, select the row of CVs above the first three rows you just modified (see Figure 6.22). Move this row along the -Y axis about a foot (12 units), down toward the base of the chimney (shown in progress in Figure 6.22).

11. In the Front view, select the back column of the first three rows of CVs. Move them along –X by about 8 inches, as shown in Figure 6.23.

12. Select the top row of CVs and uniformly scale them down; aim for about 3 to 4 inches of reduction to make a chimney that narrows in at the top. Exit Component Selection mode (hotkey: **F8**).

13. Create a layer, name it ChimneyL, and assign the Chimney cube to the layer.

14. Translate the chimney so that the end facing the house is about 6 inches inside the inner wall; to do that, change Translate X in the Channel Box to -82.

15. Open the Outliner, select all the geometry in your scene, and delete the history (Hotbox | Edit | Delete All by Type | History).

On the CD

Chapter_06\ch06tut04end.mb

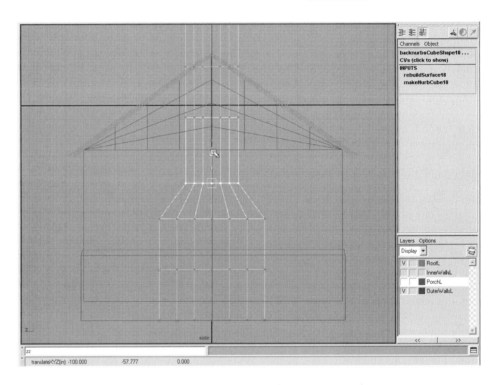

FIGURE 6.22   *Editing the chimney CVs to make a steeper angle.*

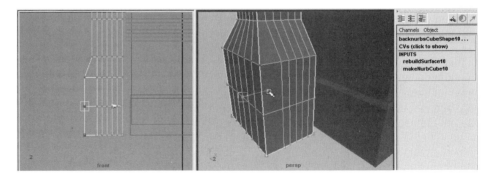

FIGURE 6.23   *Pulling out the rear of the chimney.*

Tutorial: Intersecting the Chimney and Back Walls

Now you'll use more projection curves to cut holes in the walls so that the chimney pokes through.

1. To trim off the part of the house walls that overlap the chimney, first hide the RoofL layer. Select the back outer and inner walls that are going through the chimney, and then Shift-select one of the two chimney sides that's penetrating the walls (not the flat side, but the two sides with the angled kink in them).

On the CD

Chapter_06\movies\ch06tut05.wmv

2. You need to intersect these surfaces so that you can trim them (Alt+z+LMB-click | Intersect Surfaces | option box). In the Intersect Surfaces Options dialog box, change the Create Curves option to First Surface, and click the Intersect button. Curves have now been created on both of the back walls, exactly where they intersect with the chimney, as shown in Figure 6.24. Select the two back walls again, select the other side of the chimney, and intersect them again.

Figure 6.24   *The two lines created on the inner and outer walls by the intersect.*

3. Select the outside back wall. With the intersections defined, you can now perform a trim (Alt+z+LMB-click | Trim Tool). A white grid should appear; if not, click on the back wall. This grid defines areas that can be trimmed, with bold white lines tracing the outline of the chimney.

The Trim tool works by letting you select surfaces to keep, and then discarding the surfaces that aren't selected when you complete the trim by pressing Enter. The trim relies on curves that completely intersect the surface and divide it into parts.

4. Click on the wall on one side of the chimney. A yellow diamond appears, indicating your selection of the area you want to keep. Click on the wall on the other side of the chimney. Another diamond should be placed where you click, as shown in Figure 6.25. Notice that the original diamond turns blue. Press Enter to delete the center section that's not selected. Next, select the inside wall and trim it the same way. The walls have now been trimmed from the chimney. You're cutting away only the wall because the chimney will have an inside opening for the hearth; the roof and floor intersect the chimney, but in places that won't be seen in the animation.

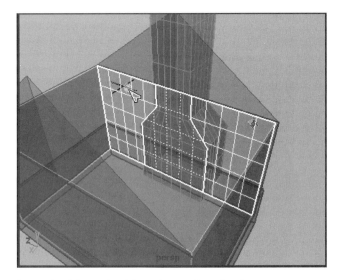

FIGURE 6.25   *The Trim tool, with surfaces selected to keep.*

5. To trim the Foundation, select the back wall of the foundation, which is a single piece because you attached the surfaces when you finished building the foundation. Shift-select one of the sides of the chimney, just as you did for the back wall. Intersect those surfaces, and then repeat for the other side of the chimney. This creates the trim lines.

6. Trim the foundation with the Trim tool. Select the two sides of the foundation to keep, and the center piece should be deleted when you complete the trim by pressing Enter (see Figure 6.26).

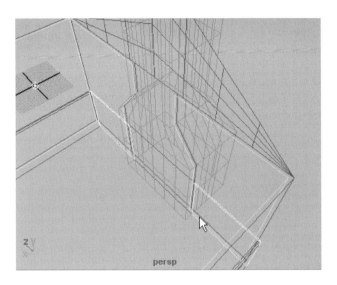

FIGURE 6.26   *The inserted chimney with completed holes cut for the inner and outer walls and the foundation.*

7. Save your scene as `ch06tut05a.mb`. It's a good idea to do occasional saves to back up your work and also so that you can revert to an earlier stage of the project, if necessary. That's why you change the filename with each save.

On the CD

Chapter_06\ch06tut05end.mb

Tutorial: Tweaking the Chimney

With the chimney created and inserted into your house, you'll add some more detail to it in this tutorial. First, you'll create a lip at the top of the chimney by putting some target rectangles above the chimney peak, and then tell the chimney to simply loft through these new shapes. You'll need four squares to do this—the outer lip requires two squares, and the inner lip requires two squares.

On the CD

Chapter_06\movies\ch06tut06.wmv

1. Hide all your layers except for ChimneyL.

2. Create a NURBS square (Ctrl+z+LMB-click | Square). Set its Translate X to –82 to center it on the chimney, and its Translate Y to 66 to put it at the top point of the chimney. Scale the square so that it is about 2 inches outside the edges of the chimney top. Because the top of the chimney was tapered in, setting Scale X and Scale Z to 40 should be about right.

3. Duplicate the square and translate it along the Y axis (above the chimney) by 4 inches.

tip   Much as the NURBS cube object is made of six planes, the NURBS square is made of four curves. You must select part of the object and press the up arrow to select the entire object.

4. Duplicate the top square and set X and Y scale to 30 in the Channel Box so that it's smaller than the top inlet of the chimney. Next, duplicate that square and move it down the Y axis by 4 inches.

   With your four squares created, you are ready to create surfaces. You will loft four times to create the completed lip. For each side, you'll loft from the top line of the chimney to each of the four lines.

5. First, you need to pick the top isoparm on one of the chimney's sides: Select a chimney side, right-click on it, and then choose Isoparm. Now you can pick the top isoparm line of the chimney. Shift-select each of the parallel curves of the squares for that side of the chimney. Be sure to follow the intended order of the curves' creation: lower outer, upper outer, upper inner, lower inner (the Perspective view in Figure 6.27 illustrates this order and how you are creating the lip starting at the top of the chimney). Then loft by clicking Ctrl+Alt+z +LMB-click | Loft | option box, setting the Surface Degree to Linear in the Loft Options dialog box, and then clicking the Loft button. You should see the new surface, as shown in Figure 6.27. Repeat on each side of the chimney.

6. Now you'll attach the four sides of the chimney lip together. Connecting the first two is easy. Select one lofted section and Shift-select a piece next to it. Attach them together with Alt+z+LMB-click | Attach | option box. In the Attach Options dialog box, make sure the Attach Method is Connect, Multiple Knots are set to Keep, and Keep Originals is unchecked. Click the Attach button, and the two lofted surfaces should become one.

7. For the other lofts, you need to select an isoparm for each part to attach them. The isoparms must be touching—that is, positioned at the joint of the two pieces. First, select the newly attached surfaces if they aren't currently selected, and then right-click and choose Isoparm. Now you can select an isoparm on the surface and drag it to the edge that will be connected. Shift-select an adjacent loft, right-click

again, choose Isoparm, and then Shift-select an isoparm on this object and drag it to the connecting edge, as shown in Figure 6.28. Because selections aren't included in the remembered commands, attach the surfaces by repeating the last command (hotkey: **g**). Repeat these steps to attach the last lofted piece. Now the lip is a single object.

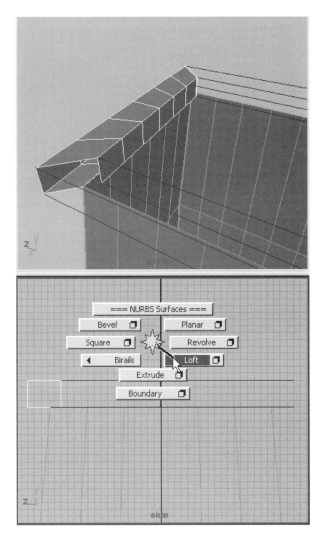

FIGURE 6.27   *One of the four sides is now lofted. The four rectangles used to create the lip are visible.*

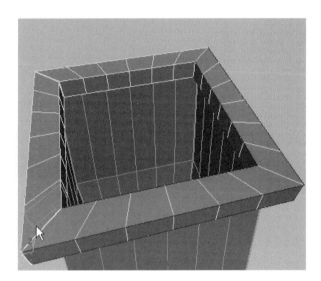

FIGURE 6.28   *All four lips are lofted and the last piece is about to be attached. The isoparm for one loft is in place, and the other is being dragged into position.*

8. Next, create a NURBS cylinder (Ctrl+z+LMB-click | Cylinder | option box, reset the settings, and click the Create button). Name it ChimneyPipe, and set Scale X and Z to 8.5 and Scale Y to 14. Move the cylinder to the center of the chimney's top edges, just as you did with the square in Step 2. We used –82, 80, and 0 for Translate X, Y, and Z.

9. Align the bottom of the cylinder to the bottom of the lip. You can move with grid snapping on (press and hold **x**) to make it easier (see Figure 6.29).

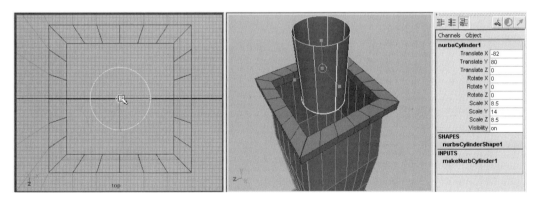

FIGURE 6.29   *A cylinder being placed in the middle of the chimney's top. Grid snapping while observing the red and blue transform handles makes placement easier.*

10. To create a planar surface between the cylinder and the lofts, select the bottom isoparm of the cylinder by selecting the cylinder, right-clicking, and choosing Isoparm, and then selecting or click-dragging to get the yellow isoparm at the bottom of the cylinder. Next, you need the other shape to connect to. Shift-select the bottom inner rectangle. Only one side turns green, so press the up arrow to get the entire rectangle, and the cylinder's isoparm remains selected. You might find it easier to select the rectangle in the Outliner. Next, open the Planar Trim Options dialog box (Ctrl+Alt+z | Planar | option box). Reset the settings, and click the Planar Trim button. Because you used snapping when placing the cylinder, it should be flush with the lip's lower inner edge, and the planar operation will produce a flat surface between the cylinder base and the rectangle (see Figure 6.30).

trap

If the operation did not work, it's probably because the two selected edges aren't planar with each other. Even though they looked like they were, they must be exact. Move the cylinder's pivot point to its base, snapping it to its own bottom curve (hotkey: **c**), and then moving the manipulator onto the curve. You will know it's snapped when the manipulator slides back and forth perfectly on the bottom of the cylinder. Now snap the cylinder base to the same grid point as the edge of your loft. If the loft edge isn't exactly at a grid point, you can select the last curve you made for your loft and snap it to the same grid point as the bottom of the cylinder. Now try to perform the planar trim. If it doesn't work, it's probably because the curves still aren't planar; some of the points might have been moved out of position.

11. You've finished detailing the chimney for now. Zoom one of the viewports out (hotkey: **a** for Frame All), and marquee-select the entire chimney. Press the up arrow to select all the parents—the top transforms of the squares, cubes, and groups. With everything selected, delete the history (Hotbox | Edit | Delete by Type | History). Assign all the new chimney parts to the ChimneyL layer: Open the Outliner and select all the new parts you created, and then MMB-drag their names in the Outliner onto the item named Chimney.

On the CD

Chapter_06\ch06tut06end.mb

12. Save your scene (hotkey: **Ctrl+s**).

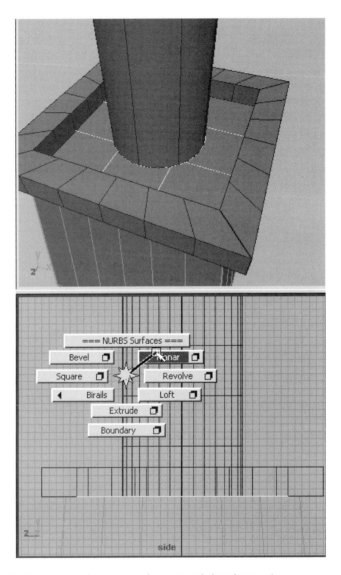

FIGURE 6.30   *The marking menu that created the planar trim.*

Going Further

If you'd like to practice your skills more and experiment with other tools, try adding more features to your house, such as trim on the side of the house. It's amazing how those small touches can make your scene look more complex.

Adding More Elements to Your House

The last details you'll add to the house are a door and some windows. In addition to modeling these objects, you'll need to create openings so that they can open and close.

Tutorial: Making a Door Opening

Before making the actual door, you'll make an opening that determines the door's size.

1. Create a NURBS cube (Ctrl+z+LMB-click | Cube). In the Channel Box, set Scale X, Y, and Z to 13, 96, and 48. Move and position the cube so that it penetrates the inner wall, outer wall, and foundation; in relation to the house, it should be next to the gap in the porch railings. We used 68, –94, and –67 for Translate X, Y, and Z.

> **On the CD**
>
> Chapter_06\movies\ch06tut07.wmv

2. When you have your cube positioned, perform the Intersect Surfaces function on all its sides with the foundation and walls: First, select the inner walls, and then Shift-select the outer walls and the side of the foundation that runs through the cube. Next, Shift-select one of the cube's four sides that's going through the walls and foundation, and intersect them (Alt+z+LMB-click | Intersect Surfaces | option box). In the Intersect Surfaces Options dialog box, select the Both Surfaces radio button next to Create Curves. Click the Intersect button to create the six curves— one on each surface for each of the three lines, as shown in Figure 6.31. Repeat this process, selecting a different side of the cube each time, until you have gone all the way around it. To select the bottom part of the door, you might need to hide the PorchL layer.

3. Next, trim the cube from the foundation and walls: Select the foundation, and then use the Trim tool (Alt+z+LMB-click | Trim). Click on the foundation side that's near but not inside the door, and press Enter. The section of the foundation that had the intersecting cube should now be gone. Trim one of the walls now, repeating the process you used for the side of the foundation. When you select the outer wall, it will have a horizontal split caused by the intersection created when you added the foundation. So for this object, select the top and bottom half to keep them before pressing Enter to perform the trim of the door hole.

FIGURE 6.31   *Shaded view in X-Ray mode to view the three curves created with the intersect.*

4. The doorway for your door is now trimmed out. Select the front and back planes of the cube and delete them (see Figure 6.32). You now have an entrance to the house!

5. The sides of your cube are sticking out of the walls, but we knew that would happen—that's why you had the intersection create curves on both surfaces. With all the curves on the cutting cube, you can trim the edges and cap the openings of the door hole. Before you trim it, open the Trim Tool Options dialog box (Alt+z+ LMB-click | Trim | option box), and change Selected State to Discard. Now the selected items are the ones that are discarded, which makes it easier to trim the sides because there are many pieces to keep. Click the Close button.

6. Click one of the sides you want to trim. Click on each side that's extruding from the wall, placing a diamond on it to signify its selection. Press Enter and watch the sides trim away. Repeat for each of the four sides.

7. Hide all the layers when you're finished, and you will see some surfaces left behind. They are the remains of the cube, which is now your perfectly cut-out door frame. Add them to the OuterWallsL layer by selecting the remaining surfaces, right-clicking on the OuterWallsL layer, and choosing Add Selected Objects.

On the CD

Chapter_06\ch06tut07end.mb

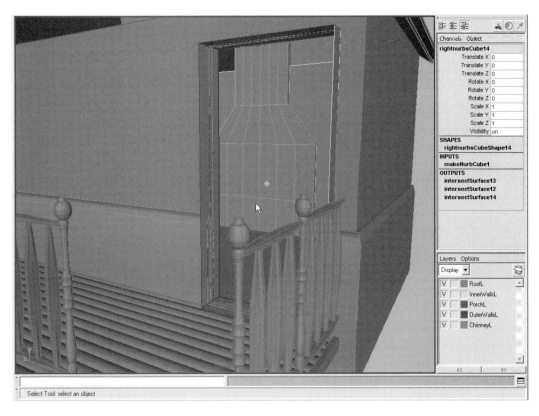

FIGURE 6.32   *The inner and outer walls and foundation have been trimmed, and the front and back of the door hole intersection cube have been deleted.*

note   If the surface looks like it has holes in it after a trim, select the surface and increase its display detail level to maximum by pressing **3**.

Tutorial: Making a Door

Now it's time to create the actual door. The easiest method is to create a cube and use it as the door. You can then project curves on the door, trim it, and add detail to it.

On the CD

Chapter_06\movies\ch06tut08.wmv

1. Create a NURBS cube, and set Scale X, Y, and Z to 2, 96, and 48 to match the door frame cutting object created earlier. Name the object Door.

2. Center the door in the door frame you made earlier. Translate X, Y, and Z are set to 67, -94, and -67. Reduce the size a little so that Scale Y is 95.5 and Scale Z is 47.5; this creates a small gap for the door.

3. Create a layer and name it DoorL. Make sure the entire door remains selected. Add the door you just created to this layer by right-clicking on the layer and choosing Add Selected Objects on the shortcut menu. Toggle the visibility for this layer to off.

4. To create the doorknob, you'll create the profile curve for it and then revolve a surface around it. Use the CV Curve Tool for the creation (Ctrl+c | CV Curve | option box). In the dialog box, be sure to set the Curve Degree to 3 Cubic so that you can make curved lines. Use the Front view to draw the profile. If you want to make a hard corner, place three sequential points in the same place. If you want a softer corner, put two sequential points in the same place. Use Figure 6.33 as a guide for drawing your doorknob profile. After you've created the curve, center the pivot point (Hotbox | Modify | Center Pivot). To move the pivot to the base of the doorknob (where it will attach to the door), press Insert to toggle the pivot adjustment, and then snap-move the pivot to the rear center point (see Figure 6.33). This sets the start point for the revolve axis. Don't forget to exit Pivot Editing mode by pressing Insert—it might be confusing if you can't see the pivot manipulator because nothing will seem to react to your selections and moves in the panels.

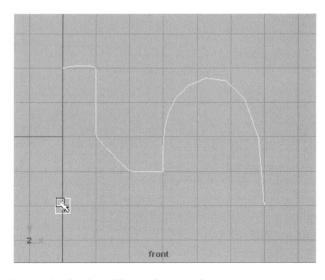

FIGURE 6.33   *A doorknob profile, ready to revolve.*

5. With the curve selected, perform a revolve on the surface (Ctrl+Alt+z | Revolve). The surface revolves and creates an unexpected shape, however, because it revolved the curve along the wrong axis. You can change the axis by modifying the revolve input because you have history enabled. In the Channel Box under Inputs, in the Revolve section, change Axis Y to 0 and then set Axis X to 1 to correct which axis the curve revolves along.

6. Tweak the source profile curve, if you like, to get the revolved doorknob looking the way you want. The revolved surface will react immediately to changes in the curve. Set the pivot for the surface to the center rear of the doorknob, as shown in Figure 6.34.

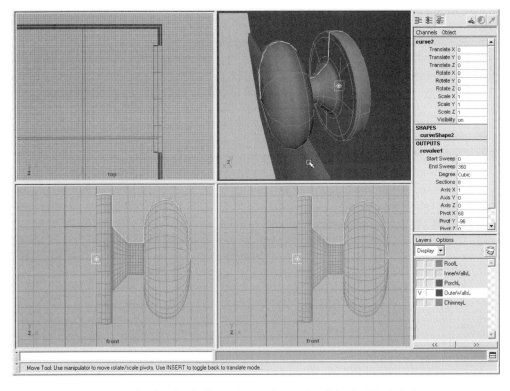

FIGURE 6.34   *The doorknob shown in maximum detail in the Shaded view.*

7. Name the doorknob surface DoorKnob.

8. Display the DoorL layer and position the handle on the door. You might need to scale the DoorKnob so that it's proportional to the rest of the door. When it's in position, delete the doorknob's history as before.

9. Duplicate the doorknob and place it on the opposite side of the door. Simply change Scale X to a negative equal value, and then move the doorknob into position. Now the door has doorknobs on both sides.

10. Select all the parts of the door in the Outliner. Group them together (hotkey: **Ctrl+g**), and name the group Door. Add the door and doorknob to the DoorL layer, and delete the doorknob's profile curve.

11. Next, you want to change the position of the door's pivot so that it can rotate from the point where a hinge would be. First, hide all layers but the DoorL layer. Next, select the Door group and press Insert to adjust the pivot. The transform gizmo changes, indicating Pivot mode.

12. Switch to Perspective view and zoom close to the door's front corner. Now you'll snap-place the pivot directly to the door's lower-right front edge, using Snap to Curves (hotkey: **c**). While still in Pivot Editing mode, press and hold c, and then MMB-click and hold on one edge of the door. The pivot snaps to the edge. While still holding the MMB, drag to the corner point, as shown in Figure 6.35. Press Insert to get out of Pivot Editing mode. Now you can rotate (hotkey: **e**; use the red circle to rotate constrained to the Y axis) the door. It should hinge as expected and take the knobs with it.

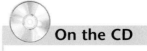
On the CD

Chapter_06\ch06tut08end.mb

Tutorial: Making Windows

The last major stage of modeling your NURBS house is making some windows. You'll create the window frame by making a window frame profile curve (like the profile of wood molding) and then lofting it around a rectangle. Adding dividers and a glass pane are then a simple matter of sizing cube objects.

On the CD

Chapter_06\movies\ch06tut09.wmv

1. Hide all layers except for InnerWallsL and OuterWallsL. Switch to the Front view so that you can see the side of your house. Create a NURBS square (Ctrl+z | Square). Next, set Rotate X to 90, Scale X to 48, and Scale Z to 36 (see Figure 6.36). Move the square along the -Z axis in the Top view so that it's outside the walls.

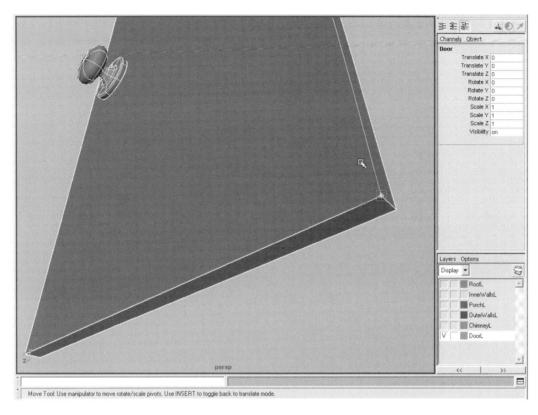

FIGURE 6.35   *Curve-snapping works by holding down c, MMB-clicking on a curve, and then dragging along the curve.*

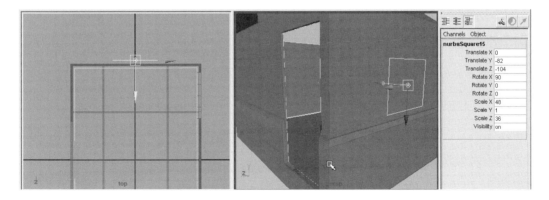

FIGURE 6.36   *The window's shape, placed on one side of the house.*

2. In the Top view, create a profile curve for the window that you will loft to create the frame. Use the EP Curve tool with the Curve Degree set to 1 Linear. Draw a frame profile like the one shown in Figure 6.37 by using snapping.

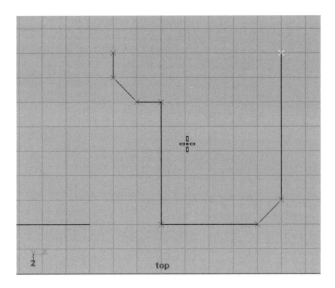

Figure 6.37   *The window frame profile shape.*

3. Center the pivot for the new curve. Move the curve to the base of the square next to the lower-right corner using curve snap (hold down **c**, then MMB-click on the rectangle shape, and drag to a corner). You are going to rotate the curve by 45 degrees and duplicate it around the square. The small leg piece of the L-shaped curve should face inward, as shown in Figure 6.38. You are creating corner curves to loft around the square, making the frame for the window. Duplicate, move, and rotate each curve to the separate corners of the square.

4. Now select each of the four curves in sequence. Open the Loft Options dialog box (Ctrl+Alt+z | Loft | option box), and reset the settings. Set Surface Degree to Linear, and select the Close check box. Then click the Loft button, and the window should appear, as shown in Figure 6.39.

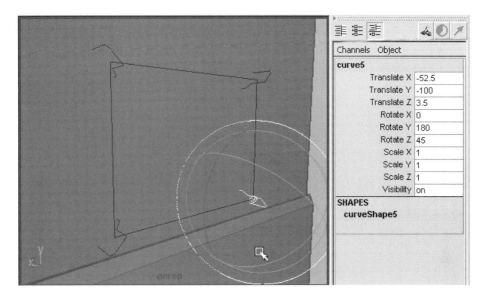

FIGURE 6.38   *Four window frame profile shapes positioned at the four corners of the rectangle.*

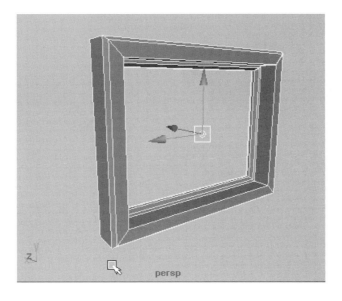

FIGURE 6.39   *The lofted window.*

5. You can add detail to the window frame with a vertical and horizontal divider. Create a cube and set Scale X to 48. Place it at the center of the window. Duplicate it and set the duplicate's Rotate Z to 90 and Scale X to 36. This creates a cross frame, evident in Figure 6.40.

FIGURE 6.40   *Two windows added to the house, with holes cut.*

6. Next, create a NURBS plane (Ctrl+z | Plane | option box, reset the settings, and click the Create button). Set Scale X to 48, Scale Z to 36, and Rotate X to 90 in the Channel Box. Position the plane where the glass in the window would be, centered on or behind the cross bars created in Step 5. Name the plane Glass.

7. To create the hole in the walls, you want to project the original window square onto the walls to prepare a trim. Select the square, press the up arrow to get all sides of the square, and then Shift-select the inner and outer walls adjacent to it. In the Front view, project the curve (Alt+z | Project Curve on Surface). You now have a curve projected onto the walls. Trim each wall out (Alt+z | Trim). Now the walls have holes in them.

8. Select all the parts of the window, including the square you used to project the curves. Group them together and name the group `Window`. Center the pivot of the group. With the history of the original square shape, you can now move the window, and the holes in the wall will move with it. That way you can move it if you aren't happy with its placement. Move the window so that it's positioned on the wall.

9. When you get the window positioned, delete its history, duplicate it, and move and rotate the window to a place on the house's front.

10. Open the Outliner (hotkey: **Shift+O**), and expand the Window1 entry to see the group listing. You should be able to find the four square sides, named topnurbsSquare, leftnurbsSquare, and so forth. Click and drag over the four names to select them. You should see the front window square shape selected. Now you can use the project curve method from Step 7 to cut a hole for this window in the inner and outer walls.

11. Create a layer and name it `WindowsL`. Add the windows to the layer, and make the other layers visible. The house is complete!

On the CD

Chapter_06\ch06tut09end.mb

12. Save your scene as `Windows`.

Summary

Having worked through the stages of creating this house, you've learned a number of complex modeling operations. You've mixed the modeling techniques of modifying simple primitives and creating surfaces from curves. These methods point the way to exploring the option boxes and experimenting with creating and modifying NURBS surfaces. Here are some of the skills you learned in this chapter that you need to keep practicing:

- **Curve snapping**   Forcing objects to track to any curve or edge in your scene.

- **Trims from projections**   Creating projected curves on two surfaces to allow for easy trimming.

- **Rebuilding surfaces**   When you need more detail for editing, rebuild the surface with more divisions.

- **Revolving surfaces**   Creating a half-profile of an object and revolving it to create a lathed effect.

- **Attaching surfaces**   Combining separately created surfaces that share edges.

- **Lofting from isoparms**   Any edge of an existing surface can be used as a starting point to loft to other curves.

- **Connecting shapes with planar surfaces**   If one curve surrounds another, and the two curves are co-planar, you can easily create a planar surface, ideal for capping holes.

- **Adjusting curves already used to make surfaces**   Surfaces based on curves change when the source curve is altered, as long as history is recorded for the object.

Maya's earliest versions focused on NURBS modeling, the more versatile approach for many models because of the ease of displaying a surface and changing the level of detail. For many purposes (such as creating characters for games), however, polygon modeling is the better method. Maya's polygon modeling capability has become as full-featured as NURBS modeling, and you'll explore polygon modeling in detail in the next chapter.

CHAPTER 7

Modeling with Polygons

In This Chapter

Polygonal modeling is usually employed for hard-edged surfaces that will not bend, or in situations where low polygon counts are important, such as modeling for games. However, in this chapter, we'll use polygon modeling with smoothing to learn about both polygon modeling and the similar methods of subdivision surfaces modeling. Of course, you can model any type of shape with any modeling system, but in this chapter, you'll see how to use polygons to create an organic surface—the head of an ogre-like creature. NURBS used to be the preferred method for modeling characters because of its power with curves and the ability to set the detail level of the rendered model. However, because of NURBS' drawbacks—the complications of matching isoparms and getting seams to close—and with the improvements Maya developers added to the polygon toolset, polygon modeling is usually the preferred method for characters now. With Maya 4.5, you can convert easily between polygons, Sub-Ds, and NURBS patches. This allows you to model in one format and then convert to another if necessary, or to use the advantages of editing or rendering a model in another format.

Polygon modeling using the Smooth Proxy approach of this chapter is similar to sculpting with clay: You begin with a simple shape and then mold and pull it into more complex shapes. You can add divisions where needed for finer surface detail and leave broader surfaces simple for easy adjustment. Although this book does not address subdivision surface modeling, the technique is very similar to this Smooth Proxy approach.

Polygons are fast to edit and look good when created and modified correctly. In addition, they don't require any computation before rendering as NURBS do, so polygonal models are generally faster to render. To see how they work, you'll begin creating a detailed, complex character. Remember that every tutorial is demonstrated in movie form on the companion CD. Creating a character can be fun and exciting. Along the way, you'll learn about these important tasks and concepts:

- **Smooth Proxy**   You'll use a crude polygonal "cage" with Maya's Smooth Proxy feature.

- **Hypergraph**   Learn how to use this editor to see your scene element's interconnections graphically.

- **Image planes**   You can assign an image to the orthogonal cameras so that the image is fixed in space and can be seen in the 3D views. This method is ideal for working from sketches or blueprints.

- **Creating a character**   Begin with a sketch to build a detailed character from scratch.

- **MELscripts**   You'll get a quick look at using this powerful command and scripting language, which gives you more control over Maya.

- **Mirrored instance**   You'll use this feature to model only half the character, and the other symmetrical half will automatically reflect changes you make to the first half.

- **Polygon smoothing**   You'll use this feature to subdivide polygonal objects so that you get a smoother result.

- **Reference layers**   You can configure an object or group of objects so that they can be viewed in a shaded or textured mode, but cannot be selected. This method is useful for alignment procedures.

Key Terms

extrude   To move a polygonal face so that its edges are surrounded with new polygonal faces, creating an area that extends outward; this method is used to build up parts of a model. You are effectively "growing" a face out of (or into) a surface.

polygon face/edge/vertex   The three components that make up a polygon surface. A vertex is a single point in space defined by an X, Y, and Z coordinate. An edge is simply a line drawn between two vertices. When you have three edges defining an enclosed area, you can create a polygonal triangle. In Maya, a polygonal face can be made up of any number of triangles.

subdivide   Splitting a polygon to create new faces for adding detail or for further editing.

Key Terms

Instance   Duplicated objects may be set as instances, where changes to either object will be reflected in both.

selection mask   Activated by RMB-clicking on an object, this option allows you to choose components of the object for selection. For polygons, you can edit edges, vertices, faces, and UVs.

Hotkeys to Memorize

Ctrl+x   Create Polygon marking menu

Alt+x   Edit Polygon marking menu

F9   Vertex Selection mode

Ctrl+q   Lasso selection

`   set focus on a cursor in the Command Line

Insert   toggle Pivot Editing mode

Backspace   delete objects or undo one step of a multistep process

Character Modeling with Polygons

This tutorial will employ Maya's new Smooth Proxy option to allow you to make polygonal edits to a simplified object, resulting in easy control over curvy surfaces. This method, called "box modeling" by some, allows you to start with a simple box and build any complex sculpted shape through a series of vertex, face, and edge edits, often extruding or splitting polygons where additional detail is needed. It may seem a little strange at first, but after you've modeled a few characters utilizing this technique, you'll likely find it to be a fast and intuitive method for modeling organic shapes.

Before you start modeling your polygonal character, you'll take some steps to simplify the process. Most 3D characters you create are symmetrical, like creatures you find in the real world. Instead of making changes to both sides of a creature, and trying to make those changes perfectly symmetrical, Maya can help you by automatically mirroring each edit on the other side of the character. This method saves time and ensures exact symmetry. If you want to add some slight variations on each side for a more natural appearance, you still can—you simply do it as a last step after finalizing the character's symmetrical attributes.

Tutorial: Preparing to Model

Before you start, remember that you're still working with Maya as set up at the beginning of the tutorials in Chapter 5, "NURBS Modeling Basics." That is, the user interface is simplified to show only the Command Line and Help Line. Also, if

On the CD

Chapter_07\movies\ch07tut01.wmv

you skipped Chapter 5, you'll need to load the marking menus and hotkeys described there. This chapter's tutorials rely on these improvements to Maya's workflow. This tutorial starts with an empty scene. Confirm that history is active: It's the Construction History button at the right of the Status Line (the one with a scroll icon on it). When it's inactive, a red × appears over the button's scroll icon.

1. Start a new project (Hotbox | File | Projects | New). Name the project Creature, click the Use Defaults button to use the default directory, and click the Accept button.

2. Set your layout to the standard Four View mode (Hotbox | Panels | Saved Layouts | Four View).

3. Start off by creating a polygon cube (Ctrl+x | LMB-hold | Cube) with the default name of pCube1.

4. With the cube still selected, choose Hotbox | Polygons | Smooth Proxy | Option Box. Reset the settings and click the Smooth button to apply the Smooth Proxy and dismiss the dialog. A sphere-like object is apparent in your scene, nested within the cube. Display the Channel Box with layers, and you can see the two layers created by the operation. The smooth layer has an "R" in the display type, indicating that it is a reference layer—it cannot be edited, but is modified by another object. That other object is the original cube, which is in the pCube1ProxyMesh layer.

tip

Layers set to Reference mode cannot be selected. You can toggle through the other two modes—Normal and Template—by clicking on the R.

5. Switch your Perspective view to Shaded mode (hotkey: **5**), and you can observe that the Smooth Proxy operation has also set the outer object to a semitransparent state, allowing you to see the effect of edits on the outer object to the shape of the inner object.

note There are several ways to smooth a polygon shape. This tutorial uses the first method, modifying the geometry by subdividing the polygons. The second method is to globally "relax" the existing geometry to make it smoother, without adding more polygons. This method is beneficial when you want UVs that are easier to work with. The third method is using the Sculpt Polygons Tool, which allows you to interactively "paint" in the smoothness, selectively applying the same approach as in the second method.

6. With the original outer cube still selected, click the polysmoothface1 rollout in the Outputs section of the Channel Box. It will roll out to display the smooth settings for the inner object, which currently looks like a crude sphere. Set the divisions to 2 and then 3, and you'll see the inner object increase in detail. Also, disable the "keep border" option by typing 0 and then enter, as shown in Figure 7.1. Return the divisions value to 1.

tip Remember to use the Outliner when you're trying to select a particular object in your scene. The Outliner is one of the fastest and most accurate ways to select objects in your scene.

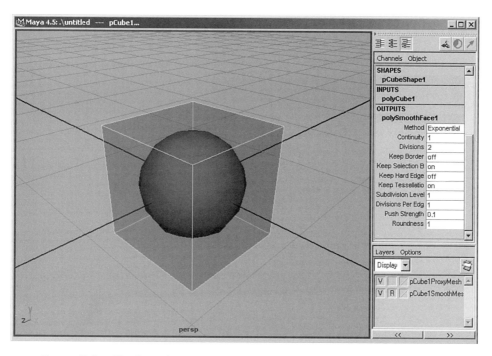

FIGURE 7.1   *The Smooth Proxy option creates the two layers and sets the inner object to a reference layer so that it is not easily editable.*

Setting Up Cubes for Modeling

Often, it's easier to view your models in Shaded mode than in Wireframe mode, but that doesn't mean modeling is more efficient in Shaded mode. The advantage of the Smooth Proxy method you're using is that you have a wireframe "cage" that surrounds a higher-resolution model. You use this simpler low-polygon cube "cage" to create a complex character by intelligently subdividing the controlling mesh cube and pulling on the new points.

When modeling a character, it's usually a lot easier to work with just one side of the figure. For that reason, the cubes in these tutorials are set up to have a mirrored version that's automatically updated with the modifications you make to the other side.

tip

As a general rule, set up orthographic viewports in Wireframe mode (hotkey: **4**) and Perspective views in Shaded mode (hotkey: **5**).

Tutorial: Symmetry Made Easy

Continue from the previous tutorial or load the scene file listed here.

1. Open the Outliner (hotkey: **shift+o**), and you'll see the two objects nested into a single group—this was also created by the Smooth Proxy. Click the "+" to roll out the group and see its members: pCube1 and pCube2.

2. Rename the objects by selecting them in the Outliner and renaming them at the top of the Channel Box. Rename pCube1 to cage and pCube2 to smooth, as shown in Figure 7.2.

On the CD

Chapter_07\movies\ch07tut02.wmv

On the CD

Chapter_07\ch07tut01end.mb

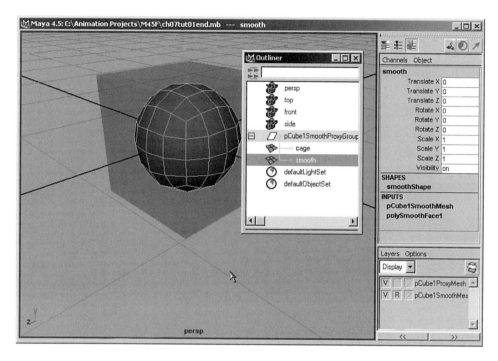

FIGURE 7.2   *The two objects are now renamed.*

3. To create the character's symmetrical left half, you'll duplicate the cube. First, to move the current geometry to the right to become the right half of the character, select Cage and Smooth, and in the Channel Box, set Translate X to 0.5.

4. Next, you need to open the side of the cube that will meet with the mirrored half by selecting and deleting the polygon faces on the cube's (soon to be) inner side, nearest the scene origin (the 0,0,0 point): To do this, select Cage, RMB-click on Cage, and choose Face. Blue-dot selector handles will appear on the cube's six sides. Select the face on the side that faces the scene origin, and press Delete. The Smooth cube is now open on one side (see Figure 7.3). Press F8 to exit Component mode.

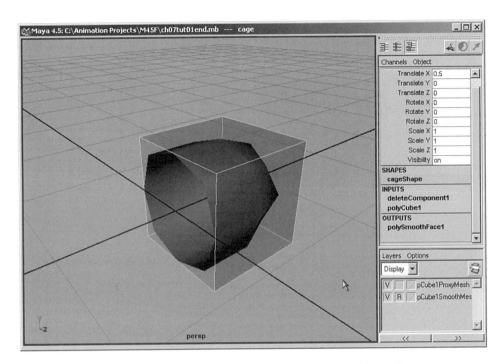

FIGURE 7.3   *In the Perspective view, the smoothed cube should now have one side open.*

5. The pivot point for the surfaces is offset from the origin, centered between the two objects you've made. Because you want to duplicate the Smooth cube and mirror it, you need to move the pivot point to the location where the objects will be mirrored, so you'll snap the pivot to the 0,0,0 origin. To do that, select Cage in the Outliner, switch to Move mode (hotkey: **w**), and press Insert to go to Pivot Editing mode. Then hold down the **x** key to snap to the grid while dragging the pivot icon in a 3D view with your MMB. Press Insert when finished to exit Pivot Editing mode. Repeat this procedure for the Smooth object.

6. Select the Smooth object in the Outliner, and duplicate it (Hotbox | Edit | Duplicate | option box). In the Duplicate Options dialog box, reset the settings, and then set Scale X to -1 and geometry type to instance. Click the Duplicate button. You should now have a duplicate beside your original, with the two visible objects forming a capsule shape. Name the duplicate smoothmirror. You can see the mirrored object in Figure 7.4.

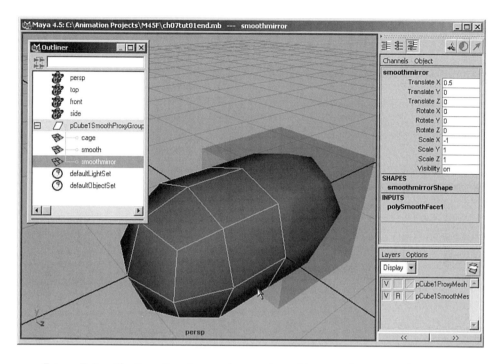

FIGURE 7.4   *The Smooth cube now has a mirrored instance for automatic symmetrical adjustment.*

note

Test out the new connection by manipulating the Proxy Mesh. To model the Smooth object, you'll adjust the Proxy Mesh, modifying vertices, edges, faces, and so on. Take a moment to play around with the Proxy Mesh to confirm the mirrored instance and see the effect of symmetry. Try selecting the Proxy Mesh and moving some of the vertices. Notice that SmoothMirror reflects the changes made to Smooth, as shown in Figure 7.5. This makes it easy to check your proportions while modeling. Use Undo (hotkey: **z**) to put the vertices back to their original position when you are done testing.

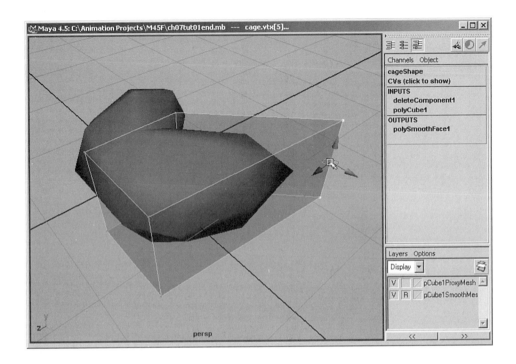

FIGURE 7.5   *The effect of pulling one of the vertices on your cage—*
SmoothMirror now moves according to the modifications.

7. Select the SmoothMirror object in the Outliner and assign it to the pCube1-
   SmoothMesh layer: right-click on the layer name and choose Add Selected
   Objects.

   Everything is set now, and you're prepared to model your creature by using the
   Smooth Proxy polygonal modeling
   method. Save your scene as SProxySetup.
   If you get stuck creating the initial setup
   for the character, you can load the file
   below the CD icon to get you started.

   On the CD

   Chapter_07\ch07tut02end.mb

Creating the Creature's Head

Before you start modeling the creature's head in Maya, you should sketch a rough drawing of what you want it to look like. It's a good idea to make front and profile view drawings. You will spend a lot more time trying to create a character if you just improvise the character model. If you plan ahead with drawings, you'll progress much faster to the results you want.

tip

You can scan in a sketch of your character and use the images as an *image plane*, a bitmap viewer in Maya that's specific to one of the views. For example, a bitmap of your character's profile sketch will appear in the Maya's Side view if it's assigned as an image plane to that view.

Loading an Image for Reference

Before you load the scans of your two sketches (front and profile drawings) in Maya, you need to make sure they're as close to the same size as possible, particularly in height. You want the model's Front and Side views to be proportional so that you can switch between the two views and use them to sculpt the creature. With this in mind, you should try to sketch both drawings at the same scale so that you can simply scan them, but if you're in doubt, just resize them to match in a bitmap editor (such as Photoshop). For this chapter, we have divided the images into several parts: face, arms, legs, and torso. This way, you can load each body part as you model those areas.

trap

When saving the file in Windows .BMP format, do not use this format's optional compressed mode. Maya cannot decode BMP image files that have been compressed.

Tutorial: Loading Image Planes for Reference

Continue from the previous tutorial or load the scene file listed here. To model your creature, you'll start off with the face, so first you need to load some reference images:

On the CD
Chapter_07\movies\ch07tut03.wmv

On the CD
Chapter_07\ch07tut02end.mb

1. RMB-click on the Front viewport to make it active. To import an image, click Hotbox | View | Image Plane | Import Image. Insert the *Maya 4.5 Fundamentals* CD, select the file below the CD icon here, and then click the Open button to create imagePlane1.

2. Open the Attribute Editor for the image (Hotbox | View | Image Plane | Image Plane Attributes | imagePlane1). Change the name of imagePlane1 to FrontFace.

3. In the Attribute Editor, expand the Placement Extras section, and set the Width to 7.5 and the Height to 7.5 (see Figure 7.6). Also, confirm that Offset is set to 0,0 and that Coverage Origin X and Y (under Placement Extras) are set to 0.

4. To load the image for the head's profile, make the Side view active (RMB-click on it), and then repeat the procedure used to load the FrontFace image, but use FaceProfile.bmp. Name the new image plane SideFace, and resize it in the Attribute Editor as before.

5. Change the layout to Three Panes Split Right (Hotbox | Panels | Layouts), and turn off the grid in the three views (Hotbox | Display | Grid). The reference images should be set up as shown in Figure 7.7.

On the CD

Chapter_07\ReferenceImages\ FaceFront.bmp

On the CD

Chapter_07\ReferenceImages\ FaceProfile.bmp

FIGURE 7.6   *With the Attribute Editor, you can load images into your scene and modify how they're displayed.*

The reference images are now set up, so you can start modeling your character. The two images should be about the same height in the viewports. If not, you can open the Attribute Editor for each one and compare them while tweaking settings.

> **tip**
>
> At the bottom of the Attribute Editor is the Copy Tab button. You can use it to make a floating window that becomes the attribute panel for a specific scene element. You can tear off a tab for one object's attributes, and then open other attributes in the Attribute Editor while still viewing the tab that was "torn off." It's an easy way to compare settings.

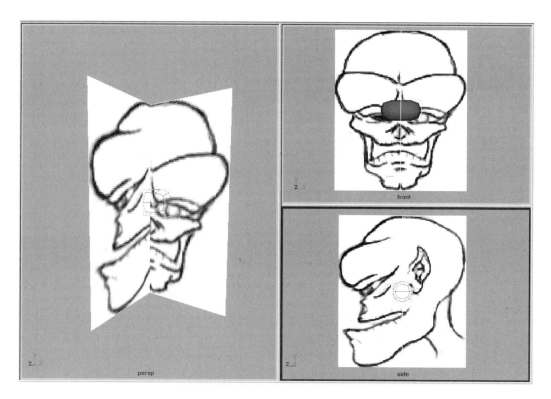

FIGURE 7.7   *The viewports with the image planes loaded.*

Modeling the Head

Using Smooth Proxy modeling is not a difficult method to master. You need only a few simple tools—Append Polygon, Extrude Faces, and Create Polygon—to model. As you create the creature, try to think in terms of working with clay. You are going to be "sculpting" your form by adding parts to it. As you build up from the original object, gradually the head's shape will take form. If you have difficulty visualizing the steps for creating parts of the face, you can always refer to this chapter's figures for help.

Tutorial: Blocking in the Head

Continue from the previous tutorial or load the scene file listed here.

1. Open the Outliner (hotkey: **Shift+O**) and select the pCube1SmoothProxyGroup. In the Side view, move this to the base of the neck because you'll build your creature from the neck up. Next, increase the Divisions setting for polySmoothFace1 to get a smoother shape. Select the Smooth cube, open the Channel Box, and in the Inputs section for polySmoothFace1, set Divisions to 2 (see Figure 7.8).

On the CD

Chapter_07\movies\ch07tut04.wmv

On the CD

Chapter_07\ch07tut03end.mb

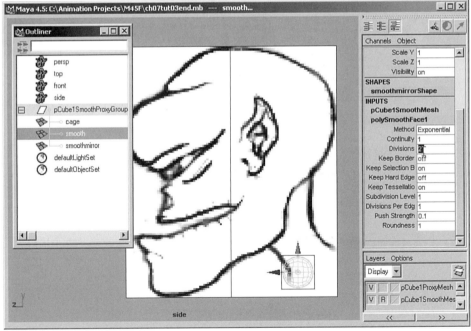

FIGURE 7.8   *Notice the cube's increased complexity after changing the Divisions setting to 2.*

tip

When modeling your character, Maya displays a more accurate representation when the divisions are set higher. However, two problems can occur. First, your computer hardware might not be able to handle the added complexity, making it difficult to manipulate the scene because of slow interaction. Second, the dense wireframe mesh of a highly subdivided surface can make it difficult to see the cage you're working with. You can always change the number of divisions, however.

You might also want to completely disable the layer with the smoothed subdivided object. Often it's too difficult and slow to work with the smooth version visible and dynamically updating as you edit. Layers are useful for this purpose; simply click the V box in the Layer Editor (below the Channel Box), and the layer disappears.

2. Now you'll start extruding faces from the Cage object so that the head shape starts to form. To do that, select Cage in the Outliner, and then select the top face of Cage by RMB-clicking on the cube's edge and choosing Face. Select the face at the top of the cage, and extrude it (Alt+x-hold | LMB-hold | Extrude Face). When the manipulator handles appear, you can change the new face's rotation, scale, and position to perform the extrusion. As you work through the upcoming edits, be careful not to translate the face in the X direction because it will separate from the mirrored copy. For this first extrusion, translate the face vertically upward about .5 of a unit, as shown in Figure 7.9.

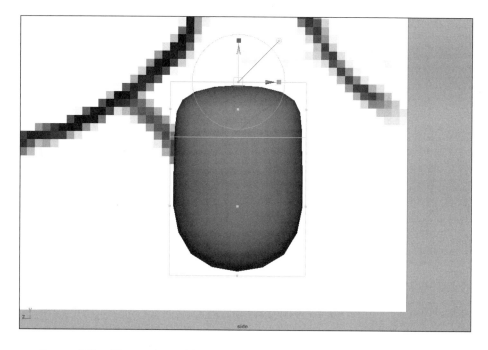

Figure 7.9   *The top face of the cube has been extruded and translated upward.*

3. Repeat the Extrude Face command (hotkey: **g**), and translate the new face about 2 units in the Y direction so that the polygon face is right in line with the base of the eyes. Repeat the extrusion one more time, and move it about 4 units to the top of the head (see Figure 7.10).

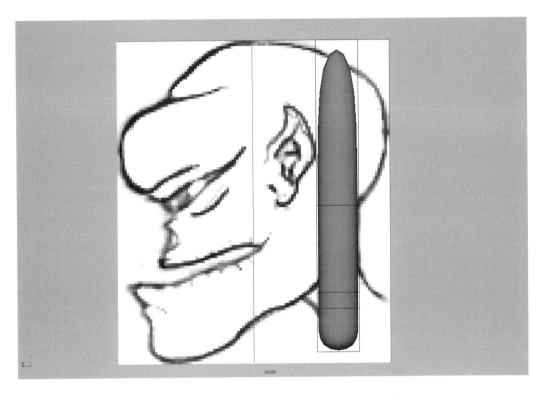

FIGURE 7.10   *The cube in the Side view after extruding in the Y direction.*

4. In the Perspective view, you can see that the extrusions created two separate pillars rising from the base of the cube. You've probably noticed that when you extruded the face, the two halves of the smooth were not connected at the center. That's because of the new faces created during the extrusion. It's easy to solve this problem, but the image planes are making it difficult to see your selections. Hide the cameras (which in turn hides the image planes) in the Perspective view (Hotbox | Show | Cameras). Now you can easily select the faces on the side of the extruded Cage object, as you are already in face editing mode. Simply select each of the three faces between the two extrusions, and press Backspace to delete them. With each deletion, the sides will come closer together (see Figure 7.11).

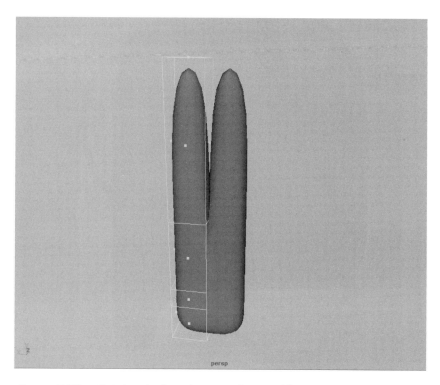

FIGURE 7.11   *Deleting the faces between the two pillars causes the sides to merge together.*

5. The next step is to extrude the faces on the front of the cubes and move them in the Z direction until they reach the front of your creature's head. Right now you have Cage divided into four sections. In the Perspective view, select the polygon faces at the front of the top two sections. Extrude them (Alt+x-hold | LMB-hold | Extrude Face) about 3 units in the positive-Z direction, and switch to the Side view to move them farther toward the front of the head, leaving a little less than one-fourth of the reference image's profile uncovered. From there, extrude one more time (hotkey: **g**), and move the faces about 1.7 units, to the left edge of the drawing (see Figure 7.12). There are now two more sections.

6. Switch to the Perspective view and delete the new faces between the two smoothed sides, as in Step 4. To make it easier, you can hide the Smooth object by clicking the V in the Layer Editor for the pCube1SmoothMesh layer.

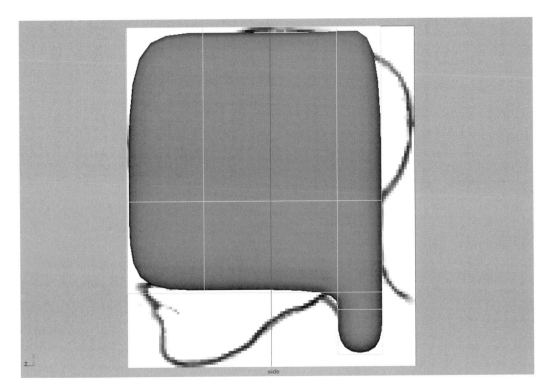

Figure 7.12   *In the Side view, you can see the new extrusions moving toward the front of the face.*

Working with the Split Polygon Tool

Now you get to be a little more creative. To add detail to the creature, you'll use the Split Polygon Tool, which divides a polygon face into two separate faces. For detail work, this tool offers an advantage over NURBS modeling because with NURBS, adding a division adds a curve that wraps around the entire model (unless you're working with NURBS patches). If you try to model a single head composed of NURBS, the result is usually divided into too many NURBS curves to be easy to work with. An exception is creating a model by placing "patches" of NURBS-based surfaces together.

The Split Polygon Tool features a setting for the number of *snapping magnets*, which refer to the number of divisions of a polygon edge that are "snappable." This is similar to the grid, curve, and point snap you've seen in prior chapters for NURBS editing. With snapping magnets set to 2, you can easily divide an edge at the 1/3 and 2/3 points because there will be two equally placed magnets on that edge. The *snapping tolerance* sets the attraction to the snap points. The higher it's set, the stronger the snap effect.

With the Split Polygon Tool, you can add localized detail. By starting off with a rough outline of the head, you can then add detailed features, such as the eyes and mouth. This method is especially effective for visual, interactive modelers who like to build their surfaces as a sculptor might with clay. The Split Polygon Tool is similar to the Create EP Curve Tool you used in NURBS modeling. If you accidentally place a point in the wrong spot, you can reposition it (hotkey: **Insert**) or delete it (hotkey: **Backspace**).

Tutorial: Adding Shape to the Head

Continue from the previous tutorial or load the scene file listed here.

1. Open the Tool Settings dialog box for the Split Polygon Tool (Alt+x | Split Polygon Tool | option box). Set the Snapping Tolerance to 50 for extra-strong snapping (see Figure 7.13), and then close the Tool Settings dialog box.

On the CD

Chapter_07\movies\ch07tut05.wmv

On the CD

Chapter_07\ch07tut04end.mb

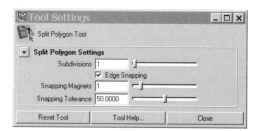

FIGURE 7.13   *In Tool Settings, you can change the settings for point snapping.*

tip

Remember that you need to switch out of Component Selection mode (hotkey: **F8**), or you will not be able to select objects. Component mode confines you to picking parts of a selected object, such as faces or vertices.

Using the Split Polygon Tool, you'll split the polygons in areas that need more detail. For now, keep it simple and add splits only where necessary. If you add too much detail early in the modeling stage, it's difficult to modify details later because you have to select so many vertices just to begin to make a new edit. To create the brow line and the areas around the eyes and mouth, you'll place points defining the beginning and end of a polygon edge. When you click one of the polygon edges, a green square appears that represents the point, and you LMB-drag the point along the edge until it's positioned at the split's starting point. You can then snap to another edge. Press Enter after you finish placing the points, and your new edges will split all the polygon faces they intersect. Notice that you automatically exit Component mode and return to Object mode when you complete a split polygon operation.

2. Switch to the Four View mode so that you can see what you're doing from all angles (Hotbox | Panels | Saved Layouts | Four View). Referring to Figure 7.14, split the upper portion all the way around (Alt+x-hold | LMB-hold | Split Polygon), and then click on the edges as you work around the mesh. Note that if you click and hold on an edge, you can move the connected point around, and it will snap to the center if you get close to an edge's center point. First follow the upper bold line shown in Perspective view in Figure 7.14; use the Perspective view to rotate around as you work. Allow the magnet snap to force you to the center point as you place each division point in the center of the edge.

tip

You can also click within a face while splitting a polygon, when you need more complex cuts.

3. Press Enter when all segments of the upper bold division line are in place and the polygons are divided. Open the Tool Settings dialog box for the Split Polygon Tool (Alt+x | Split Polygon Tool | option box), and set Snapping Magnets to 3 to get snapped divisions of edges into four parts. Next, follow the lower bold division line (see Figure 7.14). For the lower division lines, you'll need to create the points using the bottom of the three snap points.

tip

You might need to change the Snapping Magnets setting again to place a point where you need it. If you're splitting a large polygon face, try increasing the setting to 4 so that you have four possible snapping positions. This makes it easier to define areas for a mouth, brow line, or chin, for example. If you want to place split points freeform, just disable edge snapping in the Tool Settings dialog box for the Split Polygon Tool.

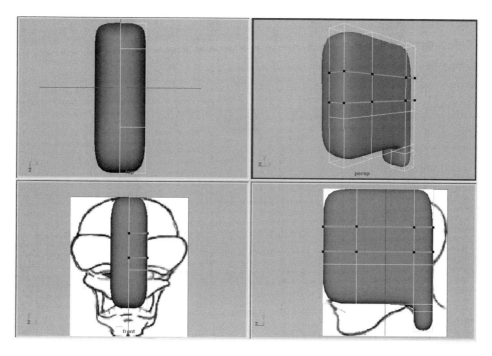

FIGURE 7.14   *Using Four View mode makes it easier to see exactly where you're placing specific points.*

4. Next, select the vertices by RMB-clicking on Cage and choosing Vertex. In both the Front and Side views, select the perimeter vertices singly or in local groups and use the Move tool to position them at the perimeter of the head drawing. Figure 7.15 shows how the vertices might be placed in the Side view. Simply LMB-drag a vertex you want to move. You can use the Lasso tool to select multiple vertices by drawing a loop around them (hotkey: **Ctrl+q**). Where possible, try to move entire rows of vertices at once to keep them in alignment. This method helps keep your model simple, and later it will be easier to animate.

trap   Keep the base of the neck flat. Do not move any vertex points at the base in the Y direction. Later you're going to extrude the body from the neck, and if the vertices are not planar, you'll have to reposition them.

5. To give the neck some roundness, you'll split the polygons up to the crown of the head and pull them out slightly. Using Figure 7.15 as a reference, apply the Split Polygon Tool from the center of the neck upward, stopping at the crown. After splitting these polygons, RMB-click the Cage object, choose Vertex, and then pull these new vertices out from the head to round the shape.

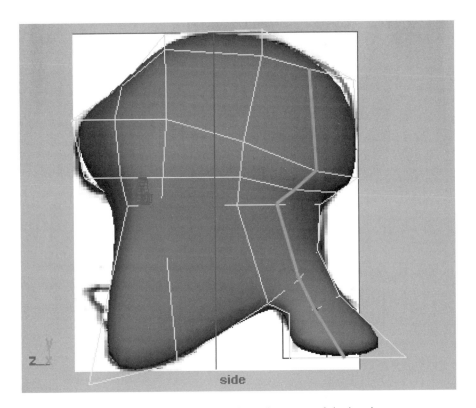

FIGURE 7.15   *The neck polygons are split to the crown of the head.*

6. The border where the two smoothed cubes meet has a sharp edge, and this obvious seam running vertically through the center of the character's head isn't going to look good. To fix it for now, you'll split the polygons all the way around the head, offsetting from the border edges one fourth of the distance of each edge. You'll need to use the Perspective view to do this. Open the Tool Settings dialog box for the Split Polygon Tool, set Snapping Magnets to 3, and close the dialog box. Start from the base of the front of the neck and work under the chin, up the head to the top, and all the way around to the back of the neck (see Figure 7.16). Don't split under the neck stub!

   With the split you just made, you can shape the head even more with the new vertices and edges. The edges where the head's two halves meet now blend more smoothly.

7. Continue to tweak the head's shape by moving vertices, faces, and edges. Remember to round off the head and adjust features such as the forehead, the back of the skull, and the chin.

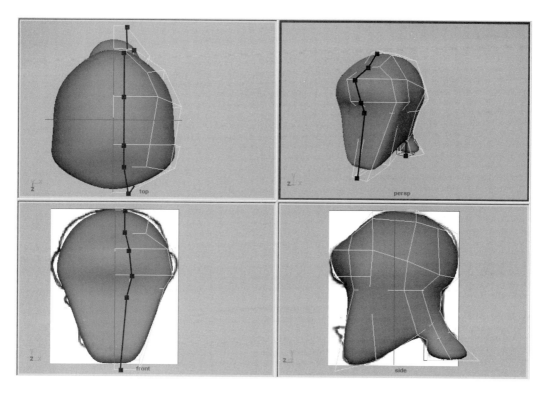

FIGURE 7.16   *By splitting the polygon faces around the seam where the mirrored cubes meet, you have a smoother connection between the two sides.*

8. After you have achieved the head's basic outline, save your scene and name it HeadShell.

   You have created just the basic shell for the creature's final head, but don't worry about it not fitting exactly the way you want. Later, you'll add detail and tweak the vertex points' positions. For now, the key is simplicity. The simpler the shape, the easier it is to modify it later.

Creating the Features

You'll begin with the eyes because creating eyes for any character is one of the most important tasks. If you are an artist, you realize how essential eyes are in creating a character. The eyes portray emotion, the essence of what brings an animated character to life.

Tutorial: Forming the Eye Sockets

Continue from the previous tutorial or load the scene file listed here. While creating the head shell, you added division lines to the upper part of the head that yield an ideal starting point for the eyebrow. You can see this area in Figure 7.17.

On the CD

Chapter_07\movies\ch07tut06.wmv

trap   If you want to load the scene file noted below the CD icon, you'll have to reload the creature's front and profile sketches for the image planes.

On the CD

Chapter_07\ch07tut05end.mb

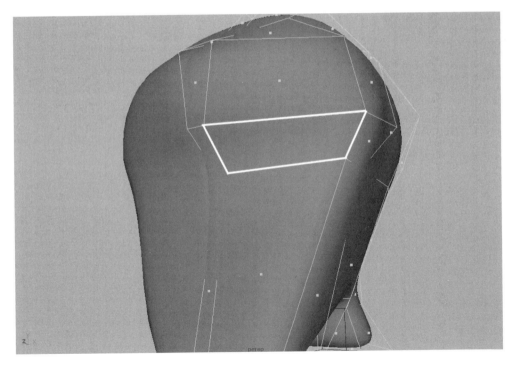

FIGURE 7.17   *The polygon face that's outlined is where you'll create the eye.*

There are a couple of methods for creating the eye socket: You can use the Bevel tool, which is faster, or use the following method, which is a little more time consuming, but is sure to work properly. As an artist, you might like using the following method because it gives you more control. What you'll do next is split the single brow polygon in a way that allows you to create a hole and add detail where needed to create the folds of the eye.

1. Select the Cage object. In the Perspective view, zoom into the polygon face where you will create the eye. Select this face by right-clicking and choosing Face, and then selecting this face by clicking on the dot that appears at the center of the face you want to divide. Now choose Hotbox | Edit Polygons | Poke Faces. This will split the polygon into four equal triangles, as shown in Figure 7.18.

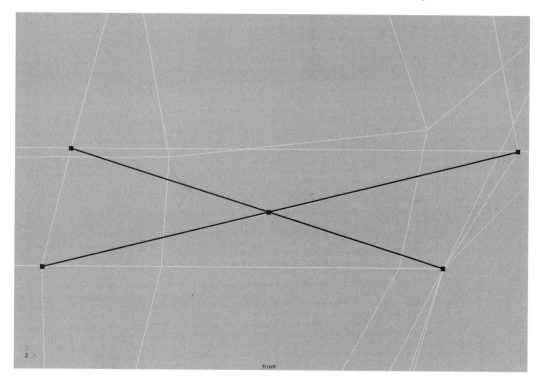

FIGURE 7.18   *Edit Polygons | Poke Faces creates an × split to start the division for the eye socket.*

2. Use the Split Polygon Tool to successively split each of these four triangles in a "+" configuration. You should end up with eight faces radiating from the same middle point, as shown in Figure 7.19.

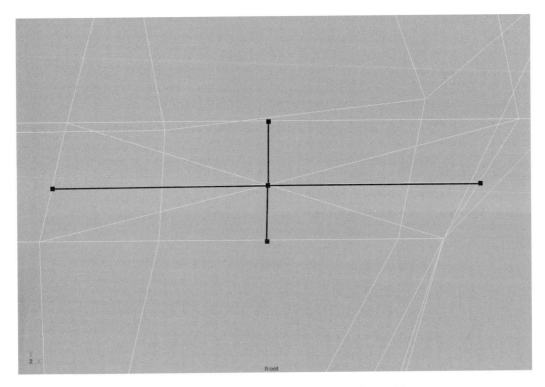

FIGURE 7.19   *This image shows the new splits; you now have eight separate edges in the original polygon face.*

3. Next, you'll use the Split Polygon Tool to split all the edges you just created so that you can create a hole for the eye. Look at a picture of an eye for reference. A good place to position the first point is where you want the corner (nearest the nose) of the eye to be. Activate the Split Polygon Tool, and click on the eight lines in sequence to make the hole. You should end by clicking on the same point where you began and pressing Enter to complete the split. Split the polygon faces so that you create a path of edges that resemble the basic outline of an eye socket (see Figure 7.20).

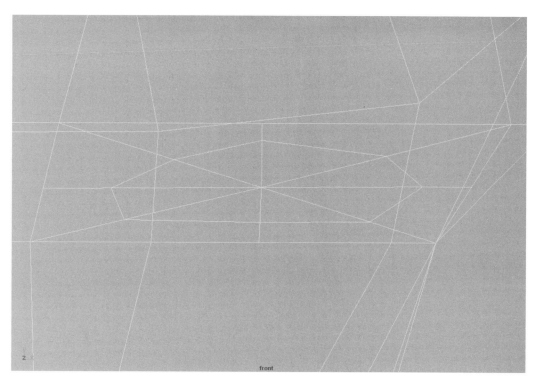

FIGURE 7.20   *By splitting the eight polygon edges, you can delete the faces within them to create a hole for the eyeball.*

4. RMB-click on any edge, choose Face, and select all eight faces within the edges you just created. You should see a spot at the center of each polygonal face. You can hold the Shift key down to select each of the faces, and then press Backspace to delete them. There should now be a hole created for the eye. You can temporarily make the pCube1SmoothMesh layer visible to see how the eye hole is mirrored on the other side.

5. Next, you'll extend some of the edges that were used to split the eye. To make the process a little easier, be sure to use edge snapping. Looking at Figure 7.21, you can see that splits are applied to the polygon faces that were directly next to the eye faces.

6. Next, select the border edges of the hole by RMB-clicking on an edge of the Cage object, selecting Edge (hotkey: **F10**), and then Shift+clicking on each edge until all eight are selected. With all the edges selected, use the Scale tool to proportion the hole. Depending on the character you're creating, you might want the proportions to be humanoid or something completely alien. Then translate the selection in the negative-Z direction until the edges are between the eye's outer profile edges.

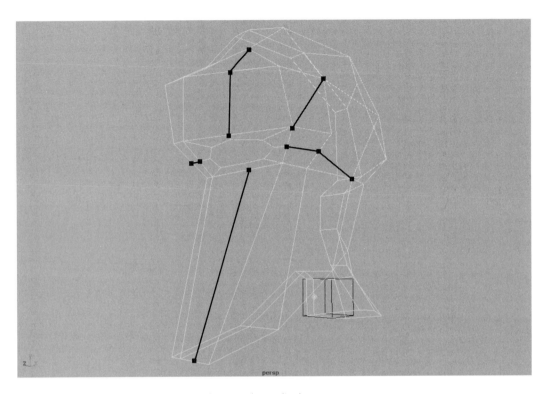

FIGURE 7.21   *Extending edges used to split the eye.*

7. To modify and shape the eye, switch the view to X-Ray mode to see through the Smooth object's surface (Hotbox | Shading | Shade Options | X-Ray). Then split the polygon faces between the initial eye face you split and the new hole you have. You can do this split in the same way you made the eye hole, by clicking around the perimeter to complete the oval. Then do it again so that you have two rings around the eye hole for manipulation (see Figure 7.22). These splits will give you an edge you can use to create the folds of skin around the eye.

   Now you'll move each of the three circles of vertices. The innermost ring will go deeper into the head to create the eyelid's rim. The middle ring will be only slightly larger than the inner ring and will be pushed less deeply into the head. The outermost ring will be pushed deeper into the head in selected areas—under and over the eye—to give the impression of eye sockets and the fatty tissue around human eyes. See Figure 7.23, which is a side cross-section of the head near the eye. Note how the eyelids are created with the two vertices of the cage nearest the eye, and the outer ring is pushed back into the head to make the eye bulge a bit.

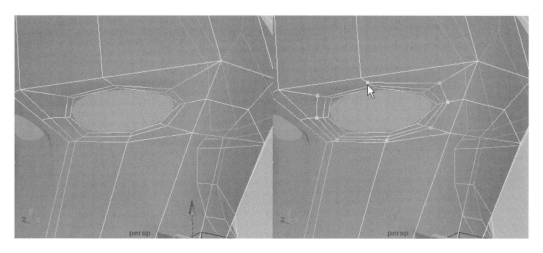

Figure 7.22   *Creating the two rings of splits; the outer ring is almost complete on the right.*

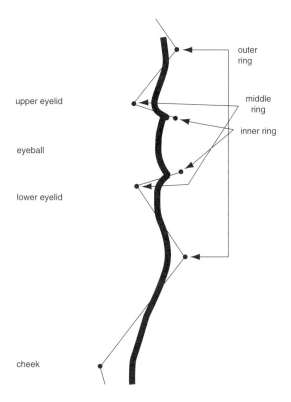

Figure 7.23   *A cross-section of the head, with the Smooth object represented by the bold line and the Cage control points represented by the thinner line.*

8. Shift-select each of the inner ring of eight vertex points around the eye (hotkey: **F9**), and push these vertices in the –Z direction (the blue arrow of the Move transform icon) about 0.1 units. The inner ring vertices you're moving should be positioned where the eyeball will touch the eyelids. Feel free to move them around the other axes to get the best positioning. Next, to create the eyelids, adjust the middle ring vertices one at a time so that they're nearly in front of the inner ring. Finally, adjust the outer ring vertices to form the outer eye socket. Push the top and bottom center vertices of the outer ring in a bit, to form indentations in the head (see Figure 7.24).

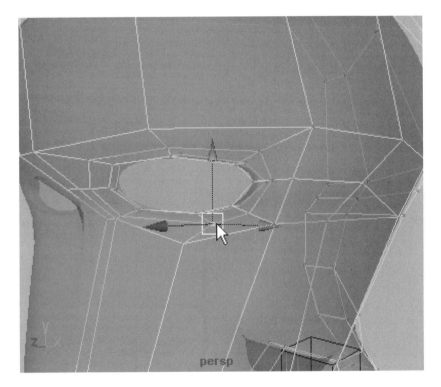

FIGURE 7.24   *The lower-center vertex of the outer ring is being pushed back into the head to form an indentation under the eye.*

You have a basic shape for the eyelids now, but it probably doesn't resemble the final shape you want. Look at drawings, yourself, or even a friend, and compare your creature's eyelids. Tweak the eyes' components until you get the results you want. You might want to get a mirror and look at the way your eyelids are formed. Try to move the vertices around and position them to improve the eyes' shape. Don't worry about splitting more polygons for detail now because you can come back to that later.

When you're finished making modifications, save your scene as HeadEyes. After you have sculpted the eyelids, you should have something that resembles Figure 7.25.

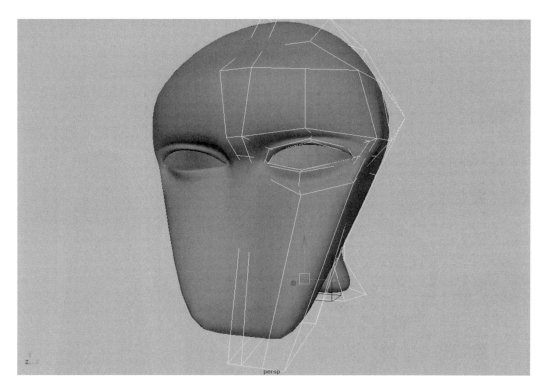

FIGURE 7.25   *The eyelids have been shaped by moving vertices to create folds for the skin.*

Tutorial: Creating the Mouth

Continue from the previous tutorial or load the scene file listed here. To create the mouth, you have to first set up some polygon faces that can be deleted. You'll create those mouth-opening polygons by splitting the existing polygons. Using the Front and Side views, you can establish the lines for the mouth boundaries.

On the CD

Chapter_07\movies\ch07tut07.wmv

1. Using the Split Polygon Tool, you'll split the polygon faces between the chin and the eye. Open the Tool Settings dialog box for the Split Polygon Tool, and deselect the Edge Snapping check box because some of these points will be close togeth-

On the CD

Chapter_07\ch07tut06end.mb

er, and snapping would tug your cursor to the wrong point. First, create a vertical split from under the chin that passes the corner of the mouth (identified as 1 in Figure 7.26). Next, using your reference images, split the polygons horizontally just under the upper lip, from the front of the face to the first split you created, indicated with 2 in Figure 7.26.

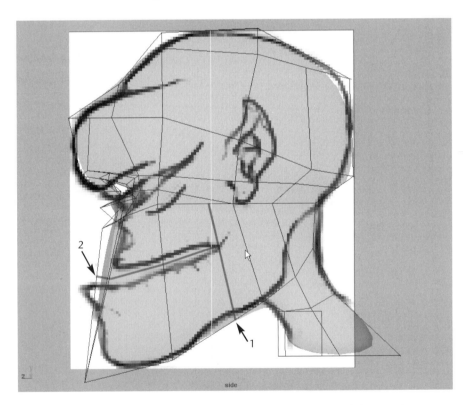

Figure 7.26   *1) The first vertical split that crosses the corner of the mouth.*
2) The horizontal split for the mouth.

2. Next, using Figure 7.27 as a guide, split an area that encircles the horizontal mouth split created in the previous step. This split line should follow the outer edge of the upper and lower lips. Click each of the 13 points, and press Enter to complete the split.

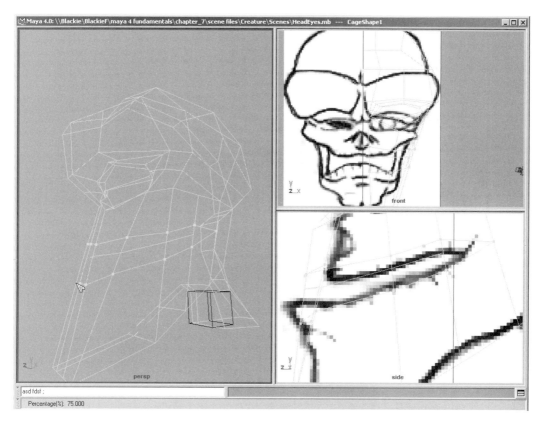

Figure 7.27   *Creating a split that follows the outer perimeter of the lips.*

3. Next, using Figure 7.28 as a guide, you'll create a split at the top of the bottom lip. This will yield a set of polygons that can be deleted to form the opening for the mouth. Using the Split Polygon Tool as before, create a horizontal split line that goes from the front of the face to the same vertical line you stopped at for the upper lip.

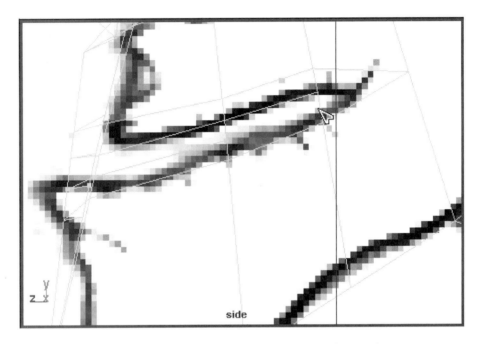

FIGURE 7.28   *Creating a set of polygons to be deleted for the mouth opening.*

4. To select and delete the polygon faces that make the mouth opening, RMB-click on Cage and choose Face. Then select the mouth polygons and delete them, as shown in Figure 7.29.

5. To make the lip lines, you'll create a horizontal split at the corner of the mouth. This gives you an anchor point for the lip splits you'll make in the next step. Split as shown in Figure 7.30.

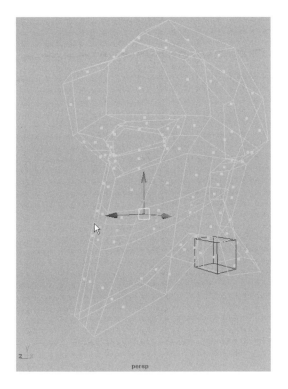

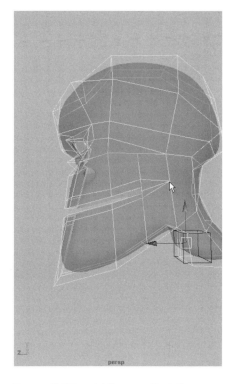

FIGURE 7.29   *Selecting the polygons to be deleted for the mouth.*

FIGURE 7.30   *Adding a split at the corner of the mouth.*

6. Now you'll add lines that enable you to create lips and other details for the mouth. You'll do this by splitting the polygons more, just as you did with the eye. Split the mouth area twice between the inner and outer lip line, and you'll have four edges to use for each lip, as shown in Figure 7.31.

7. Using the same methods as for the eyelids, create the lips. In order, the outer lip ring will mark the starting point for the lips, the next two rings will define the lip width, and the innermost ring will be pushed into the mouth to complete the lips. See Figure 7.32 for reference.

| tip | If you need to select a group of vertices, often it's difficult to select them all when using the typical drag box. By pressing Ctrl+q, you can enable the Lasso selection tool to draw the selection. |

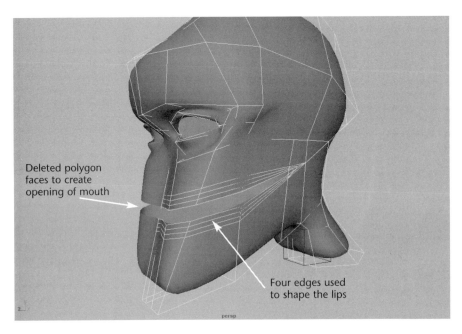

Deleted polygon
faces to create
opening of mouth

Four edges used
to shape the lips

FIGURE 7.31   *Splitting the lips lines twice to create detail from the resulting four edges.*

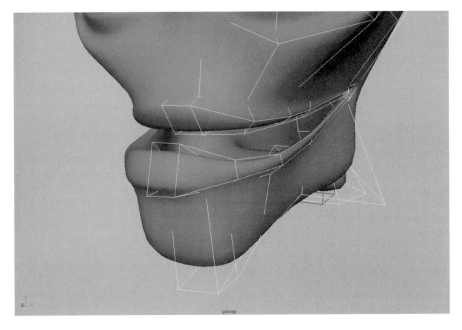

FIGURE 7.32   *This figure illustrates what the lips will look like after moving the polygons' edges/vertices.*

8. As you are creating the mouth, you'll probably find that the head's shape needs to be adjusted, too. Don't hesitate to make any changes you think are necessary. For instance, the jaw might be too wide, so you could select the vertices defining that particular area and move them until they are adjusted proportionately. At the crease of the mouth, it would be best to have the edges from the top and bottom lips come to a point so that they close together when you animate the character.

9. Save your scene as HeadMouth.

Tutorial: Creating the Nose

Continue from the previous tutorial or load the scene file listed here. Creating the nose is rather simple. It consists of several extrusions and then slight modification of the vertices.

On the CD

Chapter_07\movies\ch07tut08.wmv

On the CD

Chapter_07\ch07tut07end.mb

1. A polygon face is located at the center of the head right where the nose should go. RMB-click on Cage, choose Face, and select that polygon face. Perform an extrusion (Alt+x | Extrude Face). Move the extruded face out just a little bit, about .1 units. You can see the amount of extrusion in values shown in the Help Line. The extrusion produces four sides around the face, and you don't want the extruded side at the symmetry line. Switch to the Selection Tool (hotkey: **q**), and delete the face on the inside of the extrusion that is between the two halves of the head (see Figure 7.33).

2. Next, select the new nose face and extrude once more. This time, scale the Y down a few percent (the green box handle) and move the face farther away from the head (blue arrow handle). You're building a nasal mound. Avoid scaling along the X axis because it will separate the two smoothed cubes. Delete the inner faces between the smoothed cubes that were created when you performed the extrusion.

3. Repeat Step 2 on the new polygon face.

4. Select the last face and extrude once more. This time, do not move the polygon face at all; just scale it a few percent smaller along the Y axis. Also, do not delete the face between the two smoothed halves. The nasal mound is complete.

5. Extrude the top face of the nasal mound one more time, and scale the face down a few percent in the Y axis again. Move the face into the head (blue arrow) to create the nasal cavity (see Figure 7.34).

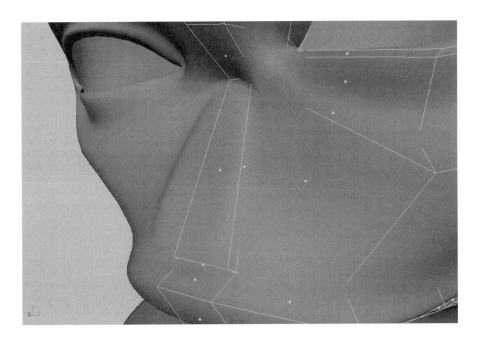

Figure 7.33   *The polygon face where the nose will go has been selected and extruded slightly.*

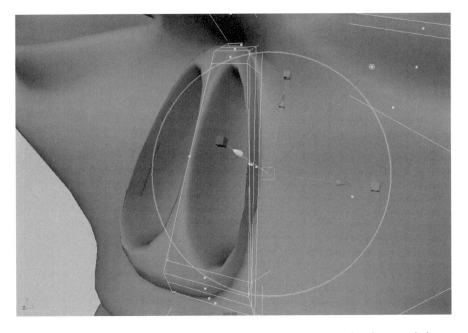

Figure 7.34   *The polygon face at the tip of the nose extrusion has been scaled down and moved into the head.*

6. Switch to Vertex Selection mode (hotkey: **F9**), and move the vertices around to get the shape you want. We moved the vertices near the bottom of the nose closer to the face and the top vertices were moved farther away for the look we were after, and to avoid any conflict with the mouth opening.

Tweaking the Shape of the Face

As a final step, you can continue to tweak the shape of the head. You might find many areas that need vertices pulled or faces moved to better approximate the original character sketch. In this example, you can see that the brow has been pulled out to Neanderthal proportions, and the chin has been given a prominent cleft (see Figure 7.35).

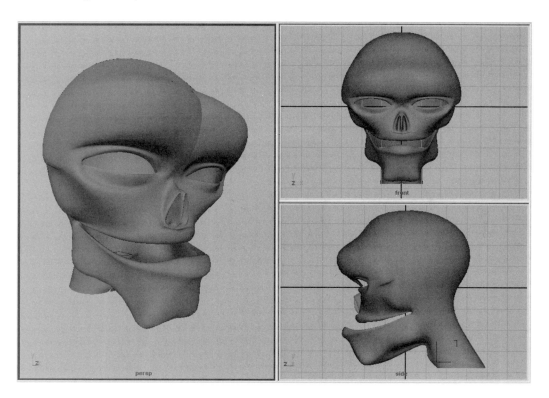

FIGURE 7.35   *The creature's head has been tweaked and shaped.*

Now that you have the shape of the head well-defined, you're ready to create the eyeballs and fit them to the eye sockets. For eyes, you'll use simple spheres.

Tutorial: Fitting the Eyeballs

Continue from the previous tutorial or
load the scene file listed here. Fitting the
eyeballs to the head is just a matter of
moving vertices so that the eyelids fit
tightly around the sphere used for
the eye.

On the CD

Chapter_07\movies\ch07tut09.wmv

1. Create a NURBS sphere (Ctrl+z | Sphere),
   and name it LeftEye.

2. Scale LeftEye to the size you want. Our
   character has large eyes like the typical
   "alien" of modern myths, so the Scale
   value for our sphere is 1.112. Position the
   sphere behind the right eyelids. In the Side view, you can translate the sphere
   until it's almost exactly at the edges of the eyelids, as shown in Figure 7.36. Try to
   position the eyeball as close as possible without moving through the front of the
   creature's face.

On the CD

Chapter_07\ch07tut08end.mb

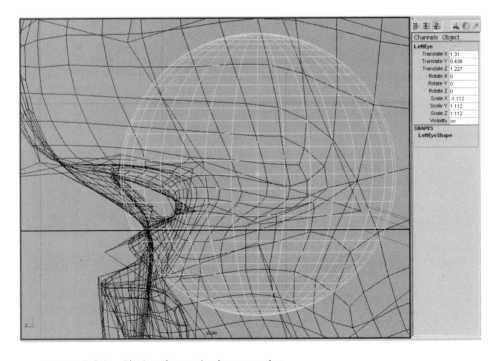

FIGURE 7.36 *Placing the eye in the eye socket.*

3. After you have the eye in position, you need to move vertices around the eyelid so that they fit almost perfectly on top of the left eye. The object is to eliminate any gaps between the eyelids and the eyeball. This can be a slow process, but it's necessary. You need to grab vertices and translate them so that they're almost perfectly on top of the eyeball. By zooming in close and using Shaded mode, you can detect and fix any gaps, as shown in Figure 7.37.

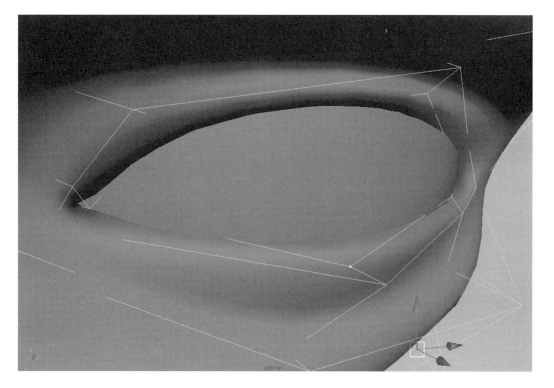

FIGURE 7.37   *By moving border vertices around the eyelids, you can make the eyelids look as though they're covering the eyeball.*

4. After you eliminate the gaps, duplicate the left eye (Hotbox | Edit | Duplicate | option box, and then reset the settings and click the Duplicate button). Next, change the Translate X value from positive to negative for the new sphere to move it into position on the other side of the head. Name the duplicate RightEye.

5. Create a new layer, name it EyesL, and assign both eyes to it. Save your scene as HeadEyeBalls.

    If you like, load the file noted below the CD icon to see the scene with the eyes finished.

On the CD

Chapter_07\ch07tut09end.mb

At this point, you have created the creature's head in some detail. Using a mix of repeated edits to a crude polygon cage, you have added surface detail where needed and fleshed out the facial features. As you might guess, creating the rest of the character is a similar process, combining splits, extrudes, and edits in a method that's a bit like sculpting. Best of all, you can increase or decrease the smoothness level for the actual renderable character by changing the number of divisions. This gives you fast interaction for animating the character when it's set at 1 or 0 divisions and ultra-smooth rendered surfaces, even in close-ups, when set at 2 or more divisions.

Going Further

We're leaving the details of creating the rest of the creature to the CD-ROM. A detailed HTML file (noted below the CD icon), viewable in any web browser, will show you the steps of finishing the head and creating the body of the creature. After making the body, arms, and legs, as a last step you stitch the two halves together to complete the character (see Figure 7.38). After you successfully create this character in detail, you should consider creating another character, perhaps something you've drawn, and attempt to model it with polygons.

On the CD

Chapter_07\html\start.html

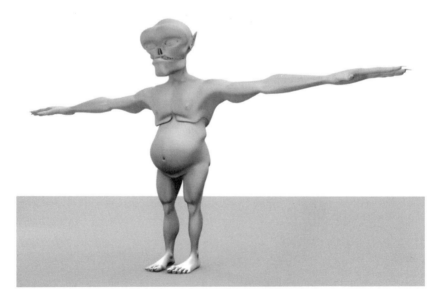

FIGURE 7.38   *The final character after modeling the ears and teeth and adding the body.*

Summary

There are many applications for modeling with polygons, but in this chapter you have learned a primary use for them—emulating Subdivision Surfaces modeling. Using the tools you learned in this chapter, you can create many kinds of detailed organic shapes. Some of the tools you've used include the following:

- **Image planes**   You can import drawings or blueprints into an orthogonal view to aid your modeling.

- **Split Polygon Tool**   This tool allows you to add detail where needed when modeling in the simulated Subdivision Surfaces technique.

- **Extruding polygons**   Using extrusions is another method for adding detail to a simulated Subdivision polygonal surface. Extrudes are ideal for adding bulges or indentations.

- **Smooth Proxy**   You used the Smooth Proxy to subdivide the Cage duplicate and create the final tessellated character.

- **Creating instances**   By duplicating as an instance, edits to one side were mirrored in the other.

You've now explored both NURBS and polygon modeling in Maya—and have seen many of the features at your disposal. Maya's subdivision surfaces modeling (now included with Maya Complete 4.5) works in a manner very similar to the Smooth Proxy technique employed in this chapter.

In the coming chapters, you'll revisit this creature and his house. You'll use them as test subjects as you explore lighting, materials, animation, rendering, and other features. Modeling is only the first step!

CHAPTER 8

Materials

In This Chapter

After you build a dollhouse or assemble a plastic airplane model, you can't wait to paint it and stick decals on it. With 3D animation, it's usually the same feeling! This chapter addresses creating and applying all manner of materials. One of the delights of 3D animation is trying out all those "what-if" material choices. What if the car was painted chrome with red leather trim, or purple plastic with chrome polka dots? Simulating these surfaces with Maya is a straightforward task when you use Maya's Hypershade—the material "laboratory." Applying revised materials and rendering the scene again is a snap. In this chapter, you'll focus first on the basics of creating materials and then learn how to add complexity and realism through mapping:

- **Using Hypershade** An overview of Maya's material creating and editing tool.
- **Creating materials** Building a surface type from scratch.
- **Using maps** Replacing a material's solid color with an image.
- **Using procedural textures** Replacing a material's solid color with a solid texture created by a mathematical formula.
- **Bump maps** A texturing method that gives the impression of bumpiness on a surface.
- **Using maps for any attribute** Replacing a solid color or a fixed number with an image to change the value across an object's surface.

Key Terms

material   The definition of all the ways a surface responds to light, including shininess, color, bumpiness, transparency, and so forth.

shader   A shader refers to both the material and the lighting of a surface with respect to rendering.

Hypershade   Maya's material editor.

texture map   A 2D image applied across a surface; typically, a bitmap image, such as a photo of wood grain, that can be tiled.

UV coordinates   Position information embedded in a 3D object, used to size and position a texture map on it. Objects can have multiple sets of UV coordinates.

environmental textures, environment map   A simulated surrounding world for a material to reflect.

volumetric material   A material type for simulating non-solid materials, such as steam, smoke, dust, or clouds.

procedural texture   A 2D or 3D texture created mathematically.

bump map   Applying a texture to create the illusion of perturbing a surface's smoothness.

Phong   A material type with sharp, tight highlights.

Lambert   A flat material type without highlights.

Blinn   A material type with softer highlights.

Anisotropic   A material type with non-uniform highlights.

transparency   The opposite of opacity; the ability to see through a material, such as glass.

translucency   Semi-transparent, but with a scattering of light, such as light seen through a green maple leaf.

specular color   The component of a material that reflects a light source—the highlight.

self-illumination   The material's sensitivity to light; fully self-illuminated materials are not affected by scene lighting, nor do they emit light.

Hotkeys to Memorize

Shift+T   open Hypershade

Shift+S   open the Script Editor

6   enable Hardware Texturing

t   show Manipulator Tool

Materials Overview

Novice animators often gloss over applying materials and lighting to scenes. "Add a few lights, make this red, that blue—we're done!" The results are typically washed out, flat, and harsh. Much of traditional media artists' criticism of computer art is based on seeing crude, simple renderings that emphasize only the limitations of the process. Good art is possible with Maya, however. It just takes time to get more interesting and complex shading. CG artists spend as much, if not more, time on lights and materials as on modeling.

Materials are a critical part of creating attractive images and animation in a 3D program. Materials interact with lights, so lighting drives some material choices; for example, if your overall lighting is bright, you might need to make your scene materials somewhat darker. Generally, you build your scene with lighting and materials progressing together, with frequent renderings to test your adjustments. Compensating for the limitations of virtual lights to create an effective and subtle light layout is an art, one that's discussed in the next chapter. In this chapter, you'll concentrate on materials.

What do we mean by materials? It's a catch-all term to describe all aspects of what a surface looks like. At first glance, novices usually notice the surface color—red, wood brown, metallic silver. To an artist, however, there are many other factors: An object isn't just metallic silver, for example—it's a mirrored smooth finish that relies on the reflected surroundings for its appearance. In addition to factors of color, shine, and reflection, Maya also considers transparency, incandescence, translucency, refraction, bumpiness, and many other user-controlled parameters. Attention to these details gives your rendered results more subtlety and complexity.

A Tour of Hypershade

As with most 3D programs, Maya has a material builder called Hypershade that lets you see your material creations on spheres (called "swatches") as you design them. After you've perfected your material to the limits of the spherical swatch, you use Maya's IPR render to fine-tune the results on actual geometry in your scene.

Hypershade uses a free-form approach to material design. Swatches connect to one another to create effects; for example, a brick image might wire to the Bump attribute on a material to create bumps in the pattern of bricks. Hypershade also doubles as a kind of browser so that you can view and select existing scene lights, cameras, materials, and other elements.

To open Hypershade, choose Window | Rendering Editors | Hypershade (hotkey: **Shift+T**). The default dialog box is divided into thirds (see Figure 8.1). The left vertical panel is called the Create Bar. The top and bottom panels on the right are called simply top tabs and bottom tabs, and you can adjust the divider lines between the two tab areas.

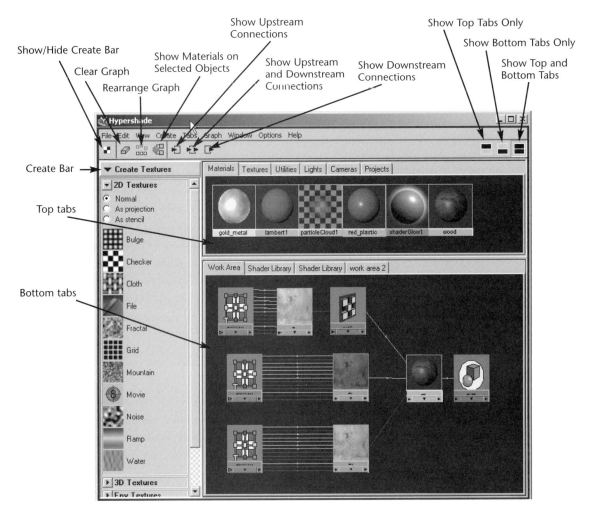

FIGURE 8.1   *Maya's Hypershade—a materials creation laboratory.*

Create Bar

At the left is the Create Bar, which displays all the material types you can create for a selected category. Simply click on a type to create that item in the Work Area. To select a category, click the down arrow on the bar at the top of the Create Bar; the options are Materials, Textures, Lights, Utilities, and All Nodes. For the tutorials in this chapter, leave the Create All Nodes category selected. To toggle the Create Bar on and off, click the checkered button to the far left (refer to Figure 8.1).

The Tab Panels

The top and bottom tab panels can be customized to include almost any type of tab. For the following descriptions, we'll describe the tab panels in the default installation mode, which uses the top tab for showing existing materials and the bottom tab for creating and editing materials. After you become familiar with Hypershade, you can customize the tabs to your liking, and even add Work Area tabs to simultaneously edit several materials.

Top Tabs

The top tab area displays all the elements that are *already part of* the current scene file in these tabs: Materials, Textures (for those that are part of existing materials), Utilities, Lights, Cameras, and Projects (to browse the project folder for other files). In this area, you can select anything that's already been created for several purposes:

- To duplicate it, so that you can modify the original when you have only slight variations to make
- To edit it
- For materials, to select objects that have been assigned a specific material or to assign a material to currently selected objects
- For lights, to make and break links to selected objects
- For textures, to reuse an existing texture with a different material, when the texture with all its parameters is identical for the materials the texture is assigned to
- To easily export a material for use in another scene

In all cases, double-clicking the swatch in the top tab area opens the Attribute Editor for that entity.

Bottom Tabs

The bottom tab area is usually used as the Work Area—the assembly point for new materials. When you start a new scene, very little appears in the top tabs until you begin creating scene elements. Therefore, the first thing you would do when you open Hypershade is put a new blank material in the Work Area and assign it to an object in the scene. You could also go to a Shader Library tab and assign materials from there. Later in this chapter, we'll show you how to create your own tab and add the materials you've created to this library.

Basic Material Types

The major material types, shown in Figure 8.2, are described in the following sections.

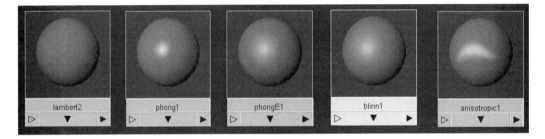

FIGURE 8.2   *In general, highlights are softer with PhongE than with Phong, and softer with Blinn than with PhongE.*

Lambert

Lambert is a flat material type that yields a smooth look without highlights. It calculates without taking into account surface reflectivity, which gives a matte, chalk-like appearance. Lambert material is ideal for surfaces that don't have highlights: pottery, chalk, matte paint, and so forth. By default, any newly created object gets the Lambert shader assigned to it. If the object should have highlights, though, it's a good idea to assign another shader. You'll want to see highlights even during the modeling stage, to see whether they are breaking across the model (indicating a seam in the surface).

Phong

The Phong material type takes into account the surface curvature, amount of light, and camera angle to get accurate shading and highlights. The algorithm results in tight highlights that are excellent for polished shiny surfaces, such as plastic, porcelain, and glazed ceramic.

Book Figures

Some of the book's black-and-white images in full color!

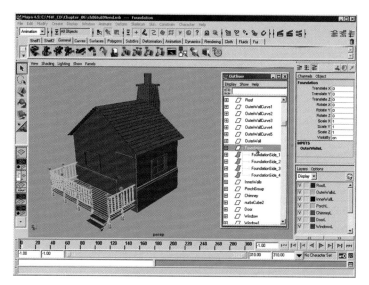

The completed house model after the tutorials in Chapters 5 and 6.

In Chapter 8, you create and assign materials in Hypershade.

Rig and animate a character walking in Chapter 11.

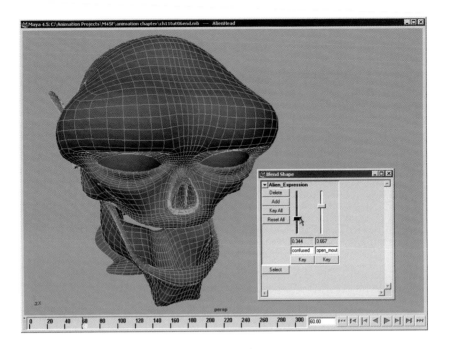

Using Maya's blend shape deformer to animate facial expressions.

Chapter 13 describes how to create trees, grass, and even the fog by painting them on the landscape with Paint Effects.

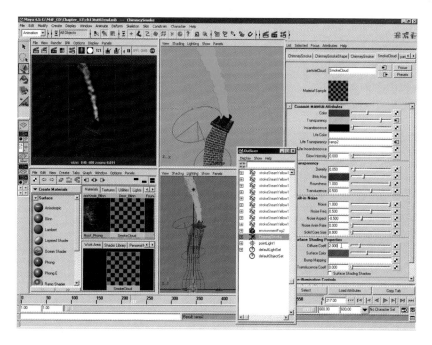

Particle setup is explained in Chapter 14, including this smoke effect for the chimney of the spooky house.

Maya offers the option to render isolated elements of an image for later compositing. From upper left, clockwise: Beauty pass (full render), diffuse only, alpha channel, shadows only, specular only (highlights), Depth Channel.

Artist Renderings

The following images were created by artists using Maya.

Provence, ©2002, Francois Rimasson, `http://perso.wandoo.fr/rimasson/`.

Human Head, ©2002, Manar Tawam, `www.manar-tawam.com`.

Neroli, ©2002, Alyssia G. Kim, www.3dspacecadet.com.

Old Toy, ©2002, Jean-Charles Kerninon.

Autumnal, ©2002, Rico Holmes, `www.ricoholmes.com.`

Landing, ©2002, Eric Hanson, `www.visuraimaging.com.`

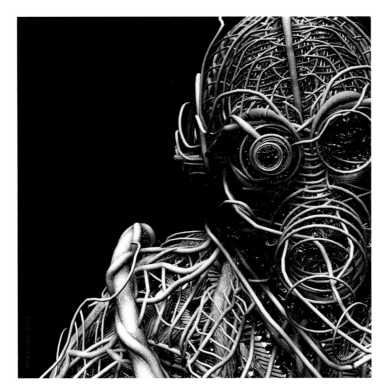

Etcher, ©2002, Meats Meier, `www.sketchovision.com.`

Halls of Ruins, ©2002, Lance Oyler, `www.26.brinkster.com/pgs2002/index.htm.`

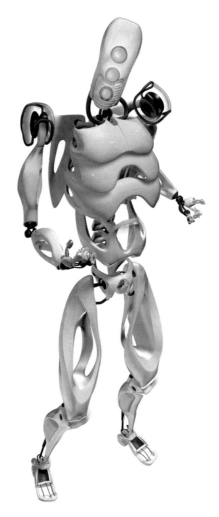

*Phius Stance, ©2001, RPM-fx, created
by Scott Peters in conjunction with
Chaz Laughlin and RPM-fx.*

City in Maya, ©2002, Garry Lewis, www.me3d.tv.

If you notice that the highlights of a surface with a phong shader applied are exhibiting flickering in your animation, or you see a "ropy" appearance from line to line, switch to a Blinn material type, which has smoother highlights. This problem can also be made worse by bump mapping.

PhongE

PhongE is a faster rendering version of Phong that yields somewhat softer highlights than Phong. Most artists use regular Phong for objects with intense highlights and Blinn for everything else.

Blinn

The Blinn material type calculates surfaces similarly to Phong, but the shape of the specular highlights in Blinn materials reflects light more accurately. Blinn is good for metallic surfaces with soft highlights, such as brass or aluminum. Because Blinn is a versatile material type and generally renders without problems, it's the primary material type we've used in these tutorials.

Anisotropic

The Anisotropic material type stretches highlights and rotates them based on the viewer's relative position. Objects with many parallel micro-grooves, such as brushed metal, reflect light differently depending on how the grooves are aligned in relation to the viewer. Anisotropic materials are ideal for materials such as hair, feathers, brushed metal, and satin.

The Others: Layered Shader, Shading Map, Surface Shader, and Use Background

The four remaining material types are for more advanced purposes, so this section just gives you an overview of what they're used for. The Layered Shader lets you combine several materials to create a more complex material. For example, if you want chrome polka dots on a wood surface, you can simply use a polka dot mask in a Layered Shader and then bring in your already-completed chrome and wood materials.

The Shading Map material is primarily designed to let you get a "cel" look in 3D, like typical animated cartoons. You can use this shader for a 2D painted-in look rather than smoothly shaded 3D. The Ramp Shader, new in version 4.5, is a material designed to make it easier to create and control a cel or illustration-style look. The Shading Map material can be used for special effects. Its prior application for cel style shading is now taken over by the Ramp Shader.

The Surface Shader is used when you want to control a material's color, transparency, and/or glow with something else in Maya. For example, you could link color to any object's XYZ position, and the material would then change colors as that object moved around the scene.

The Use Background shader applies the background (image plane or environment) color to the surface that it has been applied to. This allows you, for example, to have shadows cast on an image of a road used as an image plane. This shader type can also be used to cut a "hole" in the image's alpha channel where objects with the material appear. This material is useful for a technique in which separate rendered images are combined in a compositing program to create the final results (for more information, see Chapter 15, "Your Next Steps: Efficiency and Artistry"). CG artists usually do this to divide a large, complex animation into more manageable parts or to combine 3D animation with photographed/filmed live action.

Material Settings

Having reviewed the major material types, now take a look at the variables available in the material you'll most commonly use: Blinn. The other primary materials—Phong, PhongE, and Lambert—have many of the same variables.

To edit material settings, double-click on any material in Hypershade's top or bottom tabs. Usually you create a blank Blinn material in the Work Area of the bottom tab panel, and then double-click it to open the Attribute Editor with the material type loaded. Refer to Figure 8.3A as we travel down the Attribute Editor and discuss its sections.

Notice the material name at the top of the Attribute Editor, which Maya sets to blinn1 for a default starting name. Maya increments the number if you create more Blinn materials. You should edit this text to something more descriptive, though, to help you navigate through your scene materials.

The image next to Material Sample shows a rendered sample sphere that updates as you change the values for the attributes. You use the Type drop-down list to change a material to any other type; if the new material type has different parameters, however, it automatically has the default settings, and the name is reset to the default name.

Next is the Common Material Attributes section, followed by the Specular Shading section. These two sections, displayed by default, are used the most in material editing. The other sections remain closed unless you click to expand them.

Note that the first four variables under Common Material Attributes have a color swatch, a slider, and a checkered button. You can brighten or darken these variables with the slider, but you must click the color swatch (which opens the Color Chooser) to fine-tune a color. Use the checkered button to override a solid color with a texture.

note

Once you apply a texture, the color is no longer editable and the slider becomes locked, as shown in Figure 8.3B. The checkered button is replaced with a right-pointing arrow, and the color in the swatch is meaningless.

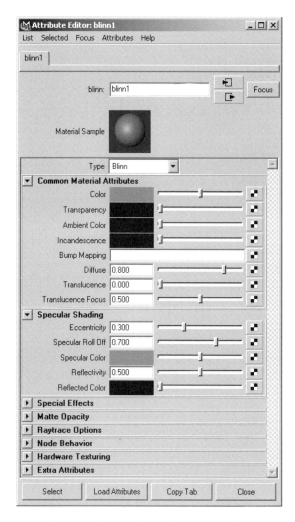

FIGURE 8.3A   *A basic Blinn material in the Attribute Editor.*

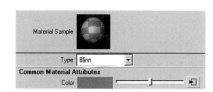

FIGURE 8.3B   *Applying a texture will make the "checker" button icon change to a connection icon, and the slider and swatch no longer are editable.*

These are the Blinn attributes in the Common Material Attributes and Specular Shading sections:

- **Color**   The base color of the surface.

- **Transparency**   Adjusts the surface opacity. As soon as it's raised above 0 (black), Maya changes the sample background to a checkerboard to help gauge the transparency effect. You can use colors to create a tinted glass effect.

- **Ambient Color**   Adds to and blends with the color value. It's a good idea to leave this value set to 0 (black) except for special effects, as it diminishes the contrast and 3D depth in your rendered results where it's applied.

- **Incandescence**   A simulation of emitted light. At low values, it tints and self-illuminates the material, and at high values, it overtakes the material's color and becomes self-illuminated. Keep in mind that the rendered material might look like it's luminous, but it doesn't cast light into the scene; you have to simulate that by adding lights.

- **Diffuse**   Intended to simulate a material scattering light, but it works like a scaling factor on the color. By default, it's set to 0.8, which dulls down the color value you've set. Often animators apply "dirt maps" in this attribute to add realistic dirt and wear that darken a surface. You'll coordinate your diffuse and specular settings, because a "dirty" object wouldn't generally be shiny.

- **Translucence**   A special attribute that lets you see shadows cast onto the back of a surface, useful for simulating materials such as frosted glass. This effect relies on the light sources around and behind the object you're applying the translucent material to.

- **Translucence Focus**   This controls how light scatters from the surface. Lower values make the light scatter heavily and results in a soft, blurry translucence.

- **Eccentricity**   The width of the highlight, simulating how polished or rough the surface appears.

- **Specular Roll Off**   The brightness/intensity of the highlight.

- **Specular Color**   The color of the highlight; usually set to white or a gray value.

- **Reflectivity**   The brightness of reflections on the object. Reflections can be raytraced or use texture maps. If no texture is assigned to the Reflected Color attribute, you need to enable raytracing to see any results from this setting. You can enable raytracing in the Render Globals window (unless you're using reflection maps).

- **Reflected Color**   For Blinn, the color swatch and slider have no effect. However, when a texture map is applied, it appears to be reflected by the material. Usually, you use one of the environmental texture types. Environment textures are used to simulate an environment surrounding the scene; when applied to a material's Reflected Color attribute, they're used to fake reflection. This technique is often used to get a shiny, reflective effect without the slower rendering caused by raytracing the actual surroundings. Also, sometimes there are no surroundings to reflect; for example, flying logo effects are often set in a black void.

Take a look at the following figures to see the differences between some of these attributes. In Figure 8.4, Transparency is applied to the square on the left so that you can see the object behind it. The square on the right has Translucence applied, so it allows only light and shadow to come through.

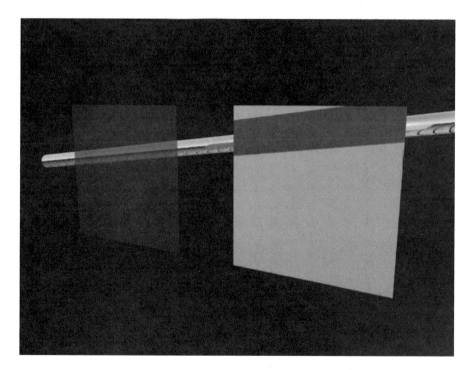

FIGURE 8.4   *Transparency versus Translucence. The red is backlit by a shadow-casting light.*

Figure 8.5 shows spheres with similar reflective materials applied, but the sphere on the right has a fractal map applied to its Diffuse attribute. The effect is apparent only where the map is darker, which causes a "dirt" effect—meaning the sphere is darker and its reflections are less intense in those areas.

In Figure 8.6, the Reflectivity attribute is always at 1 (100%), but varying approaches are used to get different effects. The leftmost image has nothing applied to the Reflected Color attribute. The next image has a chrome environment map in the Reflected Color attribute, which creates the impression of a background despite the sphere's actual surroundings. In the third image, raytracing is enabled but the Reflected Color attribute is disabled, so a perfect reflection is computed. The rightmost image shows the effect of combining raytraced reflections with environmental texture mapping to produce real reflections that have priority over the environmental (Reflected Color) reflections.

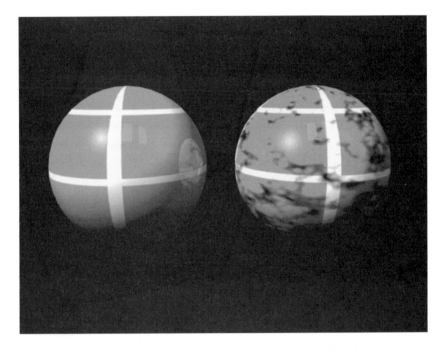

FIGURE 8.5   *The Diffuse attribute can darken the color and diminish reflectivity.*

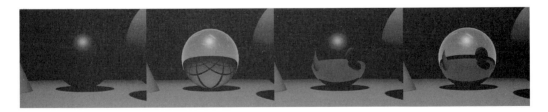

FIGURE 8.6   *Using different approaches with the Reflectivity attribute.*

The Color Chooser

The Color Chooser appears whenever you click on a color swatch. The 14 color buttons at the top are a clipboard. To select the color for a color button, you simply click on it. To replace a color button, RMB-click it. Use the eyedropper tool to pick a color anywhere in the window.

A color spectrum appears in the Wheel area. Generally, the best way to select a color is to use the sliders below the wheel (see Figure 8.7). The sliders can be set to RGB (red-green-blue) or HSV (hue-saturation-value) mode in the list box at the bottom of the Sliders section, but HSV mode is often the most useful. Pick the color tint first in the hue slider, and then select the color's intensity, as compared with gray, in the saturation slider. Finally, adjust the darkness, or black mix, with the value slider. At the bottom is the alpha slider for setting transparency, but it's rarely, if ever, used.

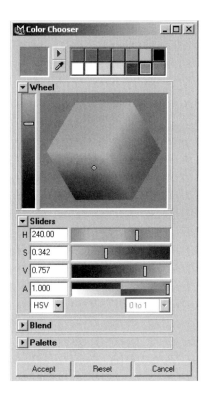

FIGURE 8.7 *Maya's Color Chooser in HSV mode.*

Tutorial: Creating Solid Materials

The most basic materials have a solid color and a consistent surface. In this tutorial, you'll use Hypershade to create some solid-colored surfaces and apply them to objects. Load the scene file noted below the CD icon so that you have a starting point for the sample world you're adding materials to.

On the CD

Chapter_08\movies\ch08tut01.wmv

Pottery

For the pot, you'll apply a pottery material created by using a dark orange color in a Lambert material.

On the CD

Chapter_08\ch08tut01begin.mb

1. Open Hypershade with **Shift+T**. Make sure the Create Bar and both tab panels are showing. Right-click the bar at the top of the Create Bar and choose Create Materials. MMB-drag a Lambert material type to the bottom tab panel. Double-click the new material and the Attribute Editor should appear with the new material loaded. If this doesn't work, you can RMB-click on the new material and choose Attribute Editor.

2. Rename the material from lambert2 to `pottery`. Set the color to dark orange in the Attribute Editor by clicking the swatch next to the Color value, and setting the color in the Color Chooser. We set the Hue to 33, Saturation to .8, and Value to .7. Click the Accept button in the Color Chooser.

3. Select the flower pot object in the scene, RMB-click the edited material in Hypershade, and choose Assign Material to Selection. You should see the pottery object in the Shaded view become dark orange.

Plastic

For plastic materials, you'll use the Blinn material with bright highlights:

4. In Hypershade, MMB-drag a Blinn material to the bottom tab panel. Open the Attribute Editor as before, and rename the material from blinn1 to `red_plastic`.

5. Set the color swatch to bright red. You can click the red color button in the Color Chooser, or use the HSV sliders to get a red you like.

6. In the Specular Shading section of the Attribute Editor, make the shine level bright and tight by setting Eccentricity to `0.1` and Specular Roll Off to `1.0`, and dragging the Specular Color slider all the way to the right to get a pure white. The material sample sphere at the top of the Attribute Editor should look like shiny red plastic.

7. Select the cylinder in the scene. In Hypershade, RMB-click on the red plastic material, and choose Assign Material to Selection. You should see the cylinder turn red in the Shaded view.

Metal

Creating metal requires a trick. The sliders in the Attribute Editor imply an upper and lower limit that doesn't really exist. You can type in any value in most of the numeric entries, and the slider will adjust its ranges. In some cases, you can get useful and unique results from "overdriving" a value in this way.

8. MMB-drag a new Blinn material type from the Create Bar to the bottom tab panel. Open the Attribute Editor for this new material, and name it gold.

9. In the Color Chooser, set the color swatch to dark brown (HSV: 40, 0.8, 0.2), and click Accept. Under the Specular Shading section in the Attribute Editor, leave the settings at their defaults: Eccentricity at 0.3 and Specular Roll Off at 0.7.

10. To get the metal look, click the Specular Color swatch and set it to orange, but with a value higher than 1 (HSV: 40, 1.0, and 2.0), as shown in Figure 8.8.

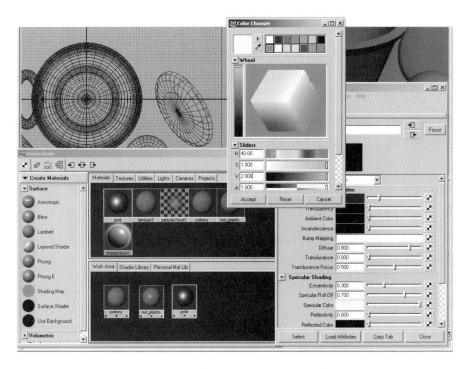

FIGURE 8.8   *Setting the highlight color for a gold material.*

11. Select the oblong sphere object in the scene, RMB-click on the gold material in Hypershade, and choose Assign Material to Selection. The object in the Shaded view should turn gold.

12. Try a test render to see what the materials really look like. RMB-click in the Perspective view, and render by clicking Hotbox | Render | Render Current Frame.

13. A Render View window appears and the image is rendered. Leave tzhis window open.

Reflective Raytraced Metal

The gold looks metallic, but what if you want it to reflect its surroundings? There's a Reflectivity slider in the Attribute Editor, but you won't see any results unless you enable raytracing in the renderer or apply an image to the Reflected Color attribute.

14. In the gold material's attributes, raise the reflectivity value to 1.0. Click the clapboard icon to the left in the Render View window, and the image will re-render. However, the gold remains non-reflective. Set the reflectivity value back to 0.5.

15. Click the Render Globals button, shown in Figure 8.9. In the Render Globals window, find the Raytracing Quality section, select the Raytracing check box, and close the Render Globals window. Render again by clicking the clapboard icon, and you should see reflective effects in the gold object. Orbit the Perspective view and render from some different angles to see the effect. Notice that the red plastic material is also reflecting. The default setting for Reflectivity is 0.5—half reflective. You need to change this value when you don't want reflections on materials.

Render Globals button

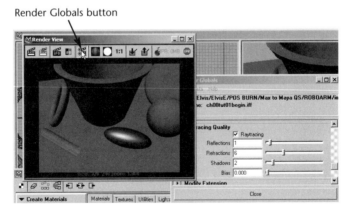

FIGURE 8.9   *Open the Render Globals window to enable raytracing for reflections and refractions.*

tip

You can zoom and pan the rendered image with the mouse as in any 3D panel. You can also zoom and pan the swatches in either tab panel in Hypershade.

Refractive Raytraced Glass

You can also have transparent materials that refract light. That is, light passes through the objects but is bent, so you see a distorted view of what's behind the refractive object.

16. MMB-drag a Blinn material to the bottom tab panel. Open the Attribute Editor and name the material glass.

17. Set the Color to black and the Transparency to white. As soon as you begin to raise the Transparency value, you'll see a checkered background appear behind the swatch in the Attribute Editor and in Hypershade, which means the material is transparent. Set the Eccentricity to 0.1, the Specular Roll Off to 1, and the Specular Color to white.

18. Now open the Raytrace Options section in the Attribute Editor. Select the Refractions check box, and set the Refractive Index to 1.5. This is similar to glass. Most materials have an index between 1 and 2. Select the ring object to the left of the pot in the scene, RMB-click on the glass material in Hypershade, and choose Assign Material to Selection.

Duplicating Materials

You can start with an existing scene material and then duplicate it so that you can use the old material as a starting point for an unassigned new material.

19. Select the gold material in Hypershade, in either tab panel, and press Ctrl+d to duplicate. A new material named gold1 appears.

20. In the Attribute Editor, rename the material as chrome. Change the Color to dark blue by setting Hue to 240 in the Color Chooser. Set Specular Color to white by changing Saturation to 0. You now have a bluish metal look. Crank the Reflectivity to .85, and assign the material to the large sphere in the scene. Render the Perspective view image. The sphere looks like a mirror, reflecting the scene around it.

21. Render the Perspective view. If it looks a bit fuzzy in the refractive and reflective areas, that's because the quality is set low for faster response. To turn the quality up, open the Render Globals window. In the Anti-aliasing Quality section, select Production Quality in the Presets drop-down list, as shown in Figure 8.10. You might also want to increase the resolution; currently, it's only 320×240 pixels. In the Presets list box, select Full 1024, which gives you a 1024×768 resolution image. This setting takes quite a bit longer to render than before, but behold the final image! To see the image at full scale, click the 1:1 button in the Render View window. You can load the final scene from the file noted below the CD icon.

On the CD

Chapter_08\ch08tut01end.mb

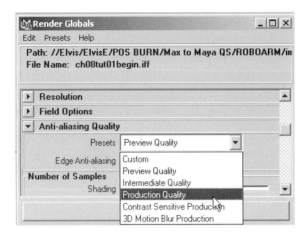

FIGURE 8.10   *Turning up the rendering quality level in the Render Globals window.*

Adding Basic Materials to Your House

In Chapters 5, "NURBS Modeling Basics," and 6, "More NURBS Modeling," you created a house with NURBS modeling techniques. In this section, you'll texture the house by following the tutorials to add materials for the doors, windows, and so forth.

Setting Up Default Lights

Before you start adding textures, you need to add some lights to the scene from various angles so that your test renderings while working on materials give you an accurate view of the fully lit house. To ease the process, we've created a MELscript that adds three Spot lights to your scene:

1. Start by opening the Script Editor (hotkey: **Shift+S**).

2. In the Chapter_08 folder on the Maya Fundamentals CD-ROM, you'll find the script file ch08Lights.mel. Open this file in the Script Editor (File | Open Script).

On the CD

Chapter_08\movies\ch08tut02.wmv

3. At the bottom of the Script Editor, you'll see some text, which is the command set you want to run. Click to get a cursor at the bottom of this command set. To run this script, press Ctrl+Enter.

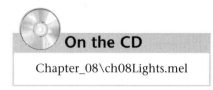

On the CD

Chapter_08\ch08Lights.mel

4. Open the Outliner (hotkey: **Shift+O**). You'll see three Spot lights listed. With some lights in the scene, now you're ready to begin creating and applying materials to the house.

Tutorial: Materials for Your House

You should load the file noted below the CD icon from the *Maya 4.5 Fundamentals* CD-ROM. If you use your own ending scene file from the previous chapter, the results might vary.

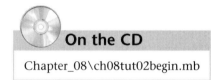

On the CD

Chapter_08\ch08tut02begin.mb

1. To work more efficiently in this tutorial, switch to the saved layout corresponding to materials and rendering (Panels | Saved Layouts | Hypershade/Render/Persp). The viewports should now be replaced with Hypershade, the Render View window, and Perspective view. If you had one of the views open as a floating window, the viewport ignores that particular window in the layout and leaves the floating window available.

2. For the doorknob's texture, you'll create a brushed metal with a worn look. First, hide all the layers in the scene, except for the DoorL layer, by clicking the "V" (for visibility) next to the layer names. If there are other objects, such as cameras or deformers, you can hide them by disabling them in the view (Hotbox | Show | Cameras, Deformers). Orbit and zoom to the DoorKnob object in the Perspective view; this is the doorknob on the outside of the house.

3. The preliminary material for the doorknob is identical to the metal you created earlier in this chapter in the "Creating Solid Materials" tutorial, so follow Steps 8–10 to create a gold metal material and change the material name to DoorKnob-Blinn.

note

When you use a hyphen (-) between words in filenames, Maya converts it to an underscore (_).

4. Make sure the doorknob is still selected, and assign the DoorKnob_Blinn material by right-clicking the new material and choosing Assign Material to Selection. IPR render the scene in the Render View window; when it's finished, marquee-select a rectangle that surrounds the doorknob. After a few seconds, this area will render again, and IPR is now set to respond instantly to your material (see Figure 8.11).

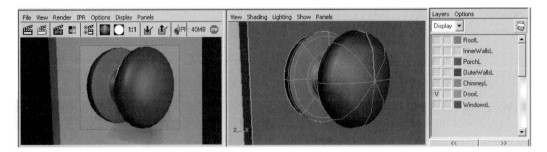

FIGURE 8.11   *Adjusting the texture of the doorknob, using IPR rendering for quick feedback.*

5. The doorknob currently has an ugly bright yellow spot, which doesn't look realistic. To fix that, select DoorKnob_Blinn again and open the Attribute Editor. Click on the swatch for Specular Color, and in the Color Chooser, change the Value setting to 0.45. The specular color looks a little duller now.

6. Save the scene as ch08TexturedHouse. It's a good idea to save your work frequently.

   The door is already visible, so even though you won't finish the texture right now, you can go ahead and add a material for it.

7. For the door, you'll create another Blinn material by MMB-dragging a new Blinn material type from the Create Bar to the bottom tab panel. Name the new material Door-Blinn.

8. Select the door object in the Perspective view. Remember that it's a NURBS cube, so after selecting one side, press the up arrow once to select the entire door.

9. In the top tab in Hypershade, RMB-click on Door_Blinn and choose Assign Material to Selection. IPR rendering will update in the Render View window.

10. Next, set up the material's attributes in the Attribute Editor. You're creating a wood material for the door, so select a light brown color (HSV: 40, 0.8, 0.3). Set Eccentricity to 0.5, thus increasing the size of the specular highlight, and set Specular Color to a lighter brown than the door in the Color Chooser (HSV 40, 0.4, and 0.5). Last, set Reflectivity to 0, and save your scene again. You'll see the updates in the Render View window after each change.

    The next step is setting up a material for the windows in your scene:

11. You're through with the door, so hide the DoorL layer in the Layer Editor, and then display the WindowsL layer.

12. Create an Anisotropic material, name it Window_Anisotropic, and set its Diffuse attribute to 1. Set the color to black, the Transparency attribute to white, and under Raytrace options, check the Refractions box and set Refractive Index to 1.5.

13. Click on the window glass object and confirm that the Channel Box lists Window_Glass. Assign Window_Anisotropic to it. Repeat for the other window's glass, and save your scene again. Notice that because the material is transparent, you can no longer see the plane representing the glass for the window. You can still select it by clicking on the area where you would normally see the plane.

To surround the window, you can add a wood trim, similar to the material you used for the door. After you create the material for the trim, you can use it for other trim on the house, such as along the porch roof or around the door. Reusing a material in this way gives your house a more realistic look—after all, the trim should match, right? This is a more efficient way to work than creating a completely new material for every element in a scene.

14. Instead of creating a new material for the trim, you'll use one you already have. In the top Materials tab in Hypershade, select Door_Blinn. Duplicate the material (hotkey: **Ctrl+d**), and change its name to Trim_Blinn.

15. Normally, you'd use the Attribute Editor to change values for the material, but this time try using the Channel Box. When a material is selected in Hypershade, its default attributes appear in the Channel Box (just as with any other object in Maya). Under Trim_Blinn in the Channel Box, change the material's color by entering values in the three text boxes for red, green, and blue: Set Color R to 0.4, Color G to 0.35, and Color B to 0.25, as shown in Figure 8.12. The material will become a darker brown, varying slightly from the original Door_Blinn.

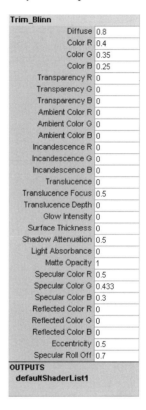

FIGURE 8.12
The Channel Box is an alternative to the Attribute Editor when modifying materials.

16. Next you need to apply the material to the window's trim. Click on one of the window's Window_Frame trim that borders the window, and assign Trim_Blinn to the selection. The wood trim intersecting the window needs to have the material applied. In the Outliner, expand the Windows group. Under either window, select Window_CrossH and Window_CrossV, and assign the material to them. Do this for both windows.

17. Now that you've finished the base materials for the windows, hide the WindowsL layer, and save the scene.

Tutorial: Creating the Remaining Base Materials

So far you've been creating a material and then immediately applying it to a designated object. That workflow method is fine when you're trying to get materials tweaked and have the details and attributes ready for specification. In this tutorial, though, you'll see how to speed up your workflow to create the rest of the base materials and assign them to the house. You need to create base materials for the following portions of the house:

On the CD

Chapter_08\movies\ch08tut03.wmv

- Vertical porch rails
- Horizontal porch rails
- Outside wall
- Outside foundation
- Chimney base
- Chimney pipe at top
- Roof

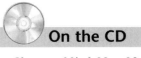

On the CD

Chapter_08\ch08tut02end.mb

Because you're just creating materials, you don't need to have the other viewports visible. With the Hypershade view active, tap the spacebar to maximize it. Increasing the workspace can help improve your productivity. You can start where you left off with the preceding tutorial or load the scene from the CD-ROM.

 tip   You can also hide the UI (user interface) to further increase the workspace (Display I UI Elements I Hide UI Elements). This removes everything from the Status Bar to the Help Line. You can turn the interface back on by selecting Restore UI Elements instead of Hide UI Elements.

1. The porch needs two separate materials for the vertical and horizontal beams on the porch. Select Trim_Blinn in the top Materials tab in Hypershade and duplicate it twice. Name Trim_Blinn1 as VertPorchRail_Blinn. Change the name of Trim_Blinn2 to HorizPorchRail_Blinn. That's all you need to do for the rails right now.

2. The house's walls are next. Create a PhongE surface material by selecting PhongE from the Create Materials Bar. Name the new material `Foundation_PhongE`. The foundation will have a wet look, so PhongE is a good material to start with. Next, create a new Blinn material and name it `Walls_Blinn`.

3. Open the Attribute Editor for Foundation_PhongE. Under the Common Material Attributes section, click the swatch next to Color to set the value in the Color Chooser (HSV: 65, 0.45, 0.35), and click Accept. Next, decrease Diffuse to 0.7. Continuing down to the Specular Shading section, increase Roughness to 0.810, decrease Highlight Size to 0.15, and set Reflectivity to 0. Finally, click the color swatch for Whiteness to set the value in the Color Chooser (HSV: 270, 0.010, 0.2), and click Accept.

4. Next, select Walls_Blinn in the top Materials tab in Hypershade. In the Channel Box (press Shift+C if it's not open), set Color R to 0.9, Color G to 0.68, and Color B to 0.4. You should have a brownish-orange color for the material.

5. Next, you'll create a Lambert material for the chimney. The chimney is made up of brick, which usually doesn't have any highlights, so Lambert is the perfect material candidate. With the new Lambert material selected (lambert2), change the name to `ChimneyBase_Lambert`. Then duplicate the material, naming the duplicate `ChimneyPipe_Lambert`. Select ChimneyBase_Lambert in the top Materials tab. Open the Attribute Editor, use the Color Chooser to set the material's color to dull red (HSV: 0, 0.6, 0.5), and click Accept. In the Attribute Editor, click on ChimneyPipe_Lambert in the Materials tab, set its Color attribute (HSV: 0, 0.4, 0.5), and click Accept.

6. The last base material you need to create is for the roof. You haven't used a Phong material yet, and the roof would look good with a mossy wet material, so create a Phong material and name it `Roof_Phong`. In the Channel Box, change the material's color by setting Color R to 0.34, Color G to 0.312, and Color B to 0.102, which results in a dark brownish-green color.

7. The Work Area bottom tab is cluttered with material nodes at this point and should be rearranged. RMB-click a blank space in the Work Area, and choose Graph | Rearrange Graph from Hypershade's menu to organize all visible materials in the Work Area.

You have now set the foundation for the materials in your scene, and can continue to apply these new materials to the corresponding objects in your scene. If you haven't saved your scene, now would be a good time because you have created quite a few materials. Your Hypershade should have all the materials shown in Figure 8.13.

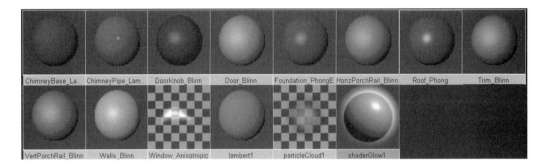

FIGURE 8.13 *The base materials you will build on for the scene.*

8. Next, you'll assign the materials you've created to your scene objects. To make it easier, switch to a predefined saved layout (Hotbox | Panels | Saved Layouts | Hypershade/Outliner/Persp). The Outliner makes it easier to select specific components, and having it open in a viewport eliminates clutter. In Hypershade, click the Show Top Tabs Only button (refer back to Figure 8.1 to see where this button is) because you don't need to see the Work Area now. For more space, hide the Create Bar by clicking the Show/Hide Create Bar button. Last, hide the UI elements in the scene (Hotbox | Display | UI Elements | Hide UI Elements). Keep the Channel Box visible (hotkey: **Shift+C**) so that you can easily work with the layers in the house. Your interface should now be set up to efficiently assign the remaining materials to objects (see Figure 8.14).

9. In the Outliner, all the scene elements are grouped under Old_House. Display all the layers in the scene. To assign a material to the house's outer walls, in the Outliner, select OuterWall and assign Walls_Blinn. You should see the green wireframe of the outer walls, indicating that they're selected. In Hypershade, RMB-click on Walls_Blinn and choose Assign Material to Selection. With the Perspective view active, press 7 to make sure textures are hardware-rendered for viewing and lighting.

10. Select Foundation in the Outliner. RMB-click on Foundation_PhongE and choose Assign Material to Selection. The outer walls of the house now have their base material assigned.

11. Select Chimney, and assign ChimneyBase_Lambert to it. Under the Chimney group in the Outliner, select Chimney_Top and assign ChimneyPipe_Lambert. Even though the material for the chimney's base had been assigned to the pipe, it had no affect on new materials being applied, which immediately override the object's existing material.

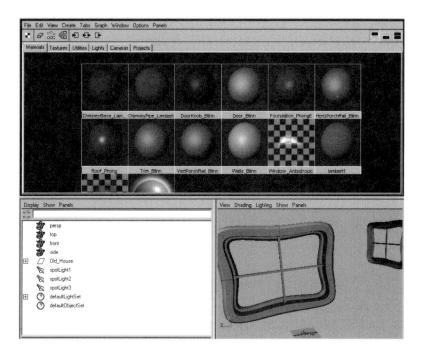

FIGURE 8.14   *By using Hypershade, the Outliner, and Perspective view, you can easily assign materials to objects in your scene.*

12. Expand the Roof group in the Outliner. Under RoofSide, select RoofSlab, and assign Trim_Blinn to it. Shingles should also be located in this group. Assign Roof_Phong to Shingles. Next, assign Trim_Blinn to RoofSlab in RoofSide1 and Roof_Phong to the Shingles in RoofSide1.

13. Close the topmost Roof parent in the Outliner. Hide the RoofL layer and save your scene.

14. The final base materials need to be assigned to the porch before you're ready to move on to texture mapping. Using the Outliner, select the three box objects that make the trim of the porch floor and assign Trim_Blinn to them. Select the horizontal parts of the porch rails, along with the stairs and the porch floor, and assign HorizPorchRail_Blinn to these. Now select the vertical elements of the porch, including the poles, the porch legs, and rail bars, and assign VertPorchRail_Blinn to these.

15. You have finished applying base materials to objects in your scene; in the following section, you'll learn how to add more detail to your textures. Hide the PorchL layer, and save your scene as usual.

On the CD

Chapter_08\ch08tut03end.mb

If you got stuck in this tutorial, load the file ch08tut03end.mb, which contains the finished scene for this tutorial.

Texture Mapping

The next step is to replace a surface's solid color with a texture. Normally, a texture refers to applying a 2D image around a 3D surface, rather like wallpapering a curvy surface. Because a 2D image can be stretched, wrapped, and projected onto a surface in many different ways, you must take control of how the image is applied.

Mapping Coordinates

Mapping coordinates, also known as UV coordinates, tell the 3D renderer how to place the 2D map across the geometry, which varies depending on whether the model is created from NURBS or polygons. For NURBS, parametric mapping is inherent to the surface and this is typically what's used. Because NURBS are already parametric surfaces, mapping can automatically flow smoothly across the surface. You can also adjust NURBS mapping, to move and rotate how the map is positioned on the object.

For polygon surfaces, mapping is normally applied by projecting 2D maps across the 3D surface in one of several ways: planar, cylindrical, spherical, and a special method called automatic mapping. As you might expect, when you apply a 2D texture to a 3D object with a planar map projection, you'll see a smearing effect in areas of the object that's perpendicular to the direction of the map projection. The cylindrical and spherical projections would seem to solve this problem, but both mapping types have their drawbacks—*singularities*. These are points at the poles of the sphere or cylinder where the mapping is pinched into a point (see Figure 8.15). Generally, you must apply the best mapping method for the surface and the areas seen during the animation. That is, if the ugly part is in an area that won't be visible to the camera during the animation, the problem is solved. In tough cases, a combination of automatic mapping, multiple mapping coordinates, and lots of photoediting work can usually fix the problem.

FIGURE 8.15   *Three teapots with planar, cylindrical, and spherical mapping (from left to right).*

Maya's Interactive Texture Placement

To make adjusting mapping on a surface less confusing, Maya offers interactive texture placement. This feature lets you see the maps move on the surface in real time as you move, rotate, and scale the manipulator for the mapping. To make this work, you need to have Hardware Texturing turned on for at least one of the 3D panels. To do that, select the panel (RMB-click over the panel) and then click Hotbox | Shading | Hardware Texturing (hotkey: **6**). By default, materials with a texture applied to the Color attribute have the color texture map set to appear in the hardware-textured panels.

Procedural Maps Explained: 2D Versus 3D

In addition to applying an image or movie to a surface, Maya provides many other texture types called *procedural textures*. Instead of using actual images for mapping, procedural textures use formulas. Many patterns, such as bricks, tiles, and gradients, are so repetitive that they can easily be represented by an equation. By using special forms of seemingly random values, many natural effects can be simulated mathematically: Marble, leather, water, granite, and many other complex and random textures are included with Maya as procedurals.

Maya's procedural textures come in two varieties: 2D and 3D. You can think of the 2D procedurals as a calculated form of a bitmap. A formula is responsible for the image, but the image must be applied to the 3D geometry with some form of mapping, so it's subject to all the benefits and drawbacks of 2D mapping. When 3D procedurals are applied, however, they exist throughout 3D space, and object surfaces define where you see the texture. It's like carving the object from a block of the material. This method has the benefit of not requiring any mapping, but if the object bends or warps, the procedural texture can seem to "swim" through the object (but Maya has an advanced option for getting around this limitation called Texture Reference Objects).

Procedural textures have several benefits. Because they are formula based, their parameters can be adjusted to instantly synthesize all kinds of different effects. Because the simulated random "noise" used for the natural textures varies at every point in space, the procedurals don't repeat, as is common with a tiled image of, say, marble. Also, because 3D procedurals exist throughout 3D space, you often get good results on objects that would otherwise be hard to map. Instead of trying to wrap a 2D texture around a complicated sculpture, you can apply a 3D procedural and it will appear to be perfectly mapped.

2D Procedurals

Maya's 2D procedurals can be divided into two categories: regular patterns and noise patterns. The regular patterns include grid, checker, bulge, cloth, and ramp. With these patterns, you can create tiles, bricks, and many other man-made repeating effects. Noise patterns include fractal, mountain, noise, and water. These psuedorandom textures are excellent for creating the complex "dirty" surfaces common in nature.

3D Procedurals

All of the 3D procedurals but snow are random types. Some, such as wood and marble, clearly imitate nature. However, all are excellent for synthesizing random effects. Even when animating a man-made world such as a building interior, you still need noisy patterns—the bump texture on ceiling tiles, some splotchy carpet patterns, and even the brushed solid-color paint on walls are slightly randomly textured.

Tutorial: Applying Textures

In this tutorial, you'll apply some textured materials to the objects and edit the placement of those textures. You can load the scene file noted here to pick up from the end of the "Creating Solid Materials" tutorial.

1. Open Hypershade (hotkey: **Shift+T**). Make sure the Create Bar and both tab panels are displayed. RMB-click the Create Bar and set it to Create Materials. MMB-drag a Blinn material to the bottom tab panel, and double-click it to open the Attribute Editor.

On the CD

Chapter_08\movies\ch08tut04.wmv

On the CD

Chapter_08\ch08tut01end.mb

2. Rename the material checkerfloor, and click the checkered button to the right of the color swatch. The Create Render Node dialog box opens to the Textures tab, displaying all the 2D and 3D procedurals and textures (see Figure 8.16). Click on the Checker type to apply it to the Color attribute.

3. Make the Perspective view full screen and set it to Shaded view (hotkey: **6**). Activate Hardware Texturing for this view (Hotbox | Shading | Hardware Texturing).

4. You'll use the drag-and-drop method to apply a material to an object. MMB-drag the checkerfloor swatch from the top tab panel of Hypershade to the scene's floor surface. You should see a checkerboard appear on the floor.

5. Double-click the checkerfloor material in Hypershade to make it active in the Attribute Editor. In the Attribute Editor for the material, open the Hardware Texturing section, and set the Texture Quality to High. You should see the checkerfloor texture sharpen in the Shaded view.

6. In the Attribute Editor for the checkerfloor material, the Color swatch is light gray, and the icon to the right of the Color slider has changed from a checkered button to a right-pointing arrow, indicating that the color has been overriden by something else. Click the right-arrow icon to have the Attribute Editor display the parameters for the Checker node.

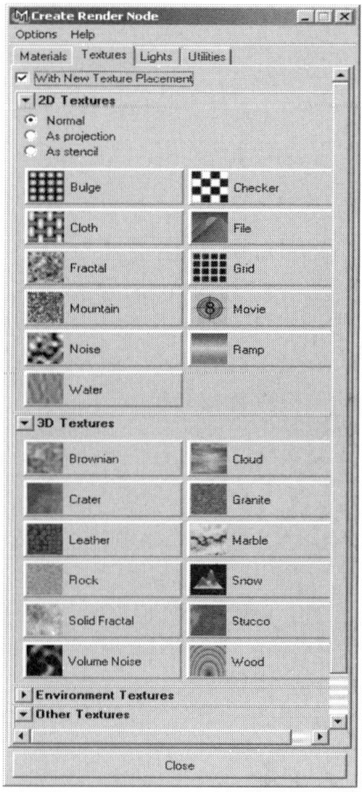

FIGURE 8.16

The Create Render Node dialog box lists all available map types.

 tip

To navigate back to the original node after you have applied a texture, click the right-arrow icon. If you need to undo a texture's assignment, RMB-click on the *name* of the entry and choose Break Connection, as shown in Figures 8.17A and 8.17B.

7. A dialog box opens where you can change the colors of the checkerfloor material from black and white to other colors, as shown in Figure 8.18. To the right of these color sliders are checkered buttons you can click to replace one of checkerfloor's solid colors with another texture. To replace the white squares in checkerfloor with a 3D marbled texture, click the checkered button to the right of Color1 (white), and then click Marble under 3D Textures in the Create Render Node dialog box.

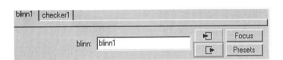

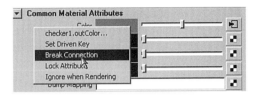

FIGURE 8.17A *Use the lower of the two connection buttons, "go to input connection," to return to the material's base properties when finished editing a texture.*

FIGURE 8.17B *Right-click over the text label for a material attribute to get a dialog option to "break connection"—removing the texture that was assigned to that attribute.*

8. The Attribute Editor now shows the settings for the marble texture. The veins in the marble are much too tiny for your scene, however. To scale the procedural marble texture higher, click the place3dTexture tab in the Attribute Editor, and set the three Scale values to 10. Render the Perspective view, and you should see a marbled checkerfloor material. The floor is somewhat reflective because the default Reflectivity value of 0.5 was assigned to checkerfloor.

FIGURE 8.18 *The Checker texture node in the Attribute Editor.*

9. Next, you'll place a 2D texture on the polygonal shield object with the text "Maya Fundamentals." Create a new Blinn material, and open the Attribute Editor. Name the material m4fshield. Click the checkered button next to Color, and in

On the CD

Chapter_08\shield_logo.tga

the Create Render Node dialog box, select File in the 2D Textures section. Next to the Image Name text box in the Attribute Editor, click the button with the folder icon to select the image you want to apply. For this object, it's the file noted below the CD icon. After selecting and accepting the file, click the m4fshield material in the top tab area of Hypershade. Then MMB-drag the material onto the shield object to the right of the flower pot. You should see the texture appear in a distorted way.

The shield is a polygonal object made with a revolve. Mapping is applied to the revolve, but it's applied circularly in the direction the spline spins to create the surface. In this case, you simply want a flat sign on the front of the shield, so you need to override the default mapping that has been applied.

10. Select the shield object and planar map it (Hotbox | Edit Polygons | Texture | Planar Mapping). You should see the mapping on the surface change immediately, and the mapping manipulator is displayed.

11. Now you can adjust the size and position of the map manipulator to make the text fit neatly on the shield. In one corner of the manipulator is a red "L"; when you click on it, it turns yellow and three manipulator handles appear: a single circle (for activating Rotate mode) and the Scale and Move icons with X, Y, and Z active, as shown in Figure 8.19. If you click on the circle, the Rotate X, Y, and Z manipulators appear, as shown in Figure 8.19. Using these manipulators, you can transform the application of the image to the shield until it's placed correctly. Note that if you click the corner "L" again, the manipulator reverts to its original mode, which is designed for easy sizing. Use the corner Ls (to the left in Figure 8.19) to adjust the map's size.

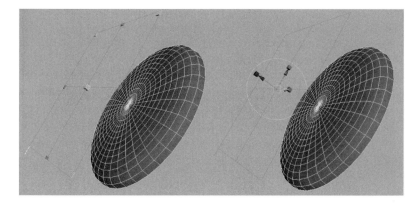

FIGURE 8.19   *The planar mapping manipulators have been pulled away from the geometry to show the two placement modes, toggled by clicking the corner "L" at the lower left of the manipulator.*

12. Now render the view to see what the materials look like. Figure 8.20 shows the planar mapping manipulator in its adjusted placement.

FIGURE 8.20   *The final scene, rendered with the shield map in place. Note that the glass torus doesn't appear in the Shaded view.*

On the CD

Chapter_08\ch08tut04end.mb

tip

If you need to bring the manipulator handles back for texture placement, you can do so by selecting the object, opening the Channel Box (hotkey: **Shift+C**), and clicking the polyPlanarProj entry. If this fails, you need to open the Tool Box (Hotbox | Display | UI Elements | Tool Box). The sixth icon from the top in the Tool Box, just below Scale, is the Show Manipulator Tool button. Click that to get your map manipulator back. The hotkey for the Show Manipulator Tool is **t**.

3D Paint

Interactive Texturing

Maya allows you to not only assign textures to your objects, but also to paint them in real time. Although this sounds like an ideal way to texture everything, in practice it is limited in its value because of the awkward man-machine interface. Most of the time, you'll paint features that are required to be in specific locations, and then take the resulting 2D image to a paint program such as Photoshop for further editing.

Interactive texturing requires a fast video card operating in shaded, hardware-textured mode so that you can see the results of your paintstrokes. Note that you can paint channels other than color, such as transparency. However, interactive shaded views do not display attributes other than color, so you must remember as you paint that you are directly editing transparency, for example, rather than color—thus, white means opaque and black means clear.

Tutorial: 3D Paint Tool

In this tutorial, we'll paint on the cylinder in the scene to create a unique color design on it. The cylinder is a NURBS primitive, so it already has inherent texture mapping across its surface. All we need to do is start the 3D paint tool, and we'll be painting!

On the CD

Chapter_08\ch08tut05.wmv

1. To ease the painting process, we'll isolate the cylinder. Select the cylinder, then choose Display | Hide | Hide Unselected Objects. Center and zoom on the cylinder by using the **a** hotkey—frame all.

On the CD

Chapter_08\ch08tut04end.mb

2. Activate 3D painting with Hotbox | Texturing | 3D Paint Tool | option box. This will bring up the interactive paint dialog, as shown in Figure 8.21. Reset the dialog with the Reset Tool button at the bottom of the dialog. Note that the cursor now appears in the 3D view as a paintbrush, but if you try to paint the cylinder at this point, you will see a red X appear over it, indicating that it is not ready for painting.

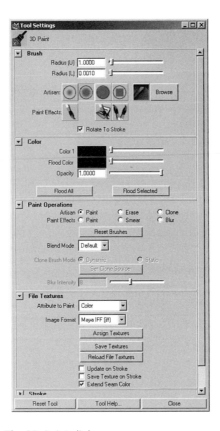

FIGURE 8.21   *The 3D Paint dialog.*

3. Go to the File Textures section of the 3D Paint dialog. This section will allow you to size and assign a new bitmap to any channel you want. Make sure that color is the selected Attribute to Paint, and click the Assign Textures button. A bitmap sizing dialog will appear—set the values to 256, and click the Assign Textures button on this dialog. Now a 256x256 pixel map has been assigned to the color channel of the material assigned to the cylinder. This new bitmap has been pre-filled with your previous solid color, so you may not notice an immediate difference. If you hold your mouse over the cylinder, you'll now see a circle cursor.

4. You can choose from many pen and paint styles that are available in Visor. Bring up Visor with shift+V. Make sure "Paint Effects" is the selected tab. Choose the "Markers" folder and pick the marker named "defaultPaint.mel." Now you can paint on the cylinder.

5. You can easily adjust the color of the markers in the 3D Paint dialog, under the Color section, using the color swatch/slider. Try adjusting this to various colors as you mark up your cylinder, as shown in Figure 8.22.

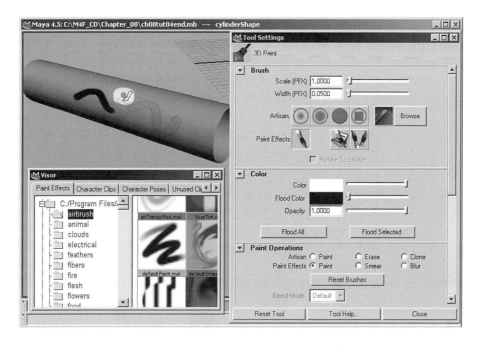

FIGURE 8.22   *Painting on the cylinder with various marker colors.*

6. Besides simple markers, you can also paint in 2D using the various other paint effects materials. You'll find these in the other folders in your Paint Effects tab in Visor. We'll explore using and editing Paint Effects in 3D in more detail in Chapter 13, "Paint Effects." For now, try switching to the blue feathers ("down4.mel") in the Feathers folder. You can size your brush by holding down the **b** key as you LMB-drag left and right. You can also size the brush by entering a value into the scale attribute of the 3D Paint dialog. As you apply blue feathers to the color channel in real time, these paint effects are applying only flat 2D image changes to the texture's color bitmap. Next, paint some more with the other presets offered in Visor—it's fun! After you've tried painting the color channel for a while, render an image to see result. The shininess and all other attributes other than color remain the same, but the solid red color is now painted (defaced?) with your handiwork.

7. Get out of 3D paint mode by switching to the cursor (hotkey: **q**). Hide the current object (hotkey: **Ctrl+h**). Unhide the cone by selecting it in the Outliner and then choosing Hotbox | Display | Show | Show Selection. Use the **a** hotkey to center and zoom on the isolated cone. Invoke 3D Paint with the option box again, and assign a 256x256 map to this object as in Steps 2 and 3 previously.

8. Now, we'll apply a background color of white to this cone by setting the Flood Color (below the Color setting in the 3D Paint dialog) to white, and clicking the Flood All button.

9. In Visor, choose the "Fun" folder, and pick cracks.mel. Now, paint some loop-de-loops on the cone—the crack direction will change based on your stroke direction. Orbit around the object to paint on its sides. You'll find that many of the complex paint effects presets work this way. Finish painting the cone using other crack colors by changing the Color attribute in the 3D Paint dialog. Finish painting with the **q** (cursor) hotkey, and close the Visor and 3D Paint dialogs.

10. Unhide the other objects with the Ouliner—select them in the Outliner (using shift to select multiple items), and then unhide them with Hotbox | Display | Show | Show Selection. Now you can render a frame after repositioning the Perspective view to something that encompasses the entire frame, as shown in Figure 8.23. The painted cone may appear more readily in the reflection from the chrome sphere.

On the CD

Chapter_08\ch08tut05end.mb

FIGURE 8.23   *The rendered result—only the color channel of the red plastic cylinder and gray cone has changed.*

11. If you select one of the painted objects, bring up the Attribute Editor, and navigate to the color channel of the material assigned to the object, you can find the bitmap created by Maya from your paint work. Note that if you want to load the book's sample textures, you'll need to redirect these image pointers to the images provided on the CD-ROM.

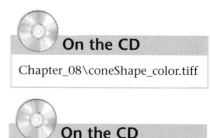

On the CD

Chapter_08\coneShape_color.tiff

On the CD

Chapter_08\cylinderShape_color.tiff

Adding Texture Mapping to Base Materials

By now, you should have a basic understanding of how textures work with the materials and how to place 2D textures on objects in your scene. In this next tutorial, you'll apply these methods to the house's base materials you created and assigned in the earlier tutorial.

Tutorial: Texturing the Doorknob, Walls, and Windows

Having a solid color for the doorknob isn't as realistic as it could be. Earlier you learned how you can use a material's Diffuse attribute to create a dirty look, which is exactly what you'll do for the doorknob.

On the CD

Chapter_08\movies\ch08tut06.wmv

1. First, load your scene into Maya. You can continue from the previous house tutorial, or load the file noted below the CD icon.

On the CD

Chapter_08\ch08tut03end.mb

2. Start by changing the layout you're working with. If you haven't already done so, hide the UI elements, and change to the saved layout for working with materials (Hotbox | Panels | Saved Layouts | Hypershade/Render/Persp).

3. Hide all the layers except DoorL. To begin, you'll modify the texture on the doorknob. By adding a map to the Diffuse attribute, you can achieve a worn metallic look for the doorknob. Select the outer doorknob and focus on it (hotkey: **f**). IPR render the doorknob and select it for update in the Render View window.

4. In Hypershade, make sure the top and bottom tabs are visible (click the Show Top and Bottom Tabs button if they aren't). Double-click the DoorKnob_Blinn material to open the Attribute Editor so that you can map a texture to the Diffuse attribute. Click the checkered button to the right of Diffuse to open the Create Render Node

dialog box. Under the 2D Textures section, make sure the Normal radio button is selected for placement, and click the Fractal type. The Attribute Editor switches to show the Fractal attributes. Looking at the IPR render, you'll see that it has updated.

5. By changing settings for the procedural texture, you can get a brushed effect on the doorknob; as you change the settings, watch the IPR render to see how the texture is affected. Click the fractal1 tab in the Attribute Editor. Under the Fractal Attributes section (see Figure 8.24), change Amplitude to 0.5, Threshold to 0.1, Ratio to 0.77, and Frequency Ratio to 8. Now click the place2dTexture tab. Under the 2D Texture Placement Attributes section, change the second text box (for V) to the right of Repeat UV to 0.15. Last, set the Noise UV to 0 and 0.75. Adding this UV noise to the Fractal attribute "swirls" it more. Close the Attribute Editor.

6. Focus on the door, and redo the IPR render with more of the door in the view. Double-click Door_Blinn in Hypershade to open the Attribute Editor. You'll assign a texture to the Diffuse attribute just as you did with the doorknob, but this time you'll create a Noise texture. To do that, in the noise1 tab, change the values under Solid Fractal Attributes (see Figure 8.25): Set Amplitude to 0.8, Ratio to 0.35, Frequency Ratio to 20, Depth Max to 3, and Noise Type to Wispy. In the place2dTexture tab, change the first text box for Repeat UV to 4. Finally, hide DoorL because you have finished applying textures to it.

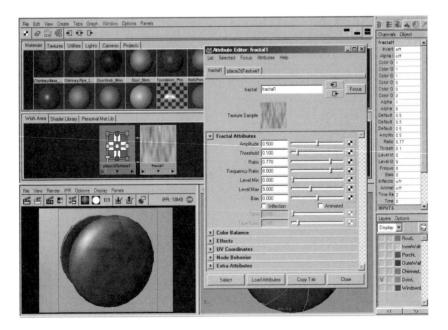

FIGURE 8.24   *Using the Attribute Editor, IPR, and Hypershade, you can easily add textures to your materials.*

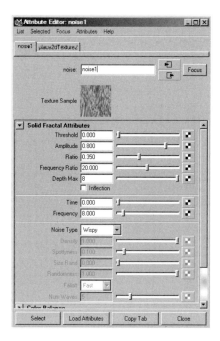

FIGURE 8.25   *Use these settings to change the Noise texture you just mapped to Door_Blinn's Diffuse attribute.*

7. Next, you'll add some texture to the walls. Display the OuterWallsL layer, and IPR render the walls so that you can see them clearly. Open Walls_Blinn in the Attribute Editor, and change the Reflectivity to 0. Map a Noise texture (again confirming that Normal is selected at the top of the Create Render Node dialog box) to the Color attribute of Walls_Blinn. Use the settings shown in Figure 8.26: Set Amplitude to 0.5, Ratio to 0.77, Frequency Ratio to 2, Depth Max to 20, Density to 5, Spottyness to 0.3, and Falloff to Bubble.

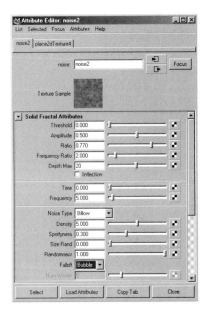

FIGURE 8.26   *Settings to change the Noise texture mapped to the Color attribute for Walls_Blinn.*

Maya provides a "color balance" option to easily adjust the brightness and contrast of the noise. You'll use that now to darken and mute the noise effect:

8. Under the Color Balance section for the Noise, set the Color Gain in the Color Chooser (HSV: 41, 0.315, 0.656). Then change the Color Offset (HSV: 45.5, 0.393, 0.120). After setting those values, click the place2dTexture tab and set Repeat UV to 1 and 5 to make the texture compress in the V direction. Save your scene.

9. Select Walls_Blinn again and map a 2D Mountain texture to the Diffuse attribute. In the place2dTexture tab, change the Repeat UV to 0 and 3 and set Noise UV to 0 and 0.005. You should also change the values in the mountain1 tab, as shown in Figure 8.27: Amplitude to 0.75, Snow Altitude to 1, and Snow Dropoff to 1.

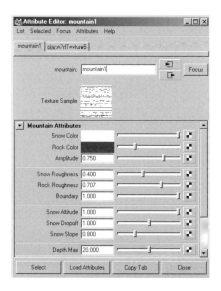

FIGURE 8.27   *Settings for the Mountain texture mapped to the Diffuse attribute of Walls_Blinn.*

10. Now you can move on to the foundation. Open the Attribute Editor for Foundation_PhongE by double-clicking on the material in Hypershade. You'll map an image file to the Color attribute by clicking on the checker button for the Color attribute. The texture list should appear. Select File. The Attribute Editor displays the file settings. We could now click the Folder button to select the image map by name, but there's an easier way, shown in the next steps.

11. In HyperShade, choose Tabs | Create New Tab. In the Create New Tab dialog box, enter M4F maps in the New Tab Name text box, select the Bottom radio button for Initial Placement, select the Disk radio button for Tab Type, and then point the root directory to the Chapter_08\Textures folder on the CD-ROM (see Figure 8.28). Click the Create button.

FIGURE 8.28   *Adding a new tab to Hypershade.*

12. In Hypershade, click on the bottom tab Shader Library, and then click the new tab you created. You should see swatches appear for all the textures in the selected folder. These are thumbnail images of the available textures that you can zoom and pan. Click cobblestones.tif to select it, and then MMB-drag the texture to the Image Name text box in the Attribute Editor. The file's location is automatically placed in the text box. Press Enter, and the Texture Sample swatch updates to show the new texture. If you do a test render, you'll see the material applied to the foundation, as in Figure 8.29.

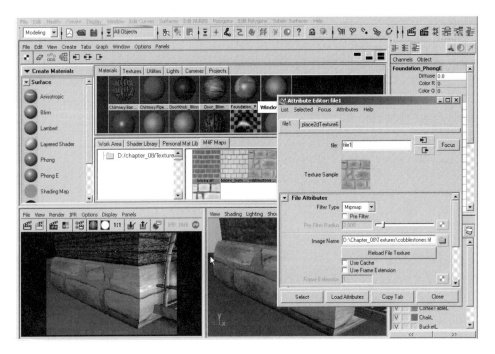

FIGURE 8.29   *The cobblestones.tif texture has been linked to the File node.*

13. Click the place2dTexture tab. Under the 2D Texture Placement Attributes section, change Repeat UV to 3 and 2. Click Foundation_PhongE again to open it in the Attribute Editor. Map the 2D texture Noise to the Diffuse attribute, and in the noise3 tab, change the Solid Fractal Attributes to match Figure 8.30: Set Amplitude to 0.7, Ratio to 0.77, Frequency Ratio to 5, Depth Max to 2, Frequency to 10, and Noise Type to Perlin Noise. This adds a heavy "grime" layer to the texture. Raising the Threshold value will lighten the noise color and therefore diminish the grime effect.

14. Hide the OuterWallsL layer and display the ChimneyL layer. Zoom in on the chimney and IPR render. If you are having trouble seeing it because some areas are not illuminated enough, select spotLight2 in the Outliner and increase its Intensity to 1.2 in the Channel Box.

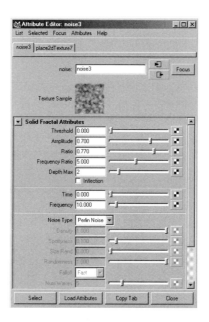

Figure 8.30   *Placing this Noise texture on the Diffuse attribute gives the cobblestone a very dirty look.*

15. Click ChimneyBase_Lambert in Hypershade. In the Attribute Editor, map a File 2D texture node (the Normal radio button should be selected for placement) to the Color attribute. Just as you loaded the cobblestone texture for the foundation, in the Shader Library tab, locate bricks.tif and MMB-drag it to the Image Name text box in the Attribute Editor.

16. The IPR updates, but the brick is stretched. To fix that, RMB-click ChimneyBase_Lambert and choose Graph Network. Click the place2dTexture node for the brick. Under the 2D Texture Placement Attributes, change the Repeat UV to 1 and 6. The brick looks too clean, so you'll add a Solid Fractal 3D Texture map to the material's Diffuse attribute. To do that, in the place3dTexture tab, click the Fit to Group bbox button. Under the Solid Fractal Attributes section, change the Amplitude to 0.8, Frequency Ratio to 5, Ripples to 2, 3, and 5, and Bias to 0.05.

17. In the Perspective view, rotate around. Notice that on two sides of the chimney, it seems as though the texture is moving in the wrong direction (see Figure 8.31). The surface's direction is going in the opposite direction as the other sides of the chimney. In other words, the U and V coordinates have been switched, which is typical of NURBS cubes in Maya. To change the direction of a surface, select the side of the chimney with the direction problem, and reverse the surface direction (Alt+z | LMB-click | Reverse Surface Direction | option box). Make sure the Surface Direction is set to Swap. Click the Reverse button to see the texture magically repositioned in the Perspective view. You'll need to IPR render again to see the change. There are two sides of the chimney with this problem, so repeat Step 17 on the opposite surface.

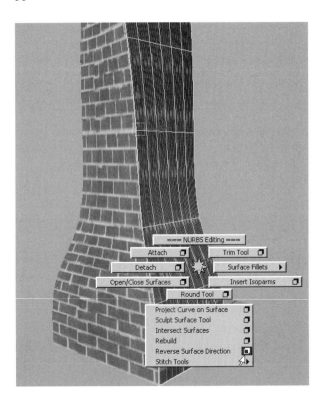

FIGURE 8.31   *Reversing the surface direction will fix the texture mapping on the NURBS object in one step.*

18. Before going any further, be sure to save your scene. The last step is to add a texture to the Transparency attribute for your Window_Anisotropic material. Make all layers visible except for PorchL because the porch isn't anywhere near the windows. You can do an IPR render of the window, but it won't show much without raytracing. In the Attribute Editor for Window_Anisotropic, map a 2D Texture Ramp (select the Normal radio button) to the Transparency attribute.

19. A Ramp texture can give you a wide range of effects. You can think of it as a gradient, with one color blending into another. Click the ramp1 tab, and select Circular Ramp in the Type drop-down list box (see Figure 8.32). The Texture Sample swatch updates to show what the Ramp looks like. You can specify the areas that will be transparent by setting a ramp color (the circular color buttons) to white. The Interpolation list box, below Type, defines how the blending (intermediate) colors change; it should be set to Linear.

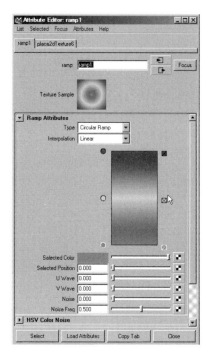

FIGURE 8.32   *The default Ramp has been changed to a Circular Ramp.*

20. After modifying all the settings, you will have a faded, more transparent look around the edges of the window. Using the IPR render can help you tweak the positions of the fading transparency. In the Attribute Editor for the Ramp texture, notice that three separate colors are displayed by default. If you click anywhere in the Ramp, you create another color. To move the colors, click on the circles to the left; to delete the colors, click the small squares on the opposite side. Click the green square to delete its color, and click the blue circle to select it. Under this color swatch, set Selected Color to almost completely black. Changed Selected Position to 0.810, U Wave to 0.150, Noise to 0.150, and Noise Freq to 0.600.

Watch the IPR render update with each change. Change the other color in the ramp to pure white by clicking the red circle and setting Selected Color to white. Change Selected Position to 0.415. Your Ramp settings should now resemble Figure 8.33. Don't forget to save your scene.

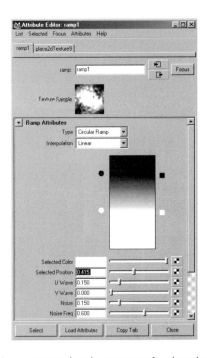

FIGURE 8.33   *The Ramp texture has been set up for the window glass.*

At this point, you can continue on your own to apply textures to the rest of the house. You have walked through applying textures for the walls, chimney, door, and glass. The next section of this chapter introduces yet another important attribute for materials—bump mapping.

On the CD

Chapter_08\ch08tut06end.mb

Bump Mapping

Another powerful and useful method to add to texture mapping is bump mapping. This kind of map does not change the geometry in any way, but it tweaks the way the surface responds to lighting to give the impression of bumpiness based on an applied map. Only the luminance of the applied bump image is used to create the bump effect, so grayscale images are the norm for bump maps. A middle gray is considered flat, lighter areas are higher, and darker areas are lower. In areas where the bump map's brightness is changing, the surface will look like it's bumpy. Because the bump map effect will not affect the silhouette of a surface, you can't use bump mapping to simulate large features that you'll get near to or the effect will be ruined. For example, you wouldn't normally bump map a character's nose; however, you might bump map the pores on that nose. For many surfaces, bump mapping is perfect—fabrics, craggy surfaces, wood grain, or even metal vents, provided the camera doesn't get too close.

tip   To see a bump effect, the material usually needs to have at least a minimal amount of shininess.

Coordinating Texture and Bump Mapping

When you combine texture mapping and bump mapping artfully, you can get an extraordinary amount of detail from even fairly simple models. Artists often create these maps in a paint program, and carefully match the placement of the bump effects in the grayscale bump map to the corresponding colored areas in the color texture map. Maya uses the bump map's luminence to set the "height," with white being all the way "out" and black being all the way "in." If you try to use an image as its own bump map, it rarely works; the shiny areas appear as large bumps and darker areas that protrude look recessed. It's important to keep bump maps slightly soft; ultra–high-contrast black-on-white images do not work as well as softer images with gradations between the extremes.

Tutorial: Applying Bump Maps

In this tutorial, you'll apply a procedural noise effect to the Bump Mapping attribute of the flower pot's clay material to give it a more natural, rough appearance.

On the CD

Chapter_08\movies\ch08tut07.wmv

1. In Hypershade, MMB-drag the pottery material to the bottom tab area. If the bottom tab area is cluttered, you can clear it by selecting the materials you are done with and clicking the Clear Graph button (refer to Figure 8.1).

On the CD

Chapter_08\ch08tut05end.mb

2. Double-click the pottery material to open the Attribute Editor. Click the checkered button to the right of the Bump Mapping attribute near the top of the Common Material Attributes section to open the Create Render Node dialog box.

3. Click the Solid Fractal type in the 3D Textures section of the Create Render Node dialog box. The Attribute Editor will show the Bump Value and Bump Depth settings. Notice that the Bump Depth defaults to 1.0. You can intensify or reduce the bump amount with this slider. Click the right-arrow icon next to Bump Value to take you to the solid fractal that's driving the bump. The Solid Fractal Attributes section will appear in the Attribute Editor.

4. Set Ratio to 1.0 to intensify the bump.

5. Click the place3dTexture tab in the Attribute Editor. You can also find this node in Hypershade, connected to the left side of the Solid Fractal swatch that connects to the pottery swatch. In the Attribute Editor, increase the scale of the Solid Fractal: Set Scale X, Y, and Z to 50. Note the size icon that appears in the 3d panels.

6. Render the scene to see the flower pot's bumpy appearance.

On the CD

Chapter_08\ch08tut07end.mb

Tutorial: Applying Bump Maps to Your House

Applying a bump map to the textures for your house requires a little more work. In this tutorial, we'll guide you through applying a bump map for three materials: the chimney, foundation, and outer walls.

On the CD

Chapter_08\movies\ch08tut08.wmv

On the CD

Chapter_08\ch08tut06end.mb

1. Load your scene with the textured house (see the file noted below the CD icon). Because bump maps are determined with values taken from a grayscale image, you can often take the color version of a texture you have and modify it to become the bump map, as shown in Figure 8.34. After you have a bump map, all you have to do is set the placement so that it lines up with the texture already applied to the object.

2. Switch into the Hypershade/Render/Persp saved layout. Hide all layers except for DoorL. The material for the door will be the easiest one to add a bump map to. There are no sharply defined lines for the door, so you can use almost any type of bump map. Maneuvering in the Perspective view, focus on the door from an angle. If you look at the door straight on, it's more difficult to see the results of the bump map. Do an IPR render.

3. Double-click the Door_Blinn material to open the Attribute Editor. Click the checkered button next to Bump Mapping. Select the Normal radio button in the

Create Render Node dialog box, and then
click File as your texture type. In the File
tab, load the file noted below the CD icon
into the Image Name text box.

On the CD

Chapter_08\BumpMaps\
planks_bump.tif

Original color
tileable
textures

Grayscale
bump maps
derived from
texture

FIGURE 8.34   *The grayscale bump maps in the bottom row were created
by desaturating and altering the original color textures in the
top row, so that "higher" areas are lighter.*

trap   If you load the bump map files from the CD-ROM, you'll need the CD-ROM every
time you load the scene. A good plan would be to copy the files from the CD-ROM
into the sourceimages folder in your project directory.

4. The bump map is applied almost perfectly, with the wood grain running vertically. In the bump2d tab, decrease the Bump Depth to 0.6. In Hypershade's Work
Area, click the place2dTexture tab for the bump map, and set Repeat UV to 1 and
0.7. Add some Noise UV set to 0.01 and 0 to make the vertical lines "wiggle" a
little. Look at Figure 8.35 to see the difference before and after the bump map was
added.

5. Now you'll add a bump map to the walls of the house. Make the OuterWallsL
layer visible. Focus on the front left side of the house in the Perspective view, and
IPR render. With Walls_Blinn open in the Attribute Editor, click the checkered
button next to Bump Mapping and click File as the texture type. In the bump2d
tab, decrease Bump Depth to around 0.5. Next, drag and drop planks_bump.tif

(see the file noted here) to the Image
Name text box as before. Double-click on
Walls_Blinn in Hypershade, and you can
find the values for the place2dTexture
node in the Channel Box (hotkey:
Shift+C) by clicking on the
place2dTexture entry under Inputs. Close
the Attribute Editor to get it out of your way.

On the CD

Chapter_08\BumpMaps\
planks_bump.tif

FIGURE 8.35   *The door, before and after adding a bump map to its material.*

6. The Inputs section of the Channel Box contains information about the material's
    connections (textures and mapping placement). There are currently three
    place2dTexture nodes, with the most recent one at the bottom. Click on the last
    place2dTexture node to see a plethora of attributes (see Figure 8.36). Change
    Rotate Frame to 90, and set Repeat U to 7 and Repeat V to 4.

7. When adding the bump map to the foun-
    dation, you have to set the map's place-
    ment to fit with the cobblestone texture.
    Open Foundation_PhongE and connect a
    2D texture File to the Bump Mapping
    attribute. Be sure the Normal radio button
    is selected for the placement. Because the
    original color texture is set up as normal

On the CD

Chapter_08\BumpMaps\
cobblestones_bump.tif

placement, the easiest way to align the two maps is to use an identical placement setup. Open the file cobblestones_bump.tif, and drag it to the Image Name text box.

8. The default placement for the bump map is way off, which you can see by doing an IPR render. The cobblestones_bump.tif file is the modified version of the foundation's texture. If the bump map is mapped overlaying the texture, you'll have a much more realistic look. RMB-click on Foundation_PhongE, and choose Graph Network. Rearrange the graph in the Work Area (RMB-click | Graph | Rearrange Graph).

9. Delete the place2dTexture node that connects to the File node for bump by clicking to select it, and then pressing Delete. Now hold down the Ctrl key while MMB-dragging from the remaining place2dTexture node to the File node for Bump. When you release the mouse button over this node, all the connections should instantly appear.

10. Select the Bump2d node, and in the Attribute Editor, adjust the Bump Depth level to around 1.2, so that it looks like stone with deep grooves. The foundation should look similar to Figure 8.37 after you're finished.

11. The last bump map you'll apply is for the chimney base. Having gone through the mapping process for the foundation, try doing the chimney on your own. The directions are basically the same, except that you'll load the bricks_bump.tif file (noted below the CD icon) and apply the bump map to the ChimneyBase_Lambert material.

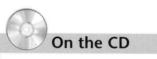

On the CD

Chapter_08\BumpMaps\
bricks_bump.tif

Surface Thickness	0
Shadow Attenuation	0.5
Light Absorbance	0
Matte Opacity	1
Specular Color R	0.5
Specular Color G	0.5
Specular Color B	0.5
Reflected Color R	0
Reflected Color G	0
Reflected Color B	0
Eccentricity	0.3
Specular Roll Off	0.7

INPUTS
 mountain1
 place2dTexture5
 noise2
 place2dTexture4
 bump2d2
 file4
 place2dTexture11

Coverage U	1
Coverage V	1
Translate Frame U	0
Translate Frame V	0
Rotate Frame	0
Mirror	off
Stagger	off
Wrap U	on
Wrap V	on
Repeat U	1
Repeat V	1
Offset U	0
Offset V	0
Rotate UV	0
Noise U	0
Noise V	0

OUTPUTS
 defaultShaderList1
 materialInfo7

FIGURE 8.36
In the Channel Box, you can modify values for your material's placement nodes.

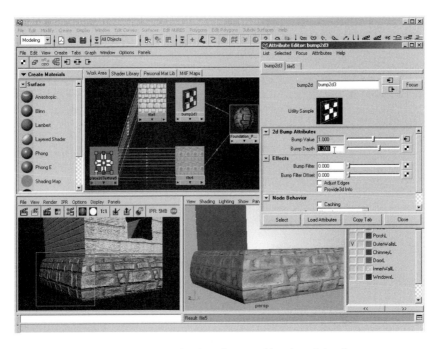

FIGURE 8.37   *Applying the bump map to the foundation adds a lot of detail.*

Going Further

To further your understanding of materials and texturing, try setting up the remaining materials for the house and experimenting with different methods of applying textures, such as projection methods, 3D textures, and so forth. You could also add some objects inside the house. You could model a coffee table, a lamp, or even a chair, or you can import a file with these objects already created for you.

To import the scene, go to File | Import | option box. Reset the settings to the default, and click the Import button. Then browse to the file's location on the CD-ROM, and click the Import button again. A ground material has been created as well as some objects for inside the house.

On the CD

Chapter_08\ch08importObjects.mb

You might have to reposition some of the objects, but if you're having trouble, you can load the scene file noted below the CD icon. Figure 8.38 shows the scene with the objects imported.

On the CD

Chapter_08\ch08tut08end.mb

FIGURE 8.38   *The objects have been imported.*

For your viewing and rendering pleasure, a fully textured version of the house is available on the CD-ROM. Load the scene file noted below the CD icon to see the objects imported and textures added.

On the CD

Chapter_08\ch08HouseComplete.mb

Summary

By working through the tutorials in this chapter, the world of materials has opened up for you. It might seem overwhelming now, but don't get discouraged. It takes time and practice to develop a thorough understanding of how nodes work together and affect your renderings. Using this fundamental knowledge of materials and texturing in Maya, you have a base to build on. Take a look at what you have learned in this chapter:

- **Blinn, Phong, PhongE, Lambert, and Anisotropic**   The basic material types are confusing at first glance, but are no longer strangers to you.

- **Working with material attributes**   Understanding the basic material attributes is vital to successfully creating a shader, such as plastic or metal.

- **Working with Hypershade**   You've learned how to use Maya's material creation tool.

- **Adding materials to the house**   Using the house from Chapters 5 and 6, you have moved closer to creating a render-worthy model.

- **Assigning materials and learning workflow**   There's no set method for creating and applying materials to a scene, but you've learned a couple of methods to give you an idea of the process.

- **Adding textures to basic materials**   A simple material can look good by itself, but adding a texture can bring the material to life!

- **Bump maps**   You learned how to fake surface deformation by changing the way that light reacts to the surface.

- **Using 3D Paint**   You learned to interactively create textures on 3D objects.

CHAPTER 9

Lighting

In This Chapter

Artists and photographers know that a beautiful image or scene owes a lot to the way it is lit. In the digital world, people often fail to give lighting the attention it deserves. To get good results in Maya, complex lighting setups are usually required. The process of skillfully lighting a scene is an art form used by photographers, cinematographers, interior designers, stage lighting designers, and other artists. In Maya, the techniques are similar but are made more complex because virtual lights behave more simply than real lights. For example, lights may or may not cast shadows, and if they don't, they pass through objects to illuminate other objects normally hidden from the light. Also, virtual lights do not reflect from surfaces, meaning that areas to be lit must be directly illuminated by a light source.

By the end of this chapter, you should have a basic understanding of lighting that allows you to experiment with different lights without working "in the dark." In this chapter, you'll explore various lighting setups to understand how to best place lights in your scene and see where to find a variety of light effects. You have several types of lights to choose from in Maya; each one has unique attributes and benefits, and you'll learn what each type is best used for. When you know how to work with lights, scenes that once rendered dull can take on a new radiance. Lighting a virtual scene is a skill that will seem easier as you get used to the limitations and advantages of virtual lights. We'll be covering the following concepts:

- **Working with lights** You'll get the opportunity to place and modify lights and become familiar with how they can light a scene.
- **Types of lights** Understand the differences between the several types of lights you can choose from.

- **Light attributes**   By learning the primary light attributes and a few related Maya variables, you can get the results you expect when you create your scenes.

- **IPR render**   Tweaking lights would take ages without IPR rendering for real-time feedback. You'll quickly see why this tool is so valuable.

- **The dark side of light—shadows**   There are two different types of shadows in Maya. Learning the differences between them could save you hours in rendering times.

Key Terms

Directional   A light type in Maya, similar to sunlight, that shines rays of light parallel to each other.

Ambient   Light type that illuminates all objects in a scene, regardless of position; it has no apparent source and casts a uniform light.

Point   Light type that emits rays of light in all directions from a single point in space.

Area   Light type that emits light from a defined rectangular area instead of a point in space.

Spot   Light type that emits rays of light in a conical fashion, similar to a flashlight or headlight.

Volume   Light type designed to fill a volume, falling off from the center to the outer boundry.

Cone Angle   A Spot light attribute that specifies how broadly to spread the light rays.

Penumbra Angle   A Spot light attribute that softens or sharpens the edge of the illuminated area (the cone).

Decay Rate   An attribute for Area, Spot, and Point lights that defines the rate at which the light intensity decreases with distance.

Light Glow   An optical effect in Maya.

Depth Map Shadows   A shadow type in Maya that creates and uses image maps to define shadows.

Raytraced Shadows   A shadow type in Maya that accurately calculates paths for the rays of light emitted from a light source resulting in shadows.

Hotkeys to Memorize

t Light Manipulator Tool	**7** enable hardware lighting, using all scene lights in a 3D panel

Why Is Lighting Important?

Virtual lighting takes a little more effort than it might appear on first glance. The reasons are both technical and creative. Technically, most of the time you're trying to get a realistic effect with your lights, and Maya's virtual lights do not work in a realistic way—in particular, lights in Maya do not reflect. In the real world, even a single light source can fully illuminate a room because it reflects from surfaces to reach areas under desks and shelves, for example, that aren't directly lit. In Maya, however, those areas are completely dark, so *diffuse reflection* must be simulated by adding many low-level lights. Lights in Maya also allow such unrealistic options as *negative lights* (to pull light from their area of influence) and *light linking* (so that lights illuminate only selected objects). These options are helpful in getting good lighting results. Also, if you're compositing a rendered image with real-world footage, the lighting for the rendered image must match the footage as closely as possible for a realistic result.

Creatively, lighting defines the scene's mood. If you're trying to create a chilling, spooky effect, you'll probably want to employ dim lighting in the scene. For a feeling of suspense, you might decide to have lights that flicker. When looking for ideas to light a specific scene, think about films in similar genres—horror, film noir, drama, and so forth. Examine the lighting in these films and look for ideas that you can carry out in your scene.

The results of a well-lit scene are worth the effort and time. Skillful lighting creates contrast between objects, enhances the colors in your scene, and gives you more control over the scene's shading. Remember that lighting in a scene creates the shadows, influences colors, and affects the appearance of shaders and materials.

Available Light Types in Maya

Several different lights are available in Maya 4, each with its own properties and uses: Directional, Ambient, Point, Volume, Spot, and Area lights. Each one has its own icon to represent it in your scene (see Figure 9.1).

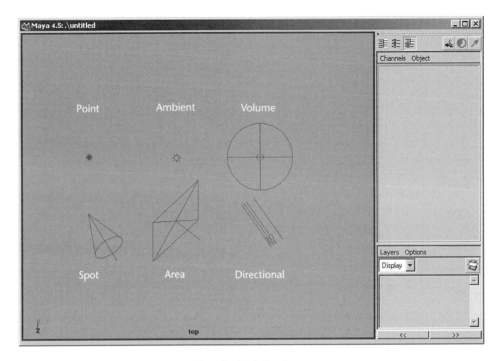

FIGURE 9.1   *Different icons identify the lights in your scene.*

Tutorial: Spot Light and Attributes

To learn to use lights, you need to work with them interactively. By using a simple scene with some NURBS primitives, you can create lights and render them to see the results of changes in attributes and other settings. The first light you'll work

On the CD

Chapter_09\movies\ch09tut01.wmv

with is the Spot light, probably the most commonly used light, with a multitude of options to adjust the settings for the areas it illuminates. The Spot light's area of illumination is defined by a cone, and within the cone's specified range, light is cast evenly. Starting from an infinitely small point in space, a Spot light spreads as it moves farther from the origin. Spot lights are useful when you're trying to create conic beams of light from, for example, a prison watch tower, a lighthouse, and so forth.

1. Start Maya, and open the scene file from
   the Maya Fundamentals CD-ROM (notcd
   below the CD icon). You'll see three primitive objects, a wall, and some ground for
   the objects.

On the CD

Chapter_09\ch09tut01.mb

2. Switch to Four View mode. Open the
   Hotbox and click Create | Lights | Spot
   Light | option box to open the Create Spot Light Options dialog box, which con-
   tains basic creation options for the Spot light. You can also access these attributes
   in the Attribute Editor.

3. Reset the values to their defaults (Edit | Reset Settings), and click the Create but-
   ton. A Spot light named spotLight1 is created at the scene's origin point. If the
   Channel Box is not visible, open it (hotkey: **Shift+C**).

   The area that a Spot light illuminates is based on its position and center of
   interest (where it's aimed), so having it located at the scene's origin isn't usually the best placement. The best way to work with a light in a scene is to switch
   to the Light Manipulator tool, which you can use to easily modify the light's
   location and center of interest.

4. Activate the Light Manipulator tool (hotkey: **t**). The Light Manipulator tool has a
   set of two manipulators: the pivot manipulator, located at the light's pivot (origin), and aim manipulator, located at the light's target—its center of interest. In
   the Top view, just as you would move an object, move the Spot light to the floor's
   lower-left corner by using its pivot manipulator.

5. The light's aim is still off. Using the aim manipulator (shown in Figure 9.2), move
   the center of interest to the floor's upper-right corner. The idea is to position
   spotLight1 so that it aims at about a 45-degree angle from the floor toward the
   objects, as seen from above.

tip

There are other manipulator options beside pivot and aim. When you're in manipulator mode, a light-blue manipulator called the Cycling Index controller (shaped like
an upside-down "Q") is visible. This is a switch to toggle through the manipulator
modes. You can get visual feedback and control over tilt, falloff, cone angle, and
other parameters with these manipulator modes.

6. Switch to the Side view and use the pivot manipulator to move it about 12.5 units
   in the Y direction. You should now have the Spot light positioned to illuminate
   the objects at about a 45-degree angle from the ground's horizontal line, as shown
   in Figure 9.2.

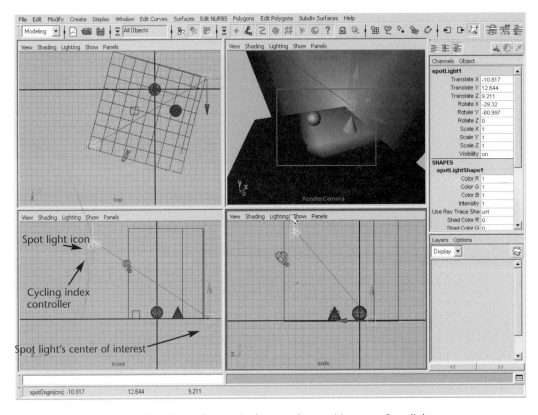

FIGURE 9.2   *Using the Light Manipulator tool to position your Spot light.*

Using the IPR Render for Tweaking

The more you work with lights, the more you'll come to appreciate IPR render. Being able to immediately update the lighting as you make adjustments is an invaluable tool in the 3D artist's hands. Lighting also affects the materials in the scene. For instance, if a particular light worked in one scene with a Lambert material, you would have no specularity. If you tried to use the same lighting in a scene with a different material, such as Blinn, the results might be unacceptable. By using the IPR render, you can easily adjust the lights for different materials. Follow these steps to try out the IPR render:

7. Open the Render View window from the Hotbox or menu bar (Window | Rendering Editors | Render View). First, you should determine the test resolution you'll use. It's currently set to 640×480. Depending on the speed of your machine, this value might be too high and can cause the IPR render to work more slowly than you would like. For this tutorial, reduce the test resolution by right-clicking in the Render View window, choosing Options | Test Resolution, and then releasing the mouse button over the 320×240 value.

8. The Render Globals settings have already been configured to render from the
   RenderCamera view. Click the IPR Render button in the Render View window.
   When the IPR render is finished, click-drag to select the entire rendered image in
   the Render View window. The IPR render should update the pixels. You can then
   change various attributes for a Spot light and see how it affects the scene (see
   Figure 9.3).

note   If you notice a warning in the Command Line about IPR not supporting non-IFF format images, it relates to the save-to file type set in the Render Globals window. It
will not cause a problem with IPR.

FIGURE 9.3   *The Spot light illuminates objects only within the cone's
specified area.*

9. If spotLight1 is not selected, open the Outliner (hotkey: **Shift+O**), and then
   click on spotLight1 to select it. Open the Attribute Editor, and click the
   spotLightShape1 tab. You now have access to the settings for a Spot light in Maya.

Attributes for Spot Lights

Each of the five light types works differently, and each one has attributes specific to its type. By understanding the attributes that differentiate the available lights in Maya, you can choose the correct light for a particular setup. Getting familiar with what these attributes do can save you some time while creating a scene, too. You should aim for being able to change a specific value and having a good idea of what the result should be. Take a look at Figure 9.4 to see the attributes for a Spot light.

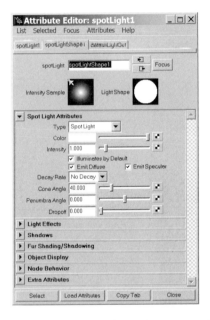

FIGURE 9.4   *Using the Attribute Editor is the easiest way to view attributes for a light.*

Tutorial: Working with Spot Light Attributes

The first attribute you're going to modify is the Cone Angle, which specifies the cone's actual width and is defined in degrees from 0.006 to 179.994. By default, the Cone Angle is set to 40. If you decrease the angle of the cone, the circular area that's lit up will decrease (see Figure 9.5). You can continue from the previous tutorial, or load the scene file noted here.

On the CD

Chapter_09\movies\ch09tut02.wmv

On the CD

Chapter_09\ch09tut01end.mb

FIGURE 9.5   *The area lit by downward-pointing Spot lights rendered from the Top view. A Cone Angle of 40 was used in the lit circle seen on the left; on the right, a Cone Angle of 25.*

1. Change the value of the Cone Angle from 40 to 60. Notice that the illuminated area increases because you increased the angle of the cone by 20 degrees.

2. Look at the edge of the area being lit. To diminish the harsh line defining the edge where the light stops, you can use the Penumbra Angle attribute. In the Attribute Editor for spotLight1, change the Penumbra Angle to -5. After the IPR updates, you can see that the edge has softened. The lighting results from the Spot light are starting to look much better. By changing a few simple settings, you now have completely different lighting.

   The Penumbra Angle can add or subtract from the Cone Angle. It softens the outer edge of the Spot light's cone. When specifying a Penumbra Angle, you're setting the angle at which the light falls off from the edge of the cone. If your Spot light has a Cone Angle of 40 and you set the Penumbra Angle to 10, the light's total spread angle will be 50 degrees (40 + 10). After the light has spread the first 40 degrees, it diminishes to darkness over the remaining 10 degrees. Simply put, the Penumbra Angle allows you to have an area intensely lit with light, but eliminates the harsh edge left by a default Spot light (see Figure 9.6). The Penumbra Angle can be set from -179.994 to 179.994 and has a default value of 0.

   The Dropoff attribute of a Spot light is similar to the Penumbra Angle, but acts from the center of the light. Therefore, you can change the softness across the entire cone (see Figure 9.7). The light starts off very bright at the center and then fades linearly to the cone's original edges. With values ranging from 0 to infinity, you can change the Dropoff attribute when the edge of the light is too solid and creates unwanted contrast. With a softer edge, you can use a Spot light without giving away its location. This gives you an opportunity to use the Spot light for general lighting as well as lighting aimed at a specific area.

FIGURE 9.6   *By raising the Penumbra Angle, the circular lit area on the right has a softer edge than the default Spot light.*

FIGURE 9.7   *By setting the Dropoff attribute to 10 in the lit circle on the right, you have a softer transition from the center lit area to the circle's edge.*

3. In the Attribute Editor for spotLight1, change the Dropoff attribute to 5. The center of interest is no longer illuminated as intensely and the area illumination seems to be more evenly distributed.

4. Render the RenderCamera view.

As you have experimented with the Spot light, you have probably noticed that you have a lot of control over aiming the light, thus allowing you to focus on a specific part of the scene. Figure 9.8 is a final render after all the attribute changes to the Spot light.

FIGURE 9.8   *The results of changing attributes for spotLight1.*

Next, for the purposes of comparison, you'll make a layer for the Spot light:

5. Create a layer for the Spot light and name it `SpotLight_L`.

6. Assign spotLight1 to the layer.

7. Take this opportunity to save the scene to your hard disk. Name the file `LightExamples`.

Other Light Types

The following tutorials walk you through the other available light types in Maya and demonstrate how to use their attributes to adjust the lighting in your scene.

Tutorial: Directional Light

The Directional light is the default light used when you create a new scene. Although this light has no special attributes, it's good for emulating the parallel rays of light coming from the sun, and does a good job of lighting the entire scene instead of just targeted areas. If you decided to skip over the first tutorial, or got lost, you can load the scene file noted next to the CD icon.

On the CD

Chapter_09\movies\ch09tut03.wmv

1. Currently, there's a layer (SpotLight_L) with spotLight1 in it. If you hide the layer, Maya will still render the light by default, so to see the effect of the Directional light by itself, you need to somehow turn the Spot light off. To do that, in the Outliner, select spotLight1. Transformation values and attributes for the Spot light should now be loaded into the Channel Box (make the Channel Box visible with **Shift+C**). In the Channel Box under Shapes, spotLightShape1, change the Visibility setting to 0, which switches it to "off" so that it doesn't illuminate the scene.

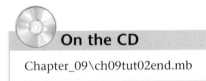

On the CD

Chapter_09\ch09tut02end.mb

2. Create a Directional light (Hotbox | Create | Lights | Directional Light). A default Directional light named directionalLight1 is placed at the scene's origin.

3. Open the Render View window (Window | Rendering Editors | Render View), and IPR render the scene with the Directional light.

> **tip**
>
> Shaded views can display geometry lit by these three methods: default lighting, all scene lighting, or selected lighting. Normally, when you begin lighting, you set shaded views to use all scene lighting (hotkey: **7**). These options appear on the Lighting menu item in each 3D panel. Remember that shaded view lighting is just a rough approximation of what the final rendered lighting will look like.

The location of the Directional light in a scene doesn't affect how objects are lit. All that matters is the angle the light is set at. Position the Directional light icon in a convenient place, scale it to a size that makes it easy to select, and rotate it to set the direction of the incoming light. For example, if it's high noon, you want the Directional light to point directly down, perpendicular to the ground.

4. Position the Render View window in a location where you can see it but still be able to modify the light. It's not easy to see the light icon because of the scene's floor plane. Confirm that the Directional light is still selected, and in the Channel Box, change Translate X to –7, Translate Y to 5, and Translate Z to 7. Rotating the light changes the angle that the light shines from, so it illuminates the scene differently. Switch to the Rotate tool (hotkey: **e**) and rotate the Directional light until the corner of the room is lit: Set Rotate X to –17 and Rotate Y to –58.

> **tip**
>
> Some people prefer to use the Light Manipulator tool to adjust the angle of rotation for a Directional light. Just press **t** and move the aim manipulator to change the rotation angle of the Directional light.

Probably the most noticeable results of the Directional light have to do with the shadows it casts. Shadows cast by a light such as a Point light vary in their angle from the object. That's just fine if you have a light source that's nearby, such as a lamp, but it won't work if you need to simulate shadows from a distant light source, such as the sun. Shadows cast from a distant object should be parallel. This is where the Directional light comes in. As a result of the Directional light shining in one specified direction and emitting light rays that are parallel to one another, the shadows are also cast in parallel (see Figure 9.9).

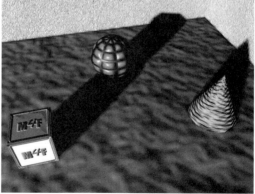

FIGURE 9.9   *The image lit with a Point light (on the left) has shadows radiating from a common point. The image lit by a Directional light (on the right) has shadows that are parallel to each other.*

5. Make sure the Directional light is selected. In the Channel Box under directionalLightShape1, change Use Depth Map Shadows setting to on (see Figure 9.10). The fast way is to type the number 1 and then press Enter, instead of typing the word on, but either method works. IPR will immediately attempt to update the addition of shadows, but will not show any. You need to IPR render again to collect data on the shadows. After IPR is set again, you'll see that the shadows the three objects cast are parallel.

6. Create a new layer and name it DirectionalLight_L. Add the Directional light to the layer, and change its Visibility setting to 0 (off) in the Channel Box.

7. Save your scene again.

Tutorial: Point Light

On the CD

Chapter_09\movies\ch09tut04.wmv

Unlike the Directional light, which has light rays that are parallel to each other, a Point light casts rays of light evenly in every direction from a point. Point lights are used for general-purpose illumination and simulating omnidirectional light sources, such as light bulbs. You can continue from the previous tutorial, or load the scene file from the Maya Fundamentals CD-ROM (see the CD icon here).

On the CD

Chapter_09\ch09tut03end.mb

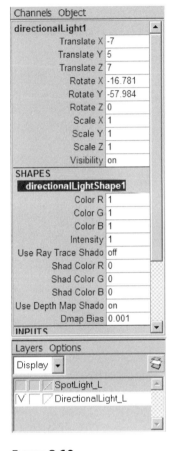

FIGURE 9.10

Enabling the Use Depth Map Shadows option in the Channel Box.

1. Create a Point light (Hotbox | Create | Lights | Point Light), which has the default name pointLight1.

2. Position pointLight1 by changing Translate Y to 3. In the Channel Box, under the pointLightShape parameters, enable the Use Depth Map Shadows option.

   Next, you'll add a light effect. Light sources have the option of having an opticalFX attribute added that can cause a particular effect to appear where the light is located. Typically, these effects are the sort that happen in cameras pointed at bright sources: lens flares, glows, and rings. When a light source is supposed to appear in the scene as a very intense object, an opticalFX flare can produce the effect convincingly.

3. Open the Attribute Editor for the Point light (hotkey: **Ctrl+a**). To add a light effect, in the PointLightShape1 tab under Light Effects, click the checkered button to the right of Light Glow. The Attribute Editor then displays a new tab called opticalFX2. Leave all the settings at their defaults for now, and keep the Attribute Editor open.

4. Render the scene from RenderCamera, and you can see that the light's origin glows. Using IPR render, you can easily use the Attribute Editor to change values for the Light Glow.

5. Experiment with the OpticalFX settings in the Attribute Editor to see their effect in the IPR render. For Figure 9.11, Glow and Halo types are set to Rim Halo, and the Lens Flare option is checked. All other values are set to default.

FIGURE 9.11   *A Point light with a Light Glow opticalFX has been positioned in the scene. Notice how the Point light emits light in every direction.*

6. Create a layer named PointLight_L and assign pointLight1 to it. Set the light's Visibility to 0 in the Channel Box, and hide the layer with the Point light.

7. Save your scene.

Tutorial: Area Light

With the release of Maya 3.0 came support for the Area light. This exciting feature enables you to have a source of light that does not just come from an infinitely small point in space. The Area light emits rays from a rectangular area in space and

On the CD

Chapter_09\movies\ch09tut05.wmv

can be scaled larger or smaller. This makes an Area light a great choice when you're looking for realistic lighting, but be forewarned that it takes longer to render. By using an Area light, you'll get shadows that soften as they're cast farther from the shadow-casting object. Maya uses only two-dimensional flat Area lights that are rectangular. You can continue from the previous tutorial, or load the scene file noted here.

1. After you have opened the file, create an Area light (Create | Lights | Area Light) with the default name areaLight1.

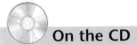

On the CD

Chapter_09\ch09tut04end.mb

2. Set Translate Y to 5 to place the light icon in the viewport. Then set Translate X to –5.5 and Translate Z to 5.5.

3. Switch to the Light Manipulator tool (hotkey: **t**), and in the Top view, position the center of interest to the back corner of the room (see Figure 9.12). Note that the Area light is above the objects and horizontally aligned.

4. Make sure the Render View window is open. With the Area light in position, make an IPR render (in the Hotbox, click Render | IPR Render Current Frame). The RenderCamera view should now be IPR rendered in the Render View window.

tip

If you think the wrong view was rendered, you can check by right-clicking in the Render View window, and then choosing IPR | IPR Render | RenderCamera. When the IPR render is complete, you'll be prompted to draw a window in the IPR image for IPR rendering to update. Select the entire image for IPR updating by marquee-selecting it.

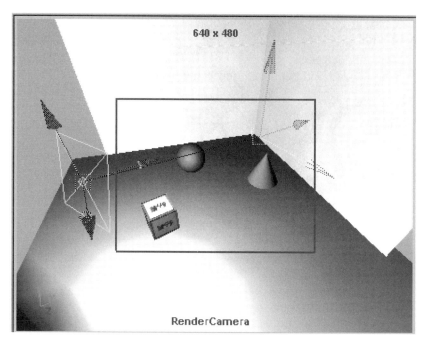

FIGURE 9.12 *Positioning areaLight1 with the center of interest at the back corner of the room.*

After IPR rendering the scene, take a look at the lighting. You can see that the light starts off very strong and then decays with distance from the light. Area lights naturally give the effect of light decay, even when the Decay Rate attribute is set to the default of No Decay. As the Area light spreads with distance, the intensity drops off because a larger area is illuminated by the same amount of light. The way you aim the Area light also varies how your scene is lit, similarly to a Spot light.

5. Using the Light Manipulator tool, with areaLight1 selected, move the center of interest to the middle of the group of objects and on the ground. The Render View window with the IPR image should quickly render again to show the moved light. The room will be more intensely lit near the front because of the angle of the light.

6. Next, try uniformly scaling (hotkey: **r**) the light smaller, to a value of about 0.5 (watch the Scale values in the Channel Box as you scale). The Area light icon in the viewport represents the light's scale. The IPR rendering will become much darker. Next, for comparison, scale the light larger, to around 2, and the IPR render will update, with the larger Area light generating far more light.

7. Again, set the Area light's Visibility to off, and then create a layer for areaLight1 with the name AreaLight_L. Add your Area light to it, and then save your scene.

Area lights can be useful for simulating the diffuse reflection of light from surfaces. This is most useful for brightly lit broad surfaces (like a ceiling) or strongly colored surfaces that reflect and tint light (a red ball near a white wall, for example). Area lights are nearly always much slower to render than the other light types, so you should use them only when necessary and can live with the loss in rendering speed. The scene file noted below the CD-ROM icon is the finished version. You might want to compare it to your final version.

 On the CD

Chapter_09\ch09tut05end.mb

Tutorial: Volume Light

Volume lights are new for Maya 4.5. This type of light has a visible range of influence that allows you to see exactly where the light dies out. By default, the light intensity falls off linearly from the center point of the light to the visible outer boundary. This type of light is ideal for interior lighting, because you will nearly always want lights to die with distance if they are primary sources of light.

 **On the CD**

Chapter_09\movies\ch09tut06.wmv

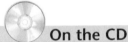 **On the CD**

Chapter_09\ch09tut05end.mb

1. Create a volume light with the default name of volumeLight1.

2. Set the Translate Y to 6 and Translate Z to 8 in the Channel Box. This should bring the volume light to the right side of the camera. However, if you render now, the image will be black. The volume light falls off to darkness before it can strike anything.

3. Switch to Scale mode (hotkey: **r**), and scale the light so that the circle circumscribes the entire scene. A scale value of about 15 will suffice.

4. Render the camera view with IPR: Hotbox | Render | IPR Render Current Frame. After the rendering completes, drag a square in the IPR render that covers the entire image.

5. Adjust the scaling of the volume light in the top view, and you can quickly see the effect in the IPR render. Note the decay of the light with distance, as shown in Figure 9.12A.

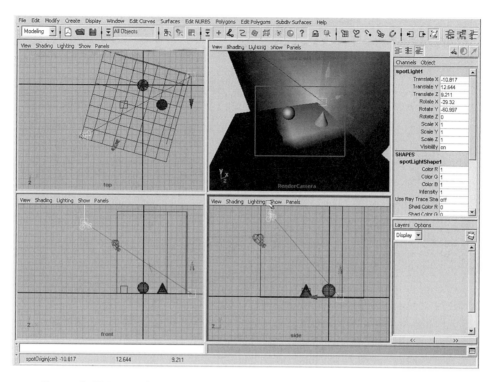

FIGURE 9.12A *Scaling the volume light to set its falloff range.*

6. Bring up the Attribute Editor while the volume light is still selected. Here you can see a number of unique variables for this light type. Under the volume light attributes, set the Light Shape to cylinder, and note that the volume light icon in the scene is now cylindrical.

7. Under color range, you'll see a gradient. The circled color dots that appear on top of the start and end of the gradient are the positioners, while the "x" boxes under the gradient allow deletion of the positioners. When a positioner is selected, the color swatch at the left of the gradient can be edited to change this point in the gradient. Clicking inside the gradient creates a new positioner. Try clicking in the center of the gradient to create a new positioner. The drag the positioner left to move this mid-gray point closer to the black end of the spectrum, as shown in Figure 9.12B. You'll see the result immediately in the IPR rendering.

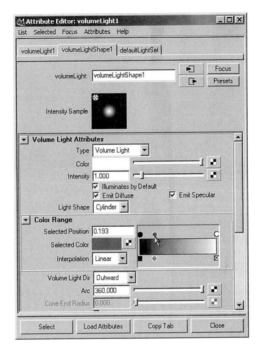

FIGURE 9.12B   *Adjusting the gradient changes the light colors as they fall off.*

8. Close IPR, set the volume light's visibility to off, and create a layer for the light named VolumeLight_L. Add your volume light to this layer and save your scene. Volume lights are excellent for simulating most man-made sources of light. You can also get a variety of bizarre and special effects by adjusting the Light Shape, the volume light direction, and the arc. Volume lights are no slower to render than point or spot lights; in most cases, you will want falloff and will therefore use the volume light in place of the point light, with the volume light shape set to spherical (to mimic the point light's omnidirectional illumination).

On the CD

Chapter_09\ch09tut06end.mb

Ambient Light

The Ambient light type creates light on all surfaces. It is in no way comparable to the real-world ambient light that creates the diffuse reflection of surfaces mentioned earlier in the chapter. Instead, it's a kind of auto–self-illumination that brightens all parts of your scene equally. For this reason, this light type should be used sparingly or for special cases only, or it will give your scene a washed-out or flat appearance.

Unique to Maya is the ability to use an Ambient light as you would a Point light. Maya's Ambient lights can also cast shadows (see Figure 9.13). In essence, these features allow you to use Ambient lights as though they were Point lights, with a variable "shine everywhere" setting. This setting is called Ambient Shade, and the light behaves more like a Point light as this value approaches 1.

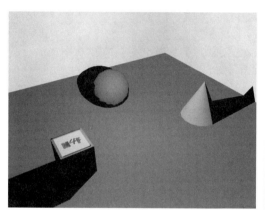 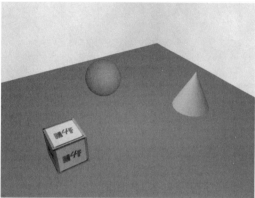

FIGURE 9.13   *Ambient lights in Maya have the option to cast shadows, but these lights shine equally on all surfaces, yielding a flat look if the Ambient light is bright.*

Shadows in Maya

Shadows in Maya can be turned on or off. The default setting for lights is to have the shadow set to off. Surfaces illuminated by the non–shadow-casting light still are shaded by it, but won't cast shadows. That means the part of an object that's exposed to light is illuminated, and the object's opposite side fades to a darker tone. It also means that the light passes through all objects, illuminating objects that are blocked by other objects.

An object's shadow can identify its size, position, and orientation in space, so by adding shadows to your scene, you can more clearly define the spatial relationships between objects. Without shadows in a scene, the render looks flat and lacks depth. Shadows add depth and realism to the scene, especially indoor scenes. Look back at Figure 9.8, and you can see that it's hard to say whether the objects are on the ground or are floating in the air between the camera and the ground!

The norm is to use only a few shadow-casting lights and many dimmer "fill" lights. Shadows require rendering time, particularly Area lights and raytraced shadows, so this guideline is partly to minimize computation. More important, however, shadows tend to wash each other out as you add more shadow-casting lights that illuminate the same area. With Maya, you have a lot of control over the way shadows are cast in a scene, which can help you reduce render times, add contrast to your renderings, and create a better-looking overall result. There are two types of shadows in Maya: depth map and raytraced shadows.

Depth Map Shadows

Depth map shadows are produced through an image map (a file with information about depth from the light's point of view). The depth map is calculated immediately before the actual render takes place. Using calculations for the distance of light to a specific point on an object, depth information is stored in the map and then passed to the rendering engine to produce a "simulated" shadow effect. The depth map tells the rendering engine which areas of the scene are illuminated by light and which aren't by specifying how far light rays will reach, stopping them as they reach points calculated from the information in the depth map.

Depth map shadows usually give good results without having to worry about a huge increase in render time. They are usually slightly softer, too, which is more natural than harsh-edged raytraced shadows. If you want, you can achieve almost the same level of sharpness as raytraced shadows (by increasing the Dmap Resolution attribute, described in the next section). The main drawback to depth map shadows is that they cannot cast soft shadows and they don't respect transparency in materials (all objects cast full shadows regardless of the transparency of their material).

Depth map shadows work in a unique way for Point, Ambient, and Area lights: Because a square bitmap is required to create shadow, and these light types cast light in all directions, they must create multiple maps to cover the area. Maya uses cubic shadow maps for these light types—that is, six shadows are cast for the six sides of a cube. This process requires six times the RAM, however, which could be a concern for large map sizes. In general, most of your shadows should be cast from Spot or Directional lights, where you can direct where the light and shadow should fall.

Depth Map Attributes

For depth map shadows, you can set the following attributes:

- **Shadow Color**   Applicable to both types of shadows in Maya. Changing the Shadow Color attribute changes the color seen in the render. It's often a good idea to bring shadow colors a little brighter than pure black, to add to the simulation of diffuse light reflection. You can also map an image file or a texture to the Shadow Color, just as you would map an image to a material, as discussed in Chapter 8, "Materials."

- **Dmap Resolution**   Specifies the resolution (accuracy) of a depth map shadow. The maps are square, so if you set this attribute to 1024, the shadow map will be produced as a 1024×1024 pixel image. At very large sizes (4096+), RAM consumption can become a problem. If your light is using a low-resolution Dmap, the shadow might have jagged edges, giving it a "step" effect (see Figure 9.14), but this is relative to the rendered image resolution. You can "fuzz up" a jagged low-resolution shadow by using a higher value for the Dmap Filter Size. Increasing the resolution also reduces the jagged effect, but creates a sharper shadow edge.

- **Dmap Filter Size**   Directly affects the edges of a depth map shadow by making them softer. This attribute, combined with the Dmap Resolution, can smoothly and gradually soften a shadow's edge. Be aware that increasing this value increases render times. Use values between 1 and 3, unless you truly need to go higher. See Figure 9.15 for a comparison of different settings.

- **Dmap Bias**   When depth map shadow–casting lights are casting long shadows, they can sometimes separate from the objects. This setting allows you to adjust the placement of the shadows, and you usually need to adjust it only for very low light angles (such as a setting sun).

FIGURE 9.14   *This depth map shadow has a very low Dmap Resolution setting, giving the shadow a jagged edge.*

FIGURE 9.15   *On the left, increasing the Dmap Resolution to 1024 defines the shadow's edge more sharply. In the middle, a low Dmap Resolution of 128 gives the shadow jagged edges. On the right, Dmap Resolution is still 128, but increasing the Dmap Filter Size to 3 smoothes the shadow's edges.*

Raytraced Shadows

Raytraced shadows are generally slower to compute, but offer the advantage of lower RAM requirements, soft shadows, and properly casting shadows for objects that are not opaque. To make raytraced shadows appear in your renderings, you must go to the Render Globals window and enable raytracing.

Like the Area light, the Spot, Directional, Ambient, and Point lights can cast area shadows. In this case, the soft shadows are created by having the light cast from a circular source. Non–Point light sources create soft shadows (known as penumbral shadows) because a variable amount of the non–Point light source is blocked as an object passes in front of the light. The light "peeks" around objects to partially illuminate the area behind them, so the shadows seem to slowly transition from pure shadow to non-shadow.

Transparent objects can affect shadows if the shadows are raytraced. However, the color values do not affect shadow color. To cast colored raytraced shadows, you must set or map the transparency color for the material. Also note that the shadows will have uniform intensity; refractive effects on light (known as caustics) are not accounted for.

Raytraced Shadow Attributes

The following list describes the attributes you'll work with when using raytraced shadows:

- **Light Radius (Shadow Radius/Light Angle)**   Sets the imaginary size of the circular Area light effect. Be aware that non-zero values for the Light Radius attribute will enable penumbral (soft) shadows, which can take much longer to render.

- **Shadow Rays**   Controls the sampling of the soft shadows. If you use a low number, the shadows will appear speckled, but render faster. This is similar to the way that Dmap Filter Size works with depth map shadows, in that increasing the Shadow Rays reduces the shadow's graininess. Unlike the Dmap Filter size, the Shadow Rays setting increases render time as you raise it, so limit the value to the bare minimum you need to get an acceptably smooth shadow (see Figure 9.16).

- **Ray Depth Limit**   This setting enables you to limit the number of times a light bounces from reflective and refractive materials. You can raise this value if you want to allow raytraced light rays to bounce around the scene before eventually creating a shadow.

FIGURE 9.16   *On the left, the default raytraced shadow. In the middle, increasing the Light Radius to 1.25 produces grainy shadow edges. On the right, Light Radius stays the same, but increasing Shadow Rays to 10 reduces the graininess.*

Area Light Shadows

If you set Area lights to cast raytraced shadows, the shadows are calculated from the rectangular Area light icon, based on its size. The results are similar to circular Area lights. As with circular Area lights, more Shadow Rays soften the shadow, but result in substantially longer render times.

Tutorial: Working with Shadows

You can continue from the previous tutorial, or load the scene file noted here.

1. First turn the spotLight1 light on by selecting it in the Outliner and switching the Visibility to on in the Channel Box. In the Attribute Editor for spotLight1, expand the shadows section. Under Depth Map Shadow Attributes, select the Use Depth Map Shadows check box.

2. Render the RenderCamera view to see the shadows you created (see Figure 9.17).

On the CD

Chapter_09\movies\ch09tut07.wmv

On the CD

Chapter_09\ch09tut06end.mb

note   IPR can give you instant feedback on changes to materials and light values, but cannot respond to some changes in shadows, including resolution. If you're changing a shadow value and not getting a visible change, try IPR rendering again.

FIGURE 9.17   *Depth map shadows have been enabled for the Spot light in the scene.*

3. In the Attribute Editor, change the Dmap Resolution from the default 512 to 128. Do an IPR render and marquee-select the image, and you'll notice jagged edges on the shadows. Keep in mind that IPR rendering won't update Dmap Resolution changes, but it will update the Dmap Filter Size changes in the next step.

4. Change the Dmap Filter Size to 3. The shadows cast by the objects are now softened to have no visible "steps."

   Next, you'll explore raytraced shadows.

5. With the Spot light still selected and the Attribute Editor open, under Depth Map Shadow Attributes, deselect the Use Depth Map Shadows check box. The IPR render should update to remove the shadows.

6. Open the Raytrace Shadow Attributes section in the Attribute Editor, and select the Use Ray Trace Shadows check box to create raytraced shadows. Looking at the IPR render, you'll see that it hasn't updated for the new shadows (just like the depth map shadows). Right-click in the Render View window, and choose Options | Render Globals. Scroll down the Render Globals window until you see Raytracing Quality. Select the Raytracing check box to turn on rendering for all raytraced parts of the scene. Raytracing Quality gives you some control over how much information is calculated for raytracing. This applies not only to shadows, but also light refractions and reflections.

7. Close the Render Globals window, and check the IPR render. It still isn't updated! Click the IPR Render button again. If you look at the Help Line, you will see this message: Error: // IPR does not support raytracing. Turn off raytracing in Render Globals and select a new region. // This explains why the IPR render doesn't work. You'll have to perform a typical render to see the raytracing in action.

8. Click the Render button in the Render View window. The render will probably take a bit longer than when you rendered with a depth map shadow. When it's done, you can actually see the shadows! The shadows have very defined edges, but that isn't the only difference. Notice any changes in the ground and the objects? The shadows for objects with bump maps have also changed.

9. Change the Light Radius to 1.25 in the Attribute Editor. Render again, and notice that the shadow seems softer at the edges. Look closely and notice that the shadow has a speckled edge. If you have a really good eye, you probably saw that the graininess increases the farther the shadow is from the object.

10. Next, you'll fix the grainy edge on the shadow. Just under the Light Radius in the Attribute Editor, you will see Shadow Rays. Change the value to 10. Render your scene once more, but prepare to wait a lot longer to get shadows without the graininess.

These tutorials have shown you the basics of light and shadow setup. Next you'll look at some of the other light controls.

On the CD

Chapter09\ch09tut07end.mb

Common Light Attributes

At the top of the Attribute Editor for lights is a set of values we haven't discussed yet: Color, Intensity, and toggles for Specular, Diffuse, and Illuminates by Default. You'll use these attributes frequently to adjust a light's intensity and appearance.

Intensity

A light's Intensity attribute controls the brightness of the source. You can set it to any value, positive or negative. If the intensity is raised, more light is emitted from the source (see Figure 9.18). Usually, you set the value between 0 and 1 for a medium-intensity fill light. For sunlight effects, you might go as high as 1.5 or so. With Decay Rate added (described later in this section), the light's Intensity might need to be set much higher because the strength can fall off rapidly with distance. By default, all Maya lights have no decay rate (although the Area light gives the impression of light decay), and illuminate objects at the light's full intensity, regardless of distance.

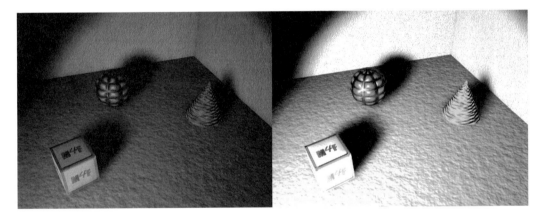

FIGURE 9.18   *By changing the Intensity from 1 to 3, the room looks much brighter and the shadows remain fully dark.*

You can also use negative values for the Intensity attribute. By setting a negative value, the light actually "absorbs" other light. If you have an area of the scene that you want to be pitch-black but light is illuminating it, you can use a light with negative Intensity to help eliminate the problem.

Illuminates by Default

By default, lights automatically illuminate all the objects in the scene. When you disable the Illuminates by Default check box, the light is removed from the defaultLightSet and affects only objects it is linked to. Light linking is handled in the

Relationship Editor for lights (Window | Relationship Editors | Light Linking). In this dialog box, you can select a light and then choose which objects it illuminates (see Figure 9.19). The "active" objects that will be illuminated are highlighted in gray on the right side of the dialog box.

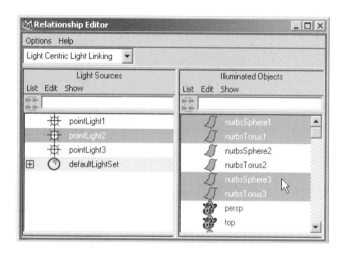

FIGURE 9.19   *Setting up light linking in the Relationship Editor.*

Emit Diffuse and Emit Specular

In special cases, a light can emit only diffuse or specular shading (see Figure 9.20). The Emit Diffuse and Emit Specular check boxes appear in the attributes for the light near the top. The Emit Diffuse and Emit Specular attributes are not available with Ambient lights. Using Emit Diffuse only is particularly useful for creating soft fill lights to simulate light reflection; you need to disable the Emit Specular attribute so that no highlights are generated. Alternatively, enabling only Emit Specular can be useful for lighting metal objects (such as chrome logos) when you want to add specular highlights to the metal without brightening other areas.

FIGURE 9.20   *The leftmost object is lit by a normal light that emits specular and diffuse components. The center shows specular only and the right shows diffuse only.*

Color

Each light can have its own color assigned, and modifying color for a light follows the same procedure and uses the same Color Chooser dialog box you see when modifying color for a material. You can also map textures to a light's color, causing the light to project the texture like a slide projector or a movie projector, if you animate the variables or use a movie as the source.

Decay Rate

Specific to Spot, Area, and Point lights, this attribute determines the rate at which the light intensity fades (decreases) at a distance. Several types of decay are available in the Attribute Editor's Decay Rate list box. The following list describes some settings to try:

- **No Decay**   The light does not diminish with distance; it reaches all objects in the scene.

- **Linear**   The intensity of emitted light decreases at a constant (linear) rate as distance from the light source increases. Linear decay is the most frequently used type because it's easier to control; you don't need to raise the light's Intensity attribute to enormously high values to compensate.

- **Quadratic**   The physically accurate mode of decay, also known as inverse square. Quadratic decay is determined by proportionally decreasing the light intensity along the square of the distance. Light intensity generally must be raised substantially with this mode.

- **Cubic**   Decreases the intensity of light faster than the rate seen in reality. Cubic Decay is evaluated by a decrease in intensity that's relatively proportional with the cube of the distance. The lit area falls off almost instantly with Cubic Decay. This type of decay can be used to have a lit area that seems as though it's burning within surrounding darkness. Light intensity must generally be raised to a very high value to make the light appear.

tip   IPR rendering is helpful for interactively adjusting light decay; it's hard to visualize otherwise.

Tutorial: Lighting the House

In this tutorial, you'll add some lights to illuminate the house you textured in the last chapter. Load the scene file noted here.

On the CD

Chapter_09\movies\ch09tut08.wmv

1. First, select all the lights in the Outliner and delete them to start with a fresh slate.

2. Create an overhead light for the scene (Create | Light | Directional Light). Name it toplight in the Channel Box, and then set Translate X, Y, and Z to -25, 1440, and -20. Then set Rotate X, Y, and Z to -270, -50, and -180 so that the light points down on the scene. Set Scale X, Y, and X to 500 so that you can easily see the icon. Open the Attribute Editor, and set the Intensity attribute to 0.2. Expand the Shadows section, and enable the Depth Map Shadows option. Set the Dmap Resolution to 1024. Disable Dmap Auto Focus so the shadows don't shift as the camera's viewpoint travels. Set the Width to 400 so that the shadow area covers the house.

3. Next, you'll create some fill lights. Create a Spot light (Create | Light | Spot Light), and rename it as front_fill. Set Translate X, Y, and Z to 3200, 570, and -1550; Rotate X, Y, and Z to 175, 64, and 180; and Scale X, Y, and Z to 500 so that you can easily see the icon. Open the Attribute Editor and deselect the Emit Specular check box so that this fill light doesn't cause highlights on objects. Set Intensity to 0.2 and Cone Angle to 90.

4. Repeat Step 3, but name the light side_fill and set its Translate X, Y, and Z to -2100, 830, and -2600 and its Rotate X, Y, and Z to 167, -38, and 180. In the Attribute Editor, set Intensity to 0.25 and Dropoff to 2 to get a gradient effect in this light.

5. Create a new Directional light and name it main_light. Set Translate X, Y, and Z to 2200, 980, and 2000 and Rotate X, Y, and Z to -16, 47, and 0. In the Attribute Editor, click the color swatch and set this light to a slightly bluish color to look like nighttime lighting (HSV: 230, .06, 0.85). Enable the Depth Map Shadows option and set Dmap Resolution to 2048. Disable Dmap Auto Focus and set the Width to 8000 so that its shadows cover the entire scene. Note that if you have limited RAM, you may need to set the shadow sizes for toplight and mainlight, currently 1024 and 2048. You can lower them to 512 and 1024 or lower if your system runs out of RAM while rendering.

    Now all the lights are in place and you can render a test frame. We've used a night lighting style for the spooky house. It's not as dark as it would be in a true nighttime scene; we've intentionally brought the light level up enough to be able to see the surroundings better. This is similar to movie makers shooting "day for night" at twilight, because true night is too dark to see anything.

    Another touch you can add to the scene is a glowing moon in the night sky. To add it, you'll make a Point light that does not shine, but uses OpticalFX to create a glowing orb in the sky.

6. Create a Point light by choosing Create | Lights | Point Light. In the Channel Box, change its name to moon-glow, and set Translate X, Y, and Z to -7500, 1500, and -4000. Open the Attribute Editor (hotkey: **Ctrl+a**). Deselect the Emit Diffuse, Emit Specular, and Illuminates by Default check boxes so that the light creates no actual light.

7. Next, in the Light Effects panel, click the checkered button to the right of the Light Glow attribute to add an optical called OpticalFX1 to the light. For the optical effect, set the Glow Type to None and the Halo Type to Exponential. In the Halo Attributes section, you can adjust the color to light blue (HSV: 230, .3, 1) and set the Halo Intensity and Halo Spread to 0.5. Select the Ignore Light check box, and close the Attribute Editor.

8. Next, you need to make sure this light is not outside the camera's far clipping plane. Select the Camera view, choose View | Camera Attribute Editor on the menu, and set the Far Clip Plane to 50000. This setting ensures that the faraway light is still within the camera's renderable view. The "moon" FX light needs to be far away to ensure that the camera doesn't show its position changing in relation to the viewer's movements (thus reducing the effect of "parallax"). The real moon is far enough away that it looks the same from any point on earth, so you don't want your virtual moon to shift position and give away its nearness too easily.

At this point, you should have a nice, spooky night effect when you render, as shown in Figure 9.21. Load the scene from the CD if you'd like to compare.

 On the CD

Chapter_09\ch09tut08end.mb

Going Further

Try adding lights to the scene with the character you modeled in Chapter 7, "Modeling with Polygons," and then rendering the scene. Lighting a character can be a lot of fun and can make a good model look spectacular. Adding lights not only illuminates objects in your scene, but also helps define the shape of the model. Using the basics you have learned in this chapter, you should be able to efficiently light your character. Try using the three-point lighting method discussed in Chapter 1, "Pre-Maya: A Primer" (see Figure 9.22).

FIGURE 9.21   *The rendered house scene with the lights added.*

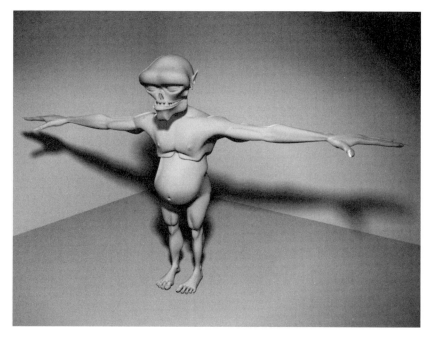

FIGURE 9.22   *The creature from Chapter 7 has been lit with three-point lighting.*

Summary

Lighting, hand in hand with materials, determines the final look of your rendering. Learning how to create and edit lighting helps you improve the quality of the renders you produce. In this chapter, you've learned the following basics:

- **The different types of lights**   You now understand the differences between Spot, Ambient, Point, Directional, and Area lights and know how the lights function.

- **Positioning lights in the scene**   Working with lights is similar to working with normal objects in Maya. With the Light Manipulator tool, you can easily control the light's pivot and center of interest.

- **Basic attributes for lights**   You can change many light attributes in Maya. By practicing with these attributes, you'll be able to predict the result of changing a value, thus saving time when trying to light your scene.

- **Raytraced and Depth Map shadows**   Understanding the two different shadow types helps you decide where they would be best used.

- **The value of IPR rendering**   Speed is an issue when you're working on an animation. With IPR rendering, you can quickly see the results of changes you have made to a scene's lighting.

CHAPTER 10

Animation Basics

In This Chapter

The most complex task in animation is the animation itself. Adding the fourth dimension of time takes the art form to a state where it's hard to make a single sketch or form a single thought to plan your animated idea. Animation requires a new kind of thinking—about motion, timing, and smoothness for a given action. It's probably where Maya most excels as a 3D tool, and in this book, unfortunately we have space to introduce you to only the fundamental aspects of animation.

Displaying several still images in sequence is what gives the illusion of motion. And just as you have been able to render still images in past chapters, you can render multiple images in sequence with the computer set to change one or more values as each image in the sequence is rendered.

When we speak of animation, there's more to animate than simple movement. Virtually anything in Maya with a number attached can be animated. Oceans can turn to wood, gravity can be inverted, and objects can tie themselves into knots. A lot of possibilities—and, therefore, a lot of complexity. We'll break down the basics of setting up, evaluating, and editing an animation, including:

- **The animation interface**   You'll learn where to find animation tools in the Maya interface and how to work with them efficiently.

- **Understanding the different types of animation**   See how the different animation types work to decide which one is best for your scene.

- **Setting up for animations**   Learn what steps you need to take before animating a scene.

- **Working with animation keys and curves**　You'll learn how to work with the Graph Editor to modify settings for animation keys and adjust animation curves.

- **Continue working with your house**　Continuing from previous chapters, you are going to animate portions of the house you have created.

- **Using the Playblast**　Learn how to use this tool to quickly judge the results of your animation efforts.

Key Terms

key　A marker that designates an attribute's value for an object at a specific point in time.

keyframe　An animation frame containing a key that has been set for an object.

keyframe-based animation　Using keys to schedule when and where events take place in the animation; these events are typically an object's "extreme" points, such as a fully extended arm and a fully flexed arm, and the computer takes care of smoothly animating the position during the time in between.

key tangent　The acceleration or deceleration of a value as you approach or leave a keyframe. Animating objects involves not only how they move, but also how the motion changes with time.

animation curve　The visual representation of the connections between keys for the same attribute; modified by adjusting the tangents for the curve in the Graph Editor.

auto keyframe　A feature that tells Maya to set a key each time an attribute's value changes, after you have manually set an initial key.

path animation　Attaching an object to a curved path to control that object's movement.

nonlinear animation　An advanced animation method that uses "clips" of animation keys on a timeline to layer and blend animation sequences independently of time. For example, a walking clip could be added over a drinking clip to get a character that drinks and walks.

Graph Editor　A tool for modifying keys and animation curves in Maya.

frame rate　Defines how many frames will be played in a period of one second; measured in frames per second (fps).

playback range　Tells Maya to play the animation from a specified starting frame to a specified ending frame.

Playblast　Maya's quick-shaded animation previewer.

Hotkeys to Memorize

Alt+v   play or stop the animation

Esc   stop playback of animation

Alt+. (period)   go to next frame

Alt+, (comma)   go to previous frame

. (period)   go to next keyframe

, (comma)   go to previous keyframe

Shift+R   set key for Scale attribute

Shift+W   set key for Translate attribute

Shift+E   set key for Rotate attribute

s   set a key at the current frame

Shift+A   frame all curves in the Graph view

The Animation Tools and Interface

Before jumping into the animation process, you should review the interface and tools that are available to you. The following sections will help you get familiar with the interface so that you can find the attributes and functions you need for animation.

Setting Up an Animation

Before you create any animation in a scene, you need to configure some standard settings. Two components of Maya's user interface are specific to animation: the Range Slider and the Time Slider. To make sure they are displayed, click Hotbox | Hotbox Controls to open a marking menu with several options for the user interface (see Figure 10.1). Use this marking menu to display the Range Slider and Time Slider in your Maya interface.

The Range Slider and Animation Preferences

Figure 10.2 shows the Range Slider with its controls. The Range Slider is used to set the total length of the animation in frames. You can also use the Range Slider to temporarily limit the range of playback and set the playback start and end frames. In the figure, frames 60–120 are focused on. After this segment has been edited, the range bar can be moved to another focus area or pulled out to show the entire animation.

Another way to control settings for your animation is to use the Preferences dialog box. To open it, click the Animation Preferences button at the far right of the Range Slider (refer to Figure 10.2) or choose Window | Settings/Preferences | Preferences on the menu. Before making any changes, reset all settings in the dialog box to defaults (Edit | Restore Default Settings). Feel free to hide the Shelf and Tool Box to minimize clutter in the Maya interface.

You use the Preferences dialog box, shown in Figure 10.3, to change values for the animation timeline and playback. You can also set the total time for your animation, the size of the timeline (the Time Slider), and other related features.

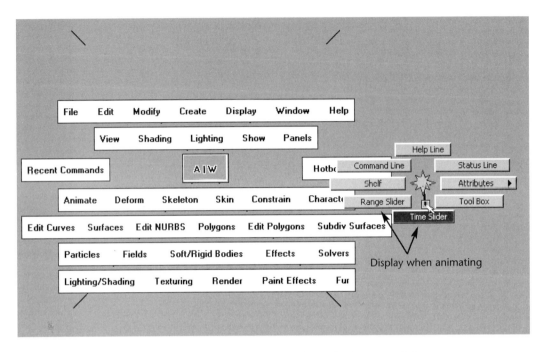

FIGURE 10.1   *Use the Hotbox to quickly toggle displaying parts of the user interface.*

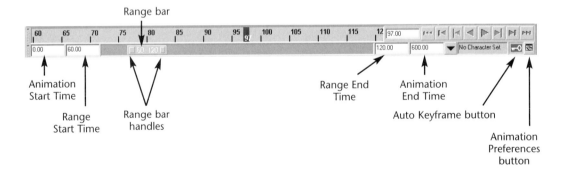

FIGURE 10.2   *Use the Range Slider to control animation length and limit playback to specific ranges.*

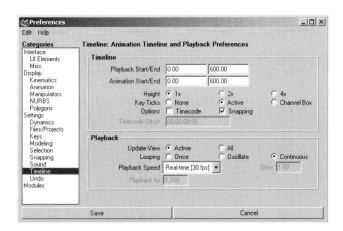

FIGURE 10.3   *Use the Preferences dialog box to specify the length of your animation and the playback speed in the viewports.*

Specifying the Frame Rate

Specifying the frame rate is the first aspect of setting up your animation. The frame rate affects the length and fluidity of your animation. By default, Maya sets your animation to Film, which plays at 24 fps. Every second of your animation, therefore, plays through 24 frames. You can see that a few minutes of animation quickly adds up to thousands of rendered images!

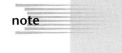

note

For animation that will be put on videotape, you typically use 30 fps in the United States and 25 fps in some other countries. NTSC (National Television Standards Committee) is a 30 fps standard developed in North America for television broadcasting. Western European and other countries use PAL (Phase Alternate Line), with a 25 fps standard. Render resolutions are also different for the two formats.

Setting the Range

The range of an animation determines the total length in frames. When determining the range, you need to decide how long you want the animation to last in seconds. Then multiply the animation's length in seconds by the frame rate (in this case, 30 fps). The animation you create in this chapter will be 20 seconds long, so you would use this calculation:

30 fps × 20 seconds = 600 frames (animation range)

The Time Slider

The Time Slider is a vital part of the animation interface in Maya. Figure 10.4 illustrates its available functions. You can use the Time Slider to play your animation, to set it to a particular frame, and even to see animation keys and where they are placed.

Click in the Time Slider area and drag left and right to "scrub" the animation back and forward in time. A black vertical line indicates the current frame. When keys have been set for the currently selected object, thin vertical red lines appear in the Time Slider area to indicate the times for those keys. In the playback controls, buttons for going forward one key or back one key are available to easily hop from key to key.

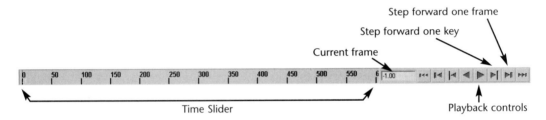

FIGURE 10.4   *The Time Slider and its controls.*

Types of Animation

You can use several different methods to animate your scene. Each method has advantages and disadvantages, of course, so before deciding which method to use, let's quickly review in the following sections what each method is capable of.

Path Animation

You got a glimpse of path animation in Chapter 4, "Diving In: Your First Animation." Generally, in this method, you create a NURBS-based curve and then attach it to an object in your scene (in Chapter 4, the object was the boat). The object then follows the curved path to simulate motion. You can choose at which time the object is positioned at any point along the path, so the object can reverse itself, pause, or oscillate, if you want. You'll revisit this method in Chapter 12, "Cameras and Rendering," to fly the camera along a path toward the house.

Nonlinear Animation

Nonlinear animation (known in Maya as the Trax Editor) is a more advanced method of animation. Unlike keyframing, nonlinear animation is completely independent of time. You blend and layer animation sequences—called clips—to set up the motion for characters. A character is a defined set of related objects you specify in Maya (see Figure 10.5). A timeline lets you drop clips of animation in wherever you like and blends clips that overlap. In addition, you can stretch or shrink clips to make the animation keys within them occur faster or slower.

You can also use this method to explore variations in parts of the animation without losing your previous work or affecting other parts of the animation. For example, if you want a character to run rather than walk, you can make the walking part of the animation a clip and then adjust the leg motion without affecting the way the rest of the character moves. If you're satisfied with the changes to the leg motion, you can make that running motion a clip and blend it with the rest of the character's animation without losing your previous work on the character. The Trax Editor is explored in more detail in Chapter 11, "Character Animation."

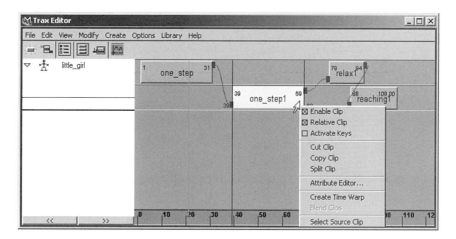

FIGURE 10.5   *Trax allows you to add and blend motion clips and poses at any point in your timeline—a novel way to build animation.*

Keyframe Animation

Keyframe animation is the standard animation method, and the one you'll use in this chapter. In this method, you set keys for an object's extreme positions and let the computer fill in the in-between motion. For instance, if you're animating an arm that will bend, you set a key with the arm fully extended and another key with the arm in a flexed position. Maya then fills in the motion—known as the *in-betweens*—between the two extremes. Keyframing also depends on time. Simply put, a key is an anchor point for a particular attribute at a designated time. When the animation reaches that specified time, the object's attribute will be at the value you set (keyed).

When preparing an animation, generally you specify the range first, as you did in the previous section. You can then place keys for numeric values throughout the range by using the Channel Box or hotkeys. As you set keys, you specify the time at which those changes in the attribute's value take place.

To set keys with the auto keyframe method, you click the Auto Keyframe button in the Range Slider (it turns red to indicate it's enabled). The idea with auto keyframing is that anything that changes creates a key. With auto keyframing, you can animate quickly by simply dragging the Time Slider to a given frame and then changing an attribute. However, you must set one initial keyframe on an attribute for the auto keyframe method to "activate" for that attribute.

 note   Maya offers the option to change an attribute based on other keyed attributes. This is called set driven key animation (discussed in Chapter 15, "Your Next Steps: Efficiency and Artistry"). For example, you could tie a bouncing ball's motion to the intensity of the light shining on it, so that the ball is more brightly lit when it bounces to its highest point.

Tutorial: The House Is Alive

To see how keyframe animation works, you're going to bring your house to life. In this tutorial, you'll key specific attributes for a bend deformer. We've already applied the bend deformer so that you'll get reliable results in this tutorial. The bend deformer lets you twist the house into different shapes to create the effect of a kind of haunted house. You'll start by loading the scene file noted below the CD icon. This scene contains your fully textured house with the lighting added and includes the imported objects on the Maya Fundamentals CD-ROM—in particular, the ground object that provides a landscape for the house to sit on.

On the CD

Chapter_10\movies\ch10tut01.wmv

1. Use the Preferences dialog box to change the actual frame rate used for your animation. In the Categories list, click Settings to display the General Application Preferences. Under Working Units, in the Time list box, select NTSC (30 fps).

On the CD

Chapter_10\ch10tut01start.mb

2. In the Categories list in the Preferences dialog box, select Timeline again. Under the Timeline section, change the Animation Start/End frames to 1 and 600; the Range Slider will be updated accordingly. Next, go down to the Playback section. In the Playback Speed list box, select Real-Time (30 fps). That means when you click the Play button in the playback controls (on the Time Slider), the active viewport regulates itself to play the animation at 30 fps. That is, it will skip frames if necessary to keep pace. To finalize the changes, click the Save button at the bottom of the dialog box.

3. There's one problem, however. If you play the scene (hotkey: **Alt+v**), you'll find that it stops and loops short of 600 frames because you never changed the specified playback range. You can change it directly in the Range Slider, though: Enter 600 in the Range End Time text box.

4. Change your current layout to the Persp/Outliner saved layout (Panels | Saved Layouts | Persp/Outliner). To make it easier to work with your scene, in the Layer Editor, hide all the layers except for OuterWallsL, ChimneyL, WindowsL, InnerWallL, DoorL, RoofL, and PorchL. Next, press **5** to enter Shaded mode.

5. Next, you need to select the deformer you're going to add keys to. In the Outliner, expand the Old_House group, and select House_Bend in that group. In the Inputs section of the Channel Box, click on bend1 to display the attributes you'll be working with for animation.

tip

The scene is quite complex at this point. If interaction seems sluggish in the Perspective view, try selecting all the objects and decreasing their level of detail by pressing **1**.

6. Using the Time Slider, set your current frame to 1. Click the Auto Keyframe button in the Range Slider to enable automatic keyframing. Under bend1 in the Channel Box, RMB-click on Curvature, and choose Key Selected to set the starting key. Now a keyframe will be set every time the Curvature value is changed. Attributes that have been keyed are represented in the Channel Box with a shaded (orange by default) text box. Look at frame 1 in the Time Slider to see the red bar representing the key that has been set.

7. With a key set at frame 1, drag on the Time Slider and you will see a slider move across it, indicating the change in frame. Drag the slider to frame 150, or just type 150 in the Current Frame text box.

8. In the Channel Box, change the Curvature to 0.6 to set another key. Go to frame 350 in the Time Slider, and change Curvature to -0.5 in the Channel Box. Then go to frame 400, and set Curvature to 0. Continue setting keys: At frame 450, set Curvature to -0.2; at frame 530, set Curvature to 0.5; and at frame 600, set Curvature to 0.3. When you're finished, click the Auto Keyframe button in the Range Slider again to turn off auto keyframing.

9. Change your animation's current frame to frame 1 by using the playback controls next to the Time Slider or by entering 1 in the Current Frame text box. Play the animation (hotkey: **Alt+v**) and watch as the house bends back and forth. Press Alt+v again to stop the animation. Everything moves fine, but some parts of the animation seem to be jerky. In the next section, you'll work with the Graph Editor to smooth out the animation. Before going any further, save your scene as ch10HouseAnimation.

Using the Graph Editor

The Graph Editor, shown in Figure 10.6, is a helpful tool for tweaking values for keys you have set. It gives you a visual representation—a curved line—of the attributes that are animated. The animation time goes from left to right, and any keyed variable appears as a line that moves up or down to indicate its value over time. It can help you visualize how things are changing and how fast. You can pan and zoom this panel like any other.

You can use the Graph Editor as a free-floating window or set it up as one of the viewports. To use it as a free-floating window, simply open it from the Hotbox (Window | Animation Editors | Graph Editor). To set it up in a viewport that displays the Perspective view and the Outliner, click Hotbox | Panels | Saved Layouts | Persp/Outliner/Graph. As you go through the next tutorial, try both layouts to see which one works better for you.

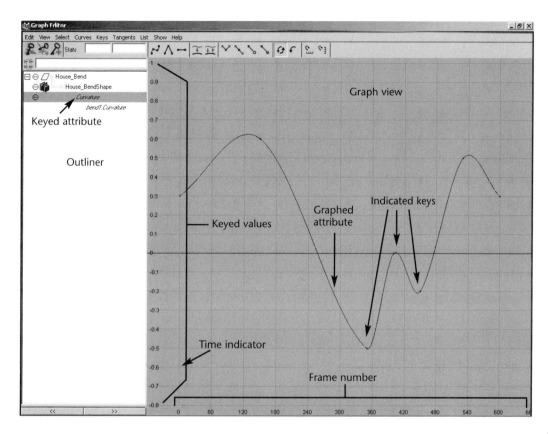

FIGURE 10.6   *You can easily work with keys in the Graph Editor.*

Let's take a brief tour through the Graph Editor's components in the following list:

- **Menu bar**   The menu bar (see Figure 10.7) contains all the commands you typically need to work with the Graph Editor. The Edit menu is much like the one in text editors or word processors, except that you're working with keys instead of text.

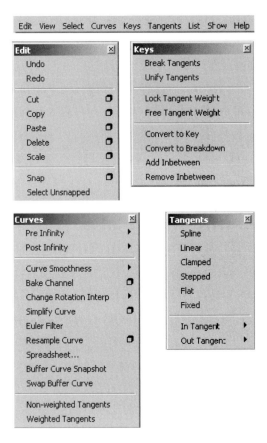

FIGURE 10.7   *The Graph Editor's menus for basic edit functions, keys, animation curves, and tangents.*

The Curves menu gives you control over how the curves are set up with the keys in your scene. For example, you can set certain keyframes to cycle over and over. To work directly with a specific key in the Graph view, you use the Keys menu. You use the Tangents menu to tell the keys how to react with the animation curve at specific keyframes.

- **Toolbar**   The toolbar (see Figure 10.8) gives you quick access to functions for modifying animation curves and keys.

- **Outliner**   The Graph Editor Outliner has the same basic function of the Outliner you have been using throughout the book. In the Graph Editor, you use it to select attributes for objects that have keys set. Keyed attributes are formatted in italics for easy identification.

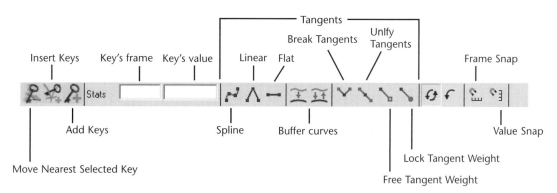

FIGURE 10.8   *The toolbar provides quick access to commonly used features of the Graph Editor.*

- **Graph view**   This section is used to display the keys, animation curves, and tangents. You can interactively adjust the displayed curves by using the typical manipulation tools (select, move, and scale). You can also use these tools to modify keys you have set. Curves are displayed with the frame number on the X axis and the numeric keyed value on the Y axis.

tip

> The Dope Sheet is another animation editor in Maya that is similar to the Graph Editor. Instead of displaying curves, the Dope Sheet displays key times as colored rectangles and lets you edit event timing and sync motion to a sound file.

Tutorial: Tweaking Keys with the Graph Editor

This tutorial gives you a chance to work with the Graph Editor. If you like, you can load the previous tutorial's scene file (see the file below the CD icon) to make sure everything's set up correctly.

1. Click Hotbox | Panels | Saved Layouts | Persp/Graph/Outliner to set up your layout. Make sure the current frame is set to 1 (the beginning of the animation) in the Time Slider. Hide the PorchL and ChimneyL layers in the Layer Editor. You don't need them now, and they'll just slow down the animation playback.

On the CD

Chapter_10\movies\ch10tut02.wmv

On the CD

Chapter_10\ch10tut01end.mb

2. In the Outliner, select the Old_House group, and click the + to expand the group. House_Bend is automatically selected, and the Graph view in the Graph Editor changes to display the animation curves for the keys you set in the previous tutorial.

3. Before editing the keys, make some changes to the Graph Editor so that it's easier to work with the curves. If needed, frame the entire curve in the Graph view by choosing View | Frame All on the Graph Editor menu bar (hotkey: **Shift+A**).

4. Each key you set is represented by a small dot along the curve. The pointed curves indicate areas with sudden reversals in direction. Play your animation (hotkey: **Alt+v**) and watch the Graph view. As the animation progresses, a red bar displaying the current frame slides across the Graph view. Play the animation again and watch the Perspective viewport and the Graph view to see how the house reacts at specific points on the curve. Checking both views is an efficient way to pinpoint problems with the animation.

5. To make the house animate more smoothly, you'll use the Graph Editor to adjust the keys and change the tangents. Click anywhere on the curve. It turns white and displays handles attached to each keyframe. These handles represent the key's tangent in relation to the curve (see Figure 10.9).

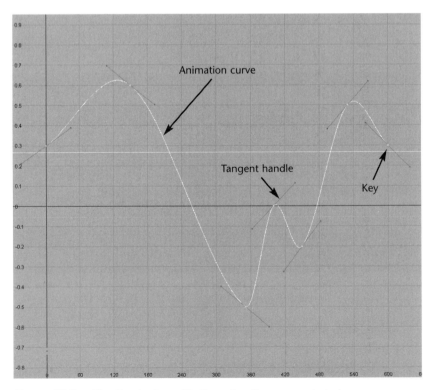

FIGURE 10.9   *The Graph view with the animation curve selected.*

6. First, you'll change the tangent for one of the keys. Marquee-select the third key at frame 350. The frame and value for the selected key are displayed on the toolbar. The tangent handles are turned at an angle, but you'll get a smoother transition if you position them horizontally. To do this, click the Flat button (refer back to Figure 10.8) or choose Tangents | Flat on the Graph Editor menu, and the handle rotates so that it's horizontal to the X axis. The animation curve changes in response, resulting in a smoother transition in and out of the key (see Figure 10.10).

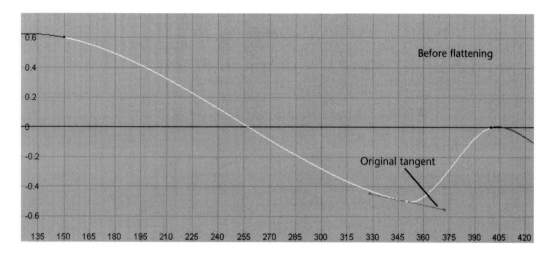

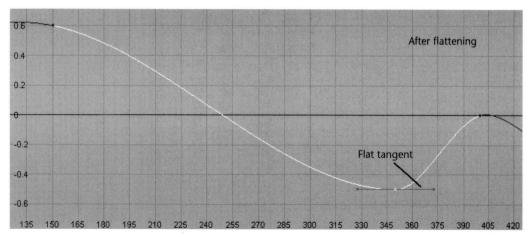

FIGURE 10.10   *The animation curve and tangent handle before and after flattening.*

You might have expected to see a more dramatic change in the animation curve after adjusting the tangent. The change in the animation curve's line is subtle in the Graph Editor, but the effects on the animation will be noticeable.

You can set several types of tangents for your keys. Feel free to experiment with them to see how they work. For example, you can click the Break Tangents button so that you can grab each side of the handle and move it independently. This creates a break, or *cusp*, in the line that equates to a sharp, jerky change in motion at the frame of that key.

7. Flattening the tangent means that the curve won't exceed the value set for the keyframe. If you look back to the Before section of Figure 10.10, you can see the dot for the key and how the curve extends past this point by a small amount. However, we were animating with the idea that the keys were set to represent the extremes. Click anywhere on the curve and then click the Flat button again to make all the handles horizontal. Play the animation again, and notice that it runs more smoothly.

8. To smooth the animation even more, you can adjust the keys with the standard manipulator tools. Use the Move tool (hotkey: **w**) and MMB-drag the keys to change their positions so that they are spaced more evenly; this makes transitions in the animation less abrupt. Use Figure 10.11 as a guide to what your final curve should look like. When you are satisfied with the animation curve and your animation, save your scene.

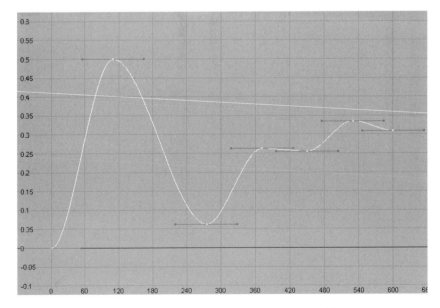

FIGURE 10.11   *Tweaking the animation curve, tangents, and keys.*

tip   If you want to insert more keys to try smoothing the animation more, simply click the Insert Keys button on the Graph Editor's toolbar and MMB-click in the Graph view.

Playblasting Your Animation

Playing your animation in the Perspective view gives you a rough idea of what your animation is going to look like. However, even the fastest computer and 3D graphics card can become bogged down and fail to display the animation smoothly at the frame rate you want. In some cases, hiding objects or setting the display quality lower can compensate. However, sometimes this isn't enough, and you must create a compiled movie of the frames to see the animation play smoothly at the target rate. Rendering the entire animation would give you this compiled movie, but it could take hours. Maya provides a faster method: the Playblast feature.

Tutorial: Using Playblast

The Playbast works by taking a screen shot, frame by frame, from a particular viewport, and then playing them back in sequence as a compiled movie. The result is an accurate interpretation of your animation's timing at final render. Playblasting can help you identify areas of your animation that might be off in timing. Follow these steps to try it out:

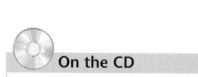

On the CD

Chapter_10\movies\ch10tut03.wmv

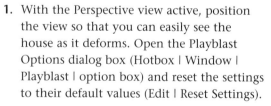

On the CD

Chapter_10\ch10tut02end.mb

1. With the Perspective view active, position the view so that you can easily see the house as it deforms. Open the Playblast Options dialog box (Hotbox | Window | Playblast | option box) and reset the settings to their default values (Edit | Reset Settings).

2. You'll notice that the Scale value is set to 0.50. Click the Playblast button. The Perspective view displays at half (50%) of normal size, and you can see the animation being played back one frame at a time. During this process, each of the animation frames is captured and stored to a buffer.

 Maya is relying on your 3D graphics card to calculate the images. If you cover the Maya interface with another window to do something else while the Playblast renders, your video card will not attempt to draw the images, and you won't have a movie to watch! You must leave the Playblast window open and unobscured while Playblast calculates.

3. When the playblast ends, your default media player opens and plays back the animation. Use this playback to decide whether you are happy with the way your house moves. If you find any problems, go back to the Graph Editor and make changes as needed.

4. Remember to save your scene again after making any changes.

 Because it takes time to evaluate your animation before you can edit it, it's essential that you keep your system responsive. Adopt the philosophy of "divide and conquer." Hide all the objects you don't need to see. Replace complex objects with simpler, faster-to-display approximations ("proxy" objects). In short, do everything you can to get your display to play back animations at the target speed so that you can easily evaluate your work by clicking the Play button. If you must resort to a Playblast or a full render every time you're ready to evaluate your animation keys, it will slow your work and also wear down your creativity.

Going Further

Having the house move is fun, but when the chimney and porch are visible, the animation doesn't look right—the chimney and porch remain still while the rest of the house warps through them. Using the skills you have learned so far, try setting them up for animation. You can group them with the house's deformations first so that they follow the house's motions. Then you can apply additional bend or other animation to make the chimney and porch more lively. If you aren't sure what the animation should look like with the porch and chimney animated, load the scene file noted here.

On the CD

Chapter_10\ch10tut03end.mb

Summary

With animation, you can make anything change over time. You can use dynamics (demonstrated in Chapter 14, "Particle Systems and Dynamics") or path animation to let Maya do the work, or you can manually key the primary settings and let Maya fill in the in-between frames. There are many other advanced ways to create animation with Maya, and this chapter has served primarily as an introduction to the methods of creating, evaluating, and editing your animation in Maya. In this chapter, you've had an overview of the following concepts:

- **Setting up a scene for animation**   You used the Preferences dialog box to set up your scene for animation.

- **Keys and animation**   Understanding how keys are set is the first step to animating your scene.

- **Editing keys and animation curves**   Sometimes settings keys doesn't give you enough control over the animation. Modifying the animation curves, tangents, and keys gives you more fine-tuned control.

- **Playblasting for a quick preview**   It would be a real pain if you spent hours setting up a scene for animation and then spent another day rendering, only to find that you don't like the way the animation plays back. However, the Playblast helps you avoid that problem.

- **Modifying your house scene**   By persevering through the previous chapters, you now have a scene that's render-worthy. Your house is gradually becoming more finished, and by the end of the book, you will have a nice animation to show off.

CHAPTER 11

Character Animation

In This Chapter

It's no secret that Maya is particularly suited to character animation—characters such as *Stuart Little* and Aki from the *Final Fantasy* film have cemented Maya's reputation for 3D character animation. Maya offers powerful and rich tools to animate characters in virtually any way desired. With this versatility and power comes a great deal of complexity.

Early animation tools didn't offer skeletons and skeletal deformation. All animation had to use simple rotations, so all the characters had doll-like arms and legs with ball sockets where they connected. Naturally, it wasn't long before animators wanted to animate something softer than an exoskeletal cockroach. The general approach is to create a continuous outer skin for a character that follows the outer surface—whether face, shoes, or shirt. Next, a set of linked joints are constructed and placed inside the character, similar to the armatures that claymation animators put in their characters. Finally, the joints are connected to the character mesh in a process known as *skinning*. By default, many of the joints will not bend "naturally" as we would like, so the animator must modify how joints bend the skin at each local trouble spot. Skinning a complex character so that it has a full range of natural motion can take several days. When complete, the bones bend within the character to deform its skin and clothes in a natural way—a perfect analogy to regular flesh-and-blood animals.

To make character animation focused and straightforward, large firms employ specialists known as technical directors to add handles, menus, dialogs, movement constraints, and other tools for a character. This process, often called "rigging," will make the character animation process straightforward, as the character behaves by default the way the animator wants; for example, knees bend forward and not backward.

Character rigging is a complex subject, by itself worthy of a book. But this chapter will cover some straightforward approaches to let you learn the basics.

In this chapter, we show you the basics of each of the major elements of character animation. Maya offers many ways to solve each task, but we'll pick the most mainstream methods for our tutorials to get you started, while still mentioning the others so you know where to explore next.

Here are some of the concepts and techniques covered in this chapter:

- **Creating skeletons**   You can build, link, and edit collections of joints to make a skeleton for any type of creature.

- **Creating Inverse Kinematics**   Easy animation is possible through Inverse Kinematics, where joints automatically rotate in response to moving an IK handle to the end of the joint chain.

- **Skinning**   The skeleton deforms the character geometry after applying the character geometry to the skeleton in a process known as *skinning*.

- **Character rigging**   Adding easily selected items for control of the character will make it much quicker to animate.

- **Adding flexors**   Rigidly bound skeletons require a special deformer called a *flexor* to modify the way the skin bends around joints.

- **AutoKey**   A way to create animation keys automatically.

- **Trax**   A tool to work with animation as "clips" and shuffle them on a timeline.

- **Blend Shapes**   A deformer that lets you blend the shape of one surface into the shape of another surface or surfaces.

Key Terms

Skinning   A kind of deformer that causes a polygonal or NURBS mesh to bend based on joints.

Skeleton   A combination of connected joints.

Joint   The pivot points of a skeleton.

Root Joint   The base joint of a skeleton

Joint Chain   Connected pivot points of a skeleton.

Forward Kinematics   In linked hierarchies, rotating joints starting at the root joint to the last joint to reach a specific pose. For example, you might pose a character's torso, then bicep, then forearm, then hand to have the character reach upward. Often abbreviated to "FK."

Key Terms

Inverse Kinematics   In linked hierarchies, moving the last joint (actually a "handle" at the end joint created for Inverse Kinematics) to cause all the in-between joints to be automatically rotated to reach a specific pose. For example, you would move a character's hand, and the forearm, bicep, and torso would adjust within defined constraints to "reach" wherever the hand was placed. Often abbreviated to "IK."

End Effector   When IK is applied in Maya, a special controller is created with handles at each end. The end that manipulates the IK chain is called the *end effector*.

Bind Pose   The position of the skeleton when it is bound to the skin; generally a neutral pose with limbs spread to facilitate skinning.

Clip   A defined set of animation for use in Trax.

Blend Shape   A deformer that allows you to assign other surfaces to the current surface as targets to be blended into. The Blend Shape deformer creates a special dialog with sliders, which are used to blend the base shape into one of the targets. This technique, known in other 3D packages as "morphing," is a popular way to animate facial expression or speech.

Hotkeys to Memorize

y   Repeat the use of the last tool—also known as the "non-sacred tool"

p   Parent all selected objects to the last selected object

k + MMB-drag   Scrub Time Slider

What Is Character Animation?

When we talk about character animation, we mean to impart anthropomorphic motion to some object. It is not necessary that it be a human or animal character; virtually anything can be a character—gas pumps, mushrooms, even sacks of flour have been animated as characters. However, in nearly every case, the animator uses various deformers in Maya to impart animal motion and intelligence (and, if the animators are successful, emotion and identity). Obviously, you can animate robots and other rigid objects in a way that still conveys that they are characters. This chapter, however, is concerned with organic, bendable characters—flesh and bone.

Deforming objects in a way that mimics nature is usually more complex than other deformations in Maya. Typically, if you are bending or twisting something, you can add the deformer and quickly get the mechanical result you desire. However, animating something with an implied skeleton overlaid with muscles, which are overlaid with skin, which is overlaid with clothing, requires a lot more adjustment to get a result that is anatomically believable. For example, a human elbow bends differently from a neck joint. Initially, all of your Maya joints will allow universal rotation. Further, real muscles "flex" when contracted, creating a bulge that is more evident for some muscles than others. Also, localized joint movement will pull and relax nearby skin in various ways. A torso doing a "crunch" will make skin do something different from the skin on fingers bending into a fist. Finally, all these variations will be different from character to character; a scrawny old wizard would be set up quite differently from a plump baby or a bodybuilder.

The general approach we'll take in this chapter is to first create joints inside the character to provide articulated movement where we will animate the character. Usually you only add joints where you will want to bend the character, so a shoe-wearing character will not have toe links for each toe. Next, these joints are connected together to create a complete linked skeleton, and adjusted to fit properly within the areas they will deform. Note that the joints themselves do not render, so if a joint protrudes through part of the character, it does not necessarily require adjustment.

Next, Inverse Kinematics is applied where desired, usually to each link chain that connects to the root joint. On a typical biped, the arms, legs, and spine/head would be connected with IK so that you can crouch the character by simply pushing the head down. To ease the animation process, we'll also create easy-to-select handles as part of our character rig.

With the skeleton now behaving in a controlled manner with IK, the character geometry is then bound to the skeleton as a smooth or rigid bind. The procedure from here varies depending on the type of binding, but the goal is to get muscles to flex and joints to bend in the desired way. In this chapter we'll use rigid binding, which then leads to using Flexors to adjust local joint bends.

With the character now set up for animation, we can set keys to make it move. In this chapter, we'll set the character to take a couple of steps forward. With IK already applied, simply posing the hands and feet will make the rest of the character move appropriately.

Maya's Trax feature lets you take any motion set from a defined character and apply it as a "clip." We'll explore this by taking a single walk cycle and using it to make the character walk for some distance.

Finally, we'll explore facial animation with blend shapes. Starting with a neutral face, we'll sculpt a new facial pose and then blend this pose with the neutral pose over time.

Creating Skeletons

The first step to setting up a character is to build its skeleton. Maya's joint tool lets you build skeleton chains directly. Where skeletons split, as in the head and arms that connect to the spine, you can build separate chains and connect them afterward. You also can build them all at once if you want.

A key consideration when building a skeleton is the root joint. This is the "trunk" of the skeleton's tree, where all the joints are affected by manipulation to this joint. Usually this joint is placed at the center of gravity of the character. For bipeds, it is the pelvis.

Tutorial: Adding a Skeleton

In this tutorial, we'll set up the skeleton's joints and position them within our character's geometry in preparation for skinning. First, we'll create the arms, legs, and spine of the skeleton, and then we'll connect them together to form a complete skeleton. The root of the skeleton will be the base of the spine, at the pelvis.

On the CD

Chapter_11\ch11tut01.wmv

On the CD

Chapter_11\ch11tut01begin.mb

When you load the scene file, you'll see a low-resolution model of a character. This was modeled using the same techniques found in Chapter 7, "Modeling with Polygons," but the smoothed mesh is not present. We'll work with this lower polygon version to keep interactivity fast, and we can apply a smooth to the character after the animation is in place.

Notice that the character is posed in a typical "bind pose"—arms horizontally outstretched from each side, legs slightly spread, head forward. This is a character position that facilitates skeleton binding.

1. Create a new layer and name it BoxBoy. Select the character mesh and assign it to this layer. Now if you need to hide the BoxBoy mesh, you can simply click on the V to toggle visibility for this layer.

2. Create the character's left leg's skeleton first. Choose Hotbox | Skeleton | Joint Tool | option box and make sure that all the X, Y, and Z options for degrees of freedom are checked, as in Figure 11.1. Click Close to dismiss the dialog and switch to the Front view. The "+" cursor indicates that you are ready to create joints. Click at the pelvis center point, and then click at the hip (top of thigh), then the knee, and then the ankle. Next, imagine the foot has turned out sideways and click where the ball of the foot would be, then the tips of the toes. Press Enter to end creation of this joint chain.

FIGURE 11.1　*The Joint Tool options.*

tip

As with drawing a curve, you can use the Backspace key to delete the last joint only, rather than the entire joint chain. Also as with curve drawing, you can use the MMB to adjust the position of a just-placed joint.

3. Adjust the joint size to make it easy to view and select. You can control this in the preferences, but it has an easier adjustment point at Hotbox | Display | Joint Size | Custom. Joints do not appear in renderings; they are like other manipulators in Maya. Simply size them to something that fits inside the mesh but is still easy to select, as shown in Figure 11.2.

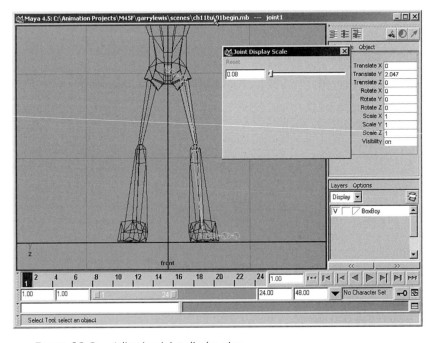

FIGURE 11.2　*Adjusting joint display size.*

4. Use the hotkey **y** to re-enter joint creation mode. This hotkey will return you to your last tool used. Now create the left leg skeleton as in Step 2, but begin at the character's right hip rather than at the pelvic center point (hereafter referred to as the root). We'll connect the right hip to the root in a later step.

5. Create the spine joints, starting at the navel (just above the root), then at the chest center point, then at the neck center, then at the mouth center, then at the eyes, and finally at the top of the head. Click the hotkey **y** to complete this joint chain and start making another.

6. Create the character's right arm skeleton next, starting with the root of the arm, then the elbow, then the wrist, then the top of the palm, and then the tips of the fingers. Take care that the joints are horizontal through the arm. Click **y** to complete this chain, and then make the left arm skeleton exactly the same. When the left-side skeleton is complete, hit Enter to finish the chain. The skeleton should appear as in Figure 11.3.

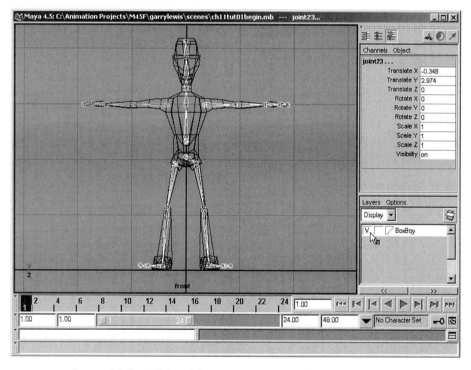

FIGURE 11.3   *All the skeleton parts are created.*

7. Toggle visibility off for the BoxBoy layer. Select the right hip joint, and then shift-select the root joint. Parent the hip to the root (hotkey: **p**). The left leg should now connect to the root.

8. Select the right arm, then shift-select the joint at the center of the chest, and parent them. Now select the left arm, then shift-select the joint at the center of the chest, and parent them. Now, select the navel joint, then shift-select the root, and parent these joints. The skeleton is now one connected linkage, as shown in Figure 11.4. The root joint moves the entire skeleton, which you can observe if you select the pelvis and move it.

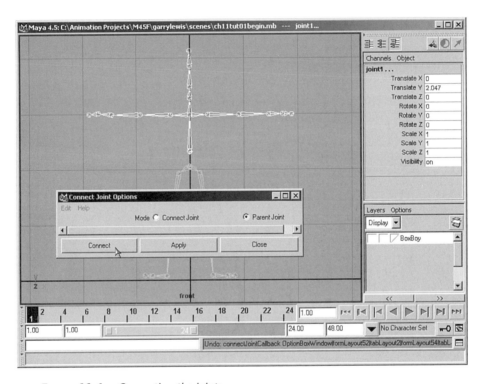

FIGURE 11.4   *Connecting the joints.*

9. Next we'll adjust joint placement. We built the skeleton in the Front view, so its z-axis position is incorrect in several places. Turn the BoxBoy layer's visibility on, switch to the Side view, and move (hotkey: **w**) the joints in the head as follows: Move the neck joint to the center of the neck, move the mouth joint to continue in the direction of the neck joints, move the eye joint closer to the eyes and the center of the head, and move the top joint to the tip of the head.

10. Move to the knee joints and marquee-select both knee joints. All joints below the knees will also highlight in green to indicate that they will move with the selected joint. Move the knee joints to the center of the BoxBoy legs. Next, marquee-select all the foot joints at the bottom of the leg joints. They are all nearly on top

of one another, so it's easy to select them. Move them back to where the BoxBoy ankle would be. Make sure that the leg joints have a slight natural bend in them.

11. Switch to the Top view and move the foot joints for each foot so that they fall at each foot's ball and tip. Switch to the Side view to align the foot joints to each other so they are similarly positioned.

12. While in the Side view, we'll add jaw-bone joints. Start the Joint Tool with Hotbox | Skeleton | Joint Tool, and click once, at the chin. Hit y to start a second joint, and click on the upper lip and press Enter to complete this joint. You will only see a circle to represent each joint. Now connect them to the spine: Shift-select the mouth joint on the spine, and choose Hotbox | Skeleton | Connect Joint. Then select the chin joint, shift-select the mouth joint on the spine, and then choose Hotbox | Skeleton | Connect Joint. The joint connects to the spine, as shown in Figure 11.5. It's a good idea to add such bones before binding the skeleton to the skin, because adding bones after that stage can sometimes cause problems.

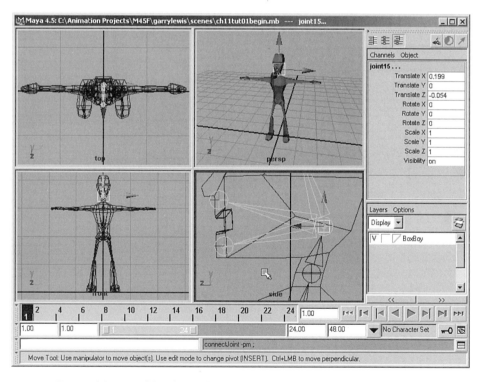

FIGURE 11.5   *Adding bones for the mouth.*

13. Switch back to the Top view and select one elbow joint, then shift-select the other. The transform icon will appear over the last selected joint, but when you move it, both joints will move together. Move the joints back slightly in the Z direction so that they are within the BoxBoy mesh. Also make sure the arm joints have a slight natural bend in them so that the elbows are slightly further back than the wrists.

At this point, you can examine the final skeleton placement. Sometimes it is easier to see if you switch the display to x-ray shading, as shown in Figure 11.6.

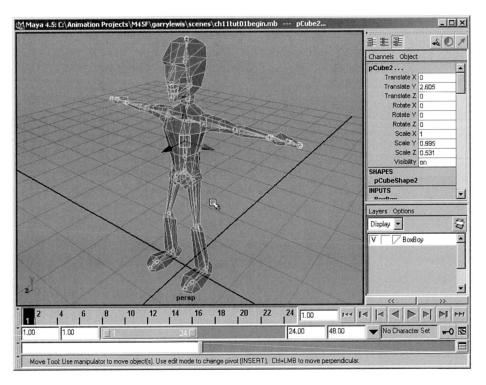

FIGURE 11.6   *Setting the display to Shading | Shade Options X-Ray lets you see through the BoxBoy mesh to the skeleton below.*

Your skeleton is now in place, but you've probably noticed that the joints move freely through space. Next, we will add some Inverse Kinematic (IK) behavior to the limbs so that they rotate in a controlled way.

On the CD

Chapter_11\ch11tut01end.mb

Inverse Kinematics

With the skeleton in place, you could now bind the character to the skeleton if you wanted. However, at this point, the skeleton only has Forward Kinematic (FK) linkages. By this, we mean that to animate, you must start at the root, and work your way to the end of the chain. For example, if a character is going to pick up a remote control, you would animate the torso leaning over, then the bicep extending, and then the forearm's rotation, and hope that the hand could approach wherever the remote control is placed (see Figure 11.7A and 11.7B). For much character animation, this type of approach is cumbersome and results in awkward character animation. Note that sometimes FK is actually more desirable—for example, if a character is bowling and the arm is to freely rotate in an arc. Maya provides tools for setting a key to toggle FK and IK for a joint.

Inverse Kinematics (or IK for short) looks at it the other way around. In our example, you would simply position the hand (now the "end effector") over the remote control, and the body from the shoulder forward would bend however necessary to reach the remote control. As you can imagine, IK might cause ridiculous contortions as it seeks a "solution" to pose the character, such that the two ends of the skeleton chain are placed as desired. There are a variety of ways to set up IK so that certain joints take precedence, and are moved before other joints. You can also set joint preferences and limits, so that knees don't bend backward and only bend to their natural limits, for example. You can also set limits and resistance levels so that as one joint nears its defined rotational limit, more of the required rotation is applied to other joints.

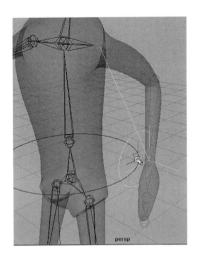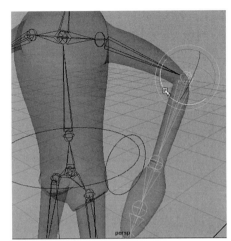

FIGURE 11.7A AND 11.7B   *Adjusting arm position with IK versus FK.*

IK in Maya comes in three types: rotate plane, single chain, and spline.

Rotate plane is best for joint chains where the individual joints tend to rotate within a plane, even though the plane itself may rotate. Think of it as starting at a ball joint, but using hinges for the remaining joints. The animator is free to set the plane orientation with this IK type. For example, the shoulder may change rotation to set the rotate plane for the forearm and bicep, but the forearm and bicep will rotate within this plane. Using rotate plane IK, you directly control the rotate plane orientation—in the previous example, the shoulder rotation. You'll use the rotate plane for typical arms and legs.

Single chain is similar to rotate plane in that the starting joint is a ball joint, free to rotate in all directions. However, instead of allowing the animator to directly pose the rotate plane for the remaining joints, the single chain type will pose all the joints according to how the IK is set up. Joints within the chain may have absolute limits beyond which they stop rotating, as well as "damping," where the joint begins to resist rotation, transferring the rotation to other joints to achieve the pose. In any case, the joint setups will completely determine how Maya poses the joints between the start and end joints of the IK chain.

Spline is a unique type of IK designed for more serpentine joint chains. Bullwhips, tentacles, and tails are ideal for this IK type. A NURBS curve serves as the handle, and the joints are repositioned as you modify the original curve.

Next we'll add IK to the character's arms and legs. We'll also add some rings around the character's hands and feet to make it easy to select and move these appendages.

Tutorial: Setting Up Inverse Kinematics

Now we'll add IK handles to the skeleton. These will allow us to control the position of the entire body by pulling on the end effectors—the hands and feet.

On the CD

Chapter_11\ch11tut01end.mb

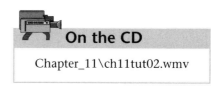

On the CD

Chapter_11\ch11tut02.wmv

1. Toggle visibility off for the BoxBoy mesh, so you can work directly with the skeleton. Switch to the Perspective view and orbit the view so that you can see from the character's right shoulder to right wrist. Bring up the IK Handle Tool options with Hotbox | Skeleton | IK Handle Tool | option box. In the dialog that appears, reset the settings. The current Solver is set to the ikRPsolver. This is the rotate plane solver, which works well for bicep-forearm relationships where the limb bends within a plane—that is, the forearm and bicep are "hinged" and rotate about one axis only. Therefore, the bicep-forearm combination rotates within one plane at all times. Close the dialog.

2. On the character's right arm, click on the shoulder joint (the ball at the end of the joint, not the linkage), followed by wrist joint. An IK handle should appear. Switch to Move mode (hotkey: **w**) and reposition the IK handle that appears at the wrist. Note how the movement stays within a plane defined by the white "pointer" in the circle that appears at the shoulder, as shown in Figure 11.8. This orientation is caused by creating the IK handle in the Top view. Undo your moves with hotkey **z**. In the Channel Box, rename the IK handle to IKrighthand.

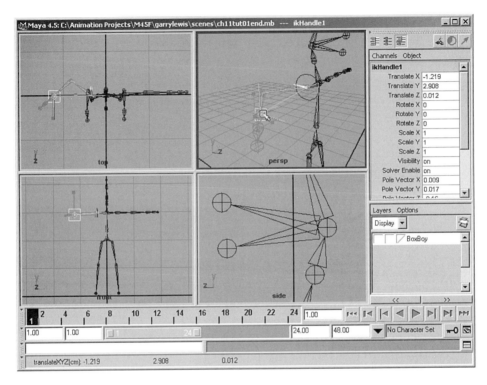

FIGURE 11.8   *The rotate plane IK handle keeps bicep-forearm motion in the plane indicated by the white pointer at the shoulder.*

Next we'll set the arm's IK pose to be the preferred angle. This is important for proper IK animation—when creating bones, you will usually want to have them slightly bent in the angle they would naturally bend in. Then you can set this as the preferred angle for the IK chain. For the right arm, simply hold down the RMB over the IK handle, which should still be selected. A marking menu will appear, and you can drag over the Set Preferred Angle option.

3. Switch to the Top view and repeat Steps 1 and 2 for the character's left arm, connecting shoulder to wrist with the IK Handle Tool. Rename the IK handle to IKlefthand and set the pose as the preferred angle.

4. Now we'll do a little character rigging: Create a NURBS circle with Hotbox | Create | NURBS Primitives | Circle. In the Channel Box, set the translate to 1.4, 3, 0; the rotate to 0, 0, 90; and the scaling to 0.2, 0.2, 0.2. The circle should now be around the character's left hand, like a bracelet. This makes for easy selection and animation. Name the circle Left_Hand.

5. Duplicate the circle with Hotbox | Edit | Duplicate | option box, reset the settings, and click Duplicate. Name the duplicate to Right_Hand. Change the Translate X value to -1.4 for this duplicated circle. Shift-select both circles, and freeze their transforms with Hotbox | Modify | Freeze Transformations. This sets the Channel Box values back to the initial state. Create a layer called SelectionRings and add the two circles to this layer.

6. Select the IK handle named IKrighthand (use the Outliner if you have trouble selecting it). Now, shift-select the Right_Hand circle in the Perspective view, and choose Hotbox | Edit | Parent | option box. Make sure that Preserve Position is checked, and click Parent. Test this by selecting the circle and moving it, as shown in Figure 11.9 (don't forget to undo). Repeat these steps for IKlefthand and the Left_Hand circle, making sure to select the parent (which is the circle) last, before typing the hotkey **p** to parent.

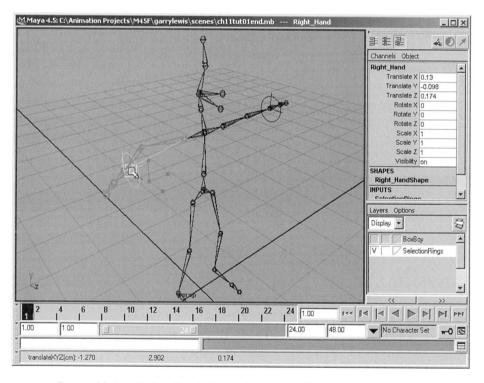

FIGURE 11.9   *Testing the circle as a hand controller.*

Next we'll add IK to the legs, but using a different type of solver—the single chain type. This type of IK will allow Maya to set the plane orientation, which will keep the knees straight ahead by default.

7. Switch to the Perspective view. Bring up the IK Handle Tool options with Hotbox | Skeleton | IK Handle Tool | option box. Set the current Solver to the ikSCsolver. Close the dialog. The "+" cursor indicates that you should now apply IK to a joint chain. Click the hip joint of the left leg, and then click the ankle joint. The IK handle will appear.

8. Switch to the Perspective view and move the IK handle around to see its effect on the leg. Name the IK handle as IKleftleg.

9. Select the thigh joint of the right leg. Switch back to the Side view, and choose Hotbox | Show | Isolate Select | View Selected. This is a fast way to hide all unselected objects. Now choose Hotbox | Skeleton | IK Handle Tool, click the hip joint, and then click the ankle joint. Name the created IK handle as IKrightLeg. Now turn off the Isolate mode by choosing Hotbox | Show | Isolate Select | View Selected, which will uncheck the option and restore all the other objects. Select each IK handle, and then RMB over the handle and choose Set Preferred Angle. This will keep the legs bending along this angle when you raise the knees.

10. Next we'll make circles for the feet: Create a NURBS circle with Hotbox | Create | NURBS Primitives | Circle. In the Channel Box, set the translate to 0.45, 0, 0.17, and the scaling to 0.3, 0.3, 0.5. The circle should now be around the character's left foot. Name the circle Left_Foot.

11. Duplicate the circle with Hotbox | Edit | Duplicate. Name the duplicate to Right_Foot. Change the Translate X value to -0.45 for this duplicated circle. Shift-select both circles, and freeze their transforms with Hotbox | Modify | Freeze Transformations. Add the two circles to the SelectionRings layer.

12. Select the IK handle named IKrightleg (use the Outliner if you have trouble selecting it). Now, shift-select the Right_Foot circle and parent (hotkey: **p**). Repeat these steps for IKleftleg and the Left_Foot circle. Test the circles and the IK by selecting each circle and moving it, as shown in Figure 11.10. Undo the moves when done. Unhide the BoxBoy layer, and try moving the ring handles again—you can observe how the skeleton is positioned within the character.

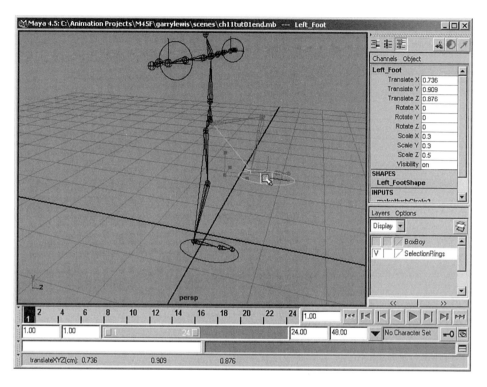

FIGURE 11.10   *Testing the leg IK and circle handles.*

13. Lastly we'll add a selection ring to the waist and connect it to the root joint for the character. Create a NURBS circle as before, and set its Translate Y to 2.2, and its scale to 0.5, 0.5, 0.5. Rename the circle to Waist. Assign this to the SelectionRings layer. Freeze the transform with Hotbox | Modify | Freeze Transformations.

14. Select any joint of the character. Because the joints are automatically created as a hierarchy, you can traverse the skeleton with the up- and down-arrow keys, just as with other grouped or parented objects. Click the up-arrow key until the entire skeleton is selected. Shift-select the circle, and parent the skeleton to the circle (hotkey: **p**). Select the circle and test the effect on the skeleton when the circle is moved, as shown in Figure 11.11. (Note: you should undo when done testing to get the character back to its neutral pose.) This circle will be very helpful when shifting the body's center of mass during an animation.

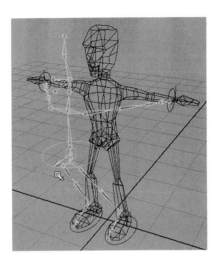

FIGURE 11.11   *Testing the waist circle handle.*

With the legs and arms moving properly, we can now attach the skin to the skeleton. Note that you can add IK to any joint at any time, even after you've attached the skin. But we're progressing directly through character setup so we don't have to go backward to make adjustments. The hands, feet, and waist selection rings will make it easier to animate the character later.

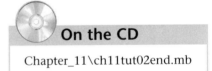

On the CD

Chapter_11\ch11tut02end.mb

Skinning

When the skeleton has been properly set up, you can bind the skeleton to the character's skin. Maya offers two direct ways to go about this:

- **Smooth Skinning**   Binds points to various joints with variable "weighting."
- **Rigid Skinning**   Binds each point of the skin to a single joint.

Maya also offers two indirect ways to attach a character to a skeleton:

- **Lattice Skinning**   Uses Lattice deformers.
- **Wrap Skinning**   Uses wrap deformers.

With Smooth Skinning, vertices (polygonal character models) or CVs (for NURBS character models) of the skin might be influenced by the position of multiple joints. After setting up Smooth Skinning, you would go through each joint and adjust the weighting on its nearby skin. You can do this by numerically editing the weights in a spreadsheet, or by visually painting the weights on the skin as a grayscale visual interaction.

For Rigid Skinning, each point is moved by one joint only. This obviously creates problems where joints bend, because a crude implosion of the character mesh will occur there—that is, the geometry attached to the bending joint will move with the joint, while the geometry where the joint attaches will remain in place, creating a collision of CVs or vertices. Maya offers a rigid mesh smoother called a *flexor* to smooth the bent areas in this case.

Lattice Skinning uses lattice deformers, skinning their influence lattices. This approach has the advantage of making it easy to adjust how the character is deformed by adjusting the influence of lattice points.

Wrap Skinning works on the wrap influence objects of wrap deformers. The advantage of this approach is that it allows for easy connection of directly animated low-resolution character models (for editing) to high-resolution models (for rendering) by allowing the low-resolution model to wrap deform the high-resolution model.

Tutorial: Binding the Character to the Skeleton

Next we'll actually bind the character's "skin"—the mesh of the BoxBoy character—to the skeleton. For this tutorial, we will use the rigid bind approach, and add flexors to fix the problems that occur at the bend points of the character.

On the CD

Chapter_11\ch11tut02end.mb

On the CD

Chapter_11\ch11tut03.wmv

1. Select the root of the skeleton by opening the Outliner (hotkey: **shift+O**) and opening the waist and transform1 objects to get to the joint1 root of the skeleton. Next, shift-select the BoxBoy character in the Perspective view. Now, bind the skeleton to the character with Hotbox I Skin I Bind Skin I Rigid Bind I option box. Reset the settings and choose Bind Skin.

2. Now try selecting the hand circles and moving the hands up in the air. You'll see a kind of "bunching" and pulling at the shoulder joint that doesn't look right, as shown in Figure 11.12. Adding a flexor will fix this. Undo any position change of the hand.

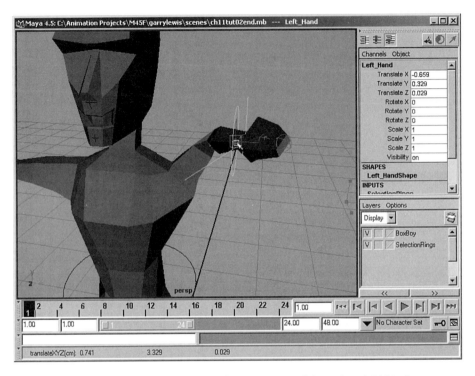

Figure 11.12   *Inhuman bending will occur at some joints after rigid binding.*

tip

Now that the character is bound to the skeleton, you may need to get the character back to this neutral pose after having applied animation to the skeleton. Flexors, for example, should always be applied to the skeleton in its bind pose. If you need to get back to this pose, you can always select the root joint of the skeleton and put it back into the bind pose with Skin | Go to Bind Pose. Usually, you must disable IK solving first, with Modify | Evaluate Nodes | IK Solvers to toggle this function on and off.

3. To fix the shoulder, select the character's left bicep joint. Now choose Hotbox | Skin | Edit Rigid Skin | Create Flexor... The Create Flexor dialog will appear. Set Flexor Type to Lattice. Check only the At Selected Joints for the Joints and none of the Bones options. Set the Flexor Lattice Options to 3x3x3 and click Create. A lattice will appear around the shoulder. The Create Flexor dialog will remain open.

4. Test the flexor by moving around the Left_Hand circle while in Shaded view. You should be able to see how the flexor adapts to the shoulder rotation and warps the nearby BoxBoy mesh, as shown in Figure 11.13.

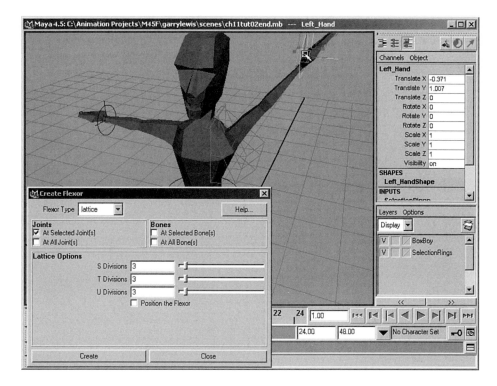

FIGURE 11.13   *The added shoulder flexor smoothes the bending effect.*

5. Make a new layer, name it flexors, and then select the new flexor and add it to this layer. Turn off the BoxBoy layer's visibility.

6. Now select the character's right bicep joint. In the Create Flexor dialog, confirm that the settings appear as before, and click Create. Leave the Create Flexor dialog open.

7. Repeat the last step for the elbows, knees, hips, and ankles of the character. Assign all the created flexors to the flexors layer. The flexors will be sized differently depending on the joint, as shown in Figure 11.14.

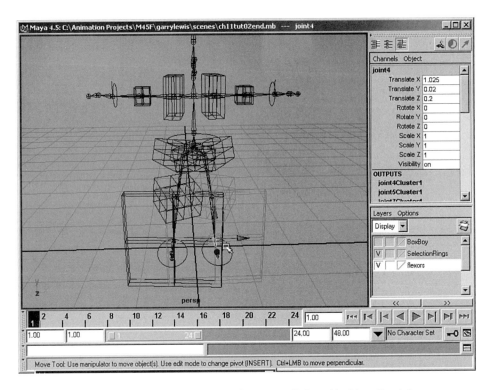

FIGURE 11.14   *The skeleton with flexors at all the critical bending joints.*

8. Now we'll adjust the flexor settings. Toggle the BoxBoy mesh visibility on. Select the Left_Hand ring and bring the arm to the side of the character. Select the right shoulder flexor for the character, and in the Channel Box, select the label "Creasing" and MMB-drag in the viewport to adjust this value in real time (Maya's Virtual slider). After you see the effect, set this value to -0.4. Try this with the Rounding variable to see its effect. Leave this value set at 1.0. Put the hand back where it was by selecting the Left_Hand ring and setting its translate to 0,0,0 in the Channel Box. Set the left shoulder flexor values to the same settings.

9. Toggle visibility off for the flexors. Now we'll create a handle for the entire character. Create a NURBS circle with Hotbox | Create | NURBS Primitives | Circle. Name the circle BoxBoy_handle. Assign the circle to the SelectionRings layer.

10. Select all the selection rings, with BoxBoy_handle last. Then choose Hotbox | Edit | Group | option box, reset the settings, and click Group. Now, any time you need to move the entire character to a starting position, you can simply select the base ring named BoxBoy_handle, and press the up arrow to select the entire group of rings. You can then move it wherever you want, as shown in Figure 11.15.

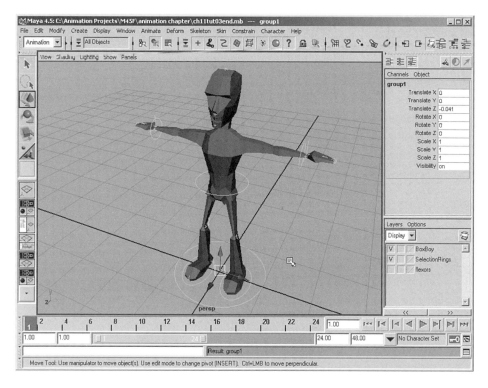

FIGURE 11.15   *An overall handle added to the base of the character allows for fast positioning.*

Now that we've got our character bending the right way, we can create some animation and make use of the hand and foot selection rings we created. When animating your own characters, sometimes you'll have to go backward and fix skinning deformation problems that were not evident until you posed the character in a position more extreme than in your prior tests.

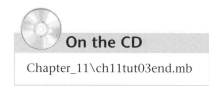

On the CD

Chapter_11\ch11tut03end.mb

Animating Your Character

After the character is bound to its skeleton, you are ready to animate with it. Because of all the built-in links and IK handles we've created, animating the character is a snap. We can simply pose the five handles (feet, hands, and waist), and IK and skinning will do the rest for us. The only part we need to be careful about is "planting" the feet—we'll need to take care to frame any time period where the foot is planted with two identical keys so it does stay put.

Also, because we'll be using Trax later to make this walk cycle repeat, we only need one full step. However, we must be careful to get the character to take one full step and end up in a position identical to an earlier starting position. We need a "tileable" walk cycle!

To make the creation of animation keys simpler, we'll use Maya's AutoKey feature. This feature acts only on objects that have at least one key on them already, so you can designate the objects you want to animate by setting a 0 frame key as you start animating.

Tutorial: Character Animation—A Short Walk

Now that our character is set up, we'll animate a walk cycle. As you animate, try to think of a walk as a kind of controlled fall. One leg is lifted and put forward, then the body shifts its center of gravity forward until it topples onto the outstretched leg, freeing the other leg to swing forward. For each leg that is put forward, the opposite arm moves forward to give the body some counter balance to the weight of the lifted leg.

On the CD

Chapter_11\ch11tut03end.mb

On the CD

Chapter_11\ch11tut04.wmv

1. In the Range Slider, set the playback end time to 120 to allow for a longer animation. The end time will be pushed out to 120 automatically. This gives four seconds at the default 30 fps playback rate.

2. To make selection easier, we'll hide the joints and IK handles, and block selection of surfaces. This will allow us to pick only on the NURBS curves that make our selection rings. Choose Display | Hide | Hide Kinematics | All, and the joints and IK handles will disappear. Next, in Selection Mask options, you can disable (mask) selection of surfaces, as shown in Figure 11.16.

Select by object type: Surfaces (RMB for more info)

Figure 11.16   *Masking selection of surfaces so that you can select only the rings.*

3. Select the selection rings for the waist, hands, and feet. Then click and drag in the Channel Box from the Translate X to the Rotate Z entries. Right-click over the darkened entries and choose Key Selected, as shown in Figure 11.17. Now that these items have keys at frame zero, you can use Maya's AutoKey feature. Enable this by clicking the key icon at the bottom right of the Maya interface; the button turns red to indicate that you are in AutoKey mode. If you move or rotate the circles, animation keys will be created.

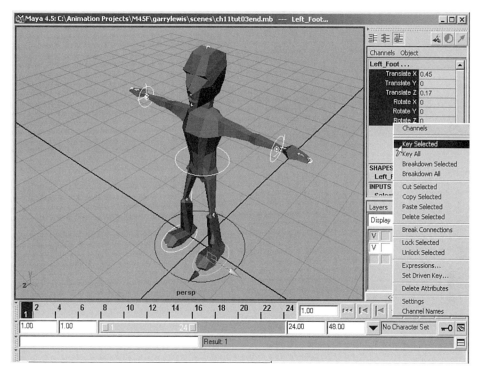

FIGURE 11.17   *Creating keys for the translate and rotate of the selection rings.*

4. Set the Time Slider to frame 10. In the Front view, bring the arms down to the sides of the character. In the Side view, bring the waist ring down to add a tiny bit of crouch to the character's posture. Raise the control circles for the hands enough to add some natural-looking bend to the arms. Bring the waist circle slightly forward to anticipate the first step. Select the same five rings, select Translate and Rotate channels in the Channel Box, and Key Selected as before. This is our starting pose, with frame 10 as a starting point, so we want keys for all five rings.

5. Set the time to frame 30. Stay in the Side view for all of the initial animation. Select the waist and both hand rings. Move them out a little less than 1/4 of the character's height. Move the right foot forward, to a position somewhat less than 1/2 of the character's height. Now raise the left hand and put it slightly forward, about one hand's length. Bring the other hand slightly back.

6. You can scrub animation in Maya by either dragging the LMB on the timeline, or by the preferred method of holding the k key while LMB-dragging anywhere in the viewport. Scrub the frames and you'll see that it's a start, but the right foot slides rather than lifts. We need another key.

tip   Remember that any animated object has some parameter that is progressing between two keys. Therefore, if you want something to stay motionless for a time, you need to create two identical keys separated in time. You usually need to flatten their curves in the Graph Editor because by default the keys will interpolate according to a spline, which can yield unexpected results.

7. Set time to frame 24. Raise the right foot ring up about the distance of 1/2 of the foot's length. Now scrub the animation for a better look.

8. Set time to frame 45. Select the waist and both hands, and bring them forward to a point that is about 1/4 the character's height beyond where the right foot is planted. Now, select the left foot and bring it to a point one full step in front of the right foot, somewhat less than 1/2 of the character's height. Now bring the right hand forward to offset the left foot, with a swinging forward stance. Take the left hand back so that it hangs down slightly behind the character's torso.

9. Scrub the Time Slider, and you'll see that the character appears to float over the first 30 frames. We had expected the left foot to remain fixed until frame 30! But we didn't set a key to keep it there. Select the left foot selection ring, and bring up the Graph Editor with Hotbox I Window I Animation Editors I Graph Editor. Make sure the left foot circle is selected. With the Graph Editor active, use hotkey **a** to frame all. Now you can see the problem—movement is beginning at frame 10 for this item. Click and drag to select the Translate X, Y, and Z entries at left. Then, marquee-select the keyframed area around frame 10 on the graph, as shown in Figure 11.18. Now change frame time for these selected keys from 10 to 30 at the top of the Graph Editor dialog, and set the tangents to flat tangents with the horizontal-bar icon button. Close the Graph Editor.

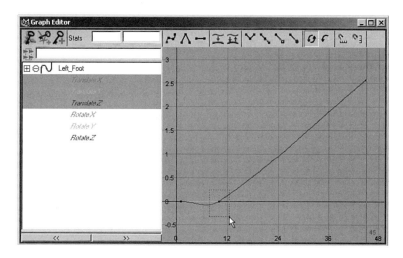

FIGURE 11.18   *Editing keys in the Graph Editor.*

10. Scrub the time again. The left foot now travels properly, but never lifts up. Fix this by setting the current frame to 40, and raising the foot up about 1/2 of the foot's length. Scrubbing now reveals that the animation looks good.

11. Now we'll add another step. Go to frame 60, select the waist and both hands, and move them about 1/4 of the character's height in front of the striding left foot. Reverse the position of the two hands. Take the right foot from behind the character to a point one full step in front of the character. Again, we see a sliding foot, caused because we expected the right foot to remain fixed to the floor between frames 45 and 60. Set the time to frame 45, select the right foot, and move it. This creates a key for the foot at frame 45. Then bring up the Graph Editor, and select the Translate X, Y, and Z entries at left. Frame all with hotkey **a**.

12. The blue or z-axis curve slopes upward. We need it to stop moving (stay horizontal) between frames 30 and 45. Do this by selecting the dot that indicates the key at frame 30, and noting the value for the key displayed at the upper left of the Graph Editor. Now select the key at frame 45 and change this key's value to the same number. Now marquee-select both keys and set them to flat tangents (the horizontal line button). Close the Graph Editor.

13. Now scrub the time, and you have a situation just like that in Step 8—the right foot drags without lifting between frames 45 and 60. Go to frame 54, and raise the right foot about 1/2 a foot length above the ground. Scrub time, and you should see good walking motion now, as shown in Figure 11.19. You might notice that one full stride occurs between frames 30 and 60.

14. Now that you are done animating, switch off Autokey. Otherwise, you may inadvertently create new animation, particularly when scrubbing time and adjusting the position of objects in the scene. It's a good idea to be aware of when you've engaged Autokey; then create your animation and exit Autokey mode.

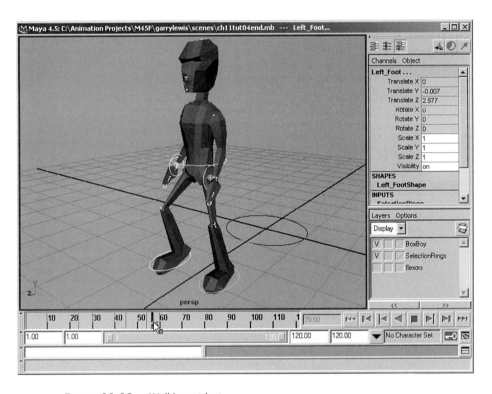

FIGURE 11.19   *Walking at last.*

With a minimum of keyframing, we've created a couple of footsteps from our starting neutral pose at frame 10. With a loop of animation occurring between frames 30 and 60, we can use Maya's Trax feature to repeat the walk for us automatically.

On the CD

Chapter_11\ch11tut04end.mb

Building Repetitive Motion with Trax

Maya offers an innovative solution to character animation called Trax, which allows you to simplify repetitive motions and build libraries of movements. Trax is Maya's version of what is known as "non-linear animation." Non-linear animation mimics the approach taken by computer-based video editors, where a timeline is displayed and footage appears as bars that can be placed, moved, copied, and layered across this timeline to compose a TV program.

With Trax, if you have a character animated to applaud, you can save this bit of animation as a clip. Then, any time the character should applaud, you simply layer this clip over the other animation that is already applied to this character. Regardless of whether the character is running, hopping, or standing still, the hands will clap where specified.

An additional method of using Trax involves poses. Here, instead of using collections of animation, you simply use still poses and blend them in as desired. You can blend any set of poses or animations in Trax. Your library of poses and animation clips reside in Visor.

Tutorial: Repeating the Walk Using Trax

Now that the character takes a single step between frames 30 and 60, we could just repeat these steps in Maya to make him walk a few more strides. But that would be mindless and boring. Instead, let's look at the Trax Editor, a way to use animation "clips" to create repetitive motion in Maya.

On the CD

Chapter_11\ch11tut04end.mb

On the CD

Chapter_11\ch11tut05.wmv

1. Select the ring handles for the hands, feet, and waist. Choose Hotbox | Animate | Create Clip | option box. Reset the dialog and change the name to one_step; then change the time range to Start/End, set the start time to 30, and set the end time to 60. Uncheck sub-characters and click the Create Clip button, as shown in Figure 11.20.

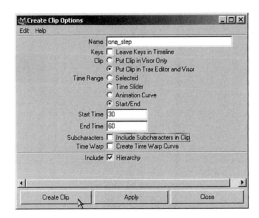

FIGURE 11.20   *Creating a clip of a single walk cycle.*

2. Open the Trax Editor with Hotbox | Window | Animation Editors | Trax Editor. You'll see the clip you created here. When you created the clip, it also created something called a character set—this is required of anything that Trax will work on. A *character set* is a group of related objects that are to be animated together—usually a character and its skeleton, IK handles, and other related nodes. The automatically created character set in this tutorial is given the default name of "MultiCh."

3. If you scrub time, you'll notice that animation now exists only for the character for frames 30-60. By creating a character set and a Trax clip, all the character's animation is now moved to the Trax clip.

4. In the Trax Editor, click the second button from right—the frame timeline range button. Now you can see the clip in context of all 120 frames. Click on the clip and drag it to frame 1. Now play back the animation, and you'll see the one walk cycle begin at frame 1.

5. Next, right click in the space to the right of the animation clip in Trax. Choose Library | Insert Clip | one_stepSource, as shown in Figure 11.21. A new clip, a copy of the original named one_step1, will appear below the original in the Trax Editor. Drag the clip to the right side of the original clip and make it start at frame 31 so that the ends of the clips touch. Drag the animation, and you'll see the walk happen twice in a row—but restarting from the same position each time!

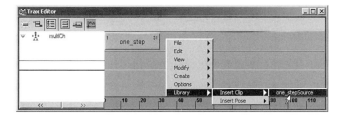

FIGURE 11.21   *The motion clip you created is now in the clip library, and right-clicking in the Trax Editor allows you to easily insert the animation.*

6. Right-click the new clip and check the relative clip box. Now play back the animation, and you'll see the walk continue as you would want. Insert two more copies of one_stepSource as in Step 4, and set these new clips to Relative mode as well. Now play back the animation, and you'll see 120 frames of walking.

7. If you'd like to see a higher-resolution BoxBoy, apply a smooth to the character by selecting the mesh and choosing Hotbox | Polygons | Smooth. In the Channel Box, click the PolySmoothFace entry and scroll to the bottom of the Channel Box. Here you can adjust the number of divisions, as shown in Figure 11.22. Set this to 1 so the animation will play back fairly fast.

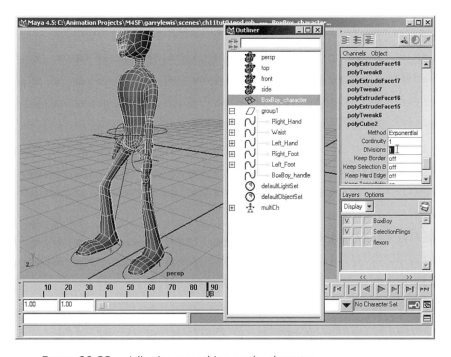

FIGURE 11.22   *Adjusting smoothing on the character.*

At this point, you can render a playblast or a full movie of the character walking. As you might surmise, you could now create libraries of other motions and mix them in using Trax to make very complicated animation. But so far, we've only touched on the methods Maya uses for character body motion. Next, we'll turn to facial animation, where characters can really come alive.

On the CD

Chapter_11\ch11tut05end.mb

Blend Shape Animation

Sometimes using skeletons to animate is problematic. This is particularly true of facial animation. The human face uses hundreds of different muscles to arrange the face into the positions with which humans communicate non-verbally. Trying to emulate this arrangement with dozens of bones strewn throughout a character's face would not make for easy animation. A better solution is the Blend Shape deformer, sometimes known as a "morph."

Blend Shapes can work on any NURBS or polygonal geometry, warping the source object to the shape of the target. In general, you copy the base object and modify the copy into a new shape. For example, you would copy the head of a character and arrange its facial features for one of the phonemes used for human speech—"ooo". You would then be able to use this as a Blend Shape target for the original neutral face. Animating the percentage of blend would make the face gradually change from the neutral pose to the "ooo" pose. You can apply any number of targets to the base object, allowing you to mix percentages of all the targets into the base. With enough phoneme poses, you can simulate speech.

In addition, you can blend any combination of poses. For example, you can have a left eyebrow-raised pose, and a right eyebrow-raised pose. These can then be independently animated *alongside* the speech animation, for truly emotive character animation.

Tutorial: Facial Expression with Blend Shapes

Animating facial expression is a snap with Blend Shapes. Facial expressions are created by making a copy of the original head, changing the facial expression, and adding this as a target to the original head on a Blend Shape deformer. Maya offers a Graphic Equalizer-style Blend Shape Editor that makes it easy to set keys for facial expression.

On the CD

Chapter_11\ch11tut06begin.mb

1. You might recognize the head shape as the cage for the creepy alien we created in Chapter 7. We'll use this same cage to create facial expressions, because editing this simple object will allow us to quickly make major changes to the character's face.

On the CD

Chapter_11\ch11tut06.wmv

2. First, we'll copy the original head to make sure we have a source for future facial expressions. Duplicate the head with Hotbox | Edit | Duplicate | option box, reset the settings, and click Duplicate. Move the duplicate to the left of the original head, and name it more_faces.

3. Select the more_faces head and duplicate it (hotkey: **Ctrl-d**). Drag this new head to the right of the original head. Name it "confused."

4. Choose Hotbox | Polygons | Smooth Proxy to see the smoothed mesh under this proxy mesh. Drag the proxy to the right of the smoothed head if you like; it might be easier to see the edits as you make them to the facial expression. Right-click on the proxy and choose Vertices. To make a concerned, worried monster, select the vertices at the four faces at the front of the brow and bring them down as in Figure 11.23.

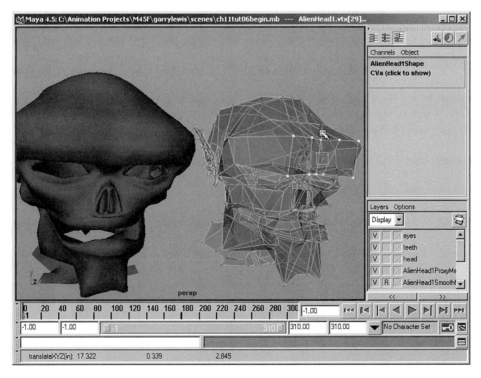

FIGURE 11.23   *Editing the proxy while observing the effect on the smoothed object.*

5. Right-click and select Face mode. Now select the center face of each eyebrow lobe and bring it slightly inward.

6. Now marquee-select an area around the nose. This will select polygons at the front *and* at the rear of the head. Orbit to the rear of the head and de-select these faces by holding down the Ctrl key as you drag a marquee over the unwanted faces. Notice how the manipulator moves to the front faces of the head once you deselect the faces in the rear. Orbit back to the front and push the nose up and scale it down vertically a slight amount. This should add to the confused facial expression. Continue editing the proxy head until you like the facial expression you've created on the smoothed face. Exit face editing (literally!) with RMB | Object Mode.

trap   The Blend Shape may give unwanted results if the target and base objects are not precisely the same geometry. Do not split, add, subtract, or otherwise change the target object in a way that would change the number of vertices or faces!

7. Select the smoothed head and delete it. Right-click on the smooth layer in the Layer Editor, named confusedSmoothMesh, and delete it. Do the same for the proxy mesh layer. Select the confused proxy head, and then shift-select the original, expressionless head. Now choose Hotbox | Deform | Create Blend Shape | option box and reset the settings. Change the BlendShapeNode name to Alien_Expression. Click Create, and the dialog disappears.

8. Open the Blend Shape Editor with Hotbox | Window | Animation Editors | Blend Shape... A dialog will appear with a "confused" slider. As you adjust this, you will see the original face move into the confused shape, as shown in Figure 11.24.

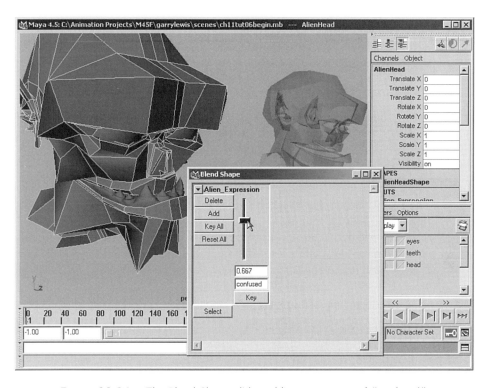

Figure 11.24   *The Blend Shape slider adds any amount of "confused" to the original head's facial expression.*

tip   You could delete the confused head if you wanted to at this point—the facial position is recorded by the Blend Shape Editor, and the actual geometry is no longer needed.

tip   Although 0 to 1 is the range created for the Blend Shape slider, you can type in other values, as we saw with other portions of Maya such as the color picker in the materials chapter. You can use negative values to bring the pose the opposite direction, or go beyond 1 to extrapolate to a more exaggerated blend.

9. You can now see the real result if you want, by applying a smooth to the head. Smooth the original AlienHead object by selecting it, and choosing Hotbox | Polygons | Smooth. Now try the slider in the Blend Shape dialog to see the real result.

10. Now we'll make another facial configuration and add it to the Blend Shape set of facial expressions. Duplicate the more_faces object and drag it to the right of the confused head. Name this head "open_mouth."

11. Make a smooth proxy of this open_mouth head, and drag the proxy object to the right of the smoothed head. Now, right-click over the proxy object and choose face mode editing. Select the faces at the front of the chin—you may need to orbit to a point where you are looking down on the face to easily select just the front of the chin.

12. Choose the marking menu activated by Ctrl+RMB (new to Maya 4.5) and choose "To Edges." Ctrl+RMB again and choose Grow Selection. Grow the selection repeatedly until the entire lower jaw is selected. Then use the Ctrl key while marquee-selecting unwanted edges to deselect them. You'll need to orbit around the head to find the unwanted edges and deselect them.

13. With just the lower jaw selected, switch to the Side view. Set it to wireframe mode (hotkey: **4**). Switch to rotate mode (hotkey: **e**). Toggle the pivot point with the Insert key. Move the pivot point to the hinge of the jaw, and exit pivot editing with the Insert key again. Now you can rotate the jaw down to open the mouth. Check your work in the Perspective view, as shown in Figure 11.25. RMB and choose Object mode to exit Component mode.

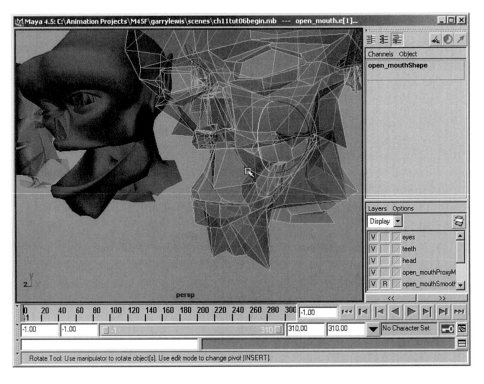

FIGURE 11.25   *Opening the mouth requires selecting edges, and then moving the rotate pivot point before rotating the edges.*

14. Select the smoothed open_mouth head and delete it. Right-click on the smooth layer in the Layer Editor, named open_mouthSmoothMesh, and delete it. Do the same for the proxy mesh layer. Select the open_mouth proxy head, and then shift-select the original, smoothed, expressionless head.

15. To add this Blend Shape to our Alien_Expression set of Blend Shapes, we need to apply this Blend Shape differently. Choose Hotbox | Deform | Edit Blend Shape | Add | option box. In the dialog that appears, reset the settings and choose Specify Node. Set this to Alien_Expression. Uncheck the option to check topology. Click Apply and Close, and go back to your Blend Shape Editor. If you closed it, you can find it under Window | Animation Editors | Blend Shape. You'll see a new slider for the open mouth. Try this slider, and the smoothed shape will open its mouth. You can also still add any amount of "confused" to the slack-jawed alien, as shown in Figure 11.26.

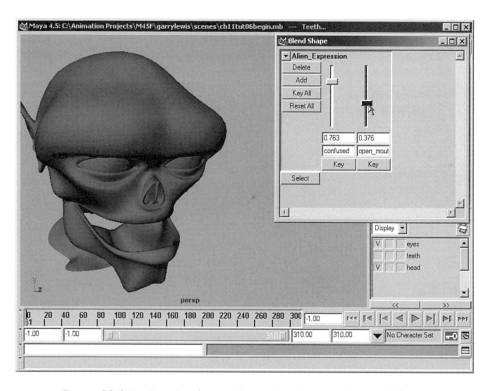

FIGURE 11.26   *Opening the mouth requires selecting edges, and then moving the rotate pivot point before rotating the edges.*

16. You can repeat Steps 10-15 to add more facial expression sliders for the alien. At this point, we'll stop creating sliders and instead create a little facial animation. Set both sliders to 0 in the Blend Shape Editor, and set the current frame to 0. In the Blend Shape Editor, click the Key All button.

17. Go to frame 35 and raise the "confused" slider to 1.0. Click Key All again. Go to frame 40. Set "confused" to 0, and raise "open_mouth" to 0.5. Click Key All again. Go to frame 60, raise "confused back to 1.0, and again click Key All.

18. Create a playblast of frames 0-60 with Hotbox | Window | Playblast | option box. Set the time range to Start/End, set start and end to 0 and 60, and click Playblast to create an AVI to see your animation.

On the CD

Chapter_11\ch11tut06end.mb

Blend Shape deformers are a delightful way to animate poses for any geometry. They provide an intuitive interface for mixing and animating poses, and you can even take any mixed configuration and "bake" it into another Blend slider (the Add function in the Blend Shape dialog).

You can mix Blend Shape deformers with characters that have been skinned with a skeleton to get walking, talking objects in Maya. You can also use Trax to animate facial poses with blended still poses or clips of motion.

Going Further

Try creating other animation clips and combining them in Trax. Try creating more facial targets and animating them doing some more complex facial animation. Try creating a skeleton for a quadruped, like a dog, and explore the unique walk cycle of these creatures.

Summary

Character animation with Maya offers a rich tablet of possibilities and immense control. In this chapter, we've explored some of the standard techniques of character animation, including the following:

- **Joint creation**   Building linked skeleton joints.
- **IK setup**   Specifying parts of a skeleton that will behave with Inverse Kinematics.
- **Rigid binding**   Attaching a skin to a skeleton with a rigid bind.

- **Applying flexors**   Smoothing the joints of a rigid bind by applying a flexor.

- **Creating character animation**   Adding animation keys to your skeleton to make your character move.

- **Using the Graph Editor**   Refining your character animation by looking at the graph of the skeleton's controllers.

- **Using Trax**   Building more complex animation from clips of simple animation.

- **Using Blend Shapes**   Making surfaces deform into another shape using Blend Shape deformers.

CHAPTER 12

Cameras and Rendering

In This Chapter

After building your scene and animating it, your final steps are usually adding a camera and rendering the animation. A camera is more than just a viewpoint, however. The camera is another part of your project's creative vision, just as movie cinematographers help tell the story by where they place and focus a camera. By working with settings such as zoom and focal length, you can make a mouse seem as big as an elephant or a skyscraper look tiny. Unlike real cameras, Maya's virtual camera has no mass or size, so it can pass through pinholes or change direction instantly. Where you position the camera and how you frame your subject matter are important details in composing your animation and adding depth to your art.

In animation, rendering is the process of generating two-dimensional images from a view of a three-dimensional scene. The images are saved as image files and can later be placed in sequence to produce an animation. You can also render still frames to sample what the final animated sequence will look like at different points. You have rendered some images in previous tutorials, but in this chapter, you'll delve into some of the options for rendering. This chapter covers the following topics:

- **Cameras and views** Learn what the three camera types are in Maya and how they work. You'll also find out how the views you're familiar with, such as Side and Perspective, differ in terms of camera setup.

- **Camera settings** Discover what attributes are available for customization so that you can fine-tune your camera setup and placement.

- **Animating cameras** Learn how to work through the process of animating a camera.
- **The Playblast revisited** You get another chance to see how the Playblast works and learn how it can save you hours of wasted render time.
- **Render Globals settings** You use the Render Globals window to define values for the Maya rendering engine. You'll get a chance to work with the most commonly used settings and understand what they do.
- **Adding a camera for your Spooky World house** Finally, you have the opportunity to add a camera to the scene you have been building and to render an animated fly-by of your scene.

Key Terms

antialiasing A rendering option that helps eliminate the "jaggies" often found between object edges and produces a smoother version of an image.

Perspective view The 3D view made up of orthographic projection.

orthographic view A 2D "flat" view of the scene, usually visualized from the front, side, or top. Perspective views exhibit foreshortening, but orthographic views do not.

focal length The Maya term for the perspective exaggeration or "wide-angle" quality of a camera. In real cameras, it's the distance from the lens to the film plane, directly proportional to the object's size in the frame.

clip planes Represent the camera's range; in Maya, cameras can see objects only within the values specified for the clip planes.

depth of field The camera's range of distance within which objects are sharply focused; also called the distance blur effect (commonly seen in photography with a subject that's in the near foreground).

Objects outside the camera's depth of field (either closer to or farther away from the camera) look blurred or out of focus.

tumble Rotate the camera about its center.

track Translate the camera up, down, left, or right without changing its aim.

dolly Move the camera toward or away from its center of interest; the scene then appears larger or smaller.

zoom Camera's focal length is changed but its position in space does not move.

roll Rotating the camera around its sight line (the line connecting the camera to its center of interest).

scrub To drag time forward and backward so you can check animation in a view. This is done by LMB-dragging in the Time Slider.

batch render A background process that allows you to render a sequence of frames (rather than a single still image) while continuing to work in Maya; these frames are stored in the Images directory for your project.

Hotkeys to Memorize

Ctrl+d   duplicate   [camera view undo

s   set an animation key   ]   camera view redo

Shift+W   set a key for Translate mode

Cameras

In Maya, every view relates to a camera. When Maya starts, you have four cameras by default: front, side, top, and perspective. Three of them are orthographic—flat, non-perspective views—and have visible icons you can use to translate or rotate the camera. The icon for the perspective camera is, by default, invisible. These four cameras are utility views that assist you in modeling and laying out your scene. When you're ready to pick the final rendered viewpoint of your scene, you should create a scene camera. If you're shooting a series of stills, you can create many cameras, one for each shot. (However, often it's easier to move a single camera to different positions in sequential frames, starting with frame 1, so that you can render the job more easily in batch rendering.) Or you might have several animated cameras that fly through the scene from varying angles, creating several different video clips of the same scene that are rendered separately.

The camera placement determines exactly what will be seen and is used to frame specific portions of the scene, in the same way artists use composition to frame certain elements in their paintings and drawings. Other key variables for cameras are focal length, rotation (orientation), and angle of view. Focal length is directly linked to angle of view; if one goes up, the other goes down. With angle of view, as the angle of the lens widens, you must move the camera closer to the subject to keep it at the same relative size in the frame. The wider the angle, the higher the value for the Angle of View setting. Figure 12.1 illustrates four settings for Angle of View.

Creating Cameras

There are three types of perspective cameras in Maya, shown in Figure 12.2. Like the lights, you can change a camera to any other camera type in the Attribute Editor.

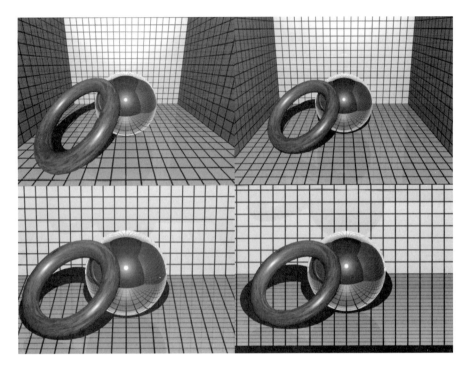

FIGURE 12.1   *Clockwise from top left: a wide-angle (90 degree) close-up view, a normal (55 degree) view, an orthographic (0 degree) view, and a zoom (17 degree) view.*

- **Camera**   With this camera type, you see only the camera icon (the next two types add manipulator handles to the camera icon). In general, because this camera freely rotates and loses track of its "up" vector (as shown in the rotating camera at far right in Figure 12.2), you should use it only when you're linking the camera to another object for movement and animation (as in the boat tutorial in Chapter 4, "Diving in: Your First Animation"), or when you're placing a camera in one fixed spot.

- **Camera and Aim**   This camera includes a camera target (in other words, what the camera is looking at) as well as an aim handle for adjusting the camera target. In addition, this camera automatically stays level in relation to the horizon, so it's the one you'll use most often. You can make this camera roll if you want, but by default it stays level except at extreme straight-up or straight-down orientations.

- **Camera, Aim, and Up**   This camera type includes two handles: the aim handle, described for Camera and Aim, and an up handle for banking (leveling) the camera. This camera type is useful when you want to bank the camera during your animation. Note that you must select both the camera and the up handle when you move the camera, or the up handle will remain in place as you move the camera, causing unwanted banking.

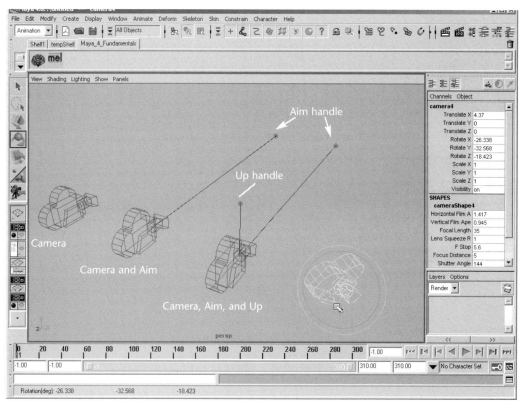

FIGURE 12.2   *The three camera types, left to right: Camera; Camera and Aim; and Camera, Aim, and Up. To rotate cameras, click in the blue circle shown at the right.*

tip

When Maya starts, you see a Perspective view with its own default "persp" camera. This Perspective view is useful for navigating around your scene to find the areas you want to focus on and to edit those areas in 3D. You can create additional cameras and use them for "official" render cameras or as additional test perspective cameras like the default perspective camera. Usually, however, it's better not to use the default perspective camera as your scene's render camera because it's too easy to unintentionally move or alter.

Camera Settings

With a camera selected, you can open the Attribute Editor and expand the Camera Attributes section to see all the variables for the camera, as shown in Figure 12.3.

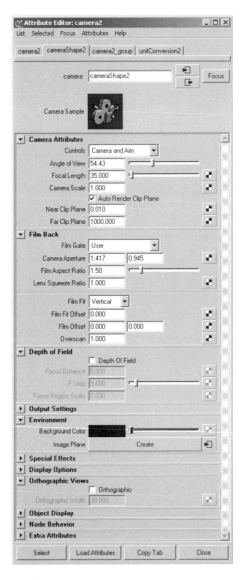

FIGURE 12.3   *The attributes for cameras.*

These are the key settings for cameras under the Camera Attributes section:

- **Controls**   In this drop-down list, you can quickly select the camera type you want.

- **Angle of View/Focal Length**   Controls the amount of perspective exaggeration. Raising the Angle of View attribute lowers the Focal Length attribute. For example, in Figure 12.1's top-left image, the angle of view has been raised to 90 degrees, so the focal length is shortened to 18, thus producing a close-up view with heightened foreshortening, most noticable in the distorted torus.

- **Camera Scale**   You can change the camera size in relation to your scene, which affects the scene objects when you render. Camera Scale is like a multiplier for the Angle of View. For example, decreasing the Camera Scale attribute to .5 halves the camera's view area, but makes the objects in the scene appear twice as large.

- **Clip Planes**   Only objects located within the values specified for the camera's clip planes appear in the scene. If distant objects are not appearing, raise the Far Clip Plane value. If nearby objects seem to be appearing in cross-section or not appearing at all, lower the Near Clip Plane value.

- **Depth of Field**   Enable distance blur with this attribute. It can be a render-intensive effect, but yields a more realistic result because objects close to and far from the focus point are progressively blurred.

- **Background Color**   The background fill color for images rendered from this camera; you can also use this section of the Attribute Editor to add an image or shader as the background.

- **Orthographic Views**   Switches the camera to an orthographic view (such as Side, Top, or Front), which has no perspective. You can create perspective cameras, rotate them into position, and then set them to orthographic to get a "flat" view for projecting textures onto an object.

tip

The Film Offset settings are helpful for architectural animators who want to avoid vertical perspective distortion. If you have set your camera to a view that causes vertical distortion (refer back to Chapter 1, "Pre-Maya: A Primer," and take another look at the rightmost image in Figure 1.10), you can adjust these values to get rid of the distortion. First, you must raise or lower the camera itself, so that it is horizontal; this removes all vertical distortion. Then use the offset settings to frame the portion of the image you want to render. The Film Offset X and Y values (X is the left text box; Y is the right) reposition where the camera "looks" in relation to the target.

Animating the Camera

When you animate the camera, you need to follow the rules of videography, such as avoiding jarring camera motions—rapid pans, zooms, or rotations of the camera. In addition, you'll usually want to give the camera the impression of having mass. The virtual camera, by default, starts and stops moving instantly, which looks unrealistic and abrupt to the viewer. To avoid this problem, adjust the tangents for the camera position start and stop keys in the Graph Editor so that motion begins and ends gradually (refer to Chapter 10, "Animation Basics," for more information on adjusting tangents). Do the same for the camera's aim point keys and any other animated camera attributes if you want to get a smooth look. Of course, if you're after the "reality TV" look, you'll have no problem creating a shaky, off-kilter camera in Maya. It's the "cinematic" look that takes some work. You'll explore smoothing the camera's action in the next tutorial.

 tip

You can make a panel "look through" any scene element (object, camera, light, and so forth). Choose Panels | Look Through Selected on the panel's menu bar, and the panel will switch to the viewpoint of the currently selected scene element. Most of the time, you do this only to check the aim of Spot and Directional lights, but this method can also be helpful when you want a quick look at the scene from an object's point of view. For objects, if you look through them, you're viewing from the object's local –Z axis.

Tutorial: Easing the Camera's Motion

In this tutorial, you'll animate a camera and then adjust its animation keys for smooth motion. You want the camera to swing left around the objects, then move left across the cylinder, cone, and torus, and finally rotate to the far side, behind

On the CD

Chapter_12\movies\ch12tut01.wmv

the tall box object. After you set the position keys for the camera and its target, you'll give the camera the appearance of mass by adjusting the tangents for the camera and the target's start and stop keys so that the transitions in motion are more gradual.

1. Make sure you're in Four View mode (if not, tap the spacebar to switch). Create a camera (Create | Cameras | Camera and Aim). In the Channel Box, set Translate X, Y, and Z to 150, 40, and 9. Set Scale X, Y, and Z to 20 so that the camera icon is

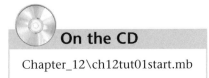

On the CD

Chapter_12\ch12tut01start.mb

bigger and easier to select. With the camera still selected, activate the Perspective view, and choose Panels | Look Through Selected. Your shaded view is now the camera's view; as you move the camera, you'll see the shaded view update. Open the Outliner, expand the Camera1_group, and select the camera's aim point, named camera1_view. Set its Translate X, Y, and Z to 50, 11, and 8 in the Channel Box.

2. Click the down arrow to the left of the Select by Object/Component Type (selection mask) buttons, and select All Objects Off, as shown in Figure 12.4. RMB-click on the Rendering selection mask button (the blue sphere), and choose Cameras. Now you can select only cameras in your scene, which will make the animation process easier.

FIGURE 12.4   *Using the selection mask buttons.*

3. Select Camera1, and then Shift-click on the aim point to select its target—camera1_view. In the Time Slider, confirm that the current frame is set to 0, and set an animation key for just the Translate values (hotkey: **Shift+W**). Deselect the camera and target by clicking in a blank area of the Camera1 view (the Perspective view).

> Normally, you set keys by using the **s** hotkey, but you can also use Shift+W, Shift+E, and Shift+R to set keys for Translate, Rotate, and Scale without affecting other keys. By default, the **s** hotkey sets keys on all the attributes, which isn't usually what you want. Adding keys to elements that aren't animated can cause a lot of trouble if you decide later that you do want to animate those attributes.

4. Drag the Time Slider to frame 60. Switch to Move mode (hotkey: **w**). In the Top view, select the camera, and move it down and to the left, so that Translate X is roughly 138 and Translate Z is about 55 (the Channel Box will reflect the camera's current position as you move it).

5. Next, you'll set a key but change the defaults so that the **s** hotkey works only for the current manipulator type—in this case, the Translate values because you're in Move mode. To do this, choose Hotbox | Animate | Set Key | option box. Change the Set Keys On radio button to Current Manipulator Handle, and then click the Set Key button. From now on, the **s** hotkey will create keys only for the current manipulator. Select camera1_view (the target), and move it slightly down and left so that it's on the cone object, and set its Translate key for frame 60 (hotkey: **s**). The Translate fields in the Channel Box turn orange to indicate that keys have been created for the selected object.

6. Drag the Time Slider to frame 120. Shift-click the aim handle to select both camera and target. In the Top view, move them together down and to the left so that the camera target is at the center of the torus. Set a key by pressing s (which will set a key for the Translate values of both the camera and target). Next, select only the camera and adjust it so that it's closer to the torus in the Top view. In the Front view, bring the camera's height down somewhat (until Translate Y is about 25). Set a key again (hotkey: **s**) to overwrite the camera's previous key.

tip   You can overwrite previously set keys by setting a new key for the same attribute on a frame that currently has a key.

7. Drag the Time Slider to frame 180. In the Top view, move the camera down to a position that's about 25 and 90 for Translate X and Z; the sight line to the target will be vertical. Check the Camera1 view and adjust the camera's position if you want it slightly closer or farther to the objects in the scene. Set a key for the camera, and then select the target and set a key for it, too.

8. With the target still selected, drag the Time Slider to frame 210, and set a key. Select the camera and move it a few degrees to the left of the torus (Translate X, 0; Translate Z, 90). Set a key.

9. Drag the Time Slider to 300. Select both camera and target. In the Top view, position the camera target at the center of the tall box by dragging the aim handle, and set a key; both will be keyed on the Translate values because both are selected and you're in Move mode. Next, select only the camera by clicking in an empty area, and then clicking the camera. In the Top view, move the camera to the far left side of the tall box. Set a key again with the **s** hotkey to key the Translate values for the camera.

10. Activate the shaded Camera1 view by RMB-clicking on it, and then click the Play button in the playback controls to the right of the Time Slider. Notice that the camera motion is fairly smooth, but it starts and stops abruptly.

11. Make sure the camera is still selected, and view the camera trajectory by choosing Hotbox | Animate | Create Motion Trail | option box. In the Motion Trail Options dialog box (see Figure 12.5), select the Line radio button for the Draw Style option, deselect the Show Frame Numbers check box, and click the Create Motion Trail button. You can now see a line that illustrates the path of the camera. Do the same for the camera target. These paths, generated by the keys you set, can be helpful to visualize what you've animated, and they are updated as you adjust keys. To see these motion trails in action, try moving the camera after activating the AutoKey feature. After you release the mouse button, the curve will update. Press z to undo, and then deactivate AutoKey.

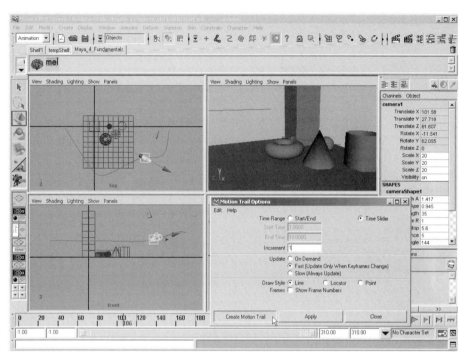

FIGURE 12.5   *Creating a motion trail for the animated camera.*

12. Make sure the camera is selected. Open the Graph Editor (Hotbox | Window | Animation Editors | Graph Editor). When it opens, you'll see lines representing the camera's motion curves. Click and drag over the three Translate labels in the Graph Editor Outliner. The graph changes to display just these three attributes. Now frame the view (hotkey: **f**) so that the motion curves fill the Graph view.

13. Marquee-select the leftmost points of the red, green, and blue motion curves in the Graph view. Hold down the Shift key and do the same for the rightmost points of each curve. RMB-click on one of the endpoints, and choose Tangents | Flat, as shown in Figure 12.6. All the tangents become horizontal at their beginning and ending points.

14. In the Graph Editor Outliner, scroll down to the bottom of the list and find the Center of Interest section. Select the three Translate entries in that section. The motion curves displayed in the Graph view will change. Repeat Step 11 to flatten the tangents for the beginning and ending points of these curves.

15. Close the Graph Editor, RMB-click the Camera1 viewport to make it active, and play the animation (hotkey: **Alt+v**). The moving camera's view should play back in a loop, and the starting and stopping

On the CD

Chapter_12\ch12tut01end.mb

action at the ends of the animation should occur much more smoothly. You can compare your final version with the finished scene file noted here, if you like.

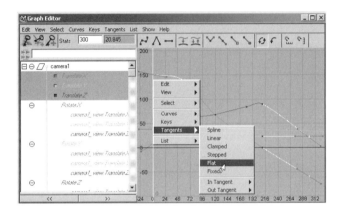

FIGURE 12.6   *Editing the tangents of the curves' endpoints in the Graph Editor.*

Previewing with Playblast

In most of the simpler examples, the scenes were so basic that even slower 3D video cards could probably keep up with changes you made to the Shaded view. However, when you have a lot of objects in your scene, use hardware texturing, or have other factors that burden a 3D video card, the responsiveness of the Shaded view suffers. Normally, this isn't a problem; you can wait for the Shaded view to catch up, or simply switch to Wireframe mode when you don't need to check for object intersections, for example. However, for gauging animation speed, you need some way to play back your animation tests in real time.

As you may recall from Chapter 10, the tool for this function in Maya is called Playblast (choose Window | Playblast on the main menu or in the Hotbox). This tool uses your 3D video card to churn out shaded frames to produce an animation; you can watch the results to help you figure out how to fine-tune your animation. This method is much faster than rendering with Maya's software renderer.

Rendering an Animation

When you're ready to render a finished animation, open Maya's Render Globals window to set up the render job. To render multiframe jobs, you use the Batch Render function, which uses the settings you've chosen in Render Globals. You can find the Render Globals button on the Status Line, just to the right of the IPR Render button. You can also activate it with Hotbox | Window | Rendering Editors | Render Globals.

Render Globals Settings

The Render Globals window, shown in Figure 12.7, can look overwhelming at first, but there are a few key areas you'll focus on to get most of your animation rendering ready.

You should make sure to configure the settings in the top section, Image File Output, when you're rendering a job unattended. Generally, you want to keep your past renders, so it's always a good idea to name the rendered output. Otherwise, it defaults to the name of the scene file. The Start/End/By Frame area is activated if you choose a movie file output format or a filename numbering extension for your saved files. The default animation render length is set to frames 1 through 10—a very short animation! Be sure to set it to the length of the animation you want to see. For the previous tutorial, you would set it to render frames 0 through 300. Select the appropriate image format and type in the Image Format list box; see Chapter 1 for a thorough explanation of these types.

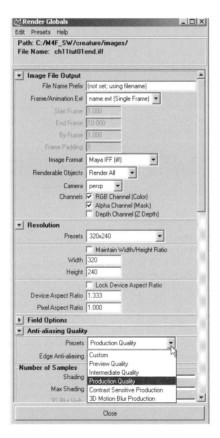

FIGURE 12.7   *Maya's Render Globals window controls how the renderer processes your scene.*

The Resolution section is where you set the image size; you can use the Presets list box to choose from a range of resolutions. Most of your tests will be at a lower resolution, typically 320×240. If your final image will be printed, you might render much higher for the final version, perhaps 2000 or more pixels wide. Your computer's RAM usually sets the ceiling for image size. Leave the Pixel Aspect Ratio set to 1.

The Anti-aliasing Quality setting has a big impact on rendering speed and image quality. Images that are poorly antialiased have a jagged appearance, particularly visible where different-colored objects overlap or in areas of high contrast. Generally, you keep this setting at a low quality level until your final render because higher settings take longer to render. For tests, you'd select the Preview Quality setting in the Presets list box; for final rendering, use the Production Quality setting.

The Raytracing section is where you configure raytraced reflections, refractions, or shadows to appear in the rendering; it's disabled by default, so expand that section to enable the options. Raytracing can also slow your rendering time dramatically. The numbers for the Reflections, Refractions, and Shadows attributes refer to the depth of raytracing—the number of bounces allowed for a ray. As the ray strikes reflective or refractive objects, it ricochets through the scene. If the number of bounces reaches the limit set here, no further raytracing is done, and the pixel is colored based on the contribution of the previous bounces added to black. These limits can save you a lot of time when rendering scenes, such as a "hall of mirrors" effect, because without the limit, a ray could bounce forever.

Rendering a Still

When you want to render a test frame, you simply activate the panel of the view you want, and click Hotbox | Render | Render Current Frame. The settings in the Render Globals window determine the resolution, antialiasing, and raytracing, but only one frame will render, and it's saved as a temporary (.tmp) file in the Images directory of your project. When the rendering is finished, you can save the rendered image to a permanent file by RMB-clicking on the Render View window and choosing File | Save Image in the Save dialog box that appears.

For images you have rendered and saved, you can view them with Maya's FCheck utility (see Figure 12.8). This handy tool can view most types of images and movies, and can also save them in other formats. To start FCheck, click its icon in the Start menu (under the menu item for Maya).

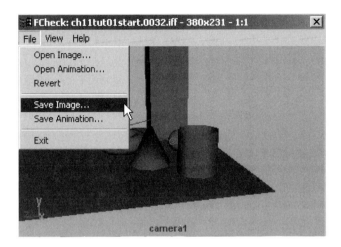

FIGURE 12.8   *FCheck is a useful file viewer and multiformat image translator.*

Setting Up a Render Job

When you're ready to render a job, follow this checklist:

- Unhide any hidden objects you want to include.

- Make visible any layers you want to include.

- In Render Globals, make sure you have set the correct filename, frame range, and image format. Make sure the Frame Padding value accommodates the frame range; for example, use a value of at least 3 (for three digits) if the frame range is under 999 but over 100.

- In Render Globals, double-check the camera or view that will be rendered from. You can render orthogonal views or any perspective camera in the scene.

- Set image resolution and antialiasing quality.

- Disable alpha channel and depth channel if you won't be compositing.

- Check the top of the window to confirm the location where the files will be saved. Make sure it's a disk drive with enough space if you're rendering a large image or a long animation. If you want to change the save-to path, choose Edit | Change Project Image Directory in the Render Globals window to open the Edit Project dialog box, where you can alter the Images setting to any path you like.

Now close the Render Globals window and click Hotbox I Render I Batch Render, and your computer will begin processing frames. You can continue working in Maya, but often the renderer requires so much of your system resources that it's difficult to work on anything else while the renderer is running. If you want to minimize this effect and you're running a multiprocessor computer, you can click the option box for Batch Render, and set the number of processors that should work on the job just assigned. More information on batch rendering multiple jobs and rendering on multiple machines is included in Chapter 15, "Your Next Steps: Efficiency and Artistry."

Tutorial: Adding a Camera for the House

Now you can apply some of what you've learned to a short tutorial that adds a camera to the house scene you've been building. You'll be continuing from the scene you worked with in Chapter 10 that includes the house deformations. If you do not have this particular scene, you can load it from the *Maya 4.5 Fundamentals* CD-ROM (see the filename below the CD icon).

On the CD

Chapter_12\movies\ch12tut02.wmv

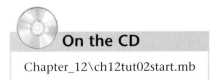

On the CD

Chapter_12\ch12tut02start.mb

Creating a Generic Path

After you have the scene loaded, you're ready to add the camera to your scene. You'll use path animation, similar to the method used in Chapter 4, to set up the movement for the camera. It's a simple method, but it gives you precise control over the camera's position and speed during playback. You'll create a path that simulates a cinematic "crane shot," in which the camera is put on a moving platform that can reach treetop heights when needed.

1. First, you need to decide which geometry should be visible as you set up the camera for animation. The camera will start off at a distance and then fly toward the house. To correctly orient the camera and path, you need the ground plane and a simple representation of the house visible. Hide all the layers except for GroundL and OuterWallsL to reduce the clutter in the scene and give you a cleaner work area.

tip   To keep things simple and uncluttered when you're working in a scene, you should keep visible only the layers you need for the current procedure you're performing.

2. Next, you'll set up the layout so that you can efficiently place the camera. To work with the camera, tap the spacebar to use the standard Four View mode (Hotbox | Panels | Saved Layouts | Four View). Lights are visible in the different views and are just more clutter, so hide their display (Hotbox | Display | Hide | Lights).

3. Next, you'll need to address the Far Clip Plane setting for certain cameras. If you see that one of the views is displaying only a portion of the scene, chances are the Far Clip Plane is set too low (see Figure 12.9). To change the Far Clip Plane value, open the Attribute Editor for the view (View | Camera Attribute Editor). Under the Camera Attributes section, increase the Far Clip Plane setting to 10000, which should work fine for this tutorial.

note

To work efficiently, cameras must have near and far cutoff points so that they display only the geometry between these values. Maya cameras have default Far Clip Plane values of 1000 units, which is often far too low for scenes of any size. If a viewport looks strange or objects are unexpectedly disappearing from 3D views, it's a good idea to check the camera clipping planes as one cause. Side, Front, and Top views are camera types that also have clipping planes. Zoom extents options in any view (such as hotkeys **a** and **f**) can also reveal this clipping issue.

4. With the layout set up, position each view so that you can see as much of the ground plane as possible. If the grid is visible, you can disable it.

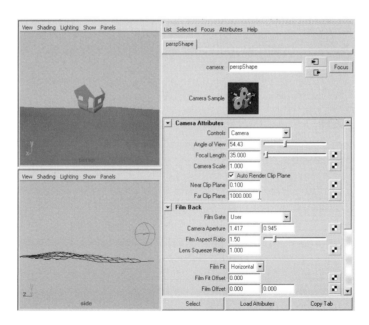

FIGURE 12.9 *Typical clipping problems in 3D shaded views. Raising the Far Clip Plane setting to 10000 solves the problem.*

trap   If you try to focus on all (hotkey: **Shift+A**) or focus on the ground plane, (hotkey: **f**) it might look as though everything in the view has disappeared, and you probably won't be able to find your scene when you adjust the view! This problem has to do with the ground plane's size—it backs the camera up so far that the clipping plane problem resurfaces. The easiest fix is to use the camera view hotkeys: **[** for undo and **]** for redo.

5. Maximize the Front view to start establishing a path for your camera. Access the CV Curve tool (Ctrl+c | CV Curve | option box). In the CV Curve Options dialog box, set the Curve Degree to 3 Cubic. Starting at the far right corner of the ground plane in the Front view, you'll place CVs that start about two house heights (about 40 feet) above the ground. Use the house as a height reference. The CVs should be placed in a gradual slope, coming closer to the ground and the house (see Figure 12.10 for reference) but no lower than 5 or 6 feet—about eye level. Remember that when making a CV curve, you must click the first four points before the curve is displayed. Continue to place CVs until you're in front of the house, and then place a couple of additional CVs to continue the curve above the house (see the far left in Figure 12.10). You can modify this basic path later, if needed. A total of 12 CVs are used for the curve.

Figure 12.10   *The basic camera path has been drawn as a CV curve.*

6. The path you just created in the Front view is flat when seen from above. To make the camera's movement more interesting, you'll add a little side-to-side motion to the curve. Restore the Four View mode by tapping the spacebar. In the Top view, you'll translate some individual CVs of this curve to create more curvature in the Y axis of this path. Switch to CV Component Selection mode (hotkey: **F8**). Using Figure 12.11 as a guide, select CVs in the middle of the path, and move them in the Top view. When positioning the CVs, try not to have any sudden sharp changes in direction so that you have a smooth curve for the camera to move along. Figure 12.11 shows the curve in the Top view after it has been modified.

7. Save the scene as ch11HouseCamera.mb.

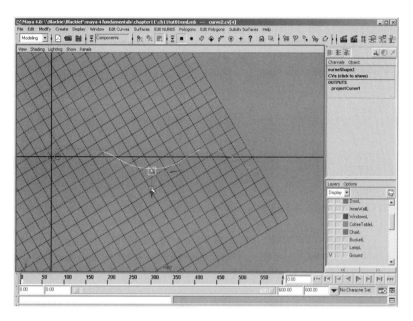

Figure 12.11   *CVs have been moved in the Top view to add more movement to the camera path.*

Tweaking the Path

Currently, the camera path is moving over the ground with little relation to elevation changes in the ground, and the curve may be higher than necessary because it's hard to gauge the camera altitude when looking through a Side view and seeing the landscape's wireframe. Continue with your scene from the last tutorial.

8. You could try to adjust each CV until it's positioned along the ground, but it would be difficult to see the height from the ground as you work. For reference, you'll project the curve onto the ground. Switch to the Top view. In the Outliner, select curve1, and then Ctrl+click on Ground to select it, too. To project the curve, in the Top view, use your NURBS Editing marking menu (Alt+z I Project Curve on Surface I option box). Reset the settings and click the Project button to place the curve directly under the path, along the ground.

9. The new reference curve is currently part of the ground's surface, so it will move only along the ground's normals. Test this with the Move tool and you'll see that the new line follows the topography everywhere it's moved. Undo with hotkey **z**. Select the projected curve, use Alt+c | Duplicate Curves | options box, reset the settings in the Duplicate Curves Options dialog box, and click the Duplicate button to create a copy of the curve that's no longer part of the surface. You can now hide the ground by clicking the V next to the Ground layer in the Layer Editor. You'll see only the two curves. The lower curve will serve as a reference for height in the Side and Front views.

10. Switch to the Front view and select the original path curve. Switch to CV Component Selection mode (hotkey: **F8**). Edit the CVs to get a better height for the camera, as shown in Figure 12.12.

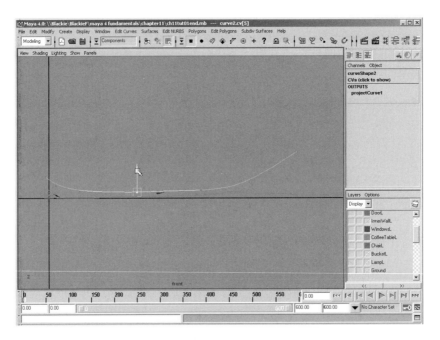

Figure 12.12   *Adjusting the camera path, using the projected path for reference.*

11. Name the final curve Camera_Path. You can also delete the reference projection curve.

Creating the Camera and Attaching It to the Path

Now that you have the curve positioned and set up, you'll create the camera and attach it to follow the curve. You can continue from the previous tutorial.

12. To keep the camera level and targeted to the house, you'll create a camera of the Camera and Aim type: Hotbox | Create | Cameras | Camera and Aim.

13. In the Outliner, notice that a new group has been created: camera1_group. Expand the group to find the camera and its view (aim). Click camera1_group, and change its name to CameraOnPath. Now select camera1_view (the aim point). The house is located at the scene's origin point, so the aim should be set to the origin, too. To do that, in the Channel Box, change Translate X, Y, and Z to 0.

tip It's possible to mistake your camera view for the Perspective view you're used to adjusting when you want to view your scene in perspective. If you orbit the camera view, it will completely change the camera aim. However, you can lock specific attributes so that the values cannot be changed by RMB-clicking an attribute in the Channel Box and choosing Lock Selected.

14. With the aim node selected (camera1_view), click the Translate X label in the Channel Box. Drag down to the Translate Z label so that all three translation settings are highlighted. RMB-click on one of the selected Translate labels, and choose Lock Selected. The Translate text boxes now have a gray background, indicating that their values are locked.

15. In Chapter 4, you attached a boat to a path created on the water. You'll use a similar method to attach the camera to the Camera_Path curve you created earlier. Select camera1 and Camera_Path in the Outliner, and then attach the camera to the path (Hotbox | Animate | Motion Paths | Attach to Motion Path | option box). Reset the settings in the Motion Path Options dialog box, uncheck the Follow check box, and then click the Attach button.

16. Switch to a shaded Perspective view, and zoom out to see the camera's entire path. (*Note:* You might need to adjust the clipping planes for the Perspective view.) The camera has been moved to the beginning of Camera_Path, and you'll notice two additions to the curve: At the beginning of the curve is the number 0 and at the end is the number 600. You can scrub the Time Slider to see the camera move along the path (see Figure 12.13). These numbers represent specific keys placed in the animation—the first at frame 0 and the last at 600, the last frame of the animation.

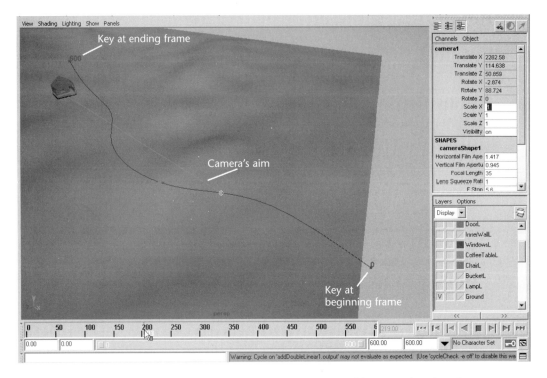

FIGURE 12.13 *The camera is attached to the curve and keys are placed at the beginning and end of Camera_Path.*

17. Now switch to the shaded Perspective view to look through the Camera1 view. Activate the Perspective view and choose Panels | Perspective | Camera1, and it will switch to the Camera1 view. Not quite what you expected? Adjust the Far Clip Plane value for the camera to 10000 by choosing View | Camera Attributes from the Camera view, and increase the Far Clip Plane value to 10000. Next turn on the Resolution Gate (View | Camera Settings | Resolution Gate), which places a small box in the viewport. This shows the exact area that will be rendered while giving the impression of a much wider angle lens to show the area outside the rendered frame.

18. With the Camera1 view active, play the animation. If the camera moves too low to the ground or exhibits other undesired behavior, edit the camera path curve as before. Don't allow the camera to dip below a medium eye-level height—roughly half the height of the door on the house. When editing your camera path curve, having fewer CVs always makes for smoother motion than having many, so use as few as possible to get the curved camera path you want.

19. Save your scene. If you want to compare your work, you can load the saved scene from the CD-ROM.

On the CD

Chapter_12\ch12tut02end.mb

Setup for Rendering

After setting up the camera path, specify the values in the Render Globals window (explained in the following tutorial) so that you can render your scene as an animation. Keep in mind, however, that you'll be adding more to the scene in Chapters 13, "Paint Effects," and 14, "Particle Systems and Dynamics." Pick a time when you won't need your computer for a while, perhaps at quitting time some evening, and set up a batch render to create an AVI, as we'll explain in the next tutorial. The next day, you'll have a fully rendered movie of the project you've created to date. It's good to do overnight renders when you're setting up animation because the machine is idle. When it's done, you'll have a fully rendered movie to view to give you a better feel for your animation's present state.

Tutorial: A Full-Length Batch-Rendered Movie

Continue from the previous tutorial, or load the scene file noted here.

On the CD

Chapter_12\movies\ch12tut03.wmv

1. Make all the layers visible in the Layer Editor.

2. To set up your scene for rendering, open the Render Globals window (Window| Rendering Editors | Render Globals).

3. In the File Name Prefix text box, enter `testfly`. In the Image Format list box, select AVI (avi), a movie format. Enter `0` in the Start Frame text box and `600` in the End Frame text box. In the Camera list box, select your scene's fly-by camera, Camera1.

On the CD

Chapter_12\ch12tut02end.mb

4. Expand the Resolution section, and in the Presets list box, select 320×240. AVI and other movie formats can be immense and sluggish if you choose a large size. Also, the lower resolution will render faster.

5. Expand the Anti-aliasing Quality section. In the Presets list box, select Production Quality, as shown in Figure 12.14.

6. Expand the Raytracing Quality section, and select the Raytracing check box. Close the Render Globals window.

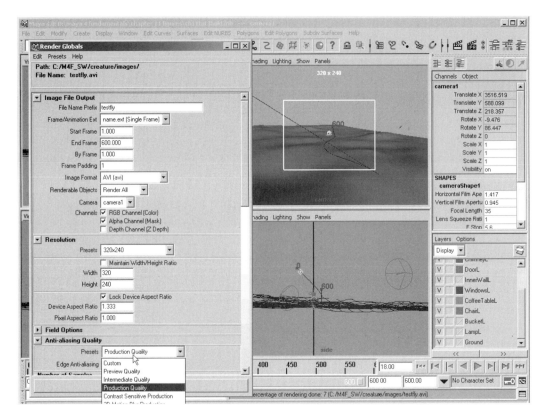

FIGURE 12.14   *A few quick changes in the Render Globals window, and you're ready to render a movie.*

7. To render the entire animation, choose Hotbox | Render | Batch Render. You can watch the progress in the Command Line or the Script Editor (if you want more detail). After starting the batch render, you can open the Script Editor by clicking the button at the far right of the

On the CD

Chapter_12\testfly.wmv

Command Line. It will probably take several hours at minimum for all 600 frames to render. The movie is created in your project's Images folder. To view the results after rendering is finished, double-click on the AVI movie file to open it in your movie player (see Figure 12.15). You can halt the batch render with Hotbox | Render | Cancel Batch Render.

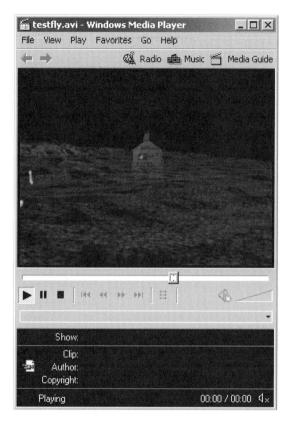

FIGURE 12.15   *Viewing your rendered animation as a movie.*

tip

Some people prefer to render to sequential still frames rather than movie formats, such as AVI, because if a movie render is interrupted, all rendering is lost and you must start the render job from the beginning. However, if you render to sequential frames, you can view the movie only by using FCheck, and you'll have a large collection of files on your drive. Also, you won't be able to show the movie on other computers or upload it anywhere unless you manually create a movie file first.

Going Further

Use the methods for easing camera motion that you learned in the first tutorial to make the camera start and stop more smoothly in the house animation. Explore creating different moods by adjusting the camera's Angle of View setting in the Attribute Editor and using different path curves for the camera path: wide angle and low, if you want a huge, ominous world, or close-up and high for a helicopter shot. Try animating the camera's aim independently of the camera to get different motion effects, or try to animate the camera to get the reality TV look, with rocking and abrupt movement. Try parenting the camera to animated objects, and rendering the resulting view.

Summary

Working through the tutorials in this chapter has given you a chance to try out some of the camera attributes and learn how to configure settings for rendering your animation. You learned the following concepts:

- **The different camera types and attributes**   You have learned the differences between the camera types and how each one gives you a different type of control, as well as the uses of the main attributes for cameras.

- **Animating cameras**   Even if no objects are moving in your scene, adding a moving camera lends a sense of action to your scene.

- **Easing camera motion**   You learned to adjust keys in the Graph Editor to give the camera a feeling of mass so that it doesn't start or stop moving too abruptly. This concept also works when you have objects that you want to seem heavy.

- **Visualizing a camera path over terrain**   You learned how to create a curve to guide your camera's height over terrain, which is important when animating the camera over a curvy surface.

- **Checking your animation**   Playing and scrubbing through your animation while looking through the Camera view can help you edit your animation.

- **Render Globals settings**   You've learned how to set up batch renders to get completed movies.

The following chapters add more exotic effects to your spooky house scene. You'll add vegetation and murky fog with Paint Effects in Chapter 13, and then make smoke emit from the chimney in Chapter 14. If you render a movie at that stage, you'll have a complex and complete animation!

PART III

Going Further with Maya

CHAPTER 13

Paint Effects

In This Chapter

Paint Effects is one of the most fun and visually impressive tools in Maya. At first, it seems like a paint program with the option to paint trees and flowers, but it can also paint 3D objects onto other 3D objects. For example, you can paint a tree onto a terrain you've painted in a viewport, and the tree's components—the branches, twigs, and leaves—will actually exist in 3D space instead of looking like a "flat," painted-on effect. You can also easily adjust and animate these elements to get a 3D environment with realistic light, movement, and shadows. With Paint Effects, you can paint a landscape with plants in a matter of minutes, and a 3D tour of that landscape is just a few clicks away! Some of the areas of Paint Effects you'll explore include the following:

- **Making objects paintable** Before you can start using Paint Effects to paint on an object, you must make it paintable.

- **Brush control** You'll learn about the controls for brushes, such as width and density, to help you get better results.

- **Picking a brush type** Before you begin making your own brushes, you'll want to explore the hundreds of preset brushes that come with Maya.

- **Optimizing the display** Paint Effects taxes your system and graphics display, so you need to control what's displayed and its level of detail to keep your visual feedback fast and accurate.

- **Modifying paint strokes** After you've created a stroke, you can change its shape and how Paint Effects uses the stroke.

- **Playblast** You can use this feature in Maya to get a reliable preview of what the animation will look like when playing at full speed.

Key Terms

stroke   The paint stroke; what's created when you drag the Paint Effects tool. The stroke, which is attached to a NURBS curve, controls how the paint is applied along the path you draw with the Paint Effects tool.

brush   The collection of Paint Effects settings that define what the stroke looks like and how it acts; can be thought of as your "paint"—daisies, hay, noodles, and so on.

template brush   Your current brush settings. You can configure these settings to affect what the next stroke looks like, or select a new brush to reconfigure the template brush settings.

Hotkeys to Memorize

8   switch to Paint Effects panel

b+LMB drag   resize the brush scale

Shift+B+LMB-drag   resize the brush width

m+LMB-drag   offset stroke from surface

Ctrl+b   open the Brush Settings dialog box

Shift+V   open the Visor

Alt+h   hide deselected objects

Ctrl+Shift+H   unhide last hidden object

Ctrt+h   hide selected objects

Paint Effects Overview

First included with Maya 2.5, Paint Effects is a compelling feature that offers the CG artist a quick and easy way to add all sorts of complex elements to a 3D scene. Simple paint effects such as Airbrush, Markers, and Swirl are included in the brush sets. You can see the potential of Paint Effects in more complex brushes, such as lightning and clouds, but it's the nature effects—including flowers, shrubs, grasses, and trees—that show off the Paint Effects capability to create fully formed, complex, and fractal 3D organics.

All this magic comes from a feature referred to as *tubes*, which follow or continue the path of the stroke to simulate organic growth. By basing the 3D portion of Paint Effects on tubes that exist in 3D space, the entire gamut of time and space changes can be applied. You can exhibit growth, dynamics, lighting, turbulence, and so forth with the 3D effects that come from the brush's paint stroke. The paint stroke is attached to a NURBS curve, so it can be fully animated. You can edit the curve to grow, undulate, change shape, and move, and the brushes applied to the stroke will follow the curve. In the same manner, the brush type applied to a paint stroke can be changed so that a row of oaks, for example, can become a row of rose bushes.

Opacity, luminosity, and other attributes can be built right into the brush; with these attributes, you can paint a luminous glowing lightning bolt in the same way you'd paint a semi-opaque raindrop or fully opaque ivy vine.

With all these varied options, the palette of available 3D brushes is boggling—stars and galaxies, fire and lightning with inherent turbulence animation, trees and grasses that can be set to rustle in the wind, flowers and bushes that can grow as though in time-lapse photography, and much more. Beginners will delight in watching an experienced animator use Paint Effects. In contrast to the sometimes painstaking process of creating an animation, using Paint Effects looks fast, fun, and easy.

Brushes and Strokes

A 3D brush is much different from a paintbrush. In Paint Effects, the brush is a collection of settings that control the appearance and behavior of the stroke. You can find all the attributes for creating the brush types in Maya under the Brush section in the Attribute Editor or in the Paint Effects Brush Settings dialog box (accessed by Hotbox | Paint Effects | Template Brush Settings; referred to in this chapter as "the Brush Settings dialog box" for simplicity). However, it's easier to create a brush by modifying one of the preset types. You can view the palette of preset brushes in a Maya dialog box called the Visor (hotkey: **Shift+V**; Window | General Editors | Visor on the menu; or Hotbox | Paint Effects | Get Brush). You might need to change the active tab in the Visor to get the brush list to appear. In Figure 13.1, the Paint Effects tab is selected, and the brush categories are listed in the Visor's left column.

tip

If the Visor doesn't show the tabs you need, you can reconfigure it to display the full set, as shown in Figure 13.1. Choose Tabs | Revert to Default Tabs on the Visor menu.

A stroke is what's created when you paint with the Paint Effects tool, and it uses the settings of the brush type you've selected. When you select a brush in the Visor, it activates the Paint Effects feature. You can paint on the grid (ground X-Y plane) or designate any NURBS object to be paintable. The cursor becomes a pencil-like icon, and when you click and drag in the viewport, a paint stroke is created. This stroke is attached to a curve drawn over the surface of the object you're painting. You can offset the stroke from the surface curve for certain effects, such as fog patches that hover over the ground. After painting the stroke, you can select its curve to adjust the settings attached to it; to do that, select the stroke, and then choose Display | Show | Show Geometry | Stroke Path Curves. All the stroke and brush settings are in the Channel Box and Attribute Editor, as with other scene elements you've created in Maya. If you drew the curve with a pressure-sensitive tablet, the pressure values are recorded along the stroke as they change. You can also use any curve you've drawn or projected in Maya as a stroke and attach a brush to it.

There are simple strokes and strokes with tubes (or "growth strokes"). Simple strokes are like paint strokes—a single line created by brush motion. With growth strokes, as you drag the mouse to create the stroke, this action creates tubes that grow, separate, or expand to continue outward in several directions from the stroke. For example, if you're painting a vine, tubes simulating leaves and tendrils can continue to "grow" from the main stalk. Tubes grow one "segment" for each step of the growth process; segments are straight, so increasing the Segments setting makes the segments in the tube smaller and thus produces a smoother appearance. Another important setting is Tube Completion. When it's enabled, the tubes continue growing automatically for their full "life span" (defined by the number of segments). When it's disabled, the tubes at the end of the stroke you draw will look more "cut off" than the tubes at the beginning of the stroke (as in half-grown trees or vines with no leaves). Usually you'll want to leave this setting enabled so that the current growth completes after you stop drawing.

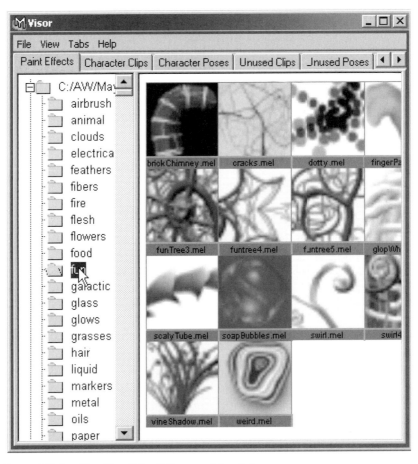

Figure 13.1   *The Visor lists all the preset brush types.*

Enabling Paint Effects

Because using Paint Effects can require a lot of system resources, some people leave it disabled when they aren't planning to use it. If it seems as though Paint Effects hasn't been enabled on your system, you can enable it by choosing Window | Settings/Preferences | Preferences on the main menu; in the Preferences dialog box, select Modules in the Categories list box. Select the Load Paint Effects on Startup check box (if it's not already), and then close the Preferences dialog box and restart Maya. Paint Effects is then added to Maya's Rendering menu.

Starting Paint Effects

When you want to apply Paint Effects to a surface, you must first designate a surface to be made paintable. This action does not modify the object; rather, it simply tells Paint Effects that this surface is prepared to receive brush strokes. If you want to paint a different surface, or if you have restarted Maya, you'll need to use the Make Paintable option again. This feature is in the Rendering menu under Paint Effects | Make Paintable. You can paint 3D Paint Effects only on NURBS surfaces, the view plane, or the ground plane. However, you can work around this by creating non-renderable NURBS surfaces that are similar to the polygonal surfaces you want, and then paint on those NURBS surfaces.

Using Paint Effects

When you have designated a surface as paintable, you can then paint in one of the following three modes:

- **Model View mode**   Painting in one of the normal 3D panels (in either Wireframe or Shaded mode). When painting in this mode, you see only a wireframe representation of your stroke and brush type (see Figure 13.2).

- **Paint Scene mode**   In this mode, when you switch into the Paint Effects panel, you'll see a shaded preview of your scene file. Paint Scene mode, shown in Figure 13.3, looks like the Perspective view, and can give you a good idea of what your paint strokes will look like by rendering them as you create them (although your display updates more slowly in this mode).

- **Paint Canvas mode**   Starts out as a white empty "canvas" when you switch into the Paint Effects panel—good for testing out brushes before trying them in your scene. Paint Canvas mode works as a sort of advanced 2D paint mode to create textures or paintings that can be saved as image files, and can store the depth and alpha channels of brushes. If you want to paint on the view plane, you need to use Paint Canvas mode.

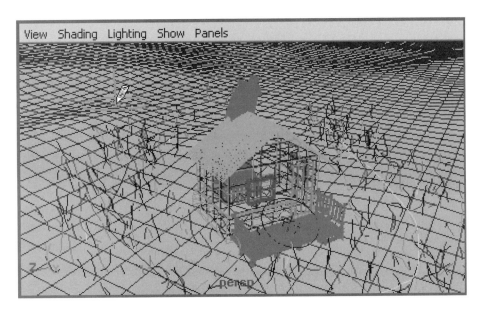

FIGURE 13.2   *Working with Paint Effects in Model View mode renders the strokes as wireframe.*

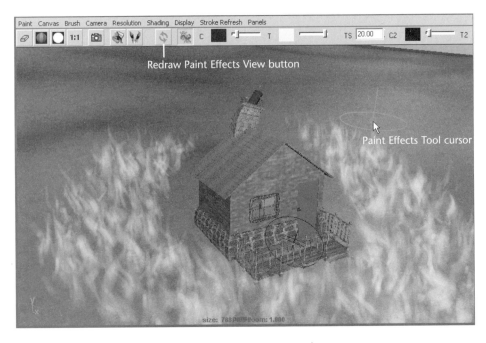

FIGURE 13.3   *Painting flames in the Paint Scene mode.*

To change the current panel to the Paint Effects panel, you press 8 or choose Hotbox | Panels | Panel | Paint Effects. You will be in Paint Scene or Paint Canvas mode (depending on the mode you were in last). To toggle between Paint Scene and Paint Canvas mode, RMB-click in the Paint Effects panel and choose Paint Scene or Paint Canvas. Paint Canvas mode is like a separate 2D painting area, and has no relation to your 3D scene. Because this chapter addresses only the 3D paint options, you'll choose Paint Scene. Paint Effects then does a quick-shade rendering of your scene file and places this 2D image into the view. It looks as though you're working in 3D, but to Paint Effects, it's only a 2D image you are painting on. When you orbit the scene to paint in another area in Paint Effects Canvas mode, the paint effects are reduced to lines. When you've found your new viewpoint, you can have Paint Effects render the previous strokes again by clicking the Redraw Paint Effects View button (refer back to Figure 13.3).

If you add many strokes of different types, redrawing can become slow. You'll find it helpful to hide strokes you don't need to see for your current Paint Effects work. To do this, open the Outliner to see all the strokes listed. Maya names the strokes with the type of brush used when the stroke was made, so it's easy to find the strokes you want to temporarily hide (see Figure 13.4). After selecting the brush strokes, you can hide them with the Ctrl+h hotkey or with Display | Hide | Hide Selection on Maya's main menu or in the Hotbox.

While working with Paint Effects, you might want to leave the Visor open to select other brushes. After you've selected a brush, Paint Effects displays a red circle cursor (refer to Figure 13.3) to give you an idea of the global scale of the objects to be "planted" when you begin painting. This cursor follows the surface of the paintable object as you move it around, and is a good indicator of whether the object you intend to paint on has truly been made paintable. You can adjust the brush size by holding down the b key and LMB-dragging left and right. You can also open the Brush Settings dialog box by pressing Ctrl+b, by choosing Brush | Edit Template Brush in the Paint Effects panel, or by clicking Hotbox | Paint Effects | Template Brush Settings. At the top of the dialog box, you'll see the Global Scale attribute.

Figure 13.4

Selecting strokes to hide in the Outliner.

trap

> Having trouble with seeing or sizing the Paint Effects brush is a common problem with video graphics card drivers. If you cannot get a red circle to appear that follows your pointer, you might want to revisit the graphics card information in this book's Introduction. In a large scene, the default brush size can cause the circle cursor to look like a tiny red point, so you might need to increase the brush size quite a bit to see it clearly.

After scaling the brush to create your stroke at the size you want, you can adjust the brush width if needed. For example, you might have set flames or trees to appear at the correct overall height for each flame or tree, but you want to fill a swath with flames or trees. To adjust the brush width, press and hold Shift+B while LMB-dragging left and right. This method works only when you're creating growth strokes; simple strokes such as "snake" will just be scaled as with Global Scale adjustments. Note that with growth strokes, stroke density is adjusted elsewhere; making the brush larger simply spreads the same number of growths over a larger area.

Another attribute to adjust is the brush offset, controlled by holding down the m key while LMB-dragging left and right. This action raises the brush stroke from the Paint Effects curve so that you can create a 3D stroke above or below the surface. For brush types such as smoke or snake, this option is invaluable.

To exit Paint Scene mode, choose Panels | Perspective on the menu. To quit the Paint Effects painting mode, simply click the arrow pointer in the Tool Box.

Tutorial: Learning Paint Effects

In this tutorial, you'll try some of the Paint Effects options on a NURBS surface you create:

On the CD

Chapter_13\movies\ch13tut01.wmv

1. Start with a blank, empty workspace in Maya. Make sure you have Paint Effects loaded (see the previous section "Enabling Paint Effects"). Tap the spacebar with the mouse over the Perspective view to switch to the Four View mode. Create a Directional light (Hotbox | Create | Lights | Directional Light), and set its Rotate X to -90. Under the light's Shape node in the Channel Box, enable the Depth Map Shadows option by typing a 1 or On and pressing Enter. Click Ctrl+z | Cone | option box, and reset the settings in the Cone Options dialog box. Set Radius to 300 and Height to 100, and then click the Create button. Press Shift+F to "fit all" so that you can see the entire cone in all four views.

If the Perspective view does not display the cone, it's likely a problem with the perspective camera's clipping plane. To fix this, choose View | Camera Attribute Editor in the Perspective view to open the perspective camera attributes, and set the Far Clip Plane to 10000.

2. Set the cone to display in high detail (hotkey: **3**), set the Perspective view to Shaded mode (hotkey: **5**), and tap the spacebar to return the Perspective panel to full screen. To make the cone paintable, select the cone, and click Hotbox | Paint Effects | Make Paintable, as shown in Figure 13.5.

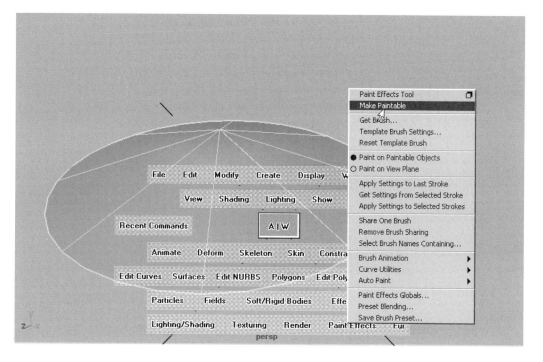

FIGURE 13.5   *The first step in Paint Effects: Making an object paintable.*

3. Switch to Paint Scene mode (hotkey: **8**). If you see a blank white panel, RMB-click in the panel and choose Paint Scene. On the Shading menu, make sure the options for Textured and Use All Lights are enabled. Choose Hotbox | Paint Effects | Get Brush on the menu in the Paint Effects panel to open the Visor (hotkey: **Shift+V**). Click the Paint Effects tab, expand the Brushes folder in the left-hand column if necessary, select the Flowers folder, and then click Daisy. Minimize the Visor.

You browse the swatches in the Visor just as you do in any Maya dialog box: Alt+MMB to pan and Alt+LMB+MMB to zoom.

4. Hold the cursor over the cone and see if the Paint Effects Tool cursor appears. The daisy's default size is quite small compared to the cone. To increase the brush's Global Scale attribute, you could press and hold the b key while clicking and dragging to the right on the cone. However, for this tutorial, you'll manually set the size to a fixed amount: Set it to 40 by opening the Brush Settings dialog box (hotkey: **Ctrl+b**) and changing the Global Scale setting. Close the dialog box, and draw a stroke on the cone, near the outer edge and about a third of the way around the cone. You should see daisies appear on the cone. Even though the last daisies you paint are only half-created when you release the mouse button, they finish growing to their full size because of the Tube Completion setting.

5. In the Channel Box, under Shapes, you'll find the settings for the stroke you created. The Sample Density attribute specifies how many daisies appear for a given length of the stroke. Try setting it to 2 or 3 to see the result.

How fast or slow you draw the stroke can affect the density, too. Because Paint Effects uses "sampling" when creating a stroke's underlying curve, a stroke drawn quickly has fewer samples and thus looks less dense than a stroke drawn more slowly.

6. Select Sunflowers from the Visor. Note that you need to adjust the brush's Global Scale setting each time you change brushes because all the brush settings (the "template brush") change when you select a new brush. Open the Brush Settings dialog box, and set Global Scale to 20. Notice that the brush size isn't necessarily related to the plant's overall size. The brush tip is small, but the sunflowers you paint are much taller than the daisies. You might want to make a few test strokes that you can undo later if needed (hotkey: **z**) to fine-tune the Global Scale settings. When you're satisfied with the plant's size, draw a stroke of sunflowers above the daisies.

If the Paint Effects panel is partially covered by another dialog box while it's rendering the stroke, the image might not be displayed in the area that's covered. Click the Redraw Paint Effects View button to regenerate the view if needed. Paint Effects are generated in the panel in the same way they appear when rendering. Therefore, the time it takes for your painted effects to "pop up" onscreen is a good indicator of how long rendering will take.

7. Use Alt+LMB to orbit the Paint Effects view. Notice how the painted objects are reduced to lines during the orbit. Select the Roses brush from the Visor, and set the Global Scale to 28 in the Brush Settings dialog box. Next, increase the brush *width* by pressing Shift+B while LMB-dragging to the right. The red brush circle will increase as though you had raised the global scale, but when you paint, you'll see that the roses are the same size as before, but appear over a broader area. Paint a new stroke above the sunflowers. Then set Sample Density in the Channel Box (under Shapes) to 3, and you'll see that the roses look denser and fill up more of the stroke area you drew, as shown in Figure 13.6.

note

The Paint Effects can be set to automatically regenerate (Rendered mode), or to regenerate only when you click the Redraw Paint Effects View button (Wireframe mode). This setting, under Stroke Refresh on the Paint Effects menu, is normally left at Wireframe mode because of the potential length of regeneration time.

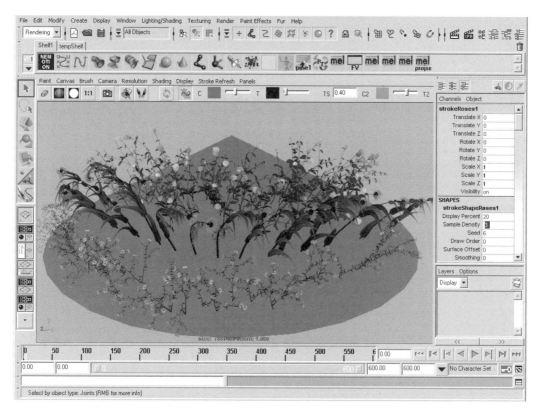

FIGURE 13.6   *Three rows of flowers.*

8. Exit Paint Effects by switching back to the Perspective panel (Panels | Perspective | Persp). The flowers' wireframe representation is noticeably thinner than it looked in Paint Effects. To see more lines for the roses, select the Roses stroke, and set the Display Percent to 100 in the Channel Box, under Shapes. If you accidentally deselect the Roses stroke, open the Outliner and select the strokeRoses1 item. You could increase the display percent for all three strokes, but interaction with Maya would slow down.

9. Orbit the Perspective view until you're looking across the cone, up close to the flowers, as shown in Figure 13.7. In the Perspective view, choose View | Camera Attribute Editor, and in the Camera Attribute Editor, set the Background Color under the Environment section to white so you can see the paint effects you added more easily. Close the Attribute Editor and render this view by clicking the Render button or choosing Hotbox | Render | Render Current Frame. Notice that the flowers cast shadows and seem thicker than the wireframe would imply.

FIGURE 13.7   *The rendered view of the three rows of flowers.*

Using Paint Effects can be quite straightforward, and it integrates well with standard geometry and lighting. To compare
your scene with ours, check the scene file
noted below the CD icon.

On the CD

Chapter_13\ch13tut01end.mb

Working with Strokes

After you've created a stroke, you can use it in many ways. You can edit the stroke,
or copy a brush to or from the stroke. You can also modify Paint Effects parameters
to, for example, make a brush have smaller flowers or more branching.

Selecting Strokes

To modify a stroke, you need to select it first, which can be challenging in Shaded or
Wireframe mode because the stroke is nearly always lying across a given object. It's
easier to select strokes in the Outliner. If you want to delete a stroke, you can press
the Delete key after selecting it in the Outliner.

Creating a Paint Effects Stroke with a NURBS Curve

You can attach a brush to any NURBS curve you've created (by projection, direct creation, or any other method) to create a new Paint Effects stroke. With the curve
selected, open the Visor, select a brush, and in the Paint Effects panel, choose Paint
Effects | Curve Utilities | Attach Brush to Curves.

Copying and Pasting Brush Settings

You can select any stroke you've already created and use its brush settings to contin-
ue painting or to paint other objects by choosing Paint Effects | Get Settings from
Selected Stroke. This action copies that stroke's brush settings into the template
brush. You can then select other strokes and apply the same settings to their brushes. To do this, you select the strokes in the scene or in the Outliner, and then choose
Paint Effects | Apply Settings to Selected Strokes.

Simplifying Curves and Strokes

To make a stroke's underlying curve easier to animate and deal with, you can remove
CVs from the curve to simplify it by choosing Paint Effects | Curve Utilities | Simplify
Stroke Path Curves.

If the stroke has a complex brush attached, however, it can slow down Maya's responsiveness. The solution is to lower the stroke's display quality (this lowers the density by reducing the numbers of tubes and segments in the stroke). With the stroke selected, choose Display | Stroke Display Quality on Maya's main menu and select one of the following: 0/25/50/75/100%/Custom. It's best to select the Custom option and set a value around 5%–20%. Usually, a percentage in this range is all you need to see where the stroke will appear and whether it's getting in the way of something else.

Tutorial: Adjusting Paint Effects

It's time to return to the scene file you've built progressively through this book. In this tutorial, you'll add a single stroke and then edit it to get the effect of dead grass blowing in the wind.

On the CD

Chapter_13\movies\ch13tut02.wmv

1. Load the scene file, and enable Hardware Texturing in the Perspective view with Shading | Hardware Texturing. If this drags down your graphics performance too much, you can work with Hardware Texturing disabled—simply toggle it off the same way you enabled it. Render a

On the CD

Chapter_13\ch13tut02start.mb

frame of the Perspective view, and you'll see that the lighting scheme is for a night scene, with the house casting soft shadows, to suit your spooky world (see Figure 13.8).

2. Open the Paint Effects Globals dialog box (Paint Effects | Paint Effects Globals). Expand the Scene section, set the Scene Scale to 200 so that the default brush sizes are at the correct scale for the scene, as shown in Figure 13.8, and then close the dialog box.

3. Select the ground and make it paintable (Paint Effects | Make Paintable). Open the Visor (hotkey: **Shift+V**) and choose the same Daisies brush you used in the previous tutorial. RMB-click in the shaded Perspective view, and you'll see the Paint Effects Tool cursor appear. Paint some daisies to check the brush size, and then undo (hotkey: **z**). Because you were painting in a Perspective view (Model View mode), the daisies look less complex than they did when you painted them in Paint Scene mode in the previous tutorial.

FIGURE 13.8   *Hardware textured and rendered view of the scene.*

4. Switch to the Paint Effects panel (hotkey: **8**). As before, if you see a white empty panel, RMB-click in the panel and choose Paint Scene. Return to the Visor, and in the Grasses category, select the grassDryBlowing.mel brush. Set the Paint Effects panel to Wireframe mode (for speedy response) by pressing 4. Orbit the view in the Paint Effects panel and zoom out until you can see most of the ground plane. Then paint a straight stroke of grass, starting from in front of the center of the porch, leading away from the house, and out to the edge of the ground plane.

5. To edit the grass stroke, open the Attribute Editor (in the following figures, the Attribute Editor is displayed instead of the Channel Box by clicking the Show Attribute Editor button at the far right of the Status Line), and select the grassDryBlowing1 tab to see the settings for the grass brush you painted with.

tip You can find the settings used in the following steps in the Channel Box, under Inputs, if you click on the grassDryBlowing1 entry. However, the values are displayed in one long list, making it difficult to find the ones you want to edit. The Attribute Editor categorizes the settings to make them easier to find.

6. The grass is a bit short for the unkempt lawn the Spooky World should have, so set the Global Scale to 200 to create taller, wider grass blades.

7. Next, you'll make a wider swath of grass for this stroke. Set the Brush Width under the Brush Profile section to 5.0 to make the blades spread out around the path. The number of blades has remained the same, however, so in the Attribute Editor, expand the Tubes section and then the Creation section. Set the Tubes Per Step setting to 60 to increase the grass density. Adjust your Perspective view to a position where you can gauge the size of the grass in relation to the house. If your display is lagging, lower the stroke's Display Percent in the Channel Box. You can also disable Stroke Refresh in the Paint Effects panel (Stroke Refresh | Off), and then refresh the display when needed by clicking the Redraw Paint Effects View button.

8. The grass is laying down, following the direction of the stroke. Although this does create a windswept grass effect, some of the grass should be standing up to create a more natural, random look. Under the Tubes section in the Attribute Editor, expand the Behavior section and then the Forces section, and then set the Path Follow attribute to 0. The grass should now be more vertical and randomly bent. To see the effect clearly, set the view to Textured mode on the Shading menu, and click the Redraw Paint Effects View button if necessary. Under the Tubes, Creation section in the Attribute Editor, set the Length Min to 0.3 and the Length Max to 0.6 to make the smallest grass blades taller, and the grass height will vary randomly between these two values. You can also reduce the Segments attribute to 6 to get a faster rendered result. Render the view to get an idea of what the grass looks like, as shown in Figure 13.9.

9. Next, you should take a look at how the grass is blowing around. To get the display to be responsive enough for a real-time preview of the wind effect, there are several steps you need to take. First, set the view to Perspective (Panels | Perspective | Persp). The paint effects will no longer be rendered and the grass will look like simple lines. Next, hide all but the currently selected object, the single grass paint stroke (hotkey: **Alt+h**, or Hotbox | Display | Hide | Hide Unselected Objects).

10. Then click the strokeShapeGrassDryBlowing1 tab in the Attribute Editor and set the Display Quality to 2, so that only 2% of the grass blades appear. Now you can click the Play button and see the wind effect in real time.

FIGURE 13.9   *The result of edits to the grass, previewed in the Paint Effects*
panel and rendered.

tip	Rendering should take no more than a minute. If your render times are extremely long, check your Render Globals settings to make sure the resolution is at 320×240 and antialiasing is set to Preview Quality.

note	You can confirm your playback speed in the Preferences dialog box (open it by clicking the Animation Preferences button at the lower right of the interface). In the Playback Speed list box, select Real-time (30 fps).

11. Leave the animation playing, return to the grassDryBlowing1 tab in the Attribute
    Editor, and expand the Tubes, Behavior, Turbulence section. Increase the
    Turbulence attribute to `0.05` to make the grass move more. Set the Frequency
    attribute to `0.3` to specify how coordinated the movement of the grass blades will
    be. If this value is set to `0`, the grass blades move in "lock step," which doesn't

look natural. Last, set Turbulence Speed to .4, which slows down the motion to give the effect of a gentle but persistent wind. With each adjustment, you should see the result in the panel as the playback loops, as shown in Figure 13.10.

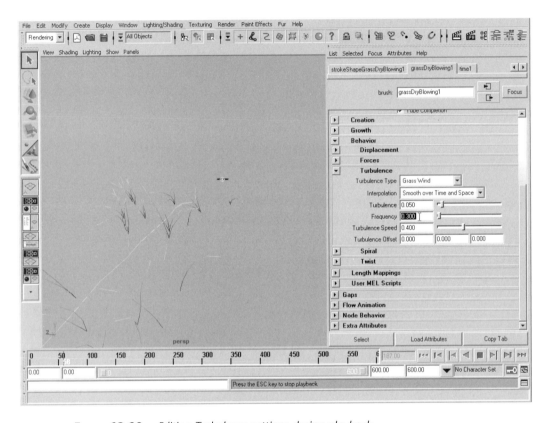

FIGURE 13.10   *Editing Turbulence settings during playback.*

12. Click the Stop button to halt playback, and unhide all the hidden objects (hotkey: **Ctrl+Shift+h**). Tap the spacebar to return to Four View mode, and configure the space on the interface's right side to display the Channel Box by clicking the button at the far right of the Status Line.

You've created and customized one grass stroke. Next, you'll sod the landscape and use the grass settings you just set up for the rest of the grass strokes. See the file on the CD if you want to compare your progress.

On the CD

Chapter_13\ch13tut02end.mb

Tutorial: More Paint Effects

Now that you've got your grass stroke the way you want it, you can fill out the rest of the landscape. In this tutorial, you'll also paint in trees and fog to complete the spooky world. You'll test it with a Playblast, and then render the scene to a movie from the fly-in Camera view. You can continue from the previous tutorial, or load the scene file from the CD.

On the CD

Chapter_13\movies\ch13tut03.wmv

On the CD

Chapter_13\ch13tut02end.mb

1. If you've restarted Maya since the previous tutorial, you'll need to make the ground surface paintable again. To do that, select the ground and choose Paint Effects | Make Paintable.

2. To increase the speed of interaction, lower the resolution of displayed NURBS objects by marquee-selecting all objects in a panel, and then pressing 1 to set the display quality to low.

3. Next, you'll make a handy tool for creating the new grass that uses the settings from the perfected grass stroke. Open the Outliner (hotkey: **Shift+O**) and select strokeGrassDryBlowing1. Then choose Paint Effects | Get Settings from Selected Stroke to copy the settings you created. Next, choose Paint Effects | Save Brush Preset. In the Save Brush Preset dialog box (see Figure 13.11), enter M4FgrassDryBlowing in the Label text box and drygrass in the Overlay Label text box. Leave the To Shelf radio button selected for the Save Preset setting, and this handy brush will appear in your Shelf. Click the Save Brush Preset button, and then click Close. The new brush icon will be displayed on the currently selected Shelf tab. If you need to get rid of some Shelf items, MMB-drag their icons to the trashcan at the far right of the Shelf.

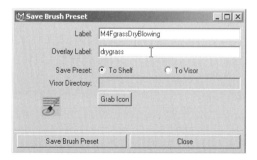

FIGURE 13.11   *Adding the custom brush type to the Shelf.*

4. Switch to the Top view, full screen. Click the new Shelf icon, and you will be working in Paint Effects. Before you begin painting, however, you need to adjust the strokes so that they display only 2% of the blades in the view. To do that, you'll use the Paint Tool settings, which define many attributes of the stroke. The Paint Tool button (shown in Figure 13.11) is in the Tool Box below the Show Manipulator Tool button. Double-click it, and set the Display Quality to 2.0. Close the Tool Settings window.

5. Now you can sod the landscape in several long strokes. As you paint, you'll see all the blades appear, but as soon as you finish a stroke, it switches to the 2% display setting. Create three long strokes on each side of the house, one behind the house that continues the stroke made in the previous tutorial, and a few other grass patches scattered around the landscape, as shown in Figure 13.12. Keep in mind that how quickly or slowly you draw the strokes affects the grass density. Overlap the broad strokes to avoid getting gaps in the grass. Also, avoid painting grass too near to the house, or it could protrude through the house geometry.

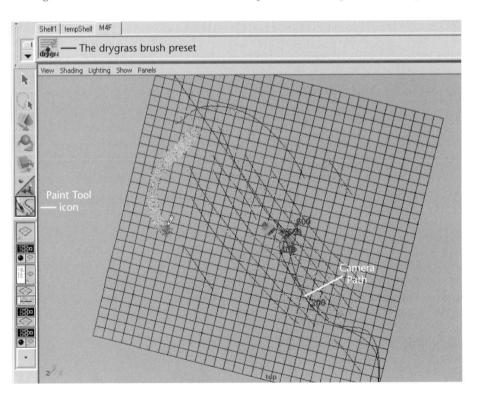

FIGURE 13.12   *The grass strokes applied.*

6. To make it easier to work in Maya, you can hide these grass strokes. Open the Outliner and select all the paint strokes, and then hide these selected objects (hotkey: **Ctrl+h**).

7. Next, you'll add some trees. Confirm that you still have your Scene Scale set to 200 in the Paint Effects Globals dialog box, as in Step 2 of the previous tutorial. In the Visor (hotkey: **Shift+V**), select the Trees folder, and click the birchDead.mel brush. To avoid placing trees directly in the camera path, you'll draw strokes that go around it. To make the trees, double-click the Paint Tool icon in the Tool Box and set the Display Quality to 25. Open the Brush Settings dialog box (hotkey: **Ctrl+b**), and set the Global Scale to 10. Now draw a looping path in the Top view that stays away from the camera path line, the camera's line of sight, and the house.

8. In the Visor, select the treeBare1.mel brush. In the Brush Settings dialog box, set the Global Scale to 3. Paint another loop of trees behind the first loop, curving around it.

9. In the Visor, select the thorn.mel brush, and set its Global Scale to 8. Paint another loop of trees behind and surrounding the one you painted in Step 8.

10. In the Visor, select the treeBare3.mel brush, and set its Global Scale to 4. Paint a shorter loop of trees, as shown in Figure 13.13.

11. You should have a real forest developing now, particularly from the camera's point of view. Check it by changing the view to the camera with Panels | Perspective | Camera1. Set the frame to 270 and render a frame.

12. You can increase the tree density easily by selecting the birchDead stroke in the Outliner, and then setting the Sample Density to 2 in the Channel Box under Shapes. The number of dead birch trees on the brush stroke will increase.

13. With the birchDead stroke still selected, hide all the objects that aren't selected (hotkey: **Alt+h**) to speed up the display. To add wind to the trees, open the Attribute Editor, and click the birchDead1 tab. Expand the Tubes, Behavior, Turbulence sections, and set the Turbulence Type to Tree Wind. Switch to the Front view, and zoom so that only a few trees are visible. Set the stroke's display quality higher so that you can see the trees in more detail (Display | Stroke Display Quality | 50%). Click the Play button. Set Turbulence, Turbulence Speed, and Frequency to 0.200. You can see in the viewports that the trees move strongly in the wind. Stop playback, and unhide the last hidden objects (hotkey: **Ctrl+Shift+h**).

14. Repeat Step 13 for the other tree strokes, using the Outliner to select each one. If you are unsure of what's hidden and want to unhide all the scene geometry, use Display | Show | Show Geometry | All to get your scene objects back.

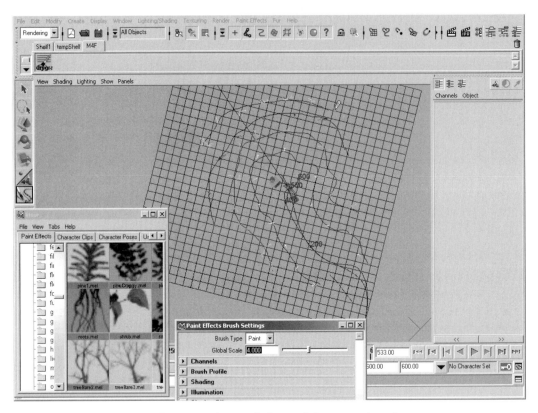

FIGURE 13.13   *The tree strokes applied, out of the camera's path.*

tip

To make sure you don't accidentally adjust the render camera's settings, you might want to lock the transforms for it. Select the camera in the Outliner, drag over all the transform names in the Channel Box (the nine entries from Translate X to Scale Z) and then RMB-click on any of them to open a shortcut menu. Choose Lock Selected to make it impossible to orbit or otherwise rotate the camera.

15. To get a preview of the camera path and all the moving trees and grass, you'll create a Playblast. First, switch back to the Camera1 view. Make sure you're in Shaded mode (hotkey: **5**) and unhide all objects, including the grass strokes; you can also have Hardware Texturing enabled, if you like. Then choose Window | Playblast | option box. In the Playblast Options dialog box, select Custom in the Display Size list box, and set the size to 480×360. Select the Save to File check box to enable the Movie File text box, and enter the name `camtest1`, as shown in

Figure 13.14. Click the Playblast button, and take a coffee break. Depending on the power of your 3D video card, the Playblast can take a few minutes up to a few hours. You can see the Time Slider's frame indicator move to show progress. When you view the resulting movie, you'll have a clear idea of what the final animated results will be.

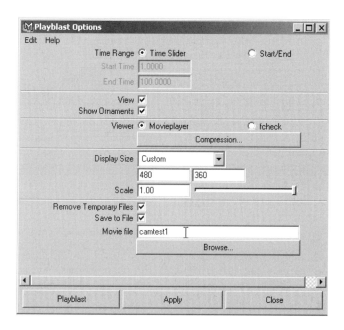

FIGURE 13.14   *The Playblast Options dialog box.*

trap   Playblast relies on your graphics card to build the 3D image for each frame. You can't obscure the Maya playback area with another window while the Playblast is being created, or your video card won't be doing any rendering, and Maya won't have a usable image for the frame. If you do cover the 3D view in Maya during Playblast recording, the movie freezes when playing back segments that were obscured during recording. To be on the safe side, find something else to do or use another machine while Maya is creating a Playblast.

tip   If the Playblast is taking too long, press the Esc key at any point to quit; any progress you've made to that point will be saved. Then you can try lowering the resolution or turning off shading or textures to get faster results. With so many paint effects in the scene, the display quality has a major effect on Playblast speed. You can select strokes in the Outliner and adjust their display quality by clicking Display I Stroke Display Quality and then choosing a percentage. Be aware that with the dense grass we've added to this scene, anything more than 3% or 4% will bring your display to a virtual halt.

Now that the animation is about right, you can add some vapor effects to help set the mood. If you want to compare your work to the sample scenes, load the file from the CD-ROM.

On the CD

Chapter_13\ch13tut03end.mb

Tutorial: Steam and Fog

Before you render the fly-through, you'll add some fog to the scene. The easy way is to apply Maya's layered fog effect. However, this fog is at a constant Z height and does not follow the contours of the landscape in a realistic way. So instead of painting on the surface, as you did with the trees and grass, you'll use the Paint Effects offset function to create a steamy fog effect that hovers in the air just above the ground plane. You'll use distance fog as well, just to blur the background. Paint Effects can create many types of effects that are otherwise difficult to simulate: rain, waterfalls, clouds, steam, fog, smoke, and so forth.

On the CD

Chapter_13\movies\ch13tut04.wmv

1. First, hide all the existing brush strokes so that they don't slow you down. In the Outliner, select all the strokes, and then hide them (hotkey: **Ctrl+h**).

On the CD

Chapter_13\ch13tut03end.mb

2. Select the Perspective view (Panels | Perspective | Persp) and make it full screen. Select the ground object and make it paintable (Paint Effects | Make Paintable) if you have restarted Maya since the previous tutorial. Switch to the Paint Effects panel (hotkey: **8**), and make sure you're in Paint Scene mode. Set the Shading menu to Textured. Open the Visor (hotkey: **Shift+V**), select the Clouds folder in the Paint Effects tab, and click the steamYellow.mel brush.

3. Open the Tool Settings window by double-clicking the Paint Tool icon in the Tool Box (or choose Hotbox | Paint Effects | Paint Effects Tool | option box). Set the Surface Offset to 120. Open the Brush Settings dialog box (hotkey: **Ctrl+b**), and set Global Scale to 12. Expand the Brush Profile section, and set Brush Width to 0.2 and Flatness1 to 0.5. Close both dialog boxes and move your mouse over the Paint Effects Shaded view landscape to see if the brush size looks right for your scene. Right-click the panel to activate it, if necessary.

4. Paint a stroke of steam over the ground, following the low-lying areas of the ground. Add several more strokes, as shown in Figure 13.15. If you have a pressure-sensitive tablet, this is a great time to use it so that the steam trails vary in width and taper off gently at their start and finish. You can get acceptable results with a mouse, however. Try varying the brush size slightly (hotkey: **b + LMB-drag left and right**) for different steam strokes.

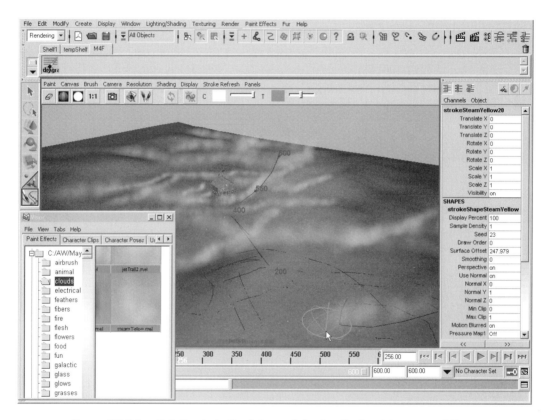

FIGURE 13.15   *Painting in trails of steam, following the low-lying areas of the landscape.*

5. Exit Paint Effects mode with Panels | Perspective | Camera1. Switch out of painting by selecting the cursor (hotkey: **q**). Render a frame (for example, around frame 270) to check your work, if you like.

6. To add some standard depth fog to the scene, open the Render Globals window. Expand the Render Options section, and click the checkered button for the Environment Fog attribute to create an environment fog. Next, select the Apply Fog in Post check box just below the EnvFogMaterial you created, so that it will render correctly with the Paint Effects.

7. You can now edit the fog effect in Hypershade. The Environment Fog is automatically selected because you just created it. Close the Render Globals window.

8. Open the Attribute Editor (hotkey: **Ctrl+a**). At the top, set Fog Color to a dark gray (HSV: **0, 0, 0.15**), and the Saturation Distance to **5000**. To affect how dense the fog remains at a distance, under the Clipping Planes section, select Fog Near/Far for the Distance Clip Planes, and set the Near Distance to **40** and the Far Distance to **10000**. Render the frame again to see the fog effect. Without the trees and grass, it should render rapidly.

9. Unhide the trees and grass (Display | Show | Show Geometry | All), and render the frame again. It will take a few minutes, but you can see one frame of the final composition (see Figure 13.16). It looks quite spooky, and the trees and grass blowing during the animation will add to the mood.

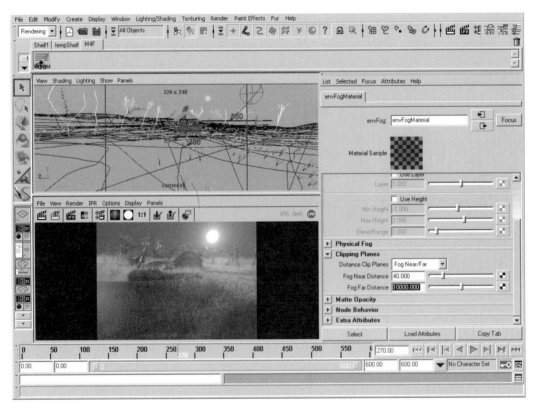

FIGURE 13.16   *The test rendering with the new glowing moon object combined with steam and fog.*

Prepare to render the movie. First, because the animation is 600 frames, you can estimate how long the render will take by multiplying your render time for one frame by 600. So if it took 3 minutes to render one frame, you can figure that it will take 1,800 minutes, or 30 hours, to render the entire animation. If you don't have 30 hours to let the computer crunch, you might want to save your scene to do it at another time. If you plan to increase the antialiasing quality or the resolution, you'll slow down the rendering speed, so you should test for a per-frame render time if you change these settings.

10. Open the Render Globals window. Set the File Name Prefix to PFXtest, select AVI in the Image Format list box, and enter 0 and 600 in the Start Frame and End Frame text boxes. Select camera1 in the Camera list box. If you like, you can raise the antialiasing quality level, but test it first for the impact it will have on rendering speed.

11. At this point, you're ready to begin batch rendering. Close the Render Globals window, and choose Render | Batch Render. If you have a multiple-processor computer, open the Batch Render Options dialog box, set it to use all available processors, and then click the Batch Render button.

In either case, your computer is now creating the frames. In a few hours to a few days, you'll have your completed movie. If you like, compare your scene to the scene file noted below the CD icon.

On the CD

Chapter_13\ch13tut04end.mb

Going Further

Because the grass and trees are moving, try making the fog move, too (to do this, you need to animate the curves the fog strokes are attached to). Try creating some brushes of your own by experimenting with the settings that appear when you edit a brush. Explore the preset brushes, and figure out how some of the more esoteric styles have been created from the set of variables that control a brush's look. Try creating some landscapes of different types, and use a variety of the brush tools. Explore the brush animation options to see how you can create effects, such as lightning and fire, that have built-in animation.

A few closing notes about Paint Effects: Everything associated with creating, rendering, and animating Paint Effects is housed within the stroke and brush. Paint Effects have their own internal shading procedures, and you can't assign your own shaders to them. They have their own Dynamics simulations, so they won't interact with Maya's Dynamic fields that are discussed in the next chapter (although they can be affected by external "control curves" to simulate it, to a degree). Paint Effects are rendered separately as a post-procedure, and then are automatically composited into the rendered frame. You can see this during rendering, when Paint Effects don't appear during the normal rendering, and then pop up at the end of rendering after some delay.

Summary

You've had a chance to try out some of the Paint Effects features and create some complex scenes with relatively little effort. Some of the methods you've learned include:

- **Preparing objects for Paint Effects**   You can't paint on an object unless it's a NURBS object and has been made paintable during the current Maya session.

- **Browsing and choosing a brush**   Maya offers a broad collection of brush presets in the Visor.

- **Editing brush settings**   You've learned how to change the way the brush paints and modify the look of the stroke after painting it.

- **Hiding and unhiding scene elements**   When you need real-time feedback in Maya, you can hide the objects you aren't working with to get maximum performance from your display.

- **Previewing your animation**   When you're animating, you need fast previews of frames, and your scene file is often larger than a graphics card can display in real time. Playblast creates a preview file using your graphics card to help you gauge your animation timing.

- **Saving your presets**   You can create brushes and add them to the Shelf or a Visor folder for later use.

CHAPTER 14

Particle Systems and Dynamics

In This Chapter

Sometimes, rather than using the keyframe animation techniques described in Chapter 10, "Animation Basics," you can allow Maya to create the animation under your direction. This feature, called Particle Systems, can be particularly helpful when you must create and animate dozens, hundreds, or thousands of similar objects that vary slightly in their geometry or animation. You can also use Maya's Dynamics mode when you just want to simulate reality in how objects behave—for example, animating the way bowling pins react when struck with a bowling ball. In Dynamics mode, you can even create "soft-body" effects, in which objects deform as though they were made from rubber or gelatin. Some of the topics covered in this chapter include the following:

- **Creating rigid-body dynamics simulations**   Setting up your scene for objects to react to forces and collide with each other.

- **Applying forces**   Dynamics simulations can take into account gravity, wind, and many other types of simulated physical effects.

- **Applying constraints**   Objects might not always be free to fly around; they can be hinged or tied down in many ways, and the simulation in Maya takes constraint factors into account.

- **Creating particles**   You can define where particles are created in Maya by painting them or by using particle emitters.

- **Particle types**   Maya offers many unique types of particles when you want to create rain, splatter, or breakup effects, among others.

- **Creating soft-body dynamics**   You'll learn the steps of setting up a soft-body effect so that objects bend and deform when they're hit by other objects or acted on by the forces in your scene.

Key Terms

active body   Objects that collide and react when collisions occur.

passive body   Objects that collide but do not react when collisions occur; however, they can serve as objects for active bodies to react to.

fields   Forces such as gravity used to animate the motion of rigid and soft bodies and particles.

constraints   A restraint on the kind of motion a dynamics object is allowed. For example, a hinge constraint restrains an object to rotating on one axis.

emitter   A particle source that controls variables such as speed and direction for particles; you can think of the emitter as a hose and particles as a stream of water.

soft body   An object that can deform during a dynamics simulation. A soft body object is influenced by a related particle system or emitter. Dynamic collisions move particles, which can then move the soft body.

goal   A position target for particles, usually defined by a NURBS or polygon object. The particles seek to distribute themselves on the CV or vertex positions of the goal object.

Hotkeys to Memorize

F4   Dynamics mode

Alt+F9   render current view

Shift+T   Hypershade

Ctrl+h   hide selected object

Alt+h   hide deselected objects

This chapter covers a set of tools in Maya that automate animation based on control parameters. These tools—particles, rigid-body dynamics, and soft-body dynamics—are related in how they function and how you control their use. To access them, you need to switch to Dynamics mode in Maya.

These functions—dynamics and particles—work together to create animation that would otherwise be difficult to hand-key. With rigid-body dynamics, the idea is to simulate physics so that objects bang into each other and deflect. With soft-body dynamics, the objects are deformed from their collisions. With particles, you can easily control the animation of large numbers of objects. For all these functions, you can create forces such as gravity or wind that affect the animation.

Rigid-Body Dynamics

With simple dynamics, also known as rigid-body dynamics, Maya simulates physics to create animation. Your scene elements are given mass and (optionally) initial velocities and spin. Then you apply forces that can affect the objects. If the objects collide, they can deflect based on the mass and friction levels assigned to them. The values for forces work much as they do in real-life physics calculations, and will give you realistic results if you set things up to mimic forces found in nature.

Dynamics in Maya can be applied as rigid body or soft body. Soft-body dynamics, discussed later in this chapter, are more complex. For now, you'll work with objects that do not deform when they collide. You can use NURBS or polygonal objects in dynamics simulations, but you must consider the objects' surface directions. Objects collide from only one side—the outward-facing direction of an object's surface normals. If you want one object to collide inside another, the outer surface must have its surface normals reversed. For example, if you put a bouncing ball inside a passive cube, you'd reverse the cube's normals (to face inward instead of outward, the default) by selecting the cube and choosing either Edit NURBS | Reverse Surface Direction (if the cube is NURBS) or Edit Polygons | Normals | Reverse (if the cube is polygons).

Active and Passive Bodies

Objects that interact can be active or passive. Passive objects can be keyframe-animated and can cause collisions (if they're in the way of a moving active body), but aren't affected by dynamics or collisions. Objects that will react to collisions must be set to active. You can switch an active object to passive and vice versa: In the Channel Box is an attribute called Active that can be set to on or off.

You can also set animation keys to trigger when dynamics takes over from keyframed animation. The switch is handled with the Soft/Rigid Bodies | Set Active Key or Set Passive Key. This lets you combine traditional keyframed animation with calculated dynamics animation. For example, you might have keyframed the animation for a ball to bounce, but you also want it to fall down a set of stairs. Setting an active key on the ball would let dynamics take over for that portion of the animation.

You can set values for Initial Velocity (speed and direction) and Initial Spin for active objects (see Figure 14.1). For both passive and active objects, you can also set values for Impulse ("push") and Impulse Spin ("twist") from an arbitrary origin point. These settings create a sort of instant force on the object. For example, you can set the Impulse Position off-center on a billiard ball to set that object moving at the precise time and place that a keyframe animated cue stick strikes it off-center.

You can also set the following attributes for active objects:

- **Mass**   The weight of the object. Heavy objects appear to push lighter objects when they collide.

- **Bounciness**   The amount of energy retained after a collision. Think in terms of a bean bag versus a superball, with the superball having a bounciness factor of 1, and the bean bag, 0. Remember that passive objects also have bounciness, and bounciness values are averaged between the colliding surfaces. A superball cannot bounce quickly off a bean bag, and a high-bounciness object will not bounce far from a low-bounciness object.

- **Damping**   An effect that produces a "drag" on an object. Values higher than 0 make the object lose directional and angular momentum over time.

- **Static Friction**   The amount of energy it takes to get a stationary object moving when it's resting against another surface. In nature, it usually takes more energy to start an object sliding along the ground than it does to keep that object sliding at a constant speed because stationary objects form a slight "glue" (a small number of atomic bonds) with the surface they're resting on. Smoother surfaces generate more of these micro-bonds, so they usually have higher static friction. For example, it's hard to start a rubber cube sliding over a steel floor, but it's rather easy to start a wood cube sliding over a concrete floor.

SHAPES	
pTorusShape1	
rigidBody17	
Initial Velocity X	0
Initial Velocity Y	0
Initial Velocity Z	0
Initial Spin X	-400
Initial Spin Y	-300
Initial Spin Z	-500
Center Of Mass X	0
Center Of Mass Y	0
Center Of Mass Z	0
Impulse X	0
Impulse Y	0
Impulse Z	0
Impulse Position X	0
Impulse Position Y	0
Impulse Position Z	0
Spin Impulse X	0
Spin Impulse Y	0
Spin Impulse Z	0
Mass	1
Bounciness	1
Damping	1
Static Friction	0.2
Dynamic Friction	0.2
Collision Layer	0
Stand In	none
Active	on
Particle Collision	off
Lock Center Of Mas	off
Ignore	off
Collisions	on
Apply Force At	boundingBo

FIGURE 14.1
Dynamics settings for active rigid bodies.

- **Dynamic Friction**   The amount of energy it takes to keep an object moving when sliding against another surface. Remember that every surface has friction settings, and the surfaces affect each other. If you want to create the effect of a slippery surface, you need to lower the static and dynamic friction of the slippery surface object and the objects that come into contact with it.

- **Stand In**   Normally, each polygon of a surface is tested at each fraction of an animation frame to see if it has touched another of the active or passive surfaces in the simulation. When objects bunch together or more complex models are used, the calculation can become so slow that it requires hours or days! The Stand In setting helps work around this problem by forcing the Dynamics engine to use a faster calculating surface in place of the current object. The options are for cube and sphere. You should always set planar wall-type objects to use the cube stand-in. Instead of simplifying the wall to a cube, it uses the wall's bounding box to calculate dynamics, thus simplifying the thousands of collision test calculations required. Similarly, spherical objects are best replaced with a sphere stand-in. Note that the object's motions reflect the stand-in, so if you use a cube stand-in for an egg, it will fall over in the simulation as though it were a rectangular slab.

tip
Complex objects that cannot be simplified to a cube or sphere can still be made to calculate much faster. Consider the option of creating a much lower complexity, non-renderable proxy object that is used for the dynamics simulation (see Figure 14.2). The original object is then parented to the stand-in proxy object so that it inherits all its motion.

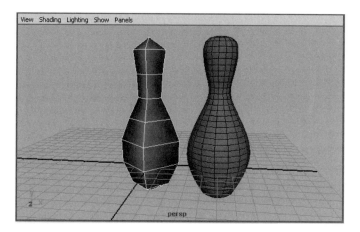

FIGURE 14.2   *A non-rendering low-resolution proxy for complex objects (left) makes for fast-calculating dynamics.*

The first step in building a dynamics simulation is to set scene elements that will be part of the simulation to passive or active bodies by choosing Soft/Rigid Bodies | Create Active Rigid Body or Create Passive Rigid Body on the menu. After creating the rigid bodies, you can adjust their settings later in the Channel Box, so you don't need to determine these values right away when you're applying rigid body attributes to an object.

After you've set objects to passive or active and optionally specified their initial conditions, you need to determine whether external forces will act on the objects and whether the objects' motion is locked in any way. In Maya, external forces are created with *fields*, and the motion-locking attributes are called *constraints*.

Fields

Fields are localized or global forces that act on objects. You might remember working with the Turbulence field in Chapter 4, "Diving In: Your First Animation." Fields have their own icons in a scene, so it's easier to select them if you want to animate a field or change its attributes. For example, you could animate the Gravity Field to make gravity turn upside down during an animation, or attach an Air Field to a boat to create a wake as it moves through a particle field. When you create a field, it affects the currently selected objects. You can later edit which objects are assigned to a field with the Dynamics Relationships Editor. These fields are included with Maya:

- **Air**   A "push" type of field, it comes with presets for Wind, Wake, and Fan.
- **Drag**   A field that slows the motion of items within its reach.
- **Gravity**   The most commonly used field, it causes objects to move and accelerate in a given direction. You can limit its reach to create localized Gravity Fields.
- **Newton**   Similar to Gravity, but operates in a spherical manner. Objects are attracted to Newton fields more strongly depending on their mass (set in rigid body attributes) and their distance from the Newton field.
- **Radial**   Like Newton, but does not take mass into account. It can be set to diminish with distance, as with the Gravity and Air fields, and it can be set to push or pull.
- **Turbulence**   Makes motion in the object more random. Turbulence is usually applied to soft bodies or particles to create the impression of wind or waves.
- **Uniform**   A field that pushes objects in a given direction. Like Gravity, but without the progressive acceleration that Gravity includes.
- **Vortex**   A kind of rotating gravity, the Vortex field pulls objects in a spiraling motion that's centered on the field's icon. Often used to create galaxies, whirlpools, or tornadoes with particle systems.

- **Volume Axis**   A complex field that lets you specify a volume shape (cube, sphere, cylinder, cone, or torus) and then create effects that work within the shape. For example, with a particle system, you might use a cylinder to create the vertical rise and a torus to create the cap of a mushroom cloud.

Constraints

Along with the forces you apply as fields, you can add constraints, which restrict an object's motion. However, constraints are applied to single objects or pairs of objects instead of to groups of objects, as with fields. After you apply constraints, they are connected to the object they're associated with. They don't have their own icons, as fields do. Maya includes the following constraints:

- **Nail**   Ties an object to a point in the scene. The object behaves as though it is tethered to the tie point by a solid rod, but it can orbit anywhere around the tie point as it collides with objects or is affected by fields. Think of it as a chandelier hanger.

- **Pin**   This type of constraint requires two objects that are tied together to a separate pivot point. Think of a rod coming from each object, with the free ends tied together in a ball joint.

- **Hinge**   As the name implies, you get free rotation constrained to an axis. You can make active objects hinge to a point in space, to another active object, or to a passive object.

- **Spring**   This constraint is like the Nail constraint, but instead of working like a chandelier on a fixed rod, it's like a chandelier on a telescoping "bungee" rod. As with the Hinge, you can use the Spring to tie an active object to another active object, to a passive object, or to a point in space.

- **Barrier**   Blocks objects from going beyond the plane it defines. You can assign this constraint to only one object. Objects can deflect, but not bounce, from the Barrier constraint, so it's recommended for objects that block other objects, such as walls or floors.

Rigid-Body Setup

The usual approach to creating a rigid-body dynamics simulation is to put objects in their starting positions for the animation, and then set them up as passive or active. You usually assign a Gravity field next, while the active bodies are still selected, so that the field is easily assigned to them. (You can assign gravity to other objects later, but it takes a few more steps.) You might want to add other fields, such as Drag or Turbulence. Finally, you can set some constraints for objects that are hinged or tethered in some way. You can view the playback during or after adjusting the objects' mass and other settings, but you shouldn't scrub the Time Slider when viewing these Dynamics simulations because each frame depends on the previous frame to calculate the simulation. When you're satisfied with the dynamics in the animation, you can cache or bake the animation (explained in the following tutorial) so that you can again scrub the animation, play it backward, skip frames, and so forth.

Tutorial: Exploring Rigid-Body Dynamics

Now you'll create some rigid dynamic effects with what you've learned. Exploring these effects is fun because Maya can respond to changes almost instantly and show you the resulting animation.

On the CD

Chapter_14\movies\ch14tut01.wmv

On the CD

Chapter_14\ch14tut01start.mb

tip

You should always take care to reset the options dialog boxes for any action if you aren't sure of its previous settings. This is especially important for dynamics, when you're often changing the values in the options dialog boxes.

1. After opening the scene file, make sure you're in Dynamics mode (select Dynamics in the drop-down list at the far left of the Status Line or use the **F4** hotkey). Note that Dynamics might not be enabled; you can check this in Window I Settings/Preferences I Preferences by selecting Modules in the Categories list. Notice that you have six plane objects and two balls suspended over the ground plane. You'll do several experiments with this scene to learn how rigid-body dynamics work.

2. Select the bottom plane, named bottom_plane, and make it a passive object (unaffected by dynamic collisions) with Soft/Rigid Bodies I Create Passive Rigid Body.

3. Marquee-select all the other items in the scene (orbit the Perspective view, if necessary, for marquee selection), and make them active with Soft/Rigid Bodies I Create Active Rigid Body.

4. While the objects are still selected, choose Fields I Gravity, and then click the Play button. All the objects will drop to the ground. Some or all of the falling planes

will pass through the bottom plane because they are one-sided and the wrong side is hitting the ground. This won't be a problem, however, because you don't intend for these objects to fall. Stop playback, and click the Rewind to Start button.

 tip

When playing back dynamics simulations, the calculations depend on each frame being calculated, so you should set Maya to play back each frame. Click the Animation Preferences button to the right of the Command Line. In the Preferences dialog box, select Play Every Frame in the Playback Speed list box, as shown in Figure 14.3.

5. Next, you'll optimize the dynamics solution to speed it up by setting all the spheres to a sphere stand-in. Marquee-select both spheres, and in the Channel Box, set the Stand In attribute to Sphere. Next, marquee-select all the planes, but set their Stand In to Cube.

6. Select the bottom right plane, named right_swing. To give it a constraint, choose Soft/Rigid Bodies | Create Constraint | option box. In the Constraint Options dialog box, reset the settings, select Nail in the Constraint Type list box, and click the Create button (see Figure 14.4). You'll see a small green spot at the center of the right_swing object. Switch to Move mode (hotkey: **w**) and raise the selected object 2 units; you can see the Translate Y value go up as you move the icon, taking it from 6 to 8.

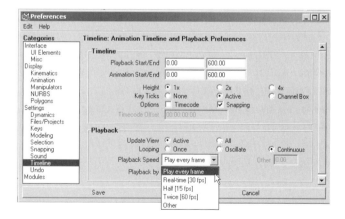

FIGURE 14.3   *Setting playback speed to play every frame ensures smooth and correct dynamics playback.*

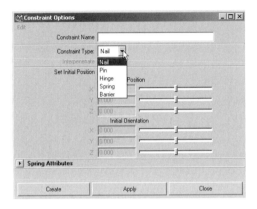

FIGURE 14.4   *Select from several types of constraints in the Constraint Options dialog box.*

7. Select the bottom left plane, named left_swing, and use the **g** hotkey to repeat the application of the Nail constraint. Translate this Nail constraint 2 units in Y also, as in Step 6.

8. Select the center plane, named center_swing, and apply a constraint to it, as in Step 6. Set the type to Hinge and click Create.

9. Select the right_spinner object, the second plane down on the right. Press g to add a hinge to this object, too. Repeat on the left_spinner object directly to the left of this object.

10. Select the top_paddle object (the top plane). Apply a constraint to it, as in Step 6, set the type to Spring, and click Create. Now click the Play button, and you can observe how the falling balls create the dynamics. While the animation is playing back, you can still rotate around the scene to observe it from different angles. Stop the animation and rewind it to the start.

11. Select the two spheres above the planes, by clicking one and then Shift-clicking to select the other. Use the Constraint Options dialog box to create another constraint, set it to Spring, and then click Create. Now the two spheres are connected with a bungee cord. Play back the animation to see the effect. Stop it and rewind to frame 0.

12. Select the line between the two spheres and the spring settings should appear in the Channel Box. As a variation, try setting the Spring Stiffness to 10 and the Spring Rest Length to 10. Play this animation and observe how the bungee cord behaves more like a stiff spring now. Stop the animation, rewind to frame 0, and set them to 2 and 6, respectively.

13. Select ball1, and in the Channel Box, change the Mass value from the default 1 to 3, as shown in Figure 14.5. Play the animation and observe the evident weight difference between the connected balls. Stop and rewind to frame 0.

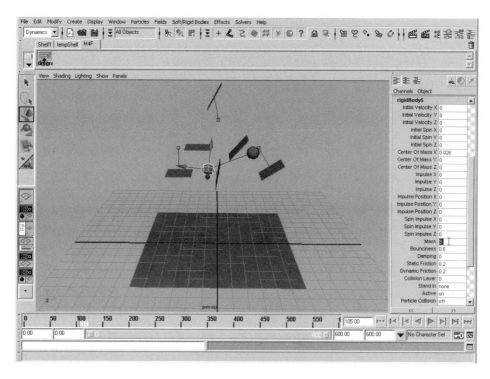

FIGURE 14.5   *Adjusting the mass of one of the spheres.*

14. At this point, you might want to cache the dynamics calculation. This records the animation in RAM so that the dynamics do not have to be calculated after you've played back the animation once. To make this work, you must select all the moving objects, and then choose Solvers | Memory Cache | Enable to turn this record mode on, and then play the animation through. When it has played through once, you can scrub or reverse-play the animation.

note

If you want to change one of the dynamics variables now, you'll find it has no effect until you clear the cache. Do this by choosing Solvers | Memory Cache | Delete or by opening the Solver in the Attribute Editor (Solvers | Rigid Body Solver) and then clicking the Delete button in the Rigid Solver States section.

15. When you like the way your animation looks, you can "bake" the solved animation so that it no longer needs to calculate. This method is helpful when you have dynamics solutions that are particularly slow to calculate. To bake the dynamics solution into keys, select all the active bodies, and then choose Edit | Keys | Bake Simulation. The animation will play, and when it's finished, you'll see that a key has been set for every frame for all the active objects. Now you can easily scrub the Time Slider with no delay; previously, there would have been long delays for each shift in time. You can also click the Reverse Play button (to the immediate left of the Play button) to see the dynamics in reverse!

On the CD

Chapter_14\ch14tut01end.mb

Particles

Maya's Particle Systems feature allows you to create complex collections of objects that look and behave similarly. Particles are ideal for animating difficult effects, such as aerosol sprays, explosions, swarms of bees, and galaxies of stars. You certainly wouldn't want to have to model and animate each member of one of those effects! With Particle Systems, it's easy to create these effects with as many particles as you want. The particles can also collide with objects and be influenced by the same fields discussed earlier in the "Rigid-Body Dynamics" section.

Creating Particles

To create particles in your scene, you can use drawn particles or particle emitters. Generally, you use drawn particles when you want them to start out in a prearranged pattern and exist throughout the animation—for example, to create a galaxy or star field. To paint particles in your scene, choose Particles | Particle Tool, which enables you to spray-paint particles where you want them. Another method called Particle Grid is available, which you use to define the corners of a 2D rectangle that will be filled with particles. Particle grids can be helpful for visualizing the effect of fields as you create them.

The more traditional approach to particle systems is using an emitter as the source that particles emanate from; eventually, the particles die. In Maya, the source can be many things:

- **Point – omni**   An emitter that sprays particles from a point in all directions.
- **Point – directional**   An emitter that sprays particles in a given direction from a point.
- **Volume**   Particles are created from some point within a defined volume, which can be a cube, sphere, cylinder, cone, or torus.

- **Surface**   You can define one of your scene NURBS or polygon objects to create particles from its surface.
- **Curve**   Any NURBS curve can emit particles.

Particle Types

In Maya, there are two types of particles: hardware-rendered and software-rendered. Most are hardware-rendered. These particle types require that you render by using the hardware rendering system (Window | Rendering Editors | Hardware Render Buffer), and the particles do not appear in any normal software render. The idea is that these particles hardware-render much faster than if they were part of the software rendering process and that anyone who owns Maya will own a compositor as well. You might think this makes using particles more difficult because when they disappear behind geometry, it could require applying complex alpha matting materials to those objects. However, the Hardware Render Buffer has an option for masking any particles that fall behind scene objects. Another issue is that most hardware rendering looks jagged (aliased). Antialiasing is similarly handled by multisampling in the Hardware Render Buffer, enabled by choosing Render | Attributes on the Hardware Render Buffer menu (see Figure 14.6). So all you need to do is overlay the rendered particles' image sequence on the scene's software-rendered image sequence to complete the effect. If you have a lot of particles or a long animation, this should save hours of rendering time because the compositor can overlay the two sequences and display the result in a few minutes.

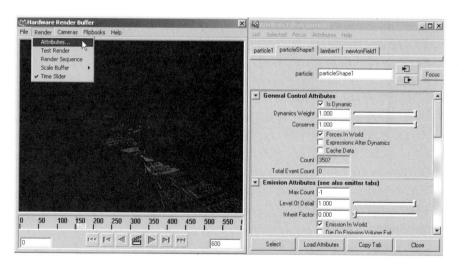

FIGURE 14.6   *Adjusting the mass of one of the spheres.*

Hardware-Rendered Particles

The following list describes the hardware-rendered particle types. Note that hardware-rendered particles cannot cast shadows or appear in reflections or refractions.

- **Point**   The default particle type, designed to render as a spot (it always faces the camera, so it has no apparent thickness). It looks like a square of pixels unless you enable a rendering option called multipass rendering, which blurs smaller particles (size lower than 5) into circular dots. When hardware rendering, the render settings are in the Hardware Render Buffer dialog box, under Render | Attributes.

- **Multipoint**   Like the Point particle type, but creates clusters of points to get a denser, clumpier appearance.

- **Streak**   Similar to the Point, but creates a streaking line instead of a dot. This type does not render until the particles are moving and you attempt to hardware-render a frame with particle motion. The size (line width) of these particles is fixed in pixels, so near particles seem to have the same width as far particles.

- **Multistreak**   Like the Streak particle type, but creates clusters of streaks to get a denser, grouped look.

- **Sprites**   Similar to Point in that Sprites always face the camera, but Sprites can have a texture and optionally an alpha (transparency) channel. In addition, these textures can be image sequences rather than still images. To create the effect of hundreds of flaming chunks of debris falling, you could use a single animated flame texture on a Sprite particle system.

- **Spheres**   These are three-dimensional spheres, and you can set the radius globally. You can apply simple flat color materials to the spheres, which are Gouraud shaded in the Hardware Render Buffer.

- **Numeric**   A test mode, this particle type displays an ID number for each particle. It's particularly useful for killing a stray particle that's going somewhere you don't want it to.

Software-Rendered Particles

The following particle types render as part of your scene when you render a frame. As such, they can also reflect, refract, and cast shadows; these options are available in the Attribute Editor for particles. There are four software-rendered particle types:

- **Blobby Surface**   A particle form of metaballs, the blobby surfaces look like spheres until they approach another, at which point they blob together like drops of mercury (see Figure 14.7). You can set the surface tension and the radius for each particle sphere. You can also texture this particle type, but you'll need to do test renderings to adjust the U and V mapping in the Attribute Editor for materials so that you can scale your textures to the right size.

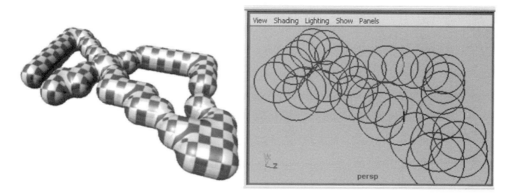

FIGURE 14.7   *Blobby objects in the viewport and rendered; notice the inherent mapping coordinates for the texturing on the blobby surface.*

- **Cloud**   Similar to the Blobby Surface type, but designed to blur and soften the edges of the Blobby Surface to get a cloud-like appearance. This particle type works specifically with the Particle Cloud material type and does not render with typical object "surface" materials.

- **Tube**   As the name implies, the source object type is a kind of uncapped cylinder. You can define the radius at the two ends. This type of particle is automatically assigned the Particle Cloud material type, and renders only with volumetric material types.

- **Instanced Geometry**   If you need to substitute any sort of object for particles, you use the Maya's Instancer, which enables you to use any kind of geometry or textures you like. For example, if you wanted to make a swarm of butterflies, you would create a single flapping butterfly type after making a particle system that animates the flight paths. Then you would open the Instancer with Particles | Instancer | option box, and configure it to substitute the prototype butterfly for the particles.

Particle Materials and Age

Particle system materials can be made to vary by using Gradient Ramps for texturing. Each particle has an inherent age (the time since it has been emitted) that Maya can use to calculate what part of the Gradient Ramp to use. Using this technique, you can make particles change color over the course of their lifespan. A typical use of this technique is to change the particle color based on its age to get the effect of sparks, for instance. The spark particles might be white at first, then cycle through yellow, orange, and red, and then fade to black, which can add to the realism of your particle effect. You can apply gradient ramps to any particle material swatch to cause it to vary with the age of the particle, where particle birth is the bottom of the gradient and particle death is the top (see Figure 14.8).

Figure 14.8 *A gradient applied to particle materials can control the particle over its lifespan; with this gradient, the particle would begin with black, and then brighten and dim twice.*

Particle Influences

Your particle systems can interact with your scene elements in several dynamic ways. Like the rigid-body dynamics discussed earlier, you can apply any of the same fields to particle systems to influence how the particles move. You can also define surfaces that act as particle collision objects. A third option allows you to specify goals, a configuration of particle positions that the particle system attempts to move to.

Fields

Fields were described in the section on rigid-body dynamics earlier in this chapter, and many of the field types are clearly oriented to apply to particle systems. Don't forget that nearly all the fields can be set to occur within a volume shape or to fall off with distance so that they have only a localized effect.

Collisions

Any particle system can collide with any scene geometry, but you have to set each collision up separately. To do so, you select the particles, Shift-select the geometry it will collide with, and choose Particles I Make Collide. The particles then collide if they hit the object. This works regardless of whether the particles or object or both are moving. For example, the particles could be stationary, and then smacked into motion by an object. You can also set particles to die (meaning the particle disappears), split (separates into several particles that each have the same particle age), or spawn (the particle dies, but new ones are created in its place) when collision occurs. These effects are typically used for splatter or breakup effects, in which particles seem to break into shrapnel when they collide with an object.

Goals

Particles can also be set to have goals, meaning that the particles try to move to a specific configuration, shape, or location. You can use this effect to make particles chase their goal object while staying in a specific relative position to the other particles. You can also create effects such as cloth in wind or seaweed in water by using particles to control geometry, described in the "Soft-Body Dynamics" section later in this chapter. When a target object is assigned to the particles as a goal, the CVs (for a NURBS target) or vertices (for a polygonal target) collect particles that are evenly distributed on the goal object.

Tutorial: Chimney Smoke

Now that you've learned some of the possibilities of particle systems, you'll try applying them to a scene you know well by now. You'll load the house scene file you added Paint Effects to in the previous chapter and add another hazy element—as though this scene weren't foggy and smoky enough! You'll make the top of the chimney on the house emit particles and configure them to move like smoke. Then you'll add a material to the particles that enables them to render like smoke.

On the CD

Chapter_14\movies\ch14tut02.wmv

On the CD

Chapter_14\ch14tut02start.mb

1. After loading the scene file, you should hide everything but the chimney so that you can focus on the particle system you'll be applying and get faster feedback from Maya when you play the animation. To do that, switch to Four View mode, and then hide all the objects but the chimney by first RMB-clicking on the V next to the ChimneyL layer and choosing Select Objects (so the chimney layer objects are selected); now you can hide all deselected objects with Display | Hide | Hide Unselected Objects (hotkey: **Alt+h**). This will leave only the objects in the ChimneyL layer selected. Center and frame the chimney in all the views (hotkey: **Shift+F**).

2. The chimney is animated to move around, so you need to use a part of the chimney, the chimney_pipe, to emit particles. Click any panel to deselect the currently selected objects, and then click the chimney_pipe to select it. Select the camera view and change it to the Perspective view with Panels | Perspective | Persp. Set this view to Shaded mode (hotkey: **5**).

3. Make sure the chimney pipe is still selected, and choose Particles | Emit from Object | option box. In the Emitter Options (Emit from Object) dialog box (see Figure 14.9), set the Emitter Name to ChimneySmoker, and select Directional in the Emitter Type list box. Also, be sure to select None in the Cycle Emission list box because you don't want to loop the smoke animation later. Expand the Distance/Direction Attributes section, and set the Spread to 0.2. Also, set DirectionX to 0 and DirectionY to 1, which means the smoke will travel upward. Click the Create button to create the smoke emitter and close the dialog box. Now play the animation, and zoom in the Perspective view to the top of the chimney. You should see the particles leaving the chimney_pipe, as shown in Figure 14.10.

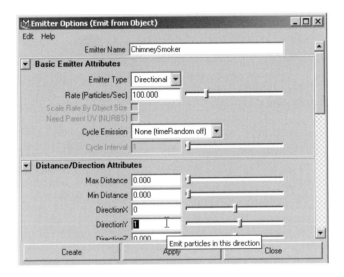

FIGURE 14.9   *Setting options for the smoke emitter.*

4. Stop playback at frame 50, and click the emitted particles. A green box will appear around the particles in the Shaded view, and the Channel Box will show the name for the particles: particle1. Change it to ChimneySmoke, and open the Attribute Editor.

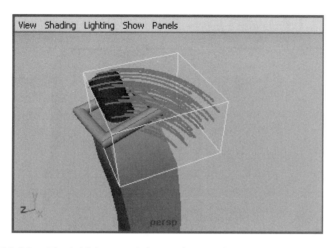

View Shading Lighting Show Panels

persp

FIGURE 14.10   *The initial state of the smoke particles.*

5. First, switch to the ChimneySmoker tab in the Attribute Editor. In the Basic
   Emitter Attributes section, select Volume in the Emitter Type list box. Farther
   down the Attribute Editor, you'll find the Volume Emitter Attributes section.
   Select Sphere in the Volume Shape list box to make the particles emit from a ball
   inside the chimney pipe, and enter 0.5 in the Volume Offset Y (the middle one)
   text box to push the ball a little higher up the pipe. In the Volume Speed
   Attributes section, enter 60 in the Along Axis text box, 10 in the Random
   Direction text box, and 60 in the Directional Speed text box (see Figure 14.11).
   Now take a look at the changed particle emission; it looks less like hair strands. If
   you can't see it, rewind the playback, and play from frame 0. You can stop it after
   roughly 100 frames to get the idea.

6. In the Attribute Editor, select the ChimneySmokeShape tab. In the Lifespan
   Attributes section, change the Lifespan mode from Live Forever to Constant,
   which means each particle is present in the scene for a certain number of frames
   and then disappears. The smoke effect should dissipate at a certain distance from
   the chimney, so set the Lifespan to 6 to make the particles disappear after six seconds. Expand the Render Attributes section, and in the Particle Render Type list
   box, select Cloud(s/w) for a software-rendered puffy cloud material type. Click the
   Add Attributes for Current Render Type button to see the cloud parameters. Enter
   15 in the Radius text box, .7 in the Surface Shading text box, and .9 in the
   Threshold text box. Surface Shading indicates how sharply the clouds are rendered, with higher values making more distinct clouds. The Threshold attribute
   controls blending between cloud "puffs," with higher values blending the particles more. Click the Play button, and you'll notice a completely different look to
   the particles, as shown in Figure 14.12.

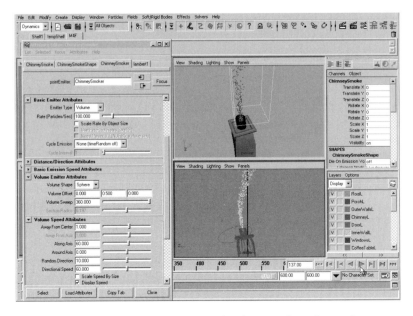

FIGURE 14.11   *The initial particle settings for changing how the smoke moves.*

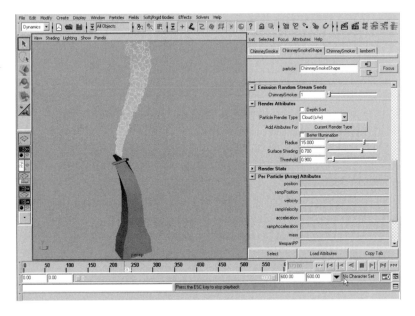

FIGURE 14.12   *The smoke particle size and type are now set up, and the particles travel upward and spread out.*

7. Next, you'll make a material for the smoke. Open the Hypershade (hotkey: **Shift+T**). Make sure the create bar is on and that Create Materials is active; right-click the Create Bar to change it if necessary. Create a new volumetric Particle Cloud material by MMB-dragging the material from the Create Bar (in the Volumetric section) to the Work Area. Select the particles in the scene, and then RMB-click on the new material in Hypershade and choose Assign Material to Selection. The scene is currently very dark, so add a Point light to make sure you're correctly evaluating the smoke as you create it. In the Channel Box, set the light's Translate X, Y, and Z to –175, 400, and 100. In the Render Globals window, set the resolution to 320×240 so that you'll get a fast render. Rewind the animation and play it through to frame 100 or higher to have some particles to render. Position the Perspective view to see the lit side of the smoke and render a frame (a normal render, not IPR, which won't work for particles). It should look like Figure 14.13.

Figure 14.13   *The initial render of the smoke particles, lit by the added Point light.*

8. Leave the rendering open, and drag a box around the smoke area. With the smoke material selected in Hypershade, open the Attribute Editor. Name the material `SmokeCloud`. Set the color to dark brown and turn the transparency up to about 75%. Click the Render Region button in the Render View window to re-render the portion inside the box you drew. You might want to resize the region (in the red rectangle) smaller to speed up rendering. It should render the area in the rectangle very quickly, enabling you to get quick feedback as you adjust settings and click the Render Region button.

9. Set the Density to `0.05` and the Blob Map color to dark gray (HSV: `0, 0, 0.3`). Render the view and you should see a more smokelike appearance. To add more complexity to the smoke, expand the Built-in Noise section. Change the Noise to `1`, the Noise Freq to `0.5`, and the Noise Aspect to `-0.5`. If you render after each change, you can see the effect of adding a subtle perturbation in the noise settings. Next, in the Surface Shading Properties section, set the Diffuse Coefficient to `2` to make the smoke look more three-dimensional. Your renderings should look similar to Figure 14.14.

In the next step, you'll use a Ramp map in the particle's Life Transparency attribute to make particles fade away as they age. That way, when the particles get to the end of their lifespan (6 seconds), they will completely fade out instead of just popping off the screen in one frame.

10. Play the animation to at least frame 200 and zoom the Perspective view back far enough to see the top of the smoke plume, where the particles should be fading out. In the Attribute Editor, with the SmokeCloud material showing, click the checkered button next to Life Transparency and click the Ramp type in the Create Render Node dialog box. Next, click the Go to Output Connection button (the right arrow icon) in the Attribute Editor. Click it again, and you'll see the Ramp Attributes. Click the color circles at the left of the gradient sample to change the color: Make the top circle white and the middle and bottom circles light gray (HSV: `0, 0, .75`). This makes the particles' transparency increase until they're completely transparent at the end of their lifespan. To extend the middle color a little higher up the gradient, select Exponential Up in the Interpolation list box. Imagine the Ramp as the transparency value from birth at the bottom to death at the top (see Figure 14.15).

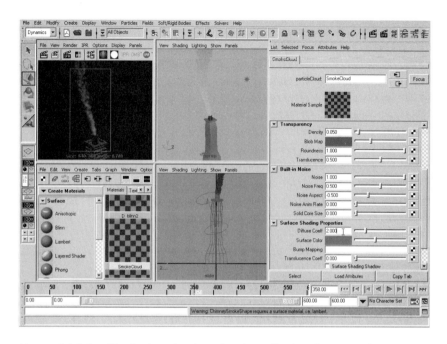

FIGURE 14.14   *The final rendered smoke after adjusting the material settings.*

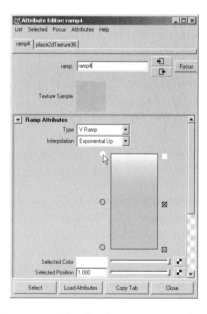

FIGURE 14.15   *The Ramp overrides the transparency value and fades each particle based on its age, mapping the Ramp over each particle's lifespan from bottom to top.*

11. Now you can delete the temporary Point light and unhide all the scene geometry to render a test of the smoke. Because you have already tested the motion of the particles when you played the animation in Step 5, you have a good idea of how the smoke will move. Rendering a single frame now will confirm what the smoke materials look like in the context of the rest of the scene. Switch the shaded Perspective view to the camera view with Panel | Perspective | Camera and set the Shading mode to Bounding Box. Click the Play button and let the animation play forward to frame 100. This ensures that the particles are emitted from the start, so that they're in the right place when you go to render the frame. You can render the camera view with the hotkey **Alt+F9** when the camera view is the active one. See the results in Figure 14.16.

Figure 14.16   *A rendering of the scene with the completed particle smoke effect.*

You should see a realistic smoke effect appearing from the chimney. You can compare your scene to the file included on the CD-ROM. If you like the still frames, you can render the entire animation, as you did in Chapter 12, "Cameras and Rendering." The smoke effect does not increase rendering time very much.

On the CD

Chapter_14\ch14tut02end.mb

Soft-Body Dynamics

Soft-body dynamics are handled in Maya by creating a set of particles that surround the object and influence it. When these particles collide with something or are moved by fields, the connected geometry moves with them. This is ideal for creating effects that mimic cloth and organic flexible materials. Soft-body dynamics are also used to create rigid yet flexible effects, such as objects that bounce and bend as though they were made of rubber or gelatin.

By default, new soft bodies infinitely inflate or deflate from almost any influence. To get a realistic response, you must add goals or springs. *Goals* give the flexible object a target shape to move toward, like a rubber squeeze toy that un-squeezes back to its original shape. Alternatively, *springs* add a lattice of tensioned springs throughout the geometry, like adding a box-spring of rigidity to the object. In this chapter, you'll explore the springs approach to soft bodies.

Creating a Soft-Body System

Any polygonal or NURBS object can be made into a soft body. The controlling particle system is created by placing a particle at each CV (for NURBS objects) or vertex (for polygonal objects), and then controlling the position of the CVs or vertices based on what happens with the particle motion. You usually make an object soft with Bodies | Create Soft Body | option box, and then determine whether the object will simply become soft or be duplicated to keep the original object as a goal. Normally, you choose the latter method so that the soft body tries to configure itself back to the shape of the original object. In either case, the object is then soft, but does not collide with other objects in the same manner as with rigid-body dynamics.

Because soft bodies are particle based, you must set these particles to specifically collide with a given object to create soft-body dynamics. For each object that will collide with the soft body, you must select the particles, Shift-select the geometry that it will collide with, and then choose Particles | Make Collide.

Adding Springs

When the object must be more resilient than a floppy soft cloth, you can add the Springs attribute to give the object a kind of support structure. This attribute creates a virtual spring object between each of the particles. Depending on how resilient you want your object to seem, you can create additional springs by increasing the Wire Walk Length setting. This parameter connects springs not only between a particle and its neighbor, but also the neighbor's neighbor, and so forth. The default setting is 2, which uses nearest neighbors, and nearest neighbors' nearest neighbors. This makes for a fairly resilient jiggle. You can also set the spring's Stiffness attribute to make the spring oscillate faster, and Damping, which absorbs energy to halt the jiggling sooner. Damping is like the shock absorbers on your car, but the Stiffness setting relates to the thickness of the spring.

Tutorial: Rubber Dumbbell

Now you'll apply soft-body attributes to a dumbbell to make it bounce around its environment as though it were made of stiff rubber. Load the scene file noted below the CD icon.

On the CD

Chapter_14\movies\ch14tut03.wmv

On the CD

Chapter_14\ch14tut03start.mb

1. First, select the dumbbell, and then choose Soft/Rigid Bodies | Create Soft Body | option box. Reset the settings in the Soft Body Options dialog box, and click the Create button.

2. While it's still selected, choose Fields | Gravity. Set the gravity's Magnitude to 50 in the Channel Box, and then click the Play button. You'll notice that the dumbbell falls but does not bounce from the cube walls.

3. Select the box object. Choose Particles | Make Collide | option box, set Resilience to .8 and Friction to .1, and click the Create button. Next, select the planar object named bouncer, and choose Particles | Make Collide. Click the Play button, and you'll see that the dumbbell continues to pass through the boxes when it falls. These objects are collision surfaces for particles, but the particles were not selected when you assigned them, so you must link the soft-body particles to the two objects in Maya's Dynamic Relationships Editor.

4. Choose Window | Relationship Editor | Dynamic Relationships. In the Dynamic Relationships Editor, open the dumbbell object so that you can see the particle system and select it. Then select the Collisions radio button, and select both the bouncerShape and the boxShape. They should turn light orange to indicate they've been assigned, as shown in Figure 14.17. Also, select the bouncer object, and enable the Gravity field for it.

5. Select the bouncer object and choose Soft/Rigid Bodies | Create Constraint | option box. Set the constraint type to Spring and click Create. In the Channel Box, set the Spring Stiffness to 2. Switch to Move mode, and raise the spring up to about 32 units in the Y axis (so that the plane is hanging by the line that indicates the spring).

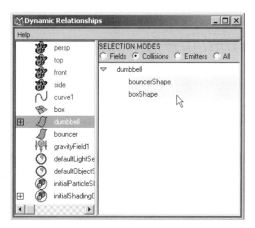

FIGURE 14.17   *The Dynamic Relationships Editor, with the collisions now enabled for the soft-body particle system on both the box and the bouncer objects.*

6. Click the Play button, and you'll get a very cartoon-like result because the dumbbell, as a soft body, is allowed to deform, and the particles interpenetrate (pass through each other) so that the dumbbell actually bounces its surfaces inside out! Adding springs will make it hold its shape more firmly.

trap   Make sure you have set your playback options to play every frame, or the object might seem to explode on playback. For all dynamics and particle systems editing you do in Maya, you must have your playback options set to play every frame and you must rewind to zero before each test playback.

7. Open the Outliner, expand the dumbbell entry, and then select the dumbbellParticle item. Choose Soft/Rigid Bodies | Create Springs | option box on the menu. Reset the settings in the Spring Options dialog box, and click the Create button. The dumbbell will be covered in green lines—the springs. You can see the springs in the Outliner, too. Use the **Ctrl+h** hotkey (hide selected objects) to hide the springs so the display is not slowed down.

8. Click the Play button and observe the result. The dumbbell moves like a gelatinous object. To make it stiffer, go to the Outliner and select the springs, named Spring1. The springs won't be displayed because they're hidden, but they are selected. In the Channel Box, set Stiffness to 20 and Damping to 0.1, and observe the results on playback, as shown in Figure 14.18. The dumbbell is now quite stiff and realistic. Lowering the Damping setting allows the object to jiggle longer after a collision.

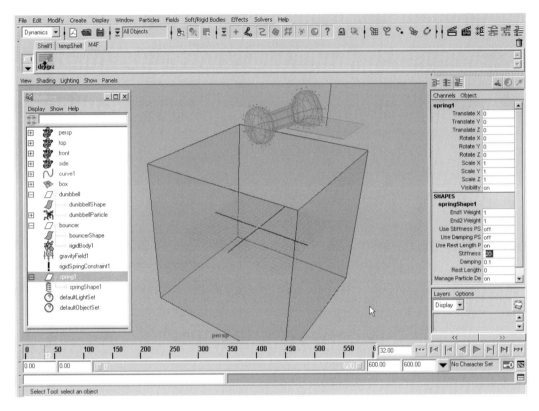

FIGURE 14.18 *The hidden springs can be selected in the Outliner and then adjusted in the Channel Box to produce all manner of boinginess in the dumbbell.*

9. Try increasing the Stiffness setting to a much higher value, such as 50. The dumbbell will oscillate and explode into chaos on playback. You can fix this by setting the Solver Oversampling. Open Solvers | Edit Oversampling or Cache Settings, and set the Oversampling value to 3. During playback, you'll see more controlled spring effects. Compare your results with the saved file on the CD-ROM.

On the CD

Chapter_14\ch14tut03end.mb

Going Further

Explore all the results of changing the masses, initial direction, and spin of objects and the friction of surfaces that touch. Try to create a simple pinball/pachinko animation that uses many different obstructions for spheres or other objects that fall from above. Explore creating particle systems that mimic other effects, such as fireworks or dripping fluid. Try each of the fields on a particle set to see how the field works and what its capabilities are. Create a NURBS sheet and use soft-body dynamics to make it react like cloth.

Summary

Particles and dynamics offer complex and realistic animation capabilities that can often make the task of creating an animation much easier. This chapter's tutorials have only touched on some of the possibilities available with particles and dynamics, but they point the way to some of the potential applications, such as hoses spraying any type of object, rain and snow effects, crash simulations, waterfalls, and so on. Some of the concepts and techniques you've learned include the following:

- **Creating rigid-body dynamics**   You learned how to set up and animate a dynamics system of non-deformable objects.

- **Caching dynamics animation**   When the dynamics simulation has played through once, you learned how to set Maya to remember the animation and play it back without recalculating.

- **Baking the animation**   After you have the animation playing the way you like, you can turn the motions into keyframes so that dynamics will not be calculated again.

- **Creating particle emitters**   You learned how to create the various types of particle emitters, and how to turn objects into particle emitters.

- **Creating fields**   You learned how to apply forces such as gravity to your particles and dynamics objects.

- **Creating soft-body dynamics**   You learned how to turn an object into a deformable object that interacts with particles and/or other objects.

Chapter 15

Your Next Steps: Efficiency and Artistry

In This Chapter

You've come to the end of the book, but there's so much more to Maya for you to explore. Because our publisher refused to allow us to issue an encyclopedic-sized set of books as *Maya 4.5 Fundamentals*, we've had to confine our subjects to those most necessary and useful to learning and using Maya. Rather than stop there, however, this last chapter points out some directions for your future growth, not only with Maya and its mechanics, but also as an animator and artist.

The subjects we'll cover include:

- **Troubleshooting slow renders** Sometimes you can unintentionally increase your render times. We'll give you a few tips on why this can happen.

- **Batch rendering** If you want to render several different animations on one or many machines, you'll need to learn how to set it up.

- **Workflow enhancements** Learn to build your own marking menus, hotkeys, Shelf buttons, and scene helpers.

- **Compositing** Professionals working on a deadline learn to divide their work into layers and use compositing to combine the layers later. We'll show you how this technique works.

- **Adding to Maya** A broad variety of free tools can be installed in Maya to add seamlessly to its functionality.

- **Future directions** We've compiled some general thoughts and tips from professional animators to guide you if you want to make a career of computer animation.

Key Terms

batch file   A text file that runs in the command prompt and includes a list of commands for the operating system.

Shelf   A convenient place in the Maya interface to set up your favorite tools or build your own.

compositing   Creating an image from several source images, layered on one another.

layer or pass or plate   One of the sources in a composite. Often described with a name, such as background plate, beauty pass, specular layer, and so forth.

Why Is It Taking So Long to Render?

By now, you've learned that rendering times are hard to predict. After you finish creating an animated scene and set Maya to render a series of frames, it's nearly always a few minutes or hours before the job is done. The scene's complexity is linked to the render time, so scenes with thousands of objects and dozens of lights are slower to render than those with fewer objects and lights. Even simple scenes can sometimes take longer than you might expect, however. What are you supposed to make of it when you come back a day later and only a few frames of a seemingly simple scene have been rendered? Something is obviously putting a heavy burden on the renderer. The following sections cover a few areas to consider as potentially expensive in terms of computation.

Render Global Settings

Resolution   Large images take longer to render than small images. If your 320×240 render took 10 minutes, you can usually count on a 640×480 render taking 40 minutes because the image has four times the number of pixels. Doubling the dimensions quadruples the pixel space and the rendering time.

Antialiasing Quality   If your renderings exhibit jagged, stair-stepped edges or reflections, you need to increase the antialiasing quality, which lengthens rendering dramatically. Generally, you use the fast, low-quality antialiasing mode for testing and a higher setting for your final production. (*Note:* If it's the depth map shadows in your scenes that exhibit aliasing, you should raise the Depth Map Resolution for sharper shadows and/or the DMap Filter Size for blurry shadows; this setting has little effect on rendering speed.)

Raytraced Shadows   This type of shadow is the sharpest, but it can slow down rendering noticeably. In particular, if the raytraced shadow must project through many small overlapping objects (such as leaves on a tree), you'll probably see a significant decrease in rendering speed.

Raytracing   The Render Globals window contains the option to raytrace, used when you are rendering reflections or refractions. It can slow down rendering speed, particularly if you turn up the reflection and refraction setting in a scene full of reflective or refractive objects. For example, if you use 10 reflections, and you are rendering a hall of mirrors, the renderer has to ping-pong the light ray for many of the image pixels through the scene to find its final color. A sample scene called slow.mb is included on the CD to illustrate this effect. Similarly, a pyramid of refractive wine goblets would be slow to raytrace if the refraction depth is set to a high number. In this case, usually you need to use a high number, such as 8 or 10, because pixels that require more bounces than the limit will be filled with a fixed color (usually black) if they do not strike a solid object in the number of bounces allotted.

Motion Blur   This option is used when you want to simulate the effect of shutter speed, as in a movie camera. If you're creating an animation in which some scene objects move rapidly through the camera's field of view, you must use motion blur to

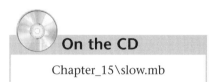

On the CD

Chapter_15\slow.mb

avoid a strobe effect. There are two types of motion blur: 2D and 3D. The 2D motion blur is a kind of intelligent post-process filter that smears pixels in the rendering and isn't usually very slow to render. The 3D motion blur blends several full-screen renders and is more realistic, but definitely requires more time to render.

Object Attributes

NURBS   All NURBS surfaces must be tessellated to polygons before the renderer can work with them, and each NURBS object can be adjusted for how finely it tessellates. If you set the tessellation level very high, you'll notice a delay while Maya processes the NURBS object into thousands of polygons. In extreme cases, an immense number of generated polygons can cause the machine to run out of memory. It's a good idea to test tessellation levels if you adjust them from the defaults. You can do this in the Attribute Editor, in the Tessellation section on the object's Shape tab. Select the Display Render Tessellation check box to see the tessellation results in the 3D panel as you adjust the settings.

Material Types

Volumetric Material Types   Maya supplies five volumetric materials for non-solid object effects: EnvFog, LightFog, Particle Cloud, Volume Fog, and Volume Shader. These special material types are usually slower to render. If you bury the camera in a Volume Fog, every pixel of the frame will be looking through a 3D fog effect and it will take much longer to render.

Camera Effects

Depth of Field   Maya's normal rendering mode is like that of a pin-hole camera: Everything is in perfect focus. You can set the camera to produce depth blurring, where objects closer to or farther away from the focus are progressively blurred. This option usually adds quite a bit to the render time when depth blurring becomes more exaggerated.

Batch Rendering in Maya

Normally, when you render stills, you simply choose the Render Current Frame option as you work. However, as you saw in Chapters 4, "Diving In: Your First Animation," and 12, "Cameras and Rendering," you can adjust the Render Globals settings to cover a range of frames, and then use the Render | Batch Render option to render the entire sequence. The renderer works on these frames in order and can store the frames in a movie format (such as AVI) or as sequentially numbered stills. For output to video or movie film, you normally output to sequential frames to avoid compression damage and a single unwieldy large file. When batch render mode begins in Maya, the rendering starts in the background and you can continue to work in Maya. Users with dual-processor machines can use the Batch Rendering Options dialog box to specify that one processor be used for background batch rendering and the other be used for continuing to work with Maya. However, you can batch render only one project at a time in Maya. If you want to render an additional project, you must cancel the current rendering or wait for it to finish.

When batch rendering starts, you get an update on its progress in the right side of Maya's Command Line. To display the entire log (see an example in Figure 15.1), click the Script Editor button to the right of the Command Line (refer back to Figure 2.1 in Chapter 2, "A Tour of Maya," to see exactly where this button is).

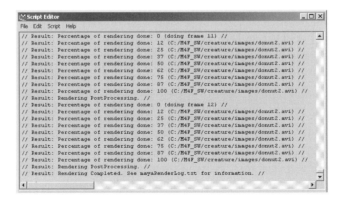

FIGURE 15.1   *The command feedback log in the Script Editor shows details of the background batch render.*

Batch Rendering as a Standalone with the Command Prompt

What if you have built 12 different scenes during your workday, and you want to have them all render during the night? One option is command-prompt batch rendering. If you look in your Maya\bin folder, you'll see the file render.exe. This utility is the standalone renderer called by the command prompt.

In Windows, you open the command prompt by clicking Start | Programs (or Programs | Accessories) | MS-DOS Prompt. At the command prompt, enter cd to change directories to the Maya\bin directory, as shown in Figure 15.2. Then you can render a job by typing the following:

```
render filename.mb
```

You might need to specify the exact pathname for the file, as shown here:

```
render c:\myjobs\maya\filename.mb
```

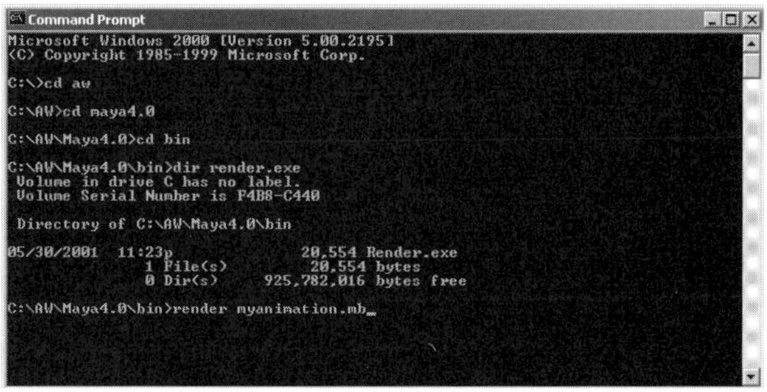

FIGURE 15.2   *Starting rendering in the command-prompt window.*

The stored Maya scene file controls which files render at what resolution and specifies where the images are saved. You can override the settings in an .mb or .ma file by using this format:

```
render <options> filename.mb
```

Here's the same line with some options filled in:

```
render -x 512 -y 512 -cam persp -im test -of sgi filename.mb
```

Note that a space is placed between each option flag and the value assigned to it, such as –x (overriding the width in pixels) and 512 (the width you want in number of pixels). A host of options are available, and you can get a full list by entering just render | more and using the spacebar to advance through each page.

How does all this help you render multiple jobs in one go? By using .bat batch files. You can create a text file with the suffix .bat that contains a number of these commands, as shown here:

```
render -x 640 -y 480 -cam persp -im testA Job1.mb

render -x 800 -y 600 -cam TopCam -im testB Job2.mb

render -x 320 -y 240 -im testC -of tga Job3.mb
```

You can run them all in sequence by simply starting the batch file from the command prompt. For example, if you took the preceding command lines and saved them in a text file called Tuesday.bat, all you need to run at the command prompt is Tuesday and the jobs are processed in order.

trap

You should use Windows Notepad to make text files. If you use MS Word or some other text editor, the file isn't raw text, but often has codes for font, pagination, and so on, and will not work when you try to run the batch file.

If you have purchased a maintenance contract from Alias|Wavefront for Maya, you can get an unlimited batch rendering license in addition to your regular Maya license. The batch rendering license allows you to install and authorize Maya's Batch Renderer on one or many other machines and to render jobs on those machines. You can give each machine a few batch render jobs to work on and they will create and save all the rendered images for each job loaded.

You might notice that although you can try to evenly distribute seven jobs across three machines, no matter what, some machines finish first and remain idle while frames of animation still need be rendered on other machines. Also, the prospect of having to walk around a room full of machines and set up .bat files on each one is going to get tiresome after a while! The next section covers true network rendering, which is the only way to go if you have several computers capable of rendering.

Batch Rendering with Slave Machines

There are a variety of third-party utilities (typically costing a few hundred dollars) for sharing Maya rendering jobs among multiple networked computers. These products enable you to manage all the network "slave" machines from one master machine. You can assign a job to all machines or just to specific machines, and you can order the jobs in the queue by priority. All the slave machines must be able to read texture map image files and other data from a shared folder. Also, all the machines need to be able to write files to one common place for output of rendered images. One other consideration is that if you intend to render to a movie file, you won't be able to share a job among several machines. However, you can render the individual frames and quickly post-process the frame sequence into any movie file format by using a compositor or other utility. Some of the available network rendering managers for Maya include:

- Render Max (rendercorp.com)
- Lemon (www.ice.org/~martin/)
- Muster (vvertex.com)
- Rush (3dsite.com/people/erco/rush/)
- Load Sharing (platform.com)

These are commercial products with a variety of pricing structures. Lemon has a free version that can split jobs among machines, and it works well for smaller productions. It leaves out such features as progress tracking and adjustment of Render Globals. For single-machine job queuing, RenderPal (www.shoran.com) is a better utility, and it's also free. There are more utilities, such as RenderPal, at the popular Maya web site www.highend3d.com.

The only critical factor when using a machine to render a job is that it must be able to load the entire scene into RAM. If your scene file is bigger than the available RAM on the slave machine, processing will bog down. If RAM is plentiful, the machine will render based solely on raw CPU horsepower.

Workflow Enhancements

This book has made custom hotkeys and marking menus an integrated part of the tutorials for good reason. Beginners who are not exposed to these workflow enhancements are missing a big part of what makes Maya so efficient. However, our marking menus and hotkeys were created to show you how to determine the tasks you perform most often and set up tools to speed or automate many of them.

Creating Your Own Marking Menu

In Chapter 5, "NURBS Modeling Basics," you started the house project by loading a set of custom marking menus into Maya. Let's go through the steps of creating one of those marking menus so that you can see how it's done. Then you can alter the existing marking menus or create your own.

Tutorial: Building a Marking Menu

1. Choose Window | Settings/Preferences | Marking Menus. In the Marking Menus dialog box that opens, click the Create Marking Menu button to open the dialog box shown in Figure 15.3.

On the CD

Chapter_15\movies\ch15tut01.wmv

Each of the nine light-gray squares represents a location on the marking menu that you attach to a function. You can add information to each block or edit it by right-clicking on one of the squares and choosing Edit Menu Item. This brings up a spot to insert MELscript, but don't panic! You're going to let Maya automatically create the MELscript you need to dump into those little boxes. The MELscript appears in the Script Editor as you use Maya, translating each of your actions into the equivalent MEL code.

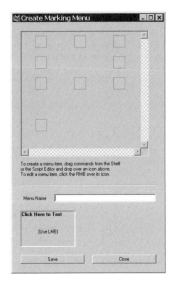

FIGURE 15.3
Maya's Create Marking Menu dialog box.

2. Open the Script Editor by clicking the button to the far right of the Command Line.

3. On the Script Editor's menu, enable the Echo All Commands setting (Script | Echo All Commands).

4. Your screen might be cluttered with all these windows open, so rearrange the Create Marking Menu dialog box and Script Editor so that you can see both. Just drag and resize the windows until you have them arranged to your liking so that you can continue working efficiently.

The following steps create the CV Curve marking menu you used in this book. For each function you add to the marking menu, you perform the function first, and then MMB-drag the MELscript from the Script Editor to one of the gray squares in the Create Marking Menu dialog box.

Remember: When you turn on Echo All Commands, you can see every script and action that Maya runs with MEL. By default, the Script Editor echoes only the most significant commands for feedback in Maya's Command Line. Maya is built on MEL, so every action you perform in Maya is carried out in this scripting language. By watching the commands in the Script Editor, you can begin to grasp how Maya works and absorb the MEL syntax.

If your Script Editor is filled with information you don't need, you can always clear its display by clicking Edit | Clear History on the Script Editor's menu.

5. First, access the CV Curve tool by clicking Create | CV Curve Tool in the Hotbox.

6. Check the new information in the Script Editor. Each line shows a different command, so you need to figure out which one actually runs the CV Curve tool. In this case, the line is CVCurveTool;, so highlight that line in the Script Editor (see

Figure 15.4). Then simply MMB-click over the highlighted text and drag it to the top center gray box in the Create Marking Menu dialog box. Maya automatically copies the necessary information to the box.

7. In the Create Marking Menu dialog box, right-click on the top center gray box and choose Edit Menu Item from the shortcut menu. The Edit North dialog box opens; it's called "North" because the gray boxes are named after compass points.

8. Next, you need to give the menu item a label that appears when you access this marking menu. In the Label text box in the Edit North dialog box, change the name to CV Curve.

9. Now you need to enable the option box to appear beside the CV Curve item in the marking menu. To do that, select the Option Box check box near the bottom of the dialog box.

FIGURE 15.4

Highlighting the correct command in the Script Editor.

10. Next, you'll tell the option box what to do when clicked. First, copy the code line from the Command(s) section and paste it in the Option Box Command(s) section. For most creation procedures in MELscript, all you have to do is add the word *Options* to the end of the standard command. In this case, the command name should be CVCurveToolOptions; (see Figure 15.5). The semicolons are critical, so make sure they don't get omitted. Also, remember that you must match the letter case exactly when entering command names because MELscript is case sensitive.

11. You've finished creating the Create CV Curve item for this marking menu. Click the Save and Close button to save your changes and close the Edit North dialog box. Make sure the Create Marking Menu dialog box is still open for the next task.

There's another method for copying the MELscript: Copy the highlighted text (hotkey: **Ctrl+c**) in the Script Editor, right-click on one of the gray boxes in the Create Marking Menu dialog box, and click Edit Menu Item on the shortcut menu. In the dialog box that opens, create a new menu item by pasting (hotkey: **Ctrl+v**) the code line in the text box right under the label Command(s).

Here's another method some Mayans prefer: Tear off the Create menu. Ctrl+Alt+Shift+LMB-click on a command, and it's added to the Shelf, complete with its icon. Finally, MMB-drag the new icon to your marking menu to add it.

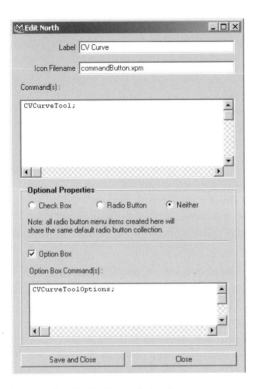

FIGURE 15.5   *The completed Edit North dialog box.*

You can test each menu item after creating it. In the lower-left corner of the Create Marking Menu dialog box, click the box that says Click Here to Test to open the menu. It's not just for show; it actually works! Click the CV Curve item in the marking menu that pops up to test it (see Figure 15.6). Then click the CV Curve option box in the marking menu, and the CV Curve Options dialog box should open.

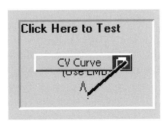

FIGURE 15.6   *Testing the first marking menu.*

Now you can add a few more items to this marking menu. Using the same methods as before, add the following actions as items on your menu:

Name of Tool	Menu Action
Pencil Curve	Create	Pencil Curve Tool
EP Curve	Create	EP Curve Tool
3 PT Arc	Create	Arc Tools	Three Point Circular Arc
2 PT Arc	Create	Arc Tools	Two Point Circular Arc

After adding these tools to your marking menu, the Create Marking Menu dialog box should look similar to Figure 15.7.

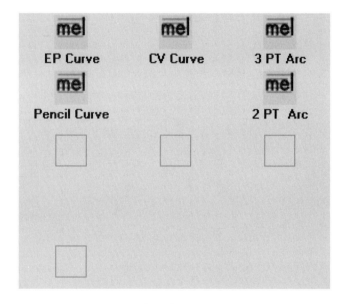

FIGURE 15.7   *Five entries are used for the CV Curve marking menu.*

Now that you have finished adding items to the marking menu, you need to name and save it. In the Create Marking Menu dialog box, type testMM in the Menu Name text box, and click the Save button. This menu is then added to the list of other menus in the Marking Menus dialog box. Select the menu in the list at the top of the dialog box. To make the marking menu accessible in the Hotkey Editor, select Hotkey Editor in the Use Marking Menu In drop-down list box (see Figure 15.8). Click the Apply Settings button, and close this dialog box and the Script Editor.

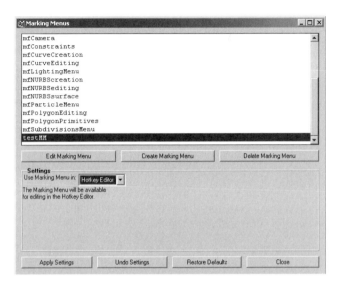

FIGURE 15.8   *Configuring the testMM marking menu to appear in the Hotkey Editor.*

You can fine-tune your marking menus by forcing the option box settings of the objects you create. Instead of just creating an object and copying the code for its creation, open the options box for that object. Configure the options box to the settings you'll use most of the time, and then create the object. In the Script Editor, to the right of the object's creation code, will be several tags, each specifying these option box settings for the object. Highlight the entire line of code and proceed as before. With option boxes for tools, the method is a little different, but you can always experiment until you find the code for the settings you want.

Tutorial: Setting Hotkeys

You've built the marking menu; now you need to set the hotkeys that will activate it:

1. Open the Hotkey Editor by choosing Windows | Settings/Preferences | Hotkeys on Maya's main menu.

2. In the Hotkey Editor, select User Marking Menus in the Categories list. All the menus should be listed under the Commands section (see Figure 15.9). You have probably noticed that each command has two names: one with a Press tag and one with a Release tag at the end of the name. With these commands, you can specify an on/off action so that Maya knows when to enable or disable a particular command action.

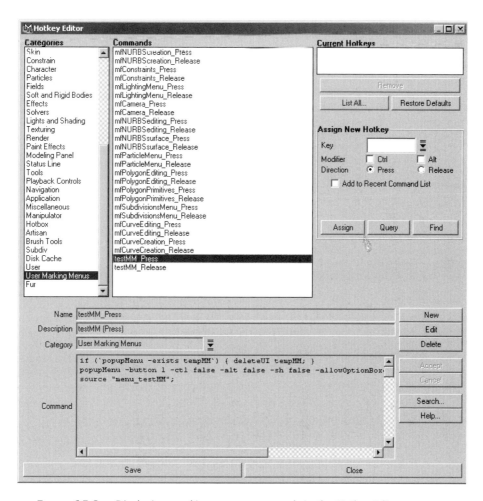

FIGURE 15.9   *Displaying marking menu commands in the Hotkey Editor.*

3. The next step is to set a hotkey for the testMM marking menu. The Current Hotkeys section to the right lists any hotkeys currently assigned to the selected command. Under that area is the Assign New Hotkey section. In the Key text box, type the letter f. Be sure to use the lowercase *f* because hotkeys are case sensitive.

4. Click the Query button to find out whether that key is already in use. In this case, it's already assigned to the Frame Selected action, so you need to add a modifier to the button.

5. To the right of the Modifier item, select the Ctrl check box. This tells Maya that when you press Ctrl+f, you want to access the testMM marking menu.

6. Now click the Assign button. Maya opens a message box telling you that the marking menu will not work unless you attach the release hotkey. Click the Yes button in the message box to have Maya set both press and release hotkeys.

7. Under Current Hotkeys, you should see the Ctrl+f hotkey combination. After you've finished assigning those hotkeys, click the Save button at the bottom of the Hotkey Editor, and then click the Close button.

8. Try the hotkeyed marking menu in a 3D view panel. Press Ctrl+f, and then LMB-click and hold in the panel. The marking menu you made should appear.

You've built a complete marking menu from scratch. The MMB drag-and-drop function from the Script Editor works for automating other tasks as well, as you'll see in the next section.

Automating Single or Multiple Tasks: Hotkey, Marking Menu, or Shelf

Almost any action you take in Maya has corresponding MELscript displayed in the Script Editor, if the Echo All Commands option is enabled. You can assign any action to a marking menu, as you learned in the previous tutorial. You can also assign an action to a hotkey or to the Shelf.

User Hotkeys

The Hotkey Editor (Window | Settings/Preferences | Hotkeys) you saw in Figure 15.9 allows you to edit the hotkeys assigned to Maya's primary functions. To view all the currently assigned hotkeys in the Hotkey Editor, click the List All button under the Current Hotkeys section to open the List Hotkeys dialog box (see Figure 15.10).

In the Hotkey Editor, the bottom half functions just as the marking menu command setup did. You click the New button in the Hotkey Editor, select command text from the Script Editor, and MMB-drag it to the Command area. You can then assign a hotkey as well as its name, description, and category. Use the catch-all "User" category if your new hotkeys don't neatly fit into the other categories.

The Shelf

Using the same MMB drag-and-drop technique as before, you can drop items on the Shelf to create a button there with a default "MEL" icon. When you click the Shelf button, that function is performed.

You can create new custom shelves for all your needs. They show up as tabs on the Shelf, and you create new shelves by clicking the down arrow at the far left of the Shelf and selecting New Shelf. You can also edit the Shelf contents and the icons used for the buttons: Click the down arrow at the far left of the Shelf and select Shelf Editor, where you can assign the graphical icon to represent the Shelf button and edit the code and labels for the Shelf.

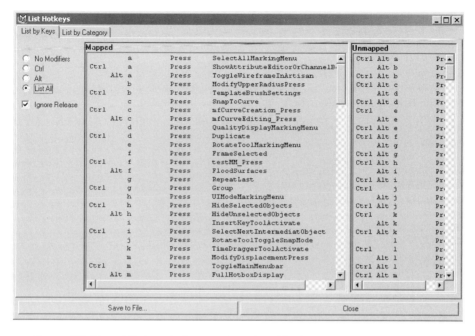

FIGURE 15.10   *A listing of all currently assigned hotkeys.*

Tutorial: Shelf and Hotkey Items

In this tutorial, you'll set up a Shelf button for making a specific torus and a hotkey for duplicating it in a unique way. You can then use this method to build your own hotkeys and Shelf items.

On the CD

Chapter_15\movies\ch15tut02.wmv

1. Open the Script Editor by clicking the Script Editor button at the right of the Command Line. Make sure there's a check mark by the Script | Echo All Commands menu option so that all your actions are recorded. Then choose Edit | Clear History from the menu so that you have a clean slate. Minimize the Script Editor so it's out of your way.

2. To create a new Shelf, click the down arrow at the far left of the Shelf, and select New Shelf. Name it `Maya_4_Fundamentals`.

3. Create the curves of a letter "A." Do this by choosing Hotbox | Create | Text | Option Box, and then reset the options and replace the default text "Maya" with a capital "A." Click the Create button, and the curves are created. Use the frame hotkey (f) to zoom to the new curves. With the curves still selected, bring up the Bevel Plus dialog with Hotbox | Surfaces | Bevel Plus | Option Box. Reset the options, and uncheck the create bevel Start and End options. This will make a

simple capped extrusion. Then click the bevel button. An extruded capital "A" appears (see Figure 15.11). Check it in shaded mode to see what it looks like.

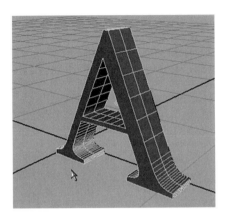

FIGURE 15.11   *Creating a beveled capital "A."*

4. Restore the Script Editor. In its text area, highlight the actions you just performed, checking to include the things that made up the creation of the extruded letter "A." Now, MMB-drag the highlighted text into the lower half of the Script Editor. Here you can remove all the lines that start with // or that were later undone. The resulting script looks like Figure 15.12. Now select this edited text, MMB-drag it to the shelf, and a MEL icon button should appear. Test this new shelf button by clearing the system with Hotbox | File | New Scene, and then clicking the MEL icon that remains in the shelf. You should get an instant re-creation of your "A."

5. To edit this shelf item, open the Shelf Editor by clicking the down arrow at the far left of the shelf, and choosing Shelf Editor. In the Shelves dialog box that opens, click the Shelf Contents tab. Enter Solid-A in the label and tooltips text box, and clear the Icon Name text box (see Figure 15.13). Click the Change Image button and select the Aicon.bmp file from the CD-ROM. This is simply a 32x32 pixel BMP directly rendered from Maya of a textured version of this very scene. You could render your own if you want, or create one from scratch in a paint program.

On the CD

Chapter_15\Aicon.bmp

6. Clear the history in the Script Editor with Edit | Clear History. Make an extruded "A" if you don't already have one in the scene. Open the Duplicate Options dialog box (Hotbox | Edit | Duplicate | Option Box), and reset the settings. Then set Translate Z to 01, Scale X to 0.9, and Scale Y to 1.1. Enter 8 in the Number of Copies text box, and click the Duplicate button. Look in the Script Editor for the line beginning with duplicate –rr and select the entire line (see Figure 15.14). If you put your mouse just to the left of the line, the mouse direction will flip, and you can easily select the entire line with one click.

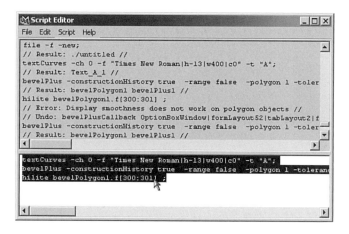

FIGURE 15.12   *The edited script, ready to drag to the Shelf.*

FIGURE 15.13   *Editing the new Shelf item.*

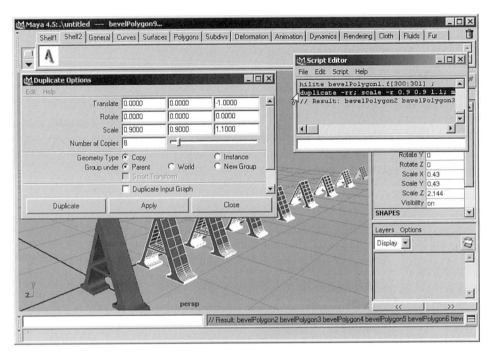

FIGURE 15.14   *The duplication settings and the selected script that caused the duplication.*

7. Open the Hotkey Editor (Hotbox | Window | Settings/Preferences | Hotkeys). In the Categories list, select User, and then click the New button. Enter ScaleDupe in the Name text box and 8 copies, stretched in the Description text box. Then MMB-drag the selected line in the Script Editor to the Command area of the Hotkey Editor, and click the Accept button. ScaleDupe is then displayed in the Commands list box. In the Assign New Hotkey area, enter o in the Key text box, select the Alt check box, and click the Assign button. You now have the Alt+o hotkey for this duplication action (see Figure 15.15). Click Save and then Close to close the dialog box. Test the hotkey by making some spheres and pressing Alt+o when they are selected. The hotkey will work on single objects or groups of objects.

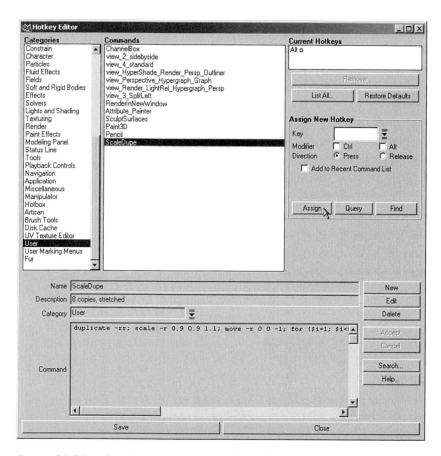

FIGURE 15.15   *Creating a new hotkey in the Hotkey Editor.*

With these methods, you can automate nearly any action in Maya. As your skills progress, notice the actions you perform often and consider whether it would benefit you to have them automated. When you're confident that you've grasped the basic skills and are ready to add workflow enhancements, try creating hotkeys, Shelf items, and marking menus for the most-used functions, in a way that makes sense for the way you work.

Maya 4.5 Shelves

Included with Maya 4.5 is a complete set of shelves to help you improve your workflow. You can load each shelf by clicking the down arrow at the far left of the shelves, and choosing "Load Shelf...," or you can run the bit of MELscript below (note: you also can find this text on the CD-ROM):

```
loadNewShelf "shelf_General.mel";
loadNewShelf "shelf_Curves.mel";
```

```
loadNewShelf "shelf_Surfaces.mel";
loadNewShelf "shelf_Polygons.mel";
loadNewShelf "shelf_Subdivs.mel";
loadNewShelf "shelf_Deformation.mel";
loadNewShelf "shelf_Animation.mel";
loadNewShelf "shelf_Dynamics.mel";
loadNewShelf "shelf_Rendering.mel";
loadNewShelf "shelf_Cloth.mel";
loadNewShelf "shelf_Fluids.mel";
loadNewShelf "shelf_Fur.mel";
saveAllShelves $gShelfTopLevel;
```

You'll find the shelves in your scripts\ startup folder, which is by default directly under your Maya 4.5 root folder. The installed shelves will look like Figure 15.16.

On the CD

Chapter_15\shelfscript.txt

FIGURE 15.16   *Although not loaded by default, you can install the Maya 4.5 shelves for added ease of use with Maya.*

Helper Objects: Organization and Control

The next workflow-assist feature you'll explore is the concept of "helper" objects—non-renderable objects in a scene that contain a set of controls for other objects. You create a simple object, disable its ability to be rendered, and hide all its existing parameters from appearing in the Channel Box. Then you add new attributes to the helper object and connect them to your critical scene variables, such as character expressions or the scene lighting mix. Helper objects can make animation and scene control much easier because all the variables you need are in the Channel Box, ready for animation.

Tutorial: Building a Helper Object

1. Reset Maya by choosing File | New Scene on the menu. Create a default polygon cube (Ctrl+x and Cube | option box). Choose Edit | Reset Settings, and then click the Create button. Set Rotate X and Z to 45. These settings make the cube a kind of diamond in any view, and easier to see.

On the CD

Chapter_15\movies\ch15tut03.wmv

2. Open the Attribute Editor for the cube (hotkey: **Ctrl+a**), and make sure the pCubeShape1 tab is selected. Expand the Render Stats section and uncheck all the boxes, as shown in Figure 15.17.

FIGURE 15.17   *Making the cube invisible, as far as the renderer is concerned.*

3. With the cube still selected, open the Channel Control Editor (Hotbox | Window | General Editors | Channel Control). In the Keyable tab of the Channel Control dialog box, the variables to be displayed in the Channel Box appear in the Keyable list. Click the first item, and drag down the list to select all the variables, as shown in Figure 15.18. Click the Move button to put all these variables in the Non Keyable list box, and then click Close. You'll notice that no variables are listed in the Channel Box now, even though the cube is selected.

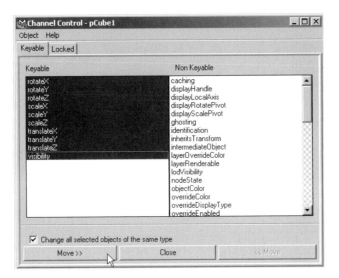

FIGURE 15.18   *Use the Channel Control dialog box to decide what can be animated (is keyable) and should appear in the Channel Box.*

4. With the cube still selected, add an attribute to it (Hotbox | Modify | Add Attribute). In the New tab of the Add Attribute dialog box, enter Steering in the Attribute Name text box. In the Numeric Attribute Properties section at the bottom, enter the following values for this attribute (see Figure 15.19): Minimum to -10, Maximum to 10, and Default to 0. Click OK.

5. Create a NURBS torus to use for a tire (Hotbox | Create | NURBS Primitives | Torus). Set Rotate X to 90, Translate X to 10, and Translate Z to 2.

6. Next, duplicate the tire (Hotbox | Edit | Duplicate | option box, choose Edit | Reset Settings in the Duplicate Options dialog box, and click the Duplicate button). The duplicate is on top of the existing tire, so change Translate Z to -2. Select both tires, and press Ctrl+d to duplicate them to get a set of four tires. Change Translate X to 4 to position the front two tires; now all four tires are in place.

7. With both tires still selected, click on the Rotate Y label in the Channel Box. RMB-click on the label and choose Set Driven Key from the shortcut menu to open the Set Driven Key dialog box. Only one tire will appear, so click the Load Driven button and both tires should appear.

8. Next, select the cube in the scene, and then click the Load Driver button. In the Driven column, select the two tire entries. In the right-hand columns of the Set Driven Key dialog box, select Steering in the Driver row, and rotateY in the Driven row, as shown in Figure 15.20.

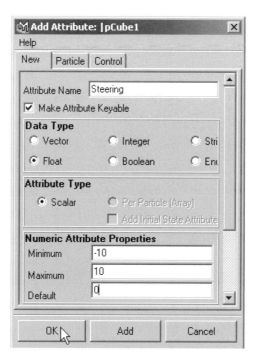

FIGURE 15.19   *Entering values for the Steering attribute in the Add Attribute dialog box.*

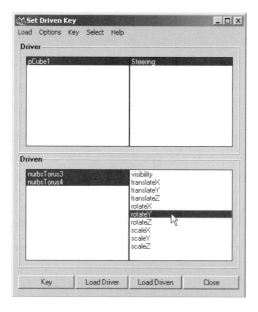

FIGURE 15.20   *Setting up the Driven keys.*

9. Now you need to tell Maya how these variables are connected. Select the cube and set its Steering value to -10 in the Channel Box. Select both tori that you loaded into the Set Driven Key dialog box and set their Rotate Y values to 45. Click the Key button in the Set Driven Key dialog box.

10. As in Step 9, select the cube and set its Steering value to 10 in the Channel Box, and then select the same two tori and set their Rotate Y values to -45. Click the Key button in the Set Driven Key dialog box. To test the setup, select the cube, click the Steering label in the Channel Box, and then MMB-drag left and right in the viewport (Maya's Virtual Slider). The tires should rotate through the range you set for it. The Steering variable on the cube now controls the Y rotation of both tires (see Figure 15.21). You can load the scene file noted below the CD icon to check out our end result.

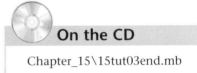

On the CD

Chapter_15\15tut03end.mb

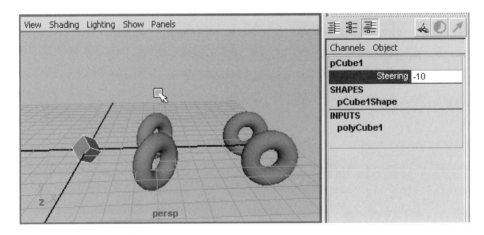

FIGURE 15.21   *The cube's Channel Box now controls the overall steering of both tires.*

You can move the cube to a position that keeps it out of the way of other objects so that it's easy to select. In this example, it's part of a car, so you would parent the helper cube to the car's root object, perhaps the body or frame that you would be modeling later. You can add more attributes and set up other Driven keys for the cube, such as the position of the steering wheel (also driven by the Steering attribute), the brightness of the headlights (on a new attribute called Headlights), the position of the seats, or any other variable you plan to animate. You could name the cube object something like aaaCar_Control so that it's easy to find in the Outliner.

Compositing

Professional animators often set up complex shots as composites. That means the shot is rendered in several different passes. They do this for several reasons:

- Huge complex scenes can become cumbersome to load, edit, and save.

- The client might request changes on specific areas of the frame that have no bearing on its three-dimensionality, and are therefore fast, easy edits in the compositor—color tints, brightness, blurriness, and so forth.

- Isolated segments of the shot might require effects that can be done much more quickly in 2D.

- Rendering one element or layer of a shot is much faster than rendering the entire shot again.

- Most of Maya's particle system effects require separate hardware rendering and compositing to the rest of the scene later.

- Compositing 2D images is nearly always faster than rendering 3D shots; usually less than one second per frame is required to composite many layers.

- Breaking a tough shot into parts allows the tasks to be divided among several animators.

- The client can judge the progress of the final shot at any time (after you do a quick composite of the layers you have rendered so far) and get a clear vision of the design.

For example, consider a shot that's going to be a first-person view from behind the windshield of an out-of-control car as it careens down a city street. The shot might consist of the following layers:

- The foreground car interior

- The car's reflective/refractive windshield

- The hood of the car seen through the windshield

- The street and buildings that the car is passing

- The other moving cars on the road

- The shadows under the other moving cars on the road

- The distant cityscape and sky

First, you need to determine the camera's motions. The trick of compositing 3D animation works because the camera sees the same 3D world in any given frame. Unlike a real-world camera positioned by hand, the computer's virtual camera always plays back exactly the same way as animated, precisely pointing where it should at each frame. Therefore, if you render a background and then a foreground from the same animated camera, the two sequences could be combined and would appear to perfectly match in camera perspective, position, and direction. For model shots, effects houses have used expensive computer-controlled cameras on rigs to get the same result, but they must be careful about the motors' tolerances; even a slight difference can cause shots in which separately filmed objects appear to slip and slide against the background they're supposed to be sitting on.

For the out-of-control car, because these shots are inside a moving car, all the car and camera motions must be decided on early because changes in the camera change the position of every object in the rendered frame and require rendering every layer again. To expedite work for the animator, proxy objects can be used if the final scene models are not finished. The buildings could be simple box objects, and the car the camera is riding in and the passing cars would also be simple shapes. A rendered test of camera and car motion is generally good enough to get approval, and then the layers can be rendered. Already there are several production-accelerating factors:

- The car's windshield glass would likely be created with 2D post-processes that can easily make refraction and reflection warping effects. Often this decision is forced because everything seen through the windshield would be altered by the glass shader properties you assigned in your 3D scene. The main action is occurring in this part of the frame, so the director will be concerned with the brightness of the glass reflections and the refraction distortion caused by the curved glass. Often the most accurate look is not acceptable and must be "bent" for the shot's aesthetic effectiveness.

- The reflections on the hood of the car can be similarly simulated in 2D. In both cases, much rendering time is saved because reflection and refraction are usually rendered by raytracing, a computationally slow method.

- The distant cityscape and sky are effectively at infinity and would be unlikely to change. This element would, therefore, be an easy model, and can be created and rendered early in the job.

If the client sees the test composite and does not like how clear or bright or colorful the sky appears, you can usually fix these factors immediately in the compositor by simply adding 2D effects, such as blur, contrast, and desaturate. The same applies to all the other layers. You can even add seemingly 3D effects, such as fog and distance blur, via the Z-depth channel (as a mask for an overlay or blur effect so that the effect is keyed by distance). A sample Z-depth channel is shown in Figure 15.22.

FIGURE 15.22   *The source image on the left yields the alpha channel (in the center) and the Z-depth channel (on the right).*

Using Compositors

Most compositors use a timeline that progresses from left to right. The elements of a shot appear in layers on the timeline and can stop or start at different points in time. Some elements might be a fixed image, but most are image sequences; a 60-frame sequence is usually set to overlay during a 60-frame period of the timeline. The top layer in the timeline overlays the second layer, and so on. The bottom layer is the background plate. Popular compositors include Adobe's After Effects, Discreet's Combustion, Nothing Real's Shake, In-Sync's Speed Razor, Puffin Design's Commotion, and Eyeon's Digital Fusion.

Using the Use Background Material and Alpha Channels

For any layer of a composite to overlay the layers beneath it, a mask is required. Instead of cutting out each object in each frame manually with a photo editor, you can have Maya render objects with mask (known as *alpha*) channels included. The alpha channel is a grayscale mask image, with black signifying transparent, white signifying opaque, and the 254 gray levels in between defining levels of semi-transparency. Besides cutting out the object, the mask supports soft masking, handling problems such as transparency (for non-opaque materials such as glass), and the antialiased edges of objects (refer back to Figure 15.22 to see the alpha channel). Alpha channels are critical for getting believable results from your composite.

Sometimes objects are not easy to overlay. For example, you might have a scene with a car pulling out from behind a building, turning into the camera, driving in front of the building, and then turning out of range, disappearing behind another building. In this case, you would not render the car object by itself. You would include the objects that obscure the car and give them a Use Background material type. This special material renders as though there's a hole in the image directly to the background, and these areas of the image do not appear in the rendered image's alpha (mask) channel. Objects with this material are "chameleon" objects that make anything they are applied to and all the objects behind them invisible. However, they can still receive shadows and reflections.

In the car example, you would bring in the outer geometry of the buildings' first floors and assign a Use Background material to them. The car would then automatically disappear as it drove behind the Use Background buildings. Use Background materials can also be used to create a surface that does not appear in renderings except for where it receives shadows. In the car example, there's no easy way to get the shadows under the car to appear on any layer. Instead, you would create a special "car shadow" layer. To do this, you would apply a Use Background material to the streets, set so that the streets appear only in the alpha channel in the areas with shadows. You would also apply a Use Background material to the entire car so that the car casts shadows but renders as transparent. This rendering pass would produce just the shadows for you to composite behind the car.

Thinking in Layers

As you can see, it takes thought and planning to pull off a complex composited shot. It's unlikely you could create a large shot such as a cityscape fly-through without resorting to compositing. As you become familiar with your compositing software's capabilities, you'll know which slower 3D functions are best handled by the fast 2D compositor. The best approach is to try some challenging test projects and experiment with methods that combine the most flexibility with the fastest revision time (edit the scene, then render and/or composite again). In production, your main challenge is to meet clients' requests for edits without missing deadlines. Magazines such as *Cinefex* and *3D World* offer advice from real-world film and television projects, and often include articles with battle-proven compositing solutions from experienced users.

Maya's Render Layers

An additional level of flexibility is built into Maya 4 in the form of render layers. If you open the Render Globals window, you'll see the Render Layer/Pass Control option, which enables you to render parts of the image to separate images. Rendered attributes, such as shadows and specularity, can be brought into your compositor separately, so that you can quickly handle changes such as blurring or colorizing shadows to simulate light changes, or blurring and brightening specular highlights for a dreamier look. Figure 15.23 illustrates the contents of the various passes.

FIGURE 15.23   *Maya's render layers, clockwise from top left: beauty pass (normal render), diffuse, specular, shadow (alpha channel).*

Installing Third-Party Plug-ins, Materials, and Scripts

An enormous free resource worth exploring comes from Maya's large user base. A mixture of plug-ins, MELscripts, material shaders, and other aids are available for download from www.AliasWavefront.com as well as third-party web sites, such as www.highend3d.com. You can find solutions for many typical problems and utilities that simplify your work. Often you'll find these solutions inspiring: They show Maya's flexibility, demonstrate techniques you might not have been aware of, and show you how other animators are solving problems similar to ones you'll probably face. You can install and use these add-ons as follows:

- **MELscripts**   Save the files in one of your MELscripts directories, typically your Maya\4.0\scripts folder under your main My Documents or Documents and Settings folder. Run the script by typing its name in the Command Line. For example, if the script is called animToolbox.MEL, run it by typing animToolbox and pressing Enter. You might need to restart Maya for it to pick up scripts added while Maya was open. You can place these scripts in hotkeys, marking menus, and shelves just like the MELscript you worked with previously. MELscripts can look as powerful and integrated as any other part of Maya (see the samples in Figure 15.24).

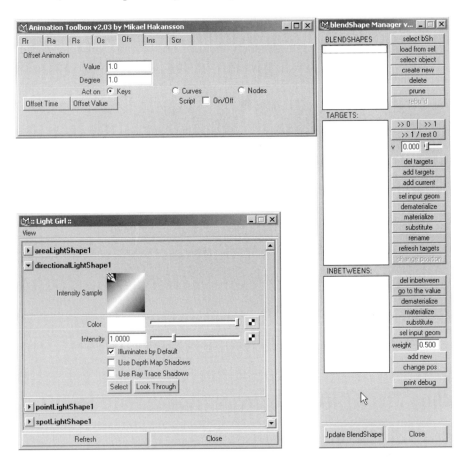

FIGURE 15.24 *Animation Toolbox (Mikael Hakansson), blendShape Manager (Sebastian Woldanski), and Light Girl (Ben Wronsky) are powerful and freely distributed MELscripts for Maya.*

- **Shaders**   They're usually .mb or .ma files, but you normally load them from Hypershade via its File | Import option. One or more shaders then appear in the top section of Hypershade. Usually no new geometry appears in your scene, but not always. Exploring the construction of the shaders you download can yield new perspectives on how to produce complex types of materials. See the "Creating Your Own Material Libraries" section for information on building a material library from your shader collection.

- **Plug-ins**   The plug-in generally includes one or more .mll files placed in the AW\Maya\bin\plug-ins folder, but they don't run until you enable them in Maya's Plug-in Manager (Window | Settings/Preferences | Plug-in Manager). You should see each .mll file listed, and enable the plug-ins once or permanently (see Figure 15.25). Because plug-ins take system resources, you can leave many of your plug-ins unloaded until needed.

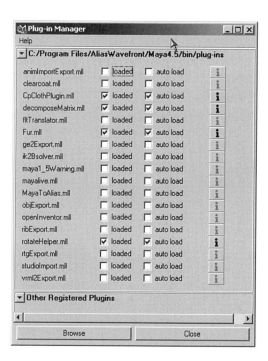

FIGURE 15.25   *Use Maya's Plug-in Manager to choose which plug-ins are running.*

Creating Your Own Material Libraries

You can build your own material libraries in Maya, but doing so takes a few steps. First, create a new tab in Hypershade by choosing Tabs | Create New Tab on Hypershade's menu. Name the new tab, and select the Bottom radio button for Initial Placement and the Disk radio button for Tab Type. Point the Root Directory text box to the folder where you're collecting your materials, and click the Create button. Set the tab to this newly created folder, and you should see a set of Maya icons, one for each material file. Normally, you want one shader stored in each .ma or .mb file in this folder.

Next, you replace those Maya icons with swatches of the rendered material. To do this, you have to actually render an IFF sample image file of the shader. You might want to make up a sample scene file, like the ball shown in Figure 15.26.

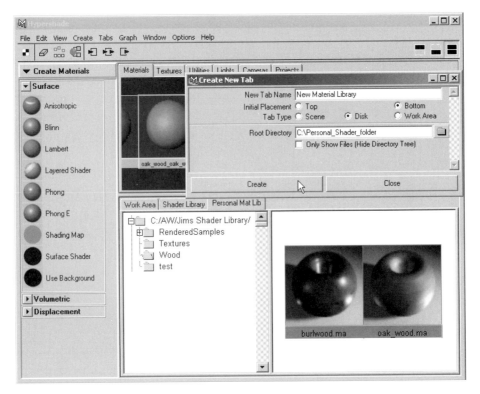

FIGURE 15.26   *Adding a material library tab to Hypershade.*

Usually you render a small (typically 200×200) pixel sample. After you render and save this IFF file, you need to rename it with the same name as the shader file, but with the suffix .swatch. So if your shader file is called darkwood.ma, your swatch is renamed from darkwood.iff to darkwood.ma.swatch. Then you copy this file to the

.MayaSwatches folder directly under the folder containing the shader files. If none exists, you can copy and paste a folder of this name from one of the AW\Maya\brushes\ folders, and then delete the contents of the duplicated folder. Windows will not let you directly create a folder with this name. When you reference the shader file in the tab, you'll see the swatch. You can then MMB-drag the swatch to the upper tabs so that the shader is ready to apply to a scene object.

Parting Thoughts

As you move forward from this book, we would like to offer you the advice of Maya artists in production settings. This advice might give you some understanding of the attitude and style of professionals who create art for a living.

On Techniques

Production animators at large studios usually work in teams of three or more. A philosophy of sharing techniques and supporting fellow animators pervades most successful studios. Some typical comments:

"You don't really know a technique until you've done it in a production setting. Several times!"

"Always be looking to improve, not only as a software user but as an artist. Inspiration can come from unlikely sources."

"Learn from everyone, and be ready to return the favor."

"Don't hoard your knowledge! Share with all those around you. It will benefit the project, and you will gain respect among your peers."

"Reference is a valuable thing. Don't have so much pride to think you don't need reference materials. It will save you time and sanity. Besides, it's always nice to show your supervisors that it *really does look that way* when they say 'But it doesn't look enough like a tree…'"

"Ask questions when you don't understand. There's no shame in not knowing every facet of the software."

"Don't always ask the Maya gurus. Occasionally, ask newer animators, too. They'll often present a unique spin on the issue that lets you see the problem from a different angle, and sometimes it's the angle you need to solve the problem."

"There is nearly always a faster, easier way. Look for it."

"In your down time, look for different ways to get things done. Faster isn't always better, and finding new ways to do things can spark new processes and creative methods for later use."

On Starting a Career in Animation

Starting a career as a professional computer animator is something of a hurdle. Aspiring animators are judged by their past work and attitude. The studio might be willing to accept some shortcomings, but in general they hire only artists who can begin producing on the first day. Some comments on the subject:

"Get apprentice work any way you can. Student and personal work is looked on very differently from production work that included an actual client and deadline. Work for free at first, if necessary, and find clients from any market that would benefit from animation."

"Study the trades (trade magazines such as *Computer Graphics World* and *Cinefex*) until you understand the business well enough to just skim them for relevant detail instead of having to read everything line by line to understand it."

"Once you've entered into the industry, help others the same way you were helped. It's a small industry and good talent moves quickly."

"See and be seen, show up at any industry events you are able to get yourself into, and introduce yourself casually."

"Admit your skill boundaries when you begin professionally. There's a tendency in new animators to overextend themselves and promise too much, too soon."

"Don't miss deadlines. Don't commit to deadlines you are likely to miss."

Going Further

This book has presented many variations and ideas on the main tutorial scene with a spooky house and a creature who lives there. Develop a variation on this theme (a character and the character's environment) as a personal project, and use the techniques you have learned to build a complex project of your own.

Use the final, rendered movies of these projects to solicit some low-stress production work—perhaps a spinning logo for a Web site or a clever graphic that a charity could use in its publications. Use your network of friends and family to find a group or business that could benefit from your animation skills, but will not demand perfection or hold you to an early deadline.

Join the online Maya community and interact.

Summary

This chapter has shown you some tips and solutions for problems you'll face as you become more expert with Maya:

- **When to expect slow render times**   Some features inevitably require more time to render. Combine enough of these features with a large scene file, and the result is usually a long render time.

- **Unattended rendering of several jobs, or combining several machines to render one job**   Batch and network rendering are the solution to slow render times.

- **Marking menus, hotkeys, and Shelf buttons**   You learned to create your own workflow enhancements in this chapter, without needing to know anything about writing MELscript code.

- **Rendering in layers**   As powerful as Maya is, you can still imagine worlds larger than what can be comfortably built in a single scene file. Rendering in layers is the answer. You also gain flexibility in changing the look of each layer if necessary.

- **Installing add-ons**   You can and should browse the available enhancements for Maya and install the ones that sound intriguing.

PART IV

Appendices

Maya Headstart for Max Users

At this writing, 3ds max (formerly known as 3D Studio and 3D Studio MAX, referred to here as simply "max") is one of the most popular 3D animation programs. Although its design and operation origins are quite different from Maya's, max has adopted many of Maya's conventions, making it easier for 3ds max users to learn Maya. For max users, this appendix summarizes where to find Maya tools and dialog boxes analogous to those they're used to working with.

Differences in Viewport Navigation

The first difference is that unlike max, Maya has overall modes that determine which menus appear. The first six menus in Maya—File, Edit, Modify, Create, Display, and Window—are always present, but the other pull-downs change depending on your mode. The modes are Animation, Modeling, Dynamics, and Rendering. If you have Maya Unlimited, Cloth and Live modes also appear.

Viewport manipulation   Maya has no buttons for zoom, orbit, pan, maximize, zoom extents, and so forth. Instead, Maya relies on a three-button mouse and hotkeys. For orbit, pan, and zoom, you must press the Alt key and simultaneously press the left (LMB), middle (MMB), or LMB *and* MMB. Max offers mouse control of viewports, too, but many users aren't aware of them: the Alt+MMB for orbit, MMB alone for pan, and scroll wheel for zoom. Maya consistently uses these zoom and pan functions for every type of browsing dialog box—graph editors, paint effects presets, and so forth. For Maya's material editor (called Hypergraph), this feature is a big plus because you can see the swatches at any size you like in the Work Area.

Zoom window   In Maya, press Ctrl+Alt and LMB-drag a rectangle of the zoom-to area. Dragging the window from upper-left to lower-right results in a zoom in, and dragging from lower-right to upper-left results in a zoom out, in which the existing frame fits into the newly drawn window. The smaller the drawn window, the more extreme the zoom.

Zoom extents and zoom extents selected   All Maya panels have a pull-down called Frame All Objects (hotkey: **a**) and Frame Selected Object (hotkey: **f**). Again, this same option works for all of Maya's other editing windows, such as Hypershade and the Graph Editor. **Shift+F** and **Shift+A** are the hotkeys for Frame Selected in all panels and Frame All in all panels.

Minimize and maximize   You simply tap the spacebar in Maya. Regardless of which window is currently selected, the panel with the mouse cursor over it toggles to full screen.

Differences in the Control Interface

Quad menu versus Hotbox   If you hold the spacebar more than a moment, the Hotbox appears (see Figure A.1); this workflow speedup device is somewhat like the right-click quad menu introduced in max 4 (see Figure A.2). Advanced Maya users often turn off the pull-downs and use just the Hotbox, activating the hot zones with a right-click.

Spinners   A handy feature in max is the spinner, the up and down arrows for each variable that let you easily scroll the values and see the results in real time. Maya's counterpart, called the Virtual Slider, is hidden. You activate it by selecting a variable in the Channel Box, and then MMB-click and drag horizontally in any panel.

Changing defaults   An important part of Maya is the option box, a square icon next to many creation and editing menu items. Clicking the option box opens a dialog box where you can adjust the menu command's default mode. Max, by contrast, always changes its creation and modifier defaults to the last settings you used for that object/modifier. Choose Edit | Reset Settings in Maya's option box pull-downs to go back to default settings for any command.

Selecting and deselecting   In max, you use the Ctrl key to add and Alt to remove items from clicked object selections. In Maya, Shift acts as a selection toggle: If the object's selected, Shift deselects it; if the object's not selected, Shift selects it. Also, you can Shift-drag to select many objects at once or to invert the selection of many objects. The Ctrl key always deselects and can also be used to drag-deselect. Note that drag selections are always in what max calls "crossing" mode, as opposed to windowed selection mode; any object that's partly in the selection rectangle is selected.

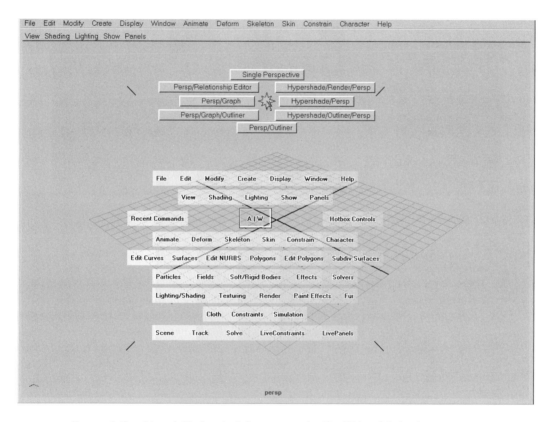

FIGURE A.1   *Maya's Hotbox in full expert mode: The UI is minimized except for the top menu bar, and all interaction is handled via the Hotbox and the hot zones above, below, and to the right and left.*

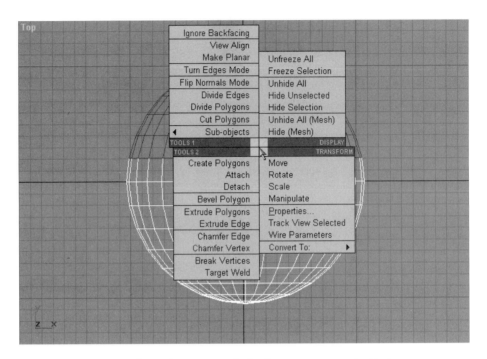

FIGURE A.2   *Max's quad menus are similar in some ways to the Hotbox.*

Differences in Viewport Mode and Layout

Orthographic and Perspective views   In max, these views are arbitrary and virtual, but in Maya there's an invisible default camera assigned for each of three orthographic views: Front, Top, and Side. To change such elements as the near/far clipping or the field of view, you must adjust this camera. To do that for any orthographic view, choose View | Camera Attribute Editor in the applicable orthographic view. The virtual camera for that view will appear, and you can adjust its values in the Attribute Editor. The orthographic views are locked and do not orbit. Any Perspective or camera view can become orthographic (like max's "user view") by selecting the Orthographic check box in the Camera Attribute Editor for that view (see Figure A.3). You access the default perspective camera attributes the same way, with View | Camera Attribute Editor.

Viewport display   In max, you right-click over the viewport name to bring up display options, such as wireframe or shaded. In Maya, it works similarly, but you use the pull-down menu at the top of any Maya panel. The Shading pull-down, shown in Figure A.4, contains most of the settings familiar to max users for viewport display modes. The Panels pull-down in Figure A.5 lists options similar to the Viewport Configuration window in max.

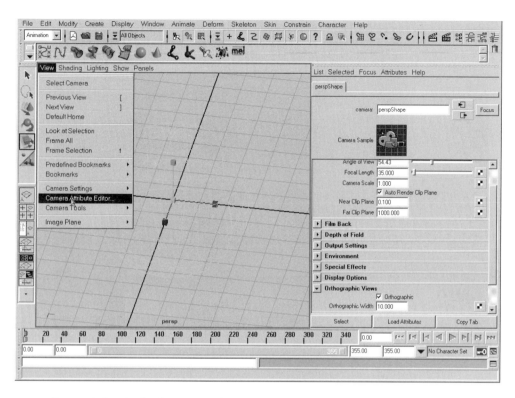

FIGURE A.3   *In the Camera Attribute Editor, you can enable the orthographic view and adjust clipping for any view.*

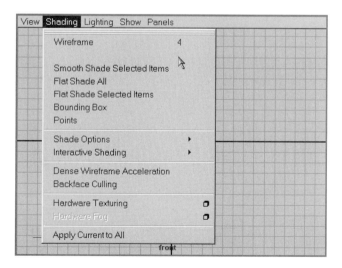

FIGURE A.4   *Adjusting a panel's display mode in Maya.*

View Shading Lighting Show Panels
Perspective
Orthographic
Look Through Selected
Panel
Layouts
Saved Layouts
Tear Off...
Tear Off Copy...
Panel Editor...
Single Pane
Two Panes Side by Side
Two Panes Stacked
Three Panes Split Top
Three Panes Split Left
Three Panes Split Bottom
Three Panes Split Right
Four Panes
Previous Arrangement
Next Arrangement

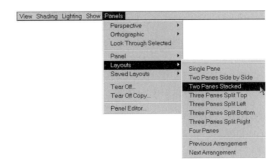

FIGURE A.5 *The layout modes available in Maya's Panels pull-down.*

Configuring panels/viewports At the left side of Maya's interface is the Tool Box, which includes a set of Quick Layout buttons (see Figure A.6) that allow you to instantly switch panel configurations. Right-clicking any of the Quick Layout buttons displays a list of many more popular layouts. In max, you change viewport layout by right-clicking in the viewport, choosing Configure | Layout Mode, and then setting up each panel. With Maya, you can also set any panel to any window by clicking the hot buttons that appear below the Quick Layout buttons.

Hot buttons used for quick changes of any panel
Top View
Side View
Front View
Persp View
Outliner
Graph Editor
Dope Sheet
Trax Editor
Hypergraph
Hypershade
Visor
UV Texture Editor
Render View
Blend Shape
Dynamic Relationships
Devices
Relationship Editor
Reference Editor
Component Editor
Paint Effects

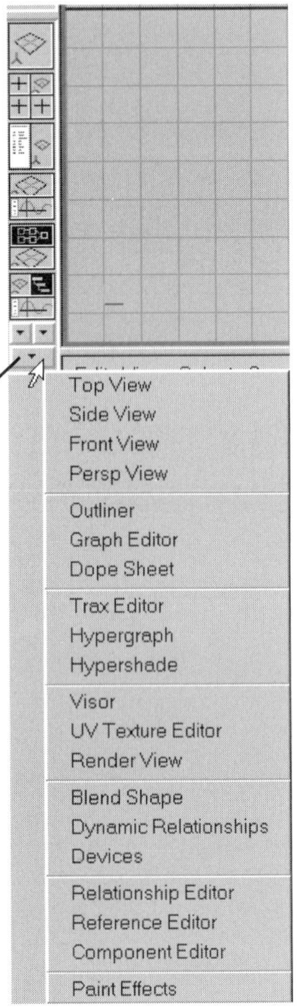

FIGURE A.6
Maya's Quick Layout buttons and hot buttons to change any panel.

Differences in Working with Objects

Creating objects/lights/cameras   In Maya, everything is created at a default size and location. Unlike max, you don't click or drag to create anything. You simply go to the Create menu to create an element; when it appears, typically it's at a size of 1 unit at the scene's origin point (0,0,0).

Numerical input   In max, you right-click a transform button to get a numerical entry field for precision adjustments. In Maya, you have full numerical control of the transform variables in the Channel Box, the dialog box usually at the far right of Maya's interface (see Figure A.7). To change a value for a setting, you simply click in the variable field and type in the value. Object transform settings are at the top of the Channel Box, with the object's creation parameters, such as number of divisions, showing up farther down the Channel Box.

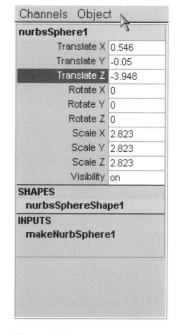

FIGURE A.7
Maya's Channel Box displays all object transforms in scene units.

Selection filters   In Maya, you can make certain object categories selectable, as with max's selection filter pull-down. Unlike max, you can mix and match selectable categories of scene elements by clicking the various buttons or right-clicking the button to toggle subcategories. Maya's selection filter buttons (see Figure A.8) are modal—in other words, they change if you're working in Hierarchy mode or Component (subobject) mode (see the "Differences in Creating and Editing Models" section later in this appendix).

Transforming objects   Object transforms are nearly identical in max and Maya. Max's Move/Rotate/Scale icons (top center of max interface; see Figure A.9) are similar to Maya's Move/Rotate/Scale icons (left side of Maya interface; see Figure A.10). The transform gizmo that appears on selected objects is also identical, except that Maya does not have the "brackets" that let you transform on x-y, y-z, or x-z planes.

FIGURE A.8   *Maya's selection filters in Object Editing mode.*

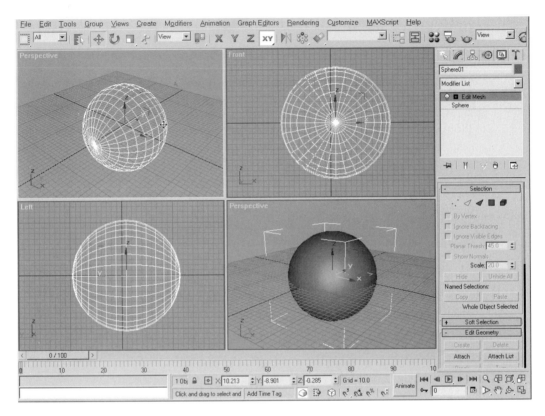

FIGURE A.9   *Max's transform buttons and transform gizmo.*

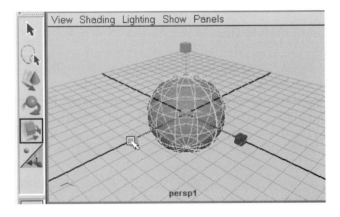

FIGURE A.10   *Maya's transform buttons and three-axis object manipulator.*

Duplicating objects   Max users are accustomed to using the Shift key during a transform to create duplicates or instances of an object, a light, or a camera. In Maya, you typically use the duplicate hotkey (**Ctrl+d**), and then adjust the new clone.

Creating instanced objects   When you duplicate, Maya applies the same settings as the previous duplication. If you want to make duplicates that are instanced (that is, changes to any instance affect all instanced copies), open the Duplicate Options dialog box (see Figure A.11), select the Instance radio button, and then click the Apply button. You can also set multiple copies and offset the copies.

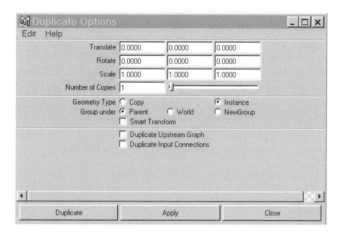

FIGURE A.11   *Switching to instanced duplication in the Duplicate Options dialog box.*

Parenting   There are no "link" or "unlink" icons in Maya. Linking is the same as Maya's parenting, which appears at the bottom of the Edit menu and has default hotkeys: lowercase **p** for parent and **Shift+P** (uppercase P) for unparent.

Differences in Creating and Editing Models

Modeling   Maya offers both NURBS and polygonal modeling. Maya's NURBS are more complex and full-featured than max's. When using NURBS, take these factors into consideration:

- **Isoparms**   Make sure areas that are supposed to smoothly seam together have an equal number of NURBS dividers, known as isoparms.

- **Computation**   NURBS can take longer to render because they must tessellate into polygons at rendering time. Generally, computation is a factor only with very complex NURBS objects.

■ **Display**   Maya displays NURBS objects in three levels of detail because these objects are parametric. When a NURBS object is selected, press 1, 2, or 3 on your keyboard to set low, medium, and high display modes. All objects are created with a low display resolution by default.

In earlier versions of Maya, some tools worked only on NURBS, such as Paint Effects and Artisan, but this is no longer the case. Keep in mind that UV mapping is inherent to NURBS, but it must be applied to polygonal surfaces.

Editing subparts of a mesh   Maya has no modifier stack, so it has no "subobject" mode. Instead, you right-click on a selected object to display its component modes in a context-sensitive menu. You can also enter the "subobject" mode with the F8 key or with the Component Selection mode button in the Status Line. When in Component Selection mode, the selection mask buttons change from object types to the appropriate component types. For polygons, they would include edges, faces, and vertices; for NURBS objects, isoparms, control vertices, and so on. You then make selections, edit the selections (with the Move, Rotate, or Scale tools), and exit the mode by right-clicking and choosing Select or by pressing the F8 key again. F8 acts as a subobject mode toggle. You can right-click on the Selection by Component Type buttons at the top of the interface to include or exclude certain types of entities, as shown in Figure A.12. Buttons are brown if the entities are disabled.

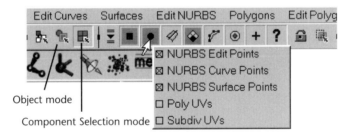

FIGURE A.12   *In Component Selection mode, the selection mask buttons change.*

Adding modifiers to a mesh   Many of the typical max modifiers, such as bend, twist, and skin, are found in the Animation mode dialog boxes. In general, Maya divides the modes of editing and deforming an object between modeling and animation. However, Maya allows almost anything to be animated, just as max does.

Object history and modifier stack   Compared to max, Maya offers much more detailed object history; every edit is stored in the object's history, as opposed to max's quantum-style modifiers that contain all edits made by the modifier in the stack. Maya's Channel Box displays a stack-like list of tweaks and source object settings for the selected object. Just as you often collapse the modifier stack for objects in max to improve load speed and file size, you should delete the object history when you're done with primary editing (Edit | Delete by Type | History on the menu). Deleting selected parts of an object's history is usually called "baking history" because you're keeping the object as is and discarding all the construction records.

Differences in Scene Organization

Groups   Maya's groups do not open or close; they simply create a hierarchically higher node that can be animated. Use the up arrow key to go from selecting a group member to selecting the entire group. You use the up arrow and down arrow keys for navigating any hierarchy.

Wireframe colors   Maya has far fewer wireframe colors than max does, but you can change them easily. Simply select an object and choose Display | Wireframe Color on the menu to get a display of eight color swatches (see Figure A.13). Note that the wireframe color isn't apparent until the object is deselected, just as in max. Instanced objects always have the same wireframe color.

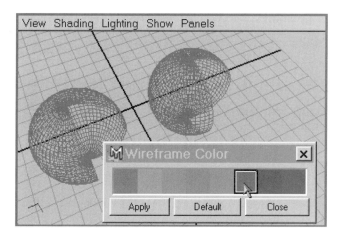

Figure A.13   *Eight colors are available for wireframes in Maya.*

Layers   Maya allows full layers as 3D Studio VIZ does; max currently does not have layers. Instead of "freezing" a layer, Maya uses the terms *Template* and *Reference*, with a T or R showing in the Layers section to indicate the display type (see Figure A.14). The V toggle is for visibility of a layer, enabling you to hide entire layers. Template and Reference are both frozen display types, but Reference allows you to snap to the frozen object. Also, Reference objects still appear in the panels but don't render. In Maya you have 32 additional colors to signify layer color in wireframes, and layer color overrides wireframe color.

FIGURE A.14   *Setting the display type for layers.*

Picking objects by name   In Maya, this is done with the Outliner window (see Figure A.15), which can appear as a floating window or be assigned to any panel. The Outliner can display every scene element, even all attributes and construction components. It can display objects alphabetically or hierarchically. It shows hidden objects (displayed in blue text), so this is where you would "unhide by name," as in max. Also, parented objects appear in green as a reminder. When selecting objects in the Outliner, Shift acts like a select macro—in a list of objects, you can Shift-click the top object, and then Shift-click the bottom object, and all the objects in between will be selected. Shift doesn't deselect objects in the Outliner. Ctrl acts as a single select toggle in the Outliner, selecting deselected objects or deselecting selected objects.

Hiding/displaying objects   Maya allows you to hide objects globally (from all panels and from Rendering) and by type, per panel (but not from Rendering). To globally hide an object, use Display | Hide. You can hide just the selected or deselected objects, or you can hide entire categories and types of objects.

To locally hide a category of object types in one of Maya's panels, use that panel's Show pull-down, where you can include or exclude scene elements, such as NURBS, polygons, lights, cameras, and so forth, in each panel. By contrast, objects can be globally hidden in max, but all max viewports respond together. The Show pull-down also offers the unique Isolate option, which forces that panel to display only the currently selected object.

Setting preferences and choosing units   Maya has a completely different set of preferences than max does, but you should look them over as you

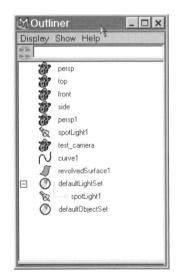

FIGURE A.15
The Outliner lists all scene entities for easy "pick by name" selections.

begin working with Maya. To display them, choose Window | Settings/Preferences | Preferences, or click the Animation Preferences button to the right of the key-shaped Auto Keyframe button at the interface's lower right. This dialog box has more options than in max, so instead of tabs at the top, there's a Categories list to the left to show preferences for each. The units setting appears under the Settings category.

Differences in Modeling Aids

Adjusting the grid   In Maya, click the option box next to Display | Grid (see Figure A.16). New in Maya 4, the grid can be color-coded and have major and minor lines.

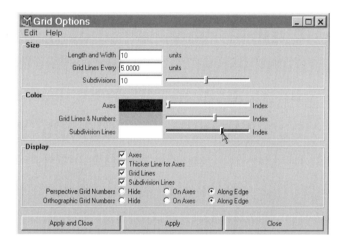

FIGURE A.16   *Features in the Grid Options dialog box.*

Snapping   Maya offers full snapping options, more powerful than those in max. The icons at the top with a U-shaped magnet (see Figure A.17) are the available snap modes; you can temporarily enable Grid, Curve, or Point snap mode with the **x**, **c**, and **v** hotkeys, for operations that demand different types of snapping. Maya can help you snap objects to lines and surfaces (the object is constrained in one or two dimensions, but otherwise floats) in addition to point snaps (the object simply locks).

Measurement helpers   Maya includes measurement tools like those in max, under Create | Measure Tools on the menu.

Aligning objects   A tool similar to max's alignment tool appears under Modify | Snap Align Objects | Align Objects.

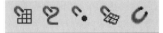

FIGURE A.17   *Maya's snapping options.*

Pivot points   In Maya, you display and move an object's pivot point by using the Insert key as an on/off toggle for this mode. The pivot point for the selected object appears as a small circle with a dot at the center (see Figure A.18). Its coordinate handles do not have arrows on the ends, but the lines function like the transform gizmo to constrain the pivot point's movement.

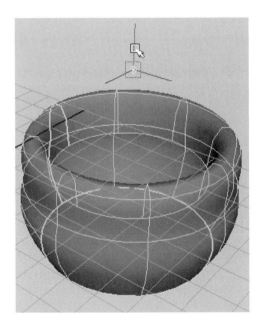

FIGURE A.18   *Display the pivot point by pressing the Insert key.*

Differences in Lighting

Lighting types   Maya includes the same primary light types and shadow modes as max. One added light type that's unique to Maya (although with max 5, area lights are possible) is called Area Light, a light source that enables you to use a rectangle- or square-shaped light source and cast soft light with penumbral shadows. This light type is invaluable for indoor scenes or any place you want soft lighting. Also, Maya's Ambient lights are nothing like the Ambient control in max's Environment dialog box. Maya's Ambient lights are like point lights that include an All Surfaces Lit variable. You can also cast shadows from Ambient lights. Max 5 also adds light reflection options called light tracer and radiosity. Maya contains no similar function.

Creating lights   Lights are created just like objects, at a fixed size (1) and place (the origin) when you choose Create | Lights | Light Type on the menu. You then position the light icon in your scene. You can scale the icons up and down without changing the rendered effect, except for the Area lights. An Area light's size is set by the icon itself, so you can use the Scale tool to stretch and size the Area light's rectangular panel. The Area light's shape affects how much light it emits.

Creating shadows   Shadow modes in Maya and max are exactly the same—mapped or raytraced shadows. As in max, mapped shadows are generally faster to calculate and appear softer. Raytraced shadows are usually hard-edged, more appropriate with intense point lights or sunlight. In Maya, you can set a radius for a raytraced shadow light to soften the edge, but that causes a severe hit on rendering speed. A unique feature in Maya for mapped shadows (*Depth Map Shadows*, in Maya's terminology) is the ability to reuse shadow maps (Dmaps; see Figure A.19), which makes rendering faster after you've rendered the shadow maps once. It even lets you edit the shadow map in an image editor. In max, shadow maps are always created on-the-fly and discarded after rendering for every frame.

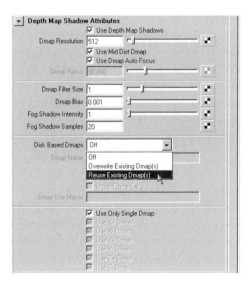

Figure A.19   *Reusing Dmaps in the Attribute Editor.*

Light include/exclude   Maya uses a special window for *light linking*, as it's called in Maya. To open it, choose Window | Relationship Editor | Light Linking on the menu. There are two ways to view these light-object relationships: object-centric or light-centric. Grouping and assignment aids are included in the Light Sets section.

Light falloff   Maya offers a new light type in version 4.5 that has similar functionality to the far falloff option in 3ds max. The new light type is called *volume light*.

It does not necessarily create volumetrics (fog effects), as you would expect. Rather, it has a visual cue as to the volume that will be illuminated by the light. This light type has traditional features, such as various shapes other than spherical: box, cylinder, and cone. Also, light color from emitter to volume edge can be controlled with a ramp.

Differences in Materials

Materials   Maya's Material Editor is completely different from max's. Called Hypershade, it's under Window | Rendering Editors | Hypershade. Instead of having a fixed number of swatches where editing is performed, Maya's interface is completely freeform, with any number of materials appearing in an open palette. In general, you create a source material type, such as Blinn or Lambert, and then assign maps to the various channels. To do that easily, MMB-drag from the palette of map types onto the material source. Then you're prompted as to which channel it's assigned to: Color, Bump, and so forth.

Material libraries   Hypershade works with materials (called *shaders* in Maya) saved as .ma or .mb (Maya ASCII or Maya binary) files. In the Hypershade window, you can load these materials into the current scene and assign them. Tabs in the Hypershade window can contain material libraries. More details on creating and editing material libraries is included in Chapter 8, "Materials."

Maps   When you are viewing a material in the Attribute Editor, a checkerboard icon appears next to any mappable variable (see Figure A.20); this icon is identical to the map button in max that shows "none" when unmapped. Most of the map types should be familiar to max users if you translate as follows for a common Blinn-type material:

Max	Maya
Diffuse	Color
Opacity	Transparency
Ambient	(none)
Self-illumination	Ambient Color
Bump	Bump Mapping
Glossiness	Eccentricity
Specular Level	Specular Roll Off
Specular	Specular Color
Reflection	Reflected Color

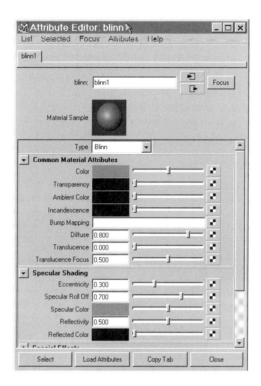

FIGURE A.20   *Blinn material in the Attribute Editor; checkerboard icons denote variables that can be mapped.*

Maya adds new map channels called Diffuse, Translucence, Incandescence, and Reflectivity:

- **Diffuse** is a darkening channel, often used to add "dirtiness" to a material.

- **Translucence** is a way to let light bleed through an object so that you can see light or shadows cast from the opposite side.

- **Incandescence** combines self-illumination and a mixed-in color. At full intensity, the mixed-in color completely overtakes the color channel.

- **Reflectivity** is the strength of the reflection map. It controls raytraced reflection if raytracing is turned on in Render Globals.

Refraction is much more complex in Maya than in max, and its many mappable variables appear under raytrace options in the material's Attribute Editor.

Procedural textures   Maya offers a full suite of 2D and 3D procedural textures. You can view and place them in a shaded viewport on any NURBS or polygonal object.

Showing textures in viewports   Any map can be displayed in the Maya panels, just as in max. Only one can be shown at a time. To enable hardware texturing, switch to Shaded mode by choosing Shading | Smooth Shade All, and then choose Shading | Hardware Texturing (see Figure A.21). You can also do this with the hotkey **6** for a selected 3D view panel. Now you can choose any applied texture in the Attribute Editor (under Hardware Texturing) for a material, and it will appear in all shaded panels with hardware texturing enabled. Unlike max, you can individually choose the texture's quality level, from default to low, medium, high, and highest.

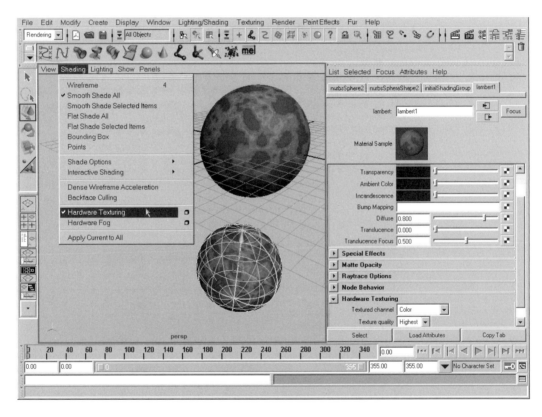

FIGURE A.21   *Showing textures in shaded panels.*

Placing textures in viewports   For polygonal objects, you can apply mapping and adjust it much as you do with the gizmo method in max. Once you have a polygonal object in a shaded, hardware-textured view, and a material with a displayed texture channel, you apply a mapping gizmo by switching to Modeling mode (hotkey: **F3**), choosing Edit Polygons | Texture, and selecting a mapping type. A transformable gizmo appears, and you can get instant feedback as you adjust it (see Figure A.22). If you click off the object, the gizmo disappears. To get it back, select the object, and then find the projection type in the Channel Box and click on the name (for example, polyPlanarProj1). If the gizmo is not visible, click the Show Manipulator button, which is with the transform buttons in the Tool Box, just below the Scale button.

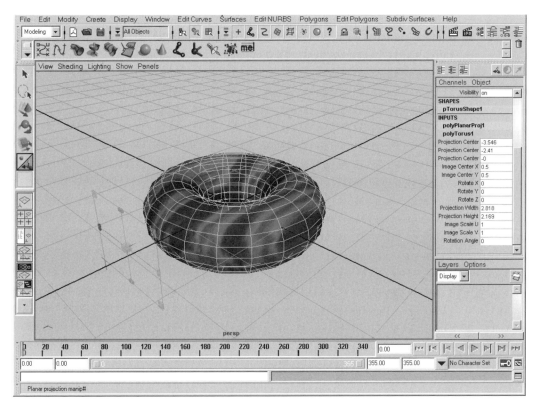

FIGURE A.22   *Maya offers interactive texture placement in a manner similar to max.*

Note that Maya does not use UV mapping channel numbers as max does. Instead, each mapping type assigned to an object is named. To pick the UV mode currently being edited, right-click the object and look under UV Sets. Every UV mapping that has been applied to the object will appear here, and you can select which one is currently active. Maya's UV Texture Editor (choose Window | UV Texture Editor on the menu) is similar to the texture editor added in 3ds max 5.

Differences in Creating Animation

Animation keyframes   Maya creates keyframes in a slightly more proactive way than max does. In Maya, you must create a key for the changed value, usually by pressing the s key. This action keys the variables you have changed to the current frame. Maya includes an Auto Keyframe button (the key icon at the lower-right corner) that's similar to max's Animate mode. However, Auto Keyframe doesn't work until an object has at least one key set for it. Be careful about which variables have had keys set; the Auto Keyframe feature can apply a key to every variable or just to the adjusted ones. This is set in the Preferences dialog box under the Keys category. In general, you should apply keys to only the adjusted parameters. In this mode, Maya behaves just like max's Animate mode except for having to manually create at least one key for a given variable. Unlike max, there is no automatic frame 0 key. Animated variables have a light orange background in the Channel Box.

Animation settings   Playback speed and other settings are in the Preferences dialog box under the Settings category. As in max, there is a hot button near the play button at the lower-right corner of the screen to open this dialog box. You set the overall animation length and focus area by adjusting the Range Slider, just below the Time Line.

Differences in Previewing and Rendering

Rendering   In Maya, click the director's clapboard icon to render the currently active panel. You can pan and zoom in the rendering panel just as in any other panel.

Rendering settings   All the adjustments for rendering are handled in the Render Globals window. To open it, click the button to the right of the IPR button or choose Window | Rendering Editors | Render Globals on the menu.

Antialiasing   Maya uses a renderer quite different from the one in max. Antialiasing settings for the raytracer and the scanline rendering appear in the Render Globals window, with four main presets for quick adjustment. Unlike max's on/off approach to antialiasing, you have to choose a quality level in Maya.

Network rendering   Maya will network render for any user who has purchased maintenance and is current. However, you must use a third-party product, such as Lemon or Muster, to control network rendering.

Render layers   Maya allows you to render separate passes for renderable, beauty, color, shadow, diffuse, and specular. They can be saved to separate directories in the chosen image file format. There is no option for combining the layers into an RPF file. Maya calls this *open compositing*, meaning that you can use any compositor you want; compositing isn't oriented to any one product.

Active Shade   3ds max 4 introduced Active Shade, which enables you to edit lighting and materials and get quick feedback. This feature originated in TDI software, a company absorbed by Wavefront before Maya was even on the drawing board. In Maya, it's called *IPR* (Interactive Photorealistic Renderer). Maya's IPR has an additional step: After IPR rendering is finished, you drag a box in the rendered view to set a rectangular area for updating (see Figure A.23). Like max, only materials and lighting changes are updated. By focusing on an area smaller than the full frame, you get faster feedback. You can MMB-click and drag and drop materials from Hypershade to an IPR window.

FIGURE A.23   *You can MMB drag and drop materials from Hypershade to an IPR view and get instant feedback.*

Previewing   In max, you can get a quick preview of your animation that uses the video card's display mode for creating an AVI file (Rendering | Make Preview on the menu). Maya offers similar functionality with Playblast, which appears under Window | Playblast.

Trackview   In Maya, you perform what max calls "trackview operations" by using two unique interfaces: the Graph Editor and the Dope Sheet Editor. The Graph Editor (see Figure A.24) is for editing curves and their tangents, and the Dope Sheet Editor, for key timing, is better for moving groups of keys or setting specific frames for individual keys. Unlike max's approach, in which every scene element is shown and you then filter objects out, in Maya you see only the currently selected object by default. Saved settings known as *bookmarks* are available to bring back your needed selection sets for either editor. These bookmarks are available in most Maya windows that display attributes of selected objects.

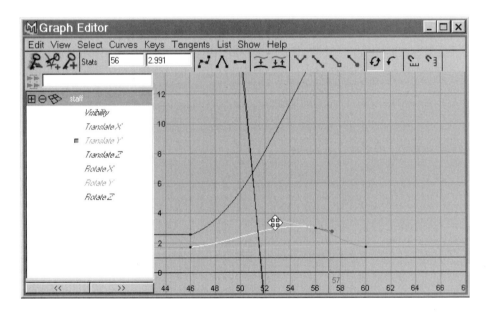

FIGURE A.24   *Maya's Graph Editor is used to tweak animation curves.*

Schematic view   This max feature has an almost identical analog in Maya's Hypergraph. Maya's can be used more because you can make all manner of "connections" in Hypergraph. For example, parts of materials could be broken off or reassigned, and object creation elements can be similarly reassigned. The right-click option is a major part of Maya's Hypergraph.

Post Effects

Video Post   Although Maya has no interface like Video Post, it still offers Glow, Depth of Field, and Lens Flare effects:

- **Glow**   You set this effect under the material's Special Effects section of the Attribute Editor for most material types. The glow intensity is mappable and usually controlled by maps if the glow shouldn't appear on the entire object.

- **Depth of Field**   This effect is set as a camera attribute. In general, the results are much better than with max's Z-buffer–based depth of field.

- **Lens Flare**   The Lens Flare effect appears in the Light Glow entry in the Light Effects Attributes for a specific light source. When you click the map icon, an Optical FX node is created (see Figure A.25). Here you can create all manner of flares, twinkles, and fiery noise effects.

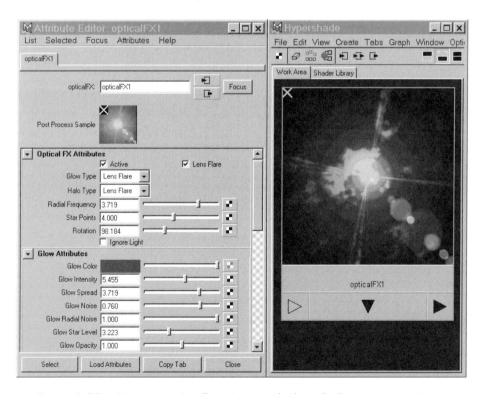

FIGURE A.25   *You can preview flares in Hypershade and edit many parameters for unique Lens Flare effects.*

Environmental Effects

Volume lights   In Maya, you can easily set these lights by using the Light Effects entry in the Attribute Editor for Spot lights. Click the icon to the right of the Light Fog entry to apply a Light Fog effect to the light. You can also set up how the dust cone should appear.

Environment Fog   This effect is part of the Render Globals window, with an option to apply the fog in post.

Scripting

Maxscript   Maya's MELscripting ability is nearly identical, with the same abilities to grab code from a listener and drag it to the Maya Shelf for often-repeated commands. MELscript is deeper into its host program than maxscript; in fact, every part of Maya runs based on MELscripts. MEL is an integral part of Maya's overall design.

Particles and Dynamics

Particles   Maya has a completely different way of creating particles than max does. You can paint them into their starting positions, use emitters, or have them emit from objects. Many of the particle types must be rendered onscreen in Maya's Hardware Render Buffer (using the quick-shaded mode that utilizes your 3D card) and then composited into your scene.

Dynamics   Maya has a mode dedicated to dynamics, with fast, complex dynamics completely built in. Instead of max's spacewarps, Maya uses *fields* that are applied to currently selected objects and generally allow much more detailed control. The Dynamic Relationships dialog box (Window | Relationship Editors | Dynamic Relationships) lets you edit the assignment of fields to objects. Like max's spacewarps, Maya's fields apply to both particles and dynamics.

Import/Export from Maya to Max

Alias/Wavefront provides a free plug-in on its web site for .3ds import that offers basic mesh translation through max's .3ds export. However, for more comprehensive translation, the best choice is Polytrans, a program by Okino (http://www.okino.com) currently selling for about $800. Its Maya version includes a plug-in for import/export within max. Okino has an interim format called .bdf; it supports translating nearly every part of your scene between max and Maya, including animation, cameras, lights, materials, NURBS, and polygons.

Maya Headstart for LightWave Users

LightWave 7 marks the addition of many new features for NewTek's venerable animation product. Although these new features like fur (Sasquatch) and SkyTracer add functionality to the product, its core methodology for creating animation remains much the same as in previous versions. LightWave users will find details in Maya that are similar to what they are used to, but overall Maya is fundamentally quite different. Also, some terminology is used differently by the two programs, such as LightWave's MetaNURBS versus Maya's NURBS. The two NURBS are completely different, but Maya's Subdivision Surfaces is the most like LightWave's MetaNURBS.

Appendix A of this book offers a thorough quick-start guide for 3ds max users that focuses on where to find the primary interface tools an animator would need. Most of the information a LightWave user would seek is already detailed in that appendix, so you should review it after reading this appendix to get additional details on commonly used functions, such as grids and snapping. This appendix covers only the major differences unique to LightWave users.

Global Differences

Unlike LightWave's Layout and Modeler modules, all scene creation and adjustment in Maya occurs in the same workspace. Objects are modeled, named, and edited at any time, concurrent with any other creating, editing, or animating. Because object creation is part of scene creation in Maya, you do not usually load individually modeled objects from outside files, as in LightWave. In Maya you usually create a single scene file that contains all objects, animation, lights, and other scene elements. Only bitmap textures and audio files are external to the scene file. An exception is the use of *references*—outside linked objects often used when working with groups of other Maya animators on a project. Referenced objects appear but the geometry cannot be edited, similar to LightWave's main Layout module.

In Maya, objects and groups of objects can be assigned to layers, but the philosophy of these layers is different from the modeling layers in LightWave. LightWave forces each unique object to reside in one of several layers, and these layers are easily chosen and activated in a pushbutton-style selector, the standard modeling method in LightWave. In LightWave, the inactive layers are visible but can't be edited—what is called Template or Reference mode in Maya. The layers in Maya are more like those used by CAD users, to facilitate organizing the scene and to allow major sections of models to be hidden and displayed as needed.

In LightWave, the GL shading settings for lights and texture detail levels are controlled globally in the display panel. In Maya, each 3D panel can be set to display lights in a unique way. Texture detail in Maya is set on a per-texture basis, with the detail set in Maya's Material Editor, called Hypershade.

In Maya, all objects and scene entities (cameras, lights, curves, joints, and so forth) can be edited in detail at any time with the Attribute Editor. This is a floating panel (accessed with Ctrl+a) that you'll use often. It's similar to the Object Properties panel in LightWave, but is much more thoroughly connected to every aspect of a selected scene entity. Navigating these scene entities can be done in schematic mode, just as in LightWave. Maya's Hypergraph panel is very similar to LightWave's Schematic view. However, the interconnections in Maya's Hypergraph are more complex and flexible.

In Maya, you do not have a fast-pick list of scene entities as you do in LightWave. Maya's Outliner window is the most similar tool for selecting objects by name. Also, in LightWave something is always selected, but in Maya it's possible to have nothing selected.

Using LightWave's Layout module, you normally edit objects, lights, cameras, and the like by selecting a tab for the entity type at the top of the interface. This selection changes all the buttons displayed in the left (or optionally right) side of the interface. Maya does have a similar function, in that when you are using the full interface, a mode selector determines which menus appear in Maya. There are only four modes in Maya Complete: Modeling, Dynamics, Animation, and Rendering. All the pull-downs other than the six to the far left change depending on the mode you are in.

Differences in Viewport Navigation

There are several ways to zoom, pan, and orbit a view in LightWave. LightWave offers keyboard hotkeys to increment in small "bumps" and three little click-and-drag buttons for navigating a viewport (see Figure B.1), and many users use these two methods for viewport navigation exclusively. Maya does not have any analogous function. LightWave also has Ctrl and Alt key options to manipulate a viewport with the mouse, and these options are available in Maya in a very similar way. In LightWave, Ctrl+Alt+LMB is zoom, Shift+Alt+LMB is pan, and Alt+LMB is orbit. For Maya, only the Alt key is used, and the LMB and MMB combinations set the mode: Alt+LMB+MMB is zoom, Alt+MMB is pan, and Alt+LMB is orbit. These mouse actions are the main way to navigate in your Maya 3D viewports, and work in all the other dialog boxes for zooming and panning.

FIGURE B.1   *LightWave's buttons for navigating a viewport.*

Differences in Control Interface

LightWave offers a Ctrl+Shift pop-up dialog box as a workflow enhancer so that you can use the left, middle, or right mouse button to open a dialog box. This feature is very similar to Maya's marking menus, but in Maya you can have dozens of them assigned to keyboard combinations, and the same menu will appear regardless of the mouse button you click. Maya's marking menus are mostly user-defined. This book includes a set of modeling marking menus to get you started on creating your own enhanced hotkeys. Maya also offers the "Hotbox"—access to all functions in one overlay that's activated with the spacebar. Many Maya users leave the interface hidden except for the 3D panels and rely on the Hotbox and their marking menus for most of their work.

Differences in Creating and Editing Models

As mentioned, the most striking difference is that Maya does not divide tasks with a separate modeler. Maya Complete offers two types of modeling, NURBS and polygons, but LightWave offers metaballs, patch modeling, and polygons. LightWave's MetaNURBS are not NURBS in the true sense; they are a kind of subdivided polygonal object. Maya NURBS are truly parametric B-spline–based surfaces that are flexible and powerful. You can edit and even animate the control points that govern the shape of NURBS objects. NURBS are ideal for complex but smooth surfaces usually seen in man-made sculpted objects, such as cell phones.

Maya has a full set of polygon modeling tools as well. Maya's Polygon Subdivide option can achieve a smoothing effect that's similar to LightWave's metaNURBS. The Maya Unlimited version of Maya includes Subdivision Surfaces modeling, which is most like metaNURBS, and this method offers a great deal of organic modeling power.

Differences in Lighting

Lighting types   Maya includes the same primary light types as LightWave except for the Linear Light type. LightWave's Distant Light type is called Directional in Maya. Maya also offers an Ambient light type, which is similar to a point light but can brighten all surfaces in the scene regardless of its location.

Maya does not offer global illumination, as LightWave does. Maya also does not have caustics built in with raytracing, but there's a downloadable utility for getting caustics on Alias|Wavefront's Web site.

Maya's raytraced and mapped shadows, controlled with the Attribute Editor, are similar to those in LightWave. As in LightWave's Properties panel, volumetrics and flares are assigned via the Attribute Editor when adjusting a light.

Differences in Materials

The LightWave Surface Editor is called Hypershade in Maya. Hypershade works in a much looser way than LightWave's Surface Editor. Hypershade uses floating swatches, which are wired together to create materials. For example, a procedural checker texture can be wired to a material's color input, thus overriding the solid-colored swatch with a checkered texture.

In Maya, materials are edited at their root in the Attribute Editor, where the familiar variables appear: diffuse, color, specularity, and so forth. Maya gives you much greater flexibility in wiring any texture to the input of any other texture. For example, a procedural checker could have a unique texture replace each of the two solid colors that normally fill the checkered squares. Maya does not have the blending modes that are part of composing textures in LightWave, but you can achieve the same effect with Maya's Layered Texture option for a texture. Maya's procedural textures don't normally leave part of the texture transparent to the underlying texture. In Maya, a texture normally overrides the value it's assigned to. For example, if you assign a checkered material in LightWave, the black squares show through to the texture below or the original color assignment. In Maya the checkered material would completely cover the previous color assignment. If you want underlying colors or textures to show through, use Maya's Layered Texture.

Both the Attribute Editor for materials and Hypershade use only spheres to preview a material as it's composed. However, in Hypershade you can zoom and pan the spherical swatches as needed to get larger, higher-resolution feedback on your material edits.

LightWave's method of having a single material type with a variety of post shaders, such as cartoon Super CEL and Thin Film, is completely alien to Maya. In Maya a material is one of several flavors at its root: Blinn, Lambert, Phong, and so forth. For effects such as a cel-shader look, a special material type called Shading Map is offered. Also, materials in Maya are created and assigned as needed instead of being dictated by the objects in the scene, as in LightWave. A simple Lambert material type is automatically assigned to any newly created object, but usually animators create a new material and assign it to the object and any other objects in the scene that consist of the same material. Materials can even be created in a scene devoid of objects.

Mapping   NURBS objects in Maya have inherent mapping that determines how texture maps are placed. Polygons offer UV mapping that is similar to that in LightWave, but you can interactively size a mapping frame to place the texture where you want it in Maya. Further, Maya offers an "automatic mapping" option that allows you to unwrap and stitch together an object's UV mapping to avoid smearing and "singularities" in which the texture seems to pinch together.

Differences in Creating Animation

Animation keyframes   Creating animation in Maya is similar to LightWave. There is no interface button for creating a key; you simply press the S key to set an animation key. A key is always set at the current frame, usually only for the attribute you're changing. Maya allows you to specify whether all animation properties or just the currently edited property has a key set. Most of the time you leave key creation set to the currently edited value so that you don't create keys on properties that aren't animated. There are many other ways to create keys in Maya, notably by right-clicking on the variable names in the Channel Box. You can click-drag several variables and key them all with one click, as shown in Figure B.2.

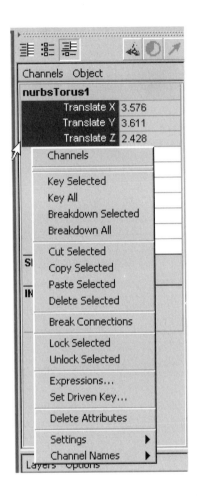

FIGURE B.2   *Setting keys in the Channel Box with a right-click.*

Animation editing windows   LightWave's Scene Editor is similar to Maya's Dope Sheet, LightWave's Graph Editor is similar to Maya's Graph Editor, and LightWave's Motion Mixer is similar to Maya's Trax editor.

Character animation   Maya creates skeletons from a series of "joints," which are similar to the bones used in LightWave.

Differences in Previewing and Rendering

Interactive renderer   Maya has a function similar to LightWave's VIPER that's called IPR (Interactive Photorealistic Renderer). Like VIPER, it allows you to have an interactively updated rendering for edits to lights and materials.

Previewing   LightWave offers a preview option near the playback controls for getting quick-shaded playback of an animated segment. In Maya this feature is called Playblast and has a similar function.

Rendering   In Maya, you simply click the director's clapboard icon to render the current frame. The settings usually assigned in LightWave as camera properties are mostly in the Render Globals window in Maya, where you set the resolution, motion blur, raytracer quality, and other rendering attributes. The camera attributes in Maya contain only field of view, depth of field, and other camera-specific settings. Also, it is possible to have orthogonal cameras in Maya and to render from them. Maya starts a scene with three fixed-direction orthographic cameras, which otherwise function like any other Maya camera and are predefined for the orthographic views: Top, Side, and Front. Rendering is always performed on the active view in Maya—the view panel with a frame around it.

Post Effects

Maya does not have a feature similar to LightWave's Compositing or Image Processing functions. In general, you use a third-party compositing program to alter Maya's rendered output, but most compositors offer more creative flexibility and power than LightWave's Compositing and Image Processing. Maya also offers the option to render elements of the image to separate files. This feature enables you to bring only the shadows, highlights, or other special layer types to your compositor. Being able to adjust such factors as shadow intensity or specular blur in a compositor is a fast way to tweak the renderer results without waiting for a new rendering.

Maya's depth of field is achieved with true raytracing, and the intensity and focus of the effect is set with camera attributes. In LightWave, the effect is achieved with post processing as an image filter.

Maya's Lens Flares are a property of the lights that create flares. Maya's Glow Effect is a property of materials. Flares and glows automatically render when the effect is enabled in their respective attributes.

Import/Export from LightWave to Maya

For translating between LightWave and Maya, the best choice is Polytrans, a program by Okino (http://www.okino.com; see Figure B.3). Its Maya version works directly within Maya and can import .lwo (object files) and .lws (scene files). Polytrans supports translation of nearly every part of your scene between LightWave and Maya, including animation, cameras, lights, hierarchies, basic materials, and polygon objects. At this writing, the Maya Polytrans utility sells for about $800.

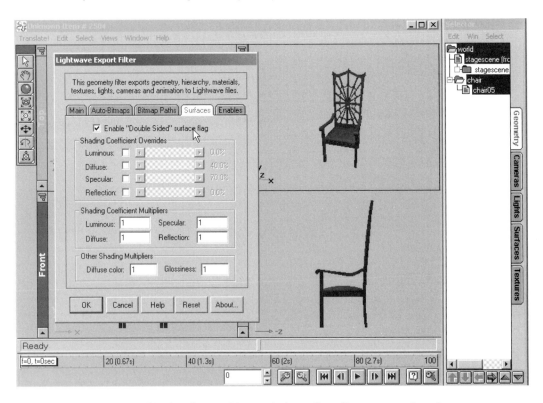

FIGURE B.3   *Okino's Polytrans 3D translation utility offers many options for LightWave file conversion.*

Index

SYMBOLS

E

F

www.informit.com

YOUR GUIDE TO IT REFERENCE

New Riders has partnered with **InformIT.com** to bring technical information to your desktop. Drawing from New Riders authors and reviewers to provide additional information on topics of interest to you, **InformIT.com** provides free, in-depth information you won't find anywhere else.

Articles

Keep your edge with thousands of free articles, in-depth features, interviews, and IT reference recommendations— all written by experts you know and trust.

Online Books

Answers in an instant from **InformIT Online Books'** 600+ fully searchable online books.

POWERED BY

Safari

Catalog

Review online sample chapters, author biographies, and customer rankings and choose exactly the right book from a selection of over 5,000 titles.

www.newriders.com

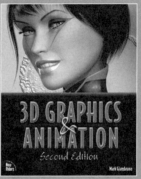
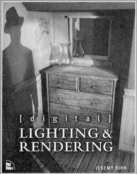

VOICES THAT MATTER

HOW TO CONTACT US

VISIT OUR WEB SITE

WWW.NEWRIDERS.COM

On our web site, you'll find information about our other books, authors, tables of contents, and book errata. You will also find information about book registration and how to purchase our books, both domestically and internationally.

EMAIL US

Contact us at: **nrfeedback@newriders.com**

- If you have comments or questions about this book
- To report errors that you have found in this book
- If you have a book proposal to submit or are interested in writing for New Riders
- If you are an expert in a computer topic or technology and are interested in being a technical editor who reviews manuscripts for technical accuracy

Contact us at: **nreducation@newriders.com**

- If you are an instructor from an educational institution who wants to preview New Riders books for classroom use. Email should include your name, title, school, department, address, phone number, office days/hours, text in use, and enrollment, along with your request for desk/examination copies and/or additional information.

Contact us at: **nrmedia@newriders.com**

- If you are a member of the media who is interested in reviewing copies of New Riders books. Send your name, mailing address, and email address, along with the name of the publication or web site you work for.

BULK PURCHASES/CORPORATE SALES

The publisher offers discounts on this book when ordered in quantity for bulk purchases and special sales. For sales within the U.S., please contact: Corporate and Government Sales (800) 382-3419 or **corpsales@pearsontechgroup.com**. Outside of the U.S., please contact: International Sales (317) 581-3793 or **international@pearsontechgroup.com**.

WRITE TO US

New Riders Publishing
201 W. 103rd St.
Indianapolis, IN 46290-1097

CALL/FAX US

Toll-free (800) 571-5840
If outside U.S. (317) 581-3500
Ask for New Riders
FAX: (317) 581-4663

New Riders

WWW.NEWRIDERS.COM

Colophon

Maya 4.5 Fundamentals was laid out and produced with the help of Microsoft Word, Adobe Acrobat, Adobe Photoshop, Collage Complete, and QuarkXpress on a variety of systems, including a Macintosh G4. With the exception of pages that were printed out for proofreading, all files—text, images, and project files—were transferred via email or FTP and edited onscreen. In addition, scene files were created with Alias|Wavefront's Maya 4.5, and the CD movie files were created with Camtasia by TechSmith.

All body text is set in the Stone Serif family. All headings, figure captions, and cover text are set in the 2 Stone Sans family. The Symbol and Sean's Symbol typefaces were used throughout for special symbols and bullets.

Maya 4.5 Fundamentals was printed on 50# Utopia Film Coat at VonHoffmann Inc., in Owensville, Missouri. Prepress consisted of PostScript computer-to-plate technology (filmless process). The cover was printed on 12pt Carolina coated one side at Moore Langen Printing in Terre Haute, Indiana.